PREACHING MARK IN TWO VOICES

PREACHING MARK
IN TWO VOICES

BRIAN K. BLOUNT

GARY W. CHARLES

Westminster John Knox Press
LOUISVILLE • LONDON

Book design by Sharon Adams
Cover design by Mark Abrams

First edition
Published by Westminster John Knox Press
Louisville, Kentucky

This book is printed on acid-free paper that meets the American National Standards Institute Z39.48 standard. ∞

PRINTED IN THE UNITED STATES OF AMERICA

03 04 05 06 07 08 09 10 11 12 — 10 9 8 7 6 5 4 3 2

Library of Congress Cataloging-in-Publication Data

Blount, Brian K., 1955–

 Preaching Mark in two voices / Brian K. Blount, Gary W. Charles.— 1st ed.
  p. cm.
 Includes bibliographical references
 ISBN 0-664-22393-1 (alk. paper)
  1. Bible. N.T. Mark—Sermons. 2. Sermons, American. 3. Sermons, African—African American authors. 4. Presbyterian church—Sermons. I. Charles, Gary W. II. Title.

 BS2585.54 .B57 2002
 252—dc21

2002028060

For
Erin, Joshua
Joe, Marguerite, and Dale

Gary

For the two places that have most nourished and nurtured my preaching:

Carver Memorial Presbyterian Church (U.S.A.)
and
Witherspoon Street Presbyterian Church (U.S.A.)

Brian

Contents

Foreword

Several years ago I had the privilege of teaching a seminary course, "Preaching the Gospel of Mark," with my friend and colleague Brian Blount. After hearing Professor Blount's lectures on Mark's Gospel and its radical, boundary-breaking Jesus, and after reading Blount's book, *Go Preach! Mark's Kingdom Message and the Black Church Today*, I realized how different this Gospel—and its Jesus—appear when viewed through the lens of the African American life experience. I emerged from that course not only with a deepened appreciation for the Gospel of Mark but also with a disturbing new awareness of how radical the call to "go preach" after the manner of Jesus really is.

In this volume, Blount (a professor of New Testament at Princeton Theological Seminary) and Gary Charles (pastor of the Old Presbyterian Meeting House in Alexandria, Virginia) team up to introduce us anew to Mark's Gospel and to its Jesus. In the process they break through any illusions we might have that Mark is the "weak stepchild of the four Gospels . . . the skeleton on which Matthew and Luke built their theological masterpieces." Instead, they open our eyes to the genius of Mark's literary technique and to the urgency of his apocalyptic message. From the opening chapter of Mark— in which God tears the heavens asunder and breaks loose in the world through the baptism and ministry of Jesus—to the closing chapter—in which we, the readers, are challenged to complete this Gospel by taking up Jesus' radically inclusive preaching mantle—Mark's distinctive voice comes through loud and clear.

But what makes this volume especially exciting is that these two authors reinterpret Mark through sermons preached out of the midst of very different sociocultural contexts. While Blount draws parallels between Mark's message and his own African American church heritage of slavery and oppression, Charles struggles with how to make this disturbing Gospel "good news" for well-educated white suburbanites living on the outskirts of our nation's capital. In a highly dialogical manner, these authors not only invite us to consider multiple possibilities for preaching Mark contextually; they also model for us—through their lively, eloquent, imaginative, and insightful sermons—how better to preach this Gospel ourselves.

If Mark is a gospel about boundary breaking, so too is this volume. Not only do we see the usual divides of race transgressed as a black man and a white man team up to write a book that honestly wrestles with the ways in which social location affects biblical interpretation. In it we also witness a seminary professor (who is an excellent preacher as well) and a local church pastor (also an excellent biblical scholar) breaking through the boundaries that frequently separate church and academy. Both scholar/preacher and preacher/scholar provide in-depth reflections on Markan texts—engaging, in the process, a diversity of contemporary Markan scholarship. Both authors struggle with the theological import of these texts for their particular faith communities. And both prepare sermons that are not only fitting and challenging for their distinctive congregations but that also sing and soar with the artful craft of imaginative language, imagery, and form. In the process, the usual pattern—in which the biblical scholar provides textual commentary while the pastor provides the sermons—is replaced by a refreshing alternative model in which the preacher is required to reveal his scholarly homework and the professor is required to bring his scholarship to fruition in the preaching moment.

Reading this book—like reading Mark's Gospel anew—is a disturbing and challenging enterprise. The Jesus we encounter here in the eloquent and provocative sermons and reflections of Blount and Charles will not let us rest easy. Indeed, this Jesus will keep on troubling us until we, too, respond to his call to "go preach." But if we are searching for models for how to proclaim the gospel we have encountered in Jesus with intelligence, imagination, pastoral sensitivity, and courage, I can think of no better guides for the journey than Brian Blount and Gary Charles. Their words inspire, even as they also unsettle.

LEONORA TUBBS TISDALE

Basking Ridge, New Jersey
Season after Pentecost, 2002

Acknowledgments

We are glad to report that we are even better friends after having written this book. This glad tiding is largely due to the wisdom, patience, and forbearance of our wives, Sharon and Jennell; our supporting institutions, Princeton Theological Seminary and the Old Presbyterian Meeting House in Alexandria, Virginia; and the contribution of two key editors: Ira Brent Driggers and Fred Morhart.

We could not write a book on Mark without the intellectual stimulation of the community of Markan scholars, living and dead. We could not write sermons on this Gospel without the years of preparation for preaching that we have received in a variety of congregations from Georgia to North Carolina to New Jersey to our home state of Virginia.

Finally, we are also grateful to colleagues and staff members who gave us both the encouragement and time to *finish the book*!

Brian K. Blount
Gary W. Charles

Introduction

And the Gospel must first be preached to all nations.

Mark 13:10

*O*kay, we're going to give it a shot. Except, this is the twenty-first century, not the first. Before we start the sermons, we must do the introductions. Readers who know Mark will better appreciate what he has written and why he has written it. That goes for us, too. Readers who know us will better appreciate what we have written and why we have written it. That is why we find it necessary to go a step beyond introducing Mark; we will also introduce ourselves.

No two people read Scripture in the same way. Contextual factors, such as who we are and where we live, determine the questions we ask of a text. They provide a unique perspective, a window, through which we gaze onto a text. They define a "space" from which we view and engage the words of Mark. Since the questions we ask of Mark, to a large extent, prefigure the answers we get, our context shapes our understanding. In other words, our context matters. Because the two of us are from different contexts, we speak from those contexts with different exegetical and homiletical voices. In this book, we work to place those two voices in conversation.

We cannot, of course, speak for Mark. We can witness to his words, we can preach from his story, but we cannot speak in his place. That means that whenever and wherever we (or anyone else for that matter!) proclaim that we are presenting Mark's voice, you can be sure that it is *his* voice as *we* understand it. All who approach Mark do so through their own cultural, social, religious, and political spectacles—through their own unique windows. Since the category fits us, so must the acknowledgment. We read Mark out of our own contexts. What follows in the rest of this book, then, are *our* views on Mark.

We share our views on Mark in three particular ways that we hope bring some fresh insight into the way *you* view this Gospel. In each chapter, one of us begins with an exegetical study of a literary/theological unit from Mark. That author then presents a sermon based on the exegesis of this Markan material. The other preacher responds to the exegesis and sermon from his own context, providing a different view of the text. Each view offers diverse ways to preach Mark in the contemporary life of the church.

Though our contexts are distinct, we share a love for Mark's Gospel. We also share a long and abiding friendship. We both grew up in the Tidewater region of southeastern Virginia. Each of us was raised by blue-collar parents whose Christian faith was contagious. We each learned to think critically about Scripture while at the College of William and Mary. After college, our paths diverged. Gary attended Union Theological Seminary in Richmond, Virginia; Brian studied at Princeton Theological Seminary in Princeton, New Jersey. In our professional lives, we have come to similar crossroads and chosen different paths. We each served Presbyterian congregations in Newport News, Virginia. Afterward, Brian entered the field of theological education, where he remains. Gary has continued to serve congregations in parish ministry. Over the years we have developed a deep respect for each other's discipleship, and both of us have been profoundly affected by Mark.

We grew up in the American South during the last official days of "separate but equal." Gary's vision of the world developed from the privileged position of a white Southern male. Brian's vision took shape as an African American whose intelligence was often questioned and whose place in the world was tightly circumscribed by the majority culture. Gary's experience of higher education required little thought as to race or social standing, since students at William and Mary were largely white and middle class. Brian could never so easily blend into the same campus life. Gary's view of the church and Christian faith was shaped by a culture tightly wedded to the institution and values of the mainline church. Brian's vision came into focus through the experience of the embattled black church.

Our two voices rise out of these strikingly similar and yet genuinely different racial, cultural, and professional contexts. That is why before we talk about Mark, we want to tell you more about ourselves.

A First View: Brian's Voice

I was having lunch in the seminary cafeteria with an African American student. He had come to talk with me about a paper he was writing for the class I was teaching on the reign of God. Before we contemplated that, though, he wanted some clarification about a conundrum that often confounds students of color caught up in the challenging circumstance of a white collegial context. How do you respond to a question about racial setting when you know more than you probably want to know about living in a white world, but the white faculty and students who surround you know next to nothing about your black one? In this particular case a white professor had asked this African American student about a sermon he might construct for his home church. Could he preach the same sermon in the church of one of the other students in the classroom? (All of the other students in the room were white.) The student responded that, except for idiomatic references or illustrations that were particular to an African American audience, he could and would preach the same sermon. That was, he was told, the wrong answer. He immediately found himself in the unenviable position of being a pedagogical object lesson. The next few minutes of the class were dedicated to the matter of his homiletical enlightenment. He wondered if I had an encouraging and instructive word for what had befallen him.

Now, there is no doubt that context plays an important role in the practice of preaching. It is certainly the case that we are what we preach. People can tell a great deal about who we are and what we believe by listening to our sermons. The opposite is just as true. We preach who and what we are! We preach from our contexts and therefore our preaching reflects those contexts. The preacher's place in life; his social, political, economic, and spiritual standing; his cultural context shapes his view of the biblical text and informs his homiletical engagement with it. But if that preaching is to be as meaningfully transformative for our hearers as one would hope it has been for us as preachers, then we must also preach with an understanding of who and what our people are. Our sermons must meet them where they live, using language that is understandable in those living spaces. That means we must spend as much time studying them and their contexts as we do studying ourselves and our biblical texts. Professor Leonora Tubbs Tisdale, with whom I have taught a course on preaching the Gospel of Mark, puts it this way:

Our quest, then, is for preaching that is more intentionally *contextual* in nature—that is, preaching which not only gives serious attention to the interpretation of biblical texts, but which gives equally serious attention to the interpretation of congregations and their sociocultural contexts; preaching which not only aims toward greater "faithfulness" to the gospel of Jesus Christ, but which also aims toward greater "fittingness" (in content, form and style) for a particular congregational gathering of hearers.[1]

1. Leonora Tubbs Tisdale, *Preaching as Local Theology and Folk Art* (Minneapolis: Fortress Press, 1997), 32–33.

That, though, is just the point. Professor Tisdale emphasizes "fittingness," not blind obedience. Our sermons must "fit" their contexts; they need not worship and, therefore, acquiesce to them. This was the word of encouragement I gave my young cafeteria colleague. In the future, I challenged, he must make *his* case, not surrender so soon *even* to the strong case being made by one of his teachers.

His case is this: In this odd reality in which African Americans find themselves, questions about context often mean something quite different than they do for white Americans. I speak in this case about the bicultural, racial reality that has always been an acute part of the black experience in the United States. W. E. B. DuBois's observations made a century ago, with some updating in the titular designations, are as appropriate now as they were then:

> After the Egyptian and Indian, the Greek and Roman, the Teuton and Mongolian, the Negro is a sort of seventh son, born with a veil, and gifted with second-sight in this American world—a world which yields him no true self-consciousness, but only lets him see himself through the revelation of the other world. It is a peculiar sensation, this double-consciousness, this sense of always looking at one's self through the eyes of others, of measuring one's soul by the tape of a world that looks on in amused contempt and pity. One ever feels his twoness,—an American, a Negro; two souls, two thoughts, two unreconciled strivings; two warring ideals in one dark body, whose dogged strength alone keeps it from being torn asunder.[2]

Through the rigors of educational and spiritual discipline, some African Americans have forged mechanisms and methodologies that enable them to evaluate their being and context with some limited sense of freedom from the dominating influence of white experience. They, though, are a fortunate minority. No doubt they, too, would acknowledge the pervasive tendency for blacks and whites still to evaluate their existences through a white cultural lens and white cultural norms and expectations.

What does all this mean for a young African American preacher contemplating the matter of preaching his black church sermon in a white church context? It means two things principally. It means, first, that unlike for his white colleagues, his context is decidedly biracial and therefore always bicultural. Unlike his white colleagues, he has had to learn the cultural context of white America in order to survive; his context is perpetually at the mercy of theirs. Neither he nor his parishioners can survive in the world if his sermons are crafted with a singular recognition of African American existence. His ser-

2. W. E. Burghardt DuBois, *The Souls of Black Folk* (Greenwich, Conn.: Fawcett Publications, 1961), 16–17.

mons must both consciously and unconsciously take into account the larger white world in which his church and his people sit even if he is preaching Sunday after Sunday to an exclusively black audience. Unlike the colleagues who sat in that preaching classroom with him, every time he went into "his" sanctuary, he was also engaging the trappings of theirs. Their sermons could afford the theoretical distinction of being written for either a black or a white setting. Given the demographic and power dynamics of American society, when they were in a white church they could assume that their parishioners had particular mono-racial demands that needed to be addressed or simply could be assumed. They could be assured, however, that were they called to preach in a black congregation the dynamics would almost completely shift. He, however, already knew what his parishioners knew—that their context, no matter how black it was, could never be completely engaged from the pulpit unless there was recognition that it was located in and influenced by a white context that therefore also always had to be addressed. His sermon, therefore, is already coded, *in the black church*, with the kinds of bicultural dynamics that make it, following idiomatic and other like adjustments, understandable in and applicable to the context of white Christianity.

It means, second, that *precisely because* white parishioners have the luxury of seeing reality only through the lens of their own racial experience, African American preachers have a prophetic mandate to preach in *their* congregations with the same kind of powerful witness that they render in black congregations. An African American preacher who goes into a white congregation and consciously changes the content and force of his sermon to adapt it to the white context loses the opportunity to help his white counterparts in the faith experience what they will otherwise probably miss—a view on the Scriptures that blossoms out of the African American experience.

For this reason, when I am invited to a church like the Old Presbyterian Meeting House in Alexandria, Virginia, where Gary pastors, I do not "change" my sermonic intent, and am, and have been, quite willing and anxious to offer there a witness to the text that I have eagerly shared with African American congregations. While the challenge such a sermon brings is often different precisely because of those different contexts, I have never found that its meaning and intent have been difficult for white Christians to understand and appreciate. In fact, I believe such a sermon is often much appreciated in white contexts because it offers a window into the reality of the text that is unique from the one they would otherwise hear. Such sermons geared for black churches may well "fit" white churches precisely because the stirring messages to hope, and challenges to transformation, are as needed in white congregations, and perhaps more so, as they are needed in black ones.

It is for this reason that when I preach, no matter in what context I find myself, I "fit" the sermon from the African American space out of which I come. Indeed, as my colleague Cleophus J. LaRue has noted, black preaching is unique because it is driven by the contextual realities that have nurtured and haunted black people in the United States. "In essence," he writes, "the distinctive power of black preaching is a matter, not merely of special techniques but of extraordinary experiences that have, among other results, forged a unique way of understanding the Bible and applying those insights in very practical ways."[3] That means that congregations must adjust to me and my particular African American interpretative spin just as much as I must adjust to them and the way they normally hear and perceive the biblical text.

In other words, context, in this case *African American* context, is key to black preaching. And what part of that context has been more influential than the one which set the foundational stage for black existence in this country, that of slavery? As LaRue reminds us, "The black church was born in slavery. Thus black preaching originated in a context of marginalization and struggle, and it is to this context that it still seeks to be relevant."[4] This is one of the reasons that I so enjoy preaching from the Gospel of Mark. Its boundary-breaking social and political emphases correspond quite provocatively with the kinds of social and political concerns I bring with me from my own history and background. LaRue points out, however, that it is not simply the experience of enslavement, and the continuing experience of trying to break beyond the oppressive circumstances that are slavery's current legacy, that marks the unique character of black preaching. "At its core the black sermon is not about what blacks have had to endure in America or their peculiar place as a people of color in this country. . . . [I]t is the Sovereign God at work in and through those experiences that characterizes the essence of powerful black preaching."[5]

And that brings me to Mark. Mark is one of those texts where the contextually driven impulses of an African American preacher like myself find meaningful contact with stories of Jesus operating on the side of those who find themselves powerless and oppressed in their first-century environments. And so, when I begin my preaching enterprise from Mark's Gospel, I begin, knowing how my own bicultural context influences what I do, by trying as best I can to reconstruct his.

---

3. Cleophus J. LaRue, *The Heart of Black Preaching* (Louisville, Ky.: Westminster John Knox Press, 2000), 1.
4. Ibid., 14.
5. Ibid., 115.

A Second View: Gary's Voice

I serve an historic, predominantly white, well-educated, prosperous congregation situated in a Virginia suburb of Washington, D.C. Many members of my congregation daily walk the halls of national and international power. We may feel oppressed by downturns in the market, legislation pending on Capitol Hill, rigorous work schedules, health struggles, or family turmoil, but on the whole, we are a privileged community far more familiar with wielding power than being threatened by it.

Listening to and preaching Mark by the banks of the Potomac is therefore more often a prophetic experience than a comforting one. Typically, I find myself, and those who hear me preaching, less in solidarity with Mark's story than in heated exchange with it. What does it mean that the "reign of God is at hand" (1:15) to those whose livelihood derives from the world's greatest "reign" of power? What sense do members, who expend no small effort to assure that they and their children *lack nothing*, make of Jesus' invitation to the rich man: "You *lack one thing*; go, sell what you own, and give the money to the poor, and you will have treasure in heaven; then come, follow me" (10:21 NRSV; my italics)? What does Jesus' assault on using the purity laws as religious and ethnic barriers have to say about those strident voices trying to purify our denomination today? What does a Gospel written to give hope and voice to marginalized people and an oppressed church in first-century society say to privileged twenty-first-century people worshiping in an historic eighteenth-century church?

The ground floor of the Flounder House—the church office of the Old Presbyterian Meeting House that I serve—hosts a new members' class for six consecutive Sundays, three times a year. Each class answers a standard set of questions, and for nearly a decade the profile has looked remarkably similar. Some new members come from a life history in the Presbyterian Church. Some come from a wide swath of other Catholic and Protestant denominations. The largest group, though, comes from the "none of the above" category. Feeling put upon to give an acceptable answer to the preacher, some identify themselves as Methodists or Lutherans or Catholics. Once we begin to talk, however there is often no substance behind the label. In reality, they have been born and raised in fast-growing unchurched America—and when they walk down the steps into the basement of the Flounder House, they enter a space—a worshiping community—that many of their friends, coworkers, gym pals, and family members have not often entered or will never enter.

The church is simply not on the radar screen for a large segment of our society. While a remnant of the former fusion of the white church and dominant

American culture remains, now both mainline white and nonwhite churches are rapidly being pushed to the margins of social relevance.[6] When people argue with me and say that millions of Americans are on a "spiritual journey," I challenge their math and then argue that the "Spiritual Special" doesn't necessarily make a stop at the entrance of any church.

The secularization and spiritualization of America often lead people to enter doors other than the church and fields other than theological education. Society says: Get a medical degree, a law degree, an MBA—not a divinity degree. We know from where the next generations of doctors and lawyers and business leaders are coming, but what about preachers, church educators, and musicians?

But, interestingly enough, despite the fact that the church and its institutions have been shoved to the precipice of irrelevancy by culture, there are those who do come, who do enter the doors of the church and the seminary. They come for a multitude of reasons, but often out of a sense of desperation, a sense of cultural void. How does the church respond?

Increasingly, I preach to a substantial number of people who feel alien in the space in which I feel most familiar. These people look familiar. Like me, they are mostly white. They are mostly well educated. They go to the same movies, read many of the same books, enjoy many of the same restaurants. Superficial looks, in this case, can be deadly for the church. To look more closely, these people are not nearly so familiar. The songs I cherish are odd to them. The words I live by are largely unknown to them. The traditions in which I was raised are not theirs. They may sit politely once, maybe twice, through our coded worship services, giving the impression that they are "one of us." But, most likely, they will not stay unless the church guides them through the particularities of tradition and language and the centuries of God-Jacob wrestling matches over scriptural interpretation. They will not stay unless the church tells them the difference between an "Amen" and a postlude and explains to them the physical maze of chancels, apses, and narthexes.

The church owes its future life to such boundary-breaking efforts as it follows its boundary-breaking Lord. When people swim against the prevailing tides of secularism and spiritualism to seek out a life of Christ in the church, the church—black, white, or multiethnic—must respond. Understanding its own context in twenty-first-century America, the church can celebrate that the risen Jesus awaits us, not in maintaining the boundary of the way the church was, not by patching holes in theological, ecclesiastical, and liturgical walls

---

6. See Gary W. Charles, *The Bold Alternative: Staying in Church in the 21st Century* (Louisville, Ky.: Geneva Press, 2001), for an extended discussion of the changing relationship between church and culture.

that were once considered inviolable, but "in Galilee" (16:7), where the church will meet its Lord and regain its voice.

The context from which I preach differs distinctly from Brian's. Ironically, though, these differences are now merging at the crossroads of marginalization. In the past, and to some extent even now, the white church in America has contributed to marginalizing black Christianity. Today, black, white, and other racial ethnic churches in America are being marginalized by the forces of secularism and even spirituality. Our two diverse voices, then, are increasingly more distinct from dismissive, secular culture and questing spirituality than they are from each other, despite our differences in race and profession.

That brings me back to Mark. Mark may seem an ironic text to preach from a prominent American pulpit to advantaged people in a proud theological tradition. In many ways, it is. However, as the church is pushed more and more to the margins of social relevance and our pews fill with people longing to hear that faith matters and can transform lives, preaching Mark seems less an option than a calling.

A Third View: Mark's Voice

The Gospel of Mark is a book about choices. Apocalyptic choices. Choices that claim to represent and reveal God's purpose for struggling humankind. While Jerusalem crumbled beneath the weight of Roman siege engines and burned from the malevolent interest of its legions, the first evangelist ignited a literary blaze of his own. He blasted the choices his oppressed people made as they plotted a strategy for Israel's future.

Some chose the path of resistance; they were passionate for political and religious independence. In their zeal to oust the Roman Gentile presence in their Jewish land and simultaneously put an end to Rome's oppressive reign in the region, they lit a fire that suddenly shifted and threatened to consume them. They continued, though, to believe. The war and the destruction it wrought were for them the appropriate markers of the coming cataclysm that would precede the inbreaking of God's reign and the reestablishment of an Israel as powerful as it had been in David's time. God was about to move. Anyone who wanted to be on God's side should anticipate the divine entry into the conflict with Rome and engage the battle on God's side, on the side that would surely bring the ancient superpower to its knees. At the darkest moment, they were sure, God would break in and break down the Roman assault against them. Israel would be what Israel once was: free.

Others, realizing the power of the Roman legions and the persistence of the empire that unleashed them, had sought the more agreeable path of accommodation. Before war had broken out, they had tried to alter the path of their people by teaching them to live alongside the Roman dominance in their region. While they believed that in the future God would vindicate Israel, they acknowledged that in some times, such as their present one, evil and oppression would hold sway. In such circumstances one tried to appease one's conquerors so that they would allow as much self-governance and normal existence as possible. Israel could be something like what Israel once was: an established, identifiable people on an identifiable land, governed under the watchful supervision of their Roman overseers, of course, but by their own identifiable law.

The Gospel of Mark offered yet another choice. This one also had the dubious distinction of being the least attractive of the three. Not only did it challenge the validity of the other two options, it also argued against the vision of a future Israel that looked as much as possible like the Israel of old. In this time of the Jewish war against Rome, about the year 70 C.E., Mark testified to the understanding that God would not move militarily into history against the Roman occupation in the interest of reestablishing Israel as Israel had once been. Neither, however, did God desire an Israel subservient to Roman interest and practice. God preferred an Israel in the image of a man who had lived four decades earlier and had died on a Roman cross because the leadership of his own people feared the kind of Israel his life and work envisioned.

The God preached by this Galilean Jesus rejected accommodation to the traditional ways of Israel's living. According to Mark, the holiness and purity laws that had once established the people as set apart before God for service to others had become divisive tools that separated the poor, the disfigured, the unhealthy, and the foreign from those who considered themselves holy and pure. Lepers, tax collectors, sinners, women, the destitute, and the ill all found that they were, according to the law, unworthy to stand before God as equal participants in the worshiping community.[7] Gentiles were considered particularly unclean;[8] those zealous for a free and independent Israel longed for the time when God would evict the Gentiles forcibly and permanently from the land.

In striking contrast, Mark offers a Jesus who embodies and preaches God's boundary-breaking, transformative message for Israel and all humankind. The message is this:

---

7. See Mark 1:40–3:6.
8. See Mark 7:24–30.

God desires a world in which the boundaries that separate people from each other, whether they be holiness and purity codes that separate Jews from other Jews or laws and traditions that separate Jews from Gentiles, be torn down and broken through. To this end, Jesus challenges laws that prohibit the touching of lepers and therefore operate against their inclusion into the full covenant community (1:40–45); Jesus embraces tax collectors and sinners (2:15–17); Jesus places the matter of human wholeness and healing above allegiance to the law (2:23–3:6); Jesus proclaims that people need no longer go through the sacrificial ritual of the Temple infrastructure to find favor with God because he can forgive sin directly (2:1–12); Jesus proclaims that the powerful reality and presence of the reign of God is as available to Gentiles as it is to Jews (7:19b; 7:24–8:10); and Jesus offers a future portrait of Israel that looks very different from Israel as it had been, even in its Davidic heyday of political independence. This Israel will not be accomplished by revolutionary zealot forces fighting Roman legions or by high priests and aristocrats accommodating to the status quo. It will be accomplished through the activities of a discipleship corps that emulates the boundary-breaking actions of Jesus in the interest of establishing a rule-of-God reality on earth that shuts out none and includes all (13:10; 11:17).

Mark, then, is a revolutionary story about a revolutionary choice. Those who preach from it must also make a choice: a homiletical one. Mark's story is not readily transparent; its key themes, its principal choices are not always apparent to the naked literary eye. In other words, its "plain sense" is not always so plain. The enterprising work of reading and understanding in light of Mark's own apocalyptic social and linguistic context must therefore be done, and done carefully. And that's where our two voices will look at Mark from our distinctive and shared contexts.

We want Mark's story to live for us and for the people to whom we preach. But we must be careful not to let our concerns and our interests co-opt Mark's story and isolate it from the lens through which it was first written and read. Those interests must interact with and help guide the insights we have gained from our long history of interpretation of his story. We must allow the interests of his story and its original audience to speak to the interests that drive us toward Mark's text today. In so doing, we find that Mark's words are more than spiritual encouragement to world-weary Sunday worshipers who come to the sanctuary in hope of finding respite from the burdens of the world around them. That reality must be recognized, but Mark was written principally for a people caught up in, and spiritually burdened by, social and political storms. His Gospel offers much more than a Jesus intended to soothe and mend the troubled soul; here is a Jesus caught up in the troubles and turmoil of a tormented world. In the midst of this Jesus story, then, the evangelist demands that we make clear sociopolitical as well as spiritual choices. The two are bound together in Mark's time; we must not separate them in ours. When we preach from his text, our spiritual voice must always be shaped with a social and political edge, informed by the politics of Mark's time, illuminated by the cultural, social, and political dynamics of our own. Otherwise, we strip this earliest Gospel of its revolutionary power and its real, transformational possibilities. From his preaching context, Brian would argue that it is at just this point that Mark's emphasis and black preaching's "heart" provocatively meet. The understanding of God moving through Christ on behalf of the marginalized today corresponds homiletically with the understanding of God moving transformatively through Jesus two millennia ago.

As in the first century, so still today, then, this Gospel is about choices. It demands that we recognize the dangers of the time in which we live and act accordingly. Not to foster the violent overthrow of those who oppose us. Not to accommodate ourselves to the way things have always been in the interest of securing a false peace devoid of justice. Not to change our sermons so that the people to whom we preach will be comfortable thinking that we see as they see, believe what they believe, want what they want. It demands instead that we carefully, through the experience of *our* context and experience, remember and then choose Jesus' way of breaking down the boundaries that separate people from one another and therefore people from God. It is through destroying those boundaries that the reign of God finds its way in and we find our way out of our chaos to God.

Mark's emphasis on God moving through Christ on behalf of marginalized people holds currency now not just for the black church, but for mainline white churches learning to live, survive, and transfigure a marginalized existence. The problem, though, is that for centuries the fullness of Mark's voice has not been heard; biblical scholars treated Mark as the weak stepchild of the four Gospels. Much of biblical scholarship since the Enlightenment has acknowledged Mark as the first Gospel, but in chronology only. At the height of the biblical criticism movement,[9] Mark's Gospel commanded minimal

---

9. The beginning of the biblical critical movement may be understood essentially as the emergence of a thoroughly historical approach to the Bible. Eighteenth-century pioneers include, among others, J. S. Semler (1725–91), G. E. Lessing (1729–81), and H. S. Reimarus (1694–1768). Around the same time, the first critical investigation of the "Synoptic problem" appeared in J. J. Griesbach's *Synopsis Evangeliorum* (1776), wherein Griesbach (Semler's pupil) argued that Mark's Gospel betrays an indebtedness to both Matthew and Luke. Although Griesbach's hypothesis was challenged in 1835 by Karl Lachmann—paving the way for later views of Markan priority—Griesbach's estimation of Mark as a poorly written and generally uninformed document carries well into the late twentieth century. Even William Wrede's *Das*

attention and respect in the academic community. Its value was assessed largely as the skeleton upon which Matthew and Luke built their theological masterpieces. The treatment of Mark as the "first in order but second in tier" Gospel is evident in how scholars[10] dealt with the story's ending. Though a significant group of nineteenth- and twentieth-century scholars argued that it is grammatically acceptable in both classical and *koine* Greek to end a sentence with a causal conjunction (*gar*, for—16:8), a preponderance of twentieth-century scholars concluded that the original ending of Mark had been lost. Paying little attention to the extant story of 16:1–8, these scholars speculated endlessly about the "missing" resurrection appearances that the "original" ending likely contained. In so doing, they treated the final eight verses of the Gospel as incomplete and the remainder of the Gospel as significant but secondary to the witness of the other Gospels.

These same scholars also criticized Mark's storytelling skills as crude, pedestrian, and even, at times, embarrassing. For example, they noted that Mark repeats stories, like the feeding of the multitudes and the calming of the sea, seemingly oblivious to this narrative redundancy. They also chided Mark for being the only Gospel writer to omit any reference to the prehistory or birth of Jesus. And they praised Matthew and Luke for "correcting" these and other literary "defects" in Mark's Gospel.

Thanks to insights from twentieth-century literary criticism and sociolinguistics, the assumptions of traditional biblical scholarship are being challenged,

---

Messiasgeheimnis in den Evangelien (1901), despite its groundbreaking claim that Mark's Gospel contains the unique theological perspective of its redactor, continued to describe the gospel itself as thoroughly lacking in artistry. Albert Schweitzer's monumental *Von Reimarus zu Wrede* (1906) belies the same assumption, using Mark only as a fragmented historical source. It is not until Willi Marxsen's form-critical analysis in *Evangelist Markus* (1956) that the scholarly world is introduced to the idea of Mark's Gospel as the unified product of a creative and original author. The interpretive implications of Marxsen's thesis, however, have only recently been understood. For a brief interpretive history of Mark's Gospel see Janice Capel Anderson and Stephen D. Moore, "Introduction: The Lives of Mark," in *Mark & Method: New Approaches in Biblical Studies* (ed. Janice Capel Anderson and Stephen D. Moore; Minneapolis: Fortress Press, 1992), 1–22. For more detailed accounts of the biblical critical movement and its subsequent scholarly trajectories, see Stephen Neill and Tom Wright, *The Interpretation of the New Testament, 1861–1986* (2d ed.; Oxford: Oxford University Press, 1988); and I. Howard Marshall, ed., *New Testament Interpretation: Essays on Principles and Methods* (Grand Rapids: Eerdmans, 1977).

10. Vincent Taylor, *The Gospel according to St. Mark* (London: Macmillan, 1966), 609: "Several scholars hold that *ephobounto gar* is the original end of the Gospel. Cf. Wellhausen, 137; Ed. Meyer, i. 13–18; Creed, 314–18, JTS, xxxi. 175–80; R. R. Ottley, JTS, xxvii. 407–9; W. K. L. Clarke, *Theol.* xxix. 106 f.; Lohmeyer, 356–60; R. H. Lightfoot, *LDG*, 1–48, *GM*, 80–97, 106–16; J. Knox, 63n.; W. C. Allen, *JTS*, xlvii. 46–9; L J. D. Richardson, *JTS*, xlix. 144f. Lightfoot gives many examples of sentences ending with *gar*, from Homer, Aeschylus, Euripides, Plato, Aristotle, the LXX." Taylor goes on to argue against this scholarly conclusion, "But none of the examples stands at the end of a book, and it is incredible that Mark intended such a conclusion. . . . The view that *ephobounto gar* is not the intended ending stands. Cf. Hort, 46; Swete, ciii–cxiii; Moffatt, 238f.; Burkitt, *Two Lectures on the Gospels*, 28; Bultmann, 309 n.; Turner, 82f.; Streeter, 337; Branscomb, 310; Schniewind, 205 f. How the Gospel ended we do not know."

while, concurrently, the oral-narrative genius of Mark is being discovered.[11] Many scholars now recognize that Mark's storytelling is anything but clumsy and his style is hardly haphazard. To the contrary, increasingly contemporary biblical scholarship appreciates the oral-narrative patterns that Mark employs to preach his "finished" Gospel.[12]

We understand the canonical Gospel of Mark as a complete story in itself. We, therefore, spend little time searching for the pre-story behind Mark, or asking why Mark includes certain stories and not others. Nor do we examine Matthean or Lucan redactions of Mark's Gospel unless such an examination adds to understanding the story Mark tells. We do not intentionally join the latest hunt for the "historical Jesus," as if the canonical Mark lacks a sufficient witness to Jesus to demand our allegiance, or as if the "historical" Jesus, if found, would speak with greater authority than the canonical Jesus. Searching for the "historical" Jesus may provide a wellspring of insight into the One the church calls Lord. Ironically, though, the search can occupy so much time and attention of the church and the academy that far too much effort is expended looking back, while the present call of the One for whom they seek—the One who calls all followers to break down boundaries, overcome fear, and live in faith on life's journey to meet him "in Galilee"—is missed.

Unlike an historian intent on recounting an objective summary of the facts, Mark feigns no such narrative neutrality. His interest is not in presenting an objective analysis of the complaints leveled against Jesus by the Pharisees, Sadducees, or scribes. Mark has even less interest in reiterating historic details and describing geographic particularities. To borrow an image from chapter 4, Mark is interested in cultivating good soil that will yield a remarkable harvest of faithfulness to God and Christian discipleship. Therefore, his

---

11. Significant literary approaches to Mark include Norman Peterson, *Literary Criticism for New Testament Critics* (Philadelphia: Fortress Press, 1978); David Rhoads, Joanna Dewey, and Donald Michie, *Mark as Story: An Introduction to the Narrative of a Gospel* (2d ed.; Minneapolis: Fortress Press, 1999); Mary Ann Tolbert, *Sowing the Gospel: Mark's World in Literary-Historical Perspective* (Minneapolis: Fortress Press, 1989); Stephen D. Moore, *Literary Criticism and the Gospels: The Theoretical Challenge* (New Haven, Conn.: Yale University Press, 1989); Robert Fowler, *Let the Reader Understand: Reader-Response Criticism and the Gospel of Mark* (Minneapolis: Fortress Press, 1991); Donald H. Juel, *A Master of Surprise: Mark Interpreted* (Minneapolis: Fortress Press, 1994); and Brian K. Blount, *Go Preach! Mark's Kingdom Message and the Black Church Today* (Maryknoll, N.Y.: Orbis, 1998).

12. Richard Horsley, *Hearing the Whole Story: The Politics of Plot in Mark's Gospel* (Louisville, Ky.: Westminster John Knox, 2001), 71–2. Horsley stresses the patterns of oral communication present in Mark's Gospel: "Within, as well as among, the various 'acts' of the narrative are echoes, repetitions, and other patterns that aid the memory of the performer and the hearing of the audience. . . . Other such techniques of 'ring' or 'chiastic' composition (inclusio), characteristic of oral narrative generally, are prevalent in Mark, both marking the boundaries of individual episodes and connecting several episodes."

communication is terse, intense, immediate,[13] and focused on bringing readers to the narrative brink of 16:8. In this way, Mark does not leave readers to mull all the facts and make one, among many, well-considered and legitimate choice. Instead, readers are left with but one unambiguous choice for how this story should end. After reading through 16:8, readers know that *they alone* must finish the story because no one else can.[14]

To accomplish this narrative goal, Mark uses some common Greco-Roman storytelling techniques, a favorite of which is repetition. In addition to his carefully crafted use of *euthus* (adverb—immediately, at once, right away), Mark repeatedly uses other crucial words and phrases in his story, such as *paradidomi* (verb—hand over, betray, permit), *euangelion* (noun—gospel, glad tidings, good news), *blepō* (verb—to see, perceive, pay attention), *akouō* (verb—to hear, listen), *parakaleō* (verb—to beg, urge, ask, summon), and *huios theou* (noun phrase—Son of God). Repetition was an *invaluable* storytelling technique to preliterate audiences, for it assisted them in remembering biblical stories, such as Mark's Gospel. As Mary Ann Tolbert explains, "Just as the visual aids of chapter titles, subheadings, and paragraphing better enable the eye to understand and comprehend material in modern books, just so repetitions, summaries, and other aural signposts aid the ear in perceiving emphasis and organization in ancient rhetorical texts."[15]

Mark also makes frequent use of irony, especially at the expense of the religious leaders of the Temple and the chosen elect of Jesus. As the tension in the story reaches a climax in Mark 15, we hear the chief priests and scribes taunt the crucified Jesus: "Let the Messiah, the King of Israel, come down

---

13. Mark uses the Greek adverb *euthus* (immediately, at once, right away) to speed the reader toward the battleground of Jerusalem. In chapters 1–10, Mark uses this adverb thirty-five times, leaving readers almost out of breath as they follow Jesus through his Galilean ministry. Once Jesus arrives in the Holy City, Mark slows his narrative speed dramatically and uses this adverb only sparingly, just six times in five chapters.

14. Donald H. Juel, *The Gospel of Mark* (Nashville: Abingdon Press, 1999), 174. Juel argues against reading 16:8 as Mark's call for faithful discipleship from his readers. "On what basis are present readers to trust that they can succeed as disciples where Jesus' chosen group failed?" Brian and I would argue that Mark's narrative and rhetorical response to Juel's question seems plain enough—because Mark's readers and listeners are the only disciples in the authorial audience who hear all the story and thus they alone know that the future of the Gospel requires that they not fear, but have faith, not be silent, but preach. See also Sharyn Dowd, *Reading Mark: A Literary and Theological Commentary on the Second Gospel* (Macon, Ga.: Smyth & Helwys, 2000), 171. Dowd concludes her book with an insightful analysis of the role of the audience in Mark's Gospel: "The audience can have had no illusions about their superiority to the disciples in the story, whether male or female, because if they have learned anything it is not to boast of one's faithfulness to Jesus and not count oneself an insider until the story is over. But they have witnessed God's ability to do 'that which is impossible for humans,' and they have also been stunned by God's amazing grace in response to cowardice and failure. So there is reason for hope, for even Peter, for even the audience, for even new audiences who hear the story told yet again, and who stand bewildered and frightened at the door of the empty tomb with nothing to do except to go and tell."

15. Tolbert, *Sowing the Gospel*, 107.

from the cross now, so that we may see and believe" (15:32 NRSV). We, the readers, realize the tragic double irony in this statement as the subject of the taunts is the very One for whom the leaders of Israel have daily prayed. Elsewhere, on three separate occasions, Jesus explains to his disciples that he must suffer, as will all disciples who follow him. Mark juxtaposes the last of these warnings by Jesus with this pretentious request from the sons of Zebedee: "Grant us to sit one at your right hand and one at your left, in your glory" (10:37 NRSV).

In addition to repetition and irony, Mark tightens his bond with us by using the classical Greek theater device of "asides." Through asides Mark conveys essential information to us as he guides us to the correct conclusions about his story. To establish the rapid popularity achieved during Jesus' Galilean ministry, Mark tells of the exorcism of a man with an unclean spirit in chapter 1 and then follows this story with an aside to us: "At once his [Jesus'] fame began to spread throughout the surrounding region of Galilee" (1:28). To accent the crowd's calamitous choice of Barabbas over Jesus, Mark tells us about a custom of political appeasement practiced each year by Pilate during the high holy days in Jerusalem.[16] These asides align us with Mark's narrator and increase the likelihood that we will make the right choice at the close of the story.

No other Gospel writer uses the "sandwich" technique—inserting a new story in the middle of an unfinished one—more often or with greater impact than Mark.[17] For example, in chapter 5, the president of the synagogue approaches Jesus on behalf of his dying daughter. We are enthralled by how Jairus, a powerful ruler of the synagogue, asks help from both a commoner and one regularly condemned by most other synagogue leaders. Just when we expect to hear how the story ends, Mark inserts a new story. More precisely, it is not so much a new story as it is a story set in the same location but viewed from another angle. In this inserted story, a bleeding woman defies Levitical teachings both by being in public and by touching Jesus.[18] Only after Mark tells about the healing of this woman do we hear about the healing of Jairus's

---

16. The historical veracity of Pilate's practice has been the object of considerable debate. See H. A. Rigg, "Barabbas," *JBL* 64 (1945): 417–56; H. Z. Maccoby, "Jesus and Barabbas," *NTS* 16 (1970): 55–60; Steven L. Davies, "Who Is Called Bar-Abbas?" *NTS* 27 (1981): 260–63; Robert L. Merritt, "Jesus Barabbas and the paschal pardon," *JBL* 104 (1985): 57–68; and C. S. Mann, *Mark* (Garden City, N.Y.: Doubleday & Co., 1986), 637–39. This debate, though, largely misses Mark's literary point. Historical or not, this narrative feature advances the plot and heightens the tragic irony.

17. Tolbert, *Sowing the Gospel,* 164–65: "For a catalogue of Markan insertions, see J. R. Donahue, *Are You the Christ? The Trial Narrative in the Gospel of Mark* (SBLDS 10; Missoula, Mont.: Scholars Press, 1973), 58–63. For a discussion of the effects of intercalation in Mark, see Kermode, *The Genesis of Secrecy,* 133–40."

18. See Leviticus 15:19–27; 22:22–25.

daughter, in which Jesus himself defies Levitical teaching by touching a corpse.[19] Donald Juel offers a tentative explanation for Mark's storytelling technique: "It may be, for example, that the whole story of Jesus' ministry is 'bracketed' by the *tearing* of the heavens at Jesus' baptism (1:10) and the *tearing* of the temple curtain at his death (15:58)."[20] In any case, Mark's literary "sandwiches" create a narrative suspense and push readers to ask what each story means and how they enrich each other.

Readers are often frustrated by what Mark's story leaves out or ignores. We want to know more about Jesus' family and his disciples, about Pilate and Herod. We want to know something more, anything more, about the intriguing cast of characters in Mark's story. Mary Ann Tolbert recognizes what should be obvious to careful readers of Mark: he pays little attention to personality profiles and character development in his story.[21] She suggests that Mark's characters are less real persons than archetypes of varied responses to the call of Jesus. For example, the disciples of Jesus serve to exemplify the rocky ground in chapter 4.[22] Mark tells us about Peter not to explain the inner psychology behind his denial but rather to urge us to do otherwise. Such an interpretative approach to Mark frees us from asking needless questions that this story simply will not answer.[23] Instead, this storytelling technique focuses on how *we* will hear and respond to the Gospel.

How *are* we to respond in faithfulness to Jesus when the major characters in Mark's story don't? Again, Mark's storytelling technique offers a solution. Through repetition, irony, asides, "sandwiching," and character typology, Mark provides no character in his story with as much vital information for faithful witness and discipleship as he does his readers. From the initial verses of the Gospel, we learn information about Jesus that no character in the story will ever fully grasp. We go down in the Jordan with Jesus and listen as God

---

19. See Leviticus 22:4; Numbers 5:2; 6:6, 11; 9:6–7, 10.

20. Juel, *Gospel of Mark,* 28.

21. Ibid., 41. Juel agrees: "As for Aristotle, plot is perhaps the most important feature of Mark's narrative. Characters are largely flat. We are given little insight into the psychological profile of any of the characters, even Jesus."

22. Tolbert, *Sowing the Gospel,* 224. Tolbert notes that this typological narrative style was commonly employed for a specific purpose by Hellenistic writers, especially Aristotle. In this case, "because the typology the disciples illustrate is a universal truth, those same weaknesses may plague the reader—or people the reader knows—as well. Character in ancient literature was revealed by choices: what one wills to do or avoids doing."

23. Horsley, *Hearing the Whole Story,* 7. Horsley notes the limited value of using modern literary analysis on ancient literature: "While claiming to recognize how different ancient literature was from modern fiction, literary interpreters of the Gospels devote considerable attention to character development. But Mark's characters do not develop; they play roles in the plot(s), with little or no attention to the 'character.'"

announces the sonship of Jesus. We travel into the wilderness with Jesus and see him survive forty days without a taste of manna or a bite of quail. When the boat tosses on the stormy sea, we rest with Jesus in the stern wondering why the Twelve understand less about the identity of Jesus than Jonah's pagan sea mates understood about him. We overhear Jesus predict his death and resurrection three times and then three times ask his disciples to keep watch while he prays. Afterward, with Jesus, we mourn the three denials of Peter. Later, sitting with Jesus before the Roman authority, we listen as Pilate pronounces sentence upon a man they all know is innocent. Finally, we walk to the tomb with the women bearing spices. We hear the young man tell about the risen Jesus going ahead of them to Galilee, back to where the story began. With this announcement, Mark leads us to think that the outcome of the story of Jesus relies on the future faithfulness of these women. Yet, once again, the hope that Mark cultivates in us is crushed when even the most faithful disciples in Mark—the women—fail the final test of faithfulness.[24] With this disappointing and "unfinished" ending, Mark leaves us in a literary quandary as we now find ourselves familiar with the greatest story "never told." Mark leads us to the cliff of 16:8 knowing that unless we make a radically different decision than the women did, his will remain forever an "unfinished" Gospel.

We write this book then with a prayer for you, the reader, the preacher, and the listener of sermons. We pray that as you read Mark from your particular cultural context and explore the exegetical viewpoints we present, you will begin to hear something new. As you listen to the Gospel proclaimed through our sermons, and debate with us which homiletical angle, if either, is best suited to enter into the Markan text, we hope you find yourself situated just where Mark wants you—persuaded by the grace of God, the power of God's Spirit, and the encouragement of the body of Christ to *finish the story yourself!*

---

24. Ibid., 203. Horsley argues for a reading of Mark that elevates the women in the story as the true disciples: "Just as Mark portrays the twelve, particularly the three intimates of Jesus, as negative examples of 'following' Jesus, so Mark portrays women in the story as both representatives of renewal and positive paradigms of faithfully responding to and 'following' Jesus." While Horsley is right to note Mark's more favorable portrait of women, especially in such a patriarchal age, he overstates his case as he neglects to address the failed discipleship of the women at the tomb in chapter 16 of the Gospel.

1

And the Walls Come Tumblin' Down
Mark 1:1–3:6

View One: From Text to Sermon
Brian K. Blount

Joshua fit de battle ob Jerico,
Jerico, Jerico,
Joshua fit de battle ob Jerico,
An' de walls come tumblin' down.[1]

*I*t was a mighty battle fought against overwhelming odds. While a ragtag assembly of former slaves reconnoitered the armed, impregnable stronghold, Joshua requisitioned God's orders. Flash traffic from above gave the "go" command to march. The enemy warriors who had hunkered down in their city, behind its fortified wall, would find no salvation. God was on the move. God's people were following close behind (Josh. 6:1–27).

That's the slave version of the story. Throughout most of their history, African American Christians have stuck to it. For the most part, contemporary scholars have not. According to Joshua's own canonical account, the vulnerable people of Jericho were paralyzed by their fear of the wilderness wanderers well before they arrived on the scene (Josh. 2:8–14). According to many skeptical historians, there wasn't even much of a wall, if there was a wall at all, for God to throw down. Apparently as much massacre as military victory, the historical event may well have unfolded in a fashion that was very different from its musical, mythical narration.

The African slaves weren't studying history, though; they were fashioning a faith. For them slavery, like walled Jericho, was a mighty fortress; all hope

---

1. James Weldon Johnson, ed., *The Book of American Negro Spirituals* (New York: Viking Press, 1931), 56.

for historical transformation languished in the bulwark's shadow. That's why, like Joshua, they hoped in God. When God moves, walls fall. Whether that was Jericho's history or not, it was certainly its truth.[2] In his first two chapters and six verses, Mark champions a similar claim. A wall of sin separated the people from God. Institutional walls alienated the people from each other. Laws which had initially been established to protect holiness and purity claimed legalistic rather than holistic force. They became weapons that targeted the broken and the lost. Detonated by pharisaic and scribal teaching, they blasted lepers, sinners, women, and the infirm out of the circle of communal living. That is why God breaks in. Working through Jesus, God wages war against the rampart of sin and the codification of purity and holiness. And the walls come tumblin' down.

It is no wonder, then, that Donald Juel titles his chapter on the theme-setting scene of Jesus' baptism "Transgressing Boundaries."[3] It is in this showcase moment of divine presence that God breaks through the barricade segregating human history from mythical reality and assigns Jesus the office of tearing down walls. The first evangelist sets the tone with his choice of words. In describing this same scene where Jesus' baptism induces a vision of the heavens parting, Matthew and Luke choose the verb "open" (*anoigō*).[4] Not Mark. In his rendering, this isn't a comforting metaphorical moment that initiates diplomatic relations between God and humankind; it is a foreboding image of the eschatological schizophrenia human history has now become. That is why Mark chooses the verb *schizō*, "tear," "rip," "rend" (1:10).[5] Its sound is as startling as its meaning. The passive formulation, "the heavens were ripped apart," indicates Mark's understanding of the truth the African American slaves took from their encounter with the Joshua story. When God moves, walls fall. This time it was the heavenly buffer that zoned God's world from the historical reality of humankind. God, who lived beyond time and promised to lead humans toward salvation at the end of time, had suddenly broken God's person and the promise that went with it directly into the present time. In what on the surface appears to be an historical delusion, that future hope and present reality can exist together at the same moment, Mark's baptism story narrates his gospel truth: in Jesus' life and ministry God's future is on the move in the human present.

---

2. For a broader interpretation of the slave spirituals as oriented toward historical liberation, see Brian K. Blount, *Cultural Interpretation: Reorienting New Testament Criticism* (Minneapolis: Fortress Press, 1995).

3. Juel, *Master of Surprise.*

4. Matthew 3:16; Luke 3:21.

5. Unless otherwise indicated, all scriptural quotations are from Mark's Gospel.

Mark's only other use of the verb *schizō*, at 15:38, confirms such an understanding. The evangelist uses it, again in the passive voice, to narrate the Temple curtain's slashing in two, from top to bottom, when Jesus died. This is God's mode of operation. God acts from above; God tears down walls that divide. In this case the curtain was most likely the one that walled off the Holy of Holies, the place of the divine presence, from the rest of the Temple. No one except the high priest entered it. And he only did so once a year in order to atone for the sins of the people. The symbolic inference was clear; God's most holy presence was sectioned off and locked away, kept secure, but also kept separate from the lives of God's people. Jesus' death symbolized the end of that division. At the moment of his son's demise, God signals one final time a note of clarity for the meaning of God's son's life; he was a boundary breaker. His life and death enabled contact between God and humankind; he opened up the possibility that the hope of participation with God in God's future reign could take place in the present Palestinian world.

But that's not all *good* news! Access to God's promise brings with it vulnerability to God's call. As Juel notes, "Viewed from another perspective, the image may suggest that the protecting barriers are gone and that God, unwilling to be confined to sacred spaces, is on the loose in our own realm. If characters in the story find Jesus' ministry threatening, then they may have good reason."[6] Why? Because God inaugurates Jesus' ministry with an act that mandates the direction for it; God breaks in and breaks through in a life-changing, transformative way. According to Mark, God's voice confirms to Jesus his special status, and therefore his special purpose. He is God's son (1:11; 9:7). Like a son, he will represent his parents in all that he does. "Jesus' ministry answers to the long deferred hope, 'O that thou wouldst rend the heavens and come down' (Isa. 64:1)."[7]

That is when, as if to bind the relationship between God and Jesus in an irrevocable manner, God's Spirit descends like a dove into Jesus (1:10). The scholarly debate that focuses on whether the dove imagery is supposed to demonstrate the bodily form of the Spirit (like a bird) or whether it is to suggest the manner in which the dove descends (like a bird) misses the point. Who cares? Mark is less concerned about what it looks like and how it glides than he is about what it does. It infiltrates Jesus. It possesses him. To be sure, as many scholars will point out, the preposition Mark uses to describe the Spirit's move "into" Jesus (*eis*) can, with an accusative object (which it has in this case) mean the same thing as another preposition, *epi*, "upon."[8] Since,

6. Juel, *Master of Surprise*, 35–36.
7. Lamar Williamson Jr., *Mark* (Interpretation; Atlanta: John Knox Press, 1983), 36.
8. Joel Marcus, *Mark 1–8* (Anchor Bible 27; New York: Doubleday, 2000), 160.

however, Mark does make widespread use of *epi*, it is clear that the evangelist knows it and knows how and when to use it. But contemporary readers are
theologically threatened by the thought of the Spirit entering "into" Jesus.
That is why so many contemporary readers make the case that Mark cannot
be saying what Mark apparently *is* saying. Having both grammatical choices
available to him, Mark *chooses* to say that the Spirit enters "into" Jesus.[9]
"That we are to understand the Spirit as inhabiting Jesus is apparent from the
dispute in Mark 3:22–30, where the charge that Jesus is possessed by unclean
spirits is characterized as blasphemy 'against the Holy Spirit.' Jesus is possessed—but by God's Spirit,"[10] argues Juel. God possesses him and God
presses him[11] toward the same ministry goal that God established in the ripping of the heavens: boundary breaking.

Preaching the reign of God is the method of that boundary breaking. Unlike
its twenty-first-century manifestation, Jesus' first-century preaching was
more than a public declaration or profession of faith. To be sure, it was that,
but it was also much more. Mark defines the concept by the way he identifies
it in relationship to Jesus' programmatic ministry act: "he came *preaching* the
gospel of God and *saying* . . ." (1:14). The preaching is defined grammatically
with the formulation of a masculine, singular, nominative participle that
relays the content of the preaching. The preaching is the public declaration,
the *saying* that the reign (*basileia*) of God has come near (1:15). Mark, however, does not end the formula there. He follows up with a succession of masculine, singular, nominative participles that refer back to Jesus and to the
programmatic act of preaching in 1:14. The preaching is not only given content by the *saying* of 1:15, but by the *passing by* of 1:16, the *entering* of 1:21,
the *approaching* of 1:31, and the *entering* of 2:1.[12] Each participle introduces
another component of the preaching act, a component that brings dramatic
transformation in the lives of the people to whom Jesus preaches. At 1:16,
Jesus' passing by initiates the call of four men who surrender their somewhat
stable present lives and follow him into his precarious future. At 1:21, Jesus'
entrance sets off a chain of authoritative teaching that redefines the notion of
authority and simultaneously touches a possessed man's life and sets him free.
At 1:31, Jesus' approach cools the fire of a woman's fever and restores her
health. At 2:1, Jesus' entrance precipitates a succession of social and political

---

9. Cf. Matthew 3:16; Luke 3:22.
10. Juel, *Master of Surprise*, 36.
11. See, e.g., the language of the wilderness scene (1:12–13) that follows directly upon the baptismal
scene. Immediately the Spirit of God thrusts, casts, propels Jesus into the wilderness and the initial
moments of his ministry.
12. For a more detailed discussion see Blount, *Go Preach!* 82–98.

boundary breaks so egregious in nature that the leadership decides this early in his ministry that he must be destroyed.

The boundary breaking begins with the descriptive content of Jesus' preached message. All of a sudden, time is filled up. "Most broadly," Williamson notes, "the coming of Jesus fulfills God's plan for the grand sweep of history. At that time ('after John was arrested') and in that place (Galilee) God stepped into human history in a unique and decisive way. The time is fulfilled, and ours is an invaded planet."[13] We have been raided by the reality that is the reign of God. The emphasis is "not so much the *place* where God rules as the *fact* that he [*sic*] rules or the *power* by which he [*sic*] manifests his [*sic*] sovereignty."[14] In Mark, God manifests that sovereignty through the preaching ministry of Jesus.

What is the appropriate response to that ministry? Transform yourself and others! Jesus makes the case with the language "repent and believe" (1:15). The parallelism in the text has been long acknowledged. The two-part indicative proclamation has a two-part imperative response. The time is filled up; repent. The reign of God has drawn near; believe the (this) good news. The imperatives demand life transformation. It is no secret that repentance involved a turning around and turning back from a misguided direction. In this case, certainly as John the Baptist professed it (1:4), the expectation was for a turn back to the ways of God. In Jesus' narrative case, matters are a bit more complex. Jesus' expectation focuses the turn more toward a future that is committed to God in a new way, a way exemplified by the narrative call of the disciples that immediately follows (1:16–20). One responds appropriately to God by leaving the old life behind and following Jesus into a new life for God. It will be a new life dedicated toward the goal of transforming others.

Jesus describes this goal in a less than amicable way; he says that he will make them fishers of people (1:17). The emphasis here is not on an evangelistic saving of souls. Instead, the metaphor conjures the harsh notion of a people who have been confronted with a new reality that they must not, under any circumstances, ignore.[15] Biblically, the image has strong linguistic ties with Jeremiah 16:16, Ezekiel 29:4, Amos 4:2, and Habakkuk 1:14–15. In each case the prophetic metaphor of fishing people is used negatively to suggest

---

13. Williamson, *Mark*, 41.

14. Marcus, *Mark 1–8*, 172.

15. "The figure is in many respects inappropriate if the mission of the disciples is thought of rescuing men or bringing them to salvation. It lacks the eminent suitability of the more widely used Biblical metaphor of the shepherd seeking the strayed sheep" (Charles W. F. Smith, "Fishers of Men," *HTR* 52 [1959]: 187).

censure and judgment. Those who argue for a positive connotation of the metaphor miss not only the Old Testament influence but also the logic inherent to the symbolism. For, as Charles Smith points out, "Fishing is a congenial diversion and perhaps occupation—for the fisherman, but scarcely for the fish. For them his coming is ominous."[16]

The censure implicit in the act of fishing, though, does not have an ultimate design of destruction. Its objective is transformation. In each OT case, the goal of the "fisher" was to effect a dramatic change in the identity of the "fished."[17] Certainly this is what happened in the lives of the four disciples "fished" in 1:16–20. They become the prototypical respondents to the arrival of the imminent reign of God in the person of Jesus. Transformed themselves, they are commissioned to go forth now and transform others (3:13–15; 6:7–13). Thus, just after Jesus tells Simon and Andrew to follow, he promises that he will *make* them become something new. He will transform them so that they can present the option of transformation to others.

Nowhere is this imagery of transformation presented more clearly than in Mark's narration of shattered sin. In Jesus' person and work, God removed the boundary that isolated humans from God. The breakthrough began with John. He came preaching a baptism of repentance into the forgiveness of sins (1:4). The language Mark uses is *aphesis*, which means "a sending away" or "a release." John is baptizing into this sending away of sins even though he believed that the actual remission of sins would only take place at the *eschaton*, or last day.[18] Baptism, then, was a present metaphorical event that signaled the anticipation of this future release in a ritual manner. In Jesus, though, the future rips open a place for itself in the present. The forgiveness (release) of (from) sins that John anticipates materializes in the present when Jesus speaks to the paralytic at 2:5: "your sins are forgiven." Jesus' person and ministry, then, represent God's move through the boundary of sin to catch hold of humankind.

This story of the paralytic (2:1–12) is filled with the imagery of God's boundary-breaking power through Jesus' person and ministry and the appropriate response to that trespass in the lives of the paralytic and his friends. The five who seek Jesus' intervention meet a wall of people who surround Jesus and thereby block their path. Undeterred, they climb to the top of the house. Faced now by the new obstacle of the roof, they proceed to dig their way

16. Ibid., 187–88.
17. William H. Wuellner, *The Meaning of "Fishers of Men"* (Philadelphia: Westminster Press, 1967), 94.
18. Marcus, *Mark 1–8*, 156.

through to Jesus. These two formidable boundaries are not enough to keep them away from a meeting with Jesus.

Jesus salutes their tenacity by extolling their faith. Theirs is precisely the kind of behavior he had come seeking. In his very first sermon (1:14–15), he proclaimed that the proper response to the indicative reality of God's reign was "believe!" Show faith! According to Jesus, these five have. Jesus responds by transforming the life of their paralyzed companion; he releases him from sin. The scribes counter with the complaint that only God can forgive sin (2:7). That, of course, is precisely Mark's point; Jesus is God's son and thus the representative of God's reign. Jesus does what God has done; he breaks open and breaks through.

The confrontation with the scribes also indicates that Jesus has done more than trespass the boundary of sin; he has also overstepped the bounds of priestly prerogative. The priestly infrastructure, of which the scribes are the representatives in this scene, was responsible for bringing the sin of the people before God and petitioning God for forgiveness. Jesus has by his mere word short-circuited that process. The Temple and the priesthood that serviced it need no longer be recognized as the way station between God and humans. That checkpoint had now been rendered meaningless; humans could reach God by going to God directly, through Jesus. It was only to make this point clear that Jesus followed up his proclamation of sin release with the physical healing of the paralytic. He demonstrated the authority to bring physical wholeness as a sign that he had the power to bestow spiritual wholeness in the form of the forgiveness of sins. This is the boundary-breaking power that his life and ministry represent.

This boundary-breaking power is on full display throughout the healing and controversy stories that follow the opening of Jesus' ministry at 1:40 and continue through the leaders' declaration that Jesus must be destroyed in 3:6. As was the case with the healing of the paralytic, Jesus' miracles are more than physical and natural transformations; they represent even more fundamentally the power of God's reign at work to revolutionize life in Israel. Institutions and laws once established to bring people closer to God and each other had taken on legalistic forms that instead divided. Just as Jesus challenged the priestly infrastructure that had been established as a gift of grace by God in the Old Testament but had now, in Mark's eyes, become a spiritual monopoly on access to God, so he also challenges the manner in which the priests and their scribal associates interpreted God's laws of holiness, purity, and Sabbath. "In sum," as Ched Myers argues, "Jesus' symbolic acts were powerful not because they challenged the laws of nature, but because they challenged the very structures of social existence. . . . Insofar as this order dehumanized life, Jesus challenged it and defied its structures: *that* is why his 'miracles' were not universally embraced."[19]

The healing of the leper at 1:40–45 is an exemplary case in point. Scholars point out that the term "leper" is probably inaccurate. The term was used by the Hebrews to indicate a variety of scaly skin diseases, some of which were incurable but most of which were not the same as the leprosy understood by modern medicine.[20] An identification of the disease, though, is not Mark's primary concern. The evangelist is concerned more with the uncleanness that the disease represents, and therefore the manner in which the contraction of the disease leads to exclusion from the circle of community (Lev. 13–14). Hooker observes, "To us, leprosy seems the most loathsome of diseases; to the Jew, it was also the most strident example of uncleanness. . . .[The leper] was not allowed to come into contact with other human beings or with their property and was thus totally cut off from society."[21] A pure people could not be tainted by such an impure person.

To be sure, Jesus responds to the man's request for cleansing by providing the cure. But significantly, he does something else first. Knowing the tradition, aware of the law, before he heals the man he reaches out and touches him (1:41). "In touching this man," Hooker notes, "Jesus did not simply run the risk of catching the leprosy, but also made himself unclean according to the regulations of the Mosaic law."[22] In a perilous act of solidarity, instead of confirming the man's exclusion by shunning him Jesus reached out and symbolically drew him in. He shattered the boundaries of purity that displaced the infirm and in the process rewrote the book on the nature of God's community.

The discipleship call at 2:13–17 is just as provocative. This time, instead of calling fishers, Jesus calls a tax collector. Historians explain that these collectors of indirect taxes, like tolls on transported goods, became collecting agents by submitting the highest bid for the privilege. Once they had obtained the office, they were then free to charge as much above that bid as they wanted. Overcharging was the norm. Generally reviled for this predatory behavior, they were also considered ritually unclean. Because of their profession they were in constant contact with Gentiles and Gentile money, both

---

19. Ched Myers, *Binding the Strong Man: A Political Reading of Mark's Story of Jesus* (Maryknoll, N.Y.: Orbis Books, 1988), 147–48.

20. Marcus, *Mark 1–8*, 205; Morna Hooker, *The Gospel according to Saint Mark* (Peabody, Mass: Hendrickson Publishers, 1991), 78.

21. Hooker, *Mark*, 78–79.

22. Ibid., 79. See also Marcus, *Mark 1–8*, 206: "Chrysostom (*Homily on Matthew 23.2*) asserts that this description is deliberately provocative, since it overlooks OT/Jewish scruples about touching ritually impure people, and he contrasts it with 2 Kings 5:1–14, where Elisha avoids contact with the man whom he cures of scale-disease."

obvious sources of ritual contagion. These were people who chose to live in manners contrary to the laws of God. Jesus not only calls *one of them* to be one of his disciples, he later reclines at meal with him and others of his kind (2:15–17). Jesus' actions were therefore a blatant display of disregard for the laws of ritual purity and social propriety. He was pulling into his community precisely those who had been legally excluded (2:17).

This new boundary-breaking effort at representing the reign of God in human history (2:18–22) climaxes in the final two scenes in which Jesus takes aim at the legalistic interpretation of none other than the Sabbath law. In the first scene, 2:23–28, Jesus allows his disciples to pluck grain and eat it on the Sabbath, despite the proscription against labor on that day (Exod. 20:10). Jesus puts the human need of hunger above the ritual prescription of the law, and thus transforms the way one prioritizes one's relationship with God. His teaching action, Hooker argues, "suggests that the Pharisees were so eager not to transgress that they lost sight of the real purpose of the commandments. In spite of all their endeavours, the will of God—that men and women should rest and enjoy the Sabbath—was not performed."[23] Jesus transgressed their legalistic interpretation and refocused the law on God's original intent for meeting human need.

He maintains that focus in the story that finishes this opening Gospel section (3:1–6). Although emergency aid was permissible on the Sabbath, it was generally not acceptable to heal. Jesus, however, "refuses to draw a distinction between saving life in the narrowest sense and the offer of full life which characterizes his whole ministry. To delay healing for a day is to deny the Torah's true intention, which is the glory of God and the benefit of man."[24] Jesus, therefore, calls the man with a withered hand into the midst of onlookers where all can see him, and where all can see what Jesus is about to do for him. In so doing, Jesus breaks through the traditional understanding of the law and opens up new, more merciful, more holistic avenues for its interpretation. Limitations on reaching out to those who are broken and infirm, even institutionalized and legally sanctioned limitations, must be overturned and broken through in this new time.

Throughout this entire opening section, then, Mark presses the thesis he established with his use of the verb rip, tear (*schizō*) at 1:10 to describe God's unruly behavior. God tears through the heavenly veil that separates God from humans. God runs loose through human history in the person and ministry of Jesus. And in that running God demands change. God transforms the

---

23. Hooker, *Mark*, 104.
24. Ibid., 107.

landscape of human living and requires transformed lives in return. God breaks down walls that separate the people of Israel from God and the people of Israel from each other. And, given Jesus' charge that his disciples follow in the same transformative task, God also directs Mark's reading disciples to become players in the same boundary-breaking movement of God's imminent reign.

View Two: "God on the Loose" (Mark 1:9–11)
Brian K. Blount

[Introduction: My good friend, the Reverend Michael Livingston, the Executive Director of the International Council of Community Churches (ICCC), asked if I would lead a series of Bible discussions on the Gospel of Mark at the ICCC's annual conference in Albuquerque, New Mexico, in the summer of 2001. Because I would be teaching each morning of the weeklong conference, he also thought it would be helpful if I preached from Mark at one of the conference's opening worship services. My sermon would give them a sense of how I proclaimed what I taught. I wrote this sermon for that occasion.]

I was thirty-eight and my wife was *thirty-something* when we had our daughter. A few friends told us jokingly, "You're too old to be having that baby. She's going to wear you out!" That probably wasn't the most tactful thing to say, but it turned out to be one of the most prophetic. When you stand and look through the glass of that nursery and see that baby hollering and screaming for dear life, you not only realize how good life *is*, you realize how different and exhausting life is *going to be*. Right from the start, well, even before the start of her life, she let it be known that things in our family were going to change. The little being trapped in her mother's womb couldn't even wait the full nine months to get out and take charge. So, not quite eight months in, when *she* was ready, she pushed her way out with such fury, such contracting force on her mommy's belly, that she forced the doctors to perform a caesarean section and cut her way free. And then, screaming bloody murder at a world that was, as far as she was concerned, centered on her, she was loose. I can still see her, just seconds after the doctor had liberated her from her mother's abdomen, her blood-streaked face, her wide eyes, her open, screaming mouth, and her arms stretched out wide, as if to say, "I am in charge of all that I survey."

From that moment on, everything changed. Her very weakness made her the strongest power in our house. Our habits, our routines, our very lives had to change to fit *her* desires and *her* schedule. When we complained to her pediatrician that she wouldn't go to sleep at night unless one of us was right there in the room with her, he said, "You've got to show her who's boss. You've got to show her who's in charge." Well, after three weeks of trying, we came to the conclusion that *she* was.

It came to me clearly one fateful and instructive December night. There I was, a thirty-eight–year-old professor at the prestigious Princeton Theological Seminary. I stand and lecture before hundreds of students. I stand and preach before great congregations. And yet, there I was, *crawling* on my hands and knees across the carpet of her bedroom floor like a scared rabbit in a futile attempt to escape before she opened her eyes, found me out, and sounded her personal, piercing cry of alarm. We couldn't domesticate her. We couldn't get her to sleep when we wanted. We couldn't get her to eat like we wanted. A mind-bending, life-altering, change-your-ways kind of force had gotten loose and was running amok in our lives.

That is what Jesus' baptism is like. In the moment of Jesus' baptism, God breaks free into the world in which we live in the same way that my little daughter broke free into ours. This is no quiet, gentle breeze, this God that comes free and loose when Jesus comes up from the waters of the Jordan. This is a wild, untamed God who breaks in on Israel the way a tiger in a zoo would, if he could, crash open his cage door just as you were walking complacently by it.

Clouds tearing. Heavens ripping. Divine voice booming. Spirit descending. This is terrible, untamed, tiger talk. It is the language of slashing and slicing, shredding and clawing until something once locked up on that safe and seldom seen heavenly side over there knifes its way free to this historical, human side we're standing on over here.

Heaven, the sky, is a firmament in the Bible. It's a buffer zone. You know what a buffer zone is. It's a place that one great power uses to separate itself from another great power. It's like the cage in which we keep tigers locked away in a zoo. That way we can still see them, but we don't have to fear them, because the bars are a buffer between them and us. Well, for human beings, the heavens are like that. The ancient Hebrews believed that no human could look upon God and live. God was too holy, too bright, too powerful. Thank heavens, then, for the heavens. It was the heavens that kept us separate from God, kept us from seeing God face to face. It kept us from being blinded and destroyed by God's holiness.

Humans tried to imitate this buffer in Jerusalem, at the Temple. They created this place in the Temple called the Holy of Holies. It was a spiritual cage that contained the dangerous presence of God. It was so holy a place that it had to be separated from the rest of the Temple by a great curtain. No one went past that curtain except the high priest. And he only went one day a year, on the Day of Atonement. And when he went it was in fear and trembling, to seek God's forgiveness for the sins of the entire people. The world needed the heavens for a buffer, the Temple needed a curtain for a buffer, lest contact with God become too direct, and therefore too dangerous. Because the power God represents was too strong, too wild.

We tend to view it all so romantically these days. We want to be closer to God. We sing songs like "Closer to Thee"; "Just a Closer Walk with Thee"; "He Touched Me." We want as much as we can to get closer to God, to walk in the garden with God, to stand next to and be touched by God. That's why so many Christians love that story of the Temple curtain tearing when Jesus died. You know the story from Mark 15:37–38, when Jesus utters his last cry and breathes that one final time, and then that Temple curtain rips. We don't like it that Jesus dies, but we do like the fact that if we had to lose our Lord, we could take comfort in knowing that with his death the Temple curtain was shredded from top to bottom. God would no longer tolerate a separation of God from God's people. Now, through Jesus, what Jesus had done, what Jesus had given, God was saying that you no longer have to put up a curtain, you no longer have to seek me out only one day a year through the high priest. Now you can seek me out yourselves, whenever you want. I've removed the buffer. I've made it possible for you to come be with me. That's how we look at it. Because that's the nice, safe way to look at it. That's how we want it. Tamely romantic. Spiritually sedate.

I have a colleague, Don Juel; he teaches Mark with me at Princeton Seminary. He tells how he once taught this story to a group of teenagers; he told them exactly what I just told you. He told them that the tearing of the Temple curtain meant that we now had access to God. As he was going on, feeling good about what he was teaching these young folk, a young man in the group raised his hand and said, "I have something." My colleague nodded and said, "Yes?" The teenager said, *"I think you have it wrong."* Imagine that. A young teenager who gets his Bible study in Sunday school one day a week tells a man who holds a Ph.D. in biblical studies, a man who has studied the Bible every day of his life for years, in Greek and Hebrew no less, that he has it wrong, and he, the teenager, has it right. Well, my colleague listened for what he had to say, and he told me what that young man said changed forever the way he looks at that passage. The young man said, "I don't think it means that we now have access to God. I think it means that all of a sudden, God has access to us." See, all of a sudden, the God we've trapped behind the curtain is on the loose.

According to Mark, though, God was already breaking loose, already getting ready to run wild through human history, at Jesus' baptism. So, when you look at the story of Jesus following that moment of his baptism, you're seeing what it looks like to have God on the loose.

It *looks* strange! The people were looking for a great Messiah, someone who would, like David, lead the people back to political freedom by kicking the Romans out of their land and reestablishing a free and independent Israel. So when John the Baptist starts talking about the one who is coming, the great one who will baptize them with the powerful and Holy Spirit of God, you can be sure they were looking for Arnold Schwarzenegger, not Little Orphan Annie. But then it's Jesus who comes. This man from that little, nowhere, orphaned town of Nazareth. It's like, you're looking for God in a great building with long halls, high ceilings, a magnificent steeple, dressed in a long robe, most likely with doctor's stripes on the sleeves . . . and then God comes sliding out of some trailer park, hanging out with people from the wrong side of the tracks.

It gets stranger still! Mark says that the Spirit of God, this force that has just ripped up the buffer zone of the heavens and clawed its way to our side of the creation fence, moves *into* Jesus. It's at this point that the translators get as nervous as people living in a neighborhood with a tiger on the loose. Check out your own English Bibles. The translators say that the Spirit descends *on* Jesus. And, to be sure, the preposition Mark uses here can sometimes be used that way. But its principal and primary definition is "into." But you rarely if ever hear anyone explain that. The most likely way to translate the Greek here is: The Spirit descends *into* Jesus. Even the buffer of Jesus' human being, his skin and bone, his human spirit and consciousness cannot stop God from moving *into* him in a way that makes the power that belongs to God the power that is going to be revealed in Jesus. The Spirit of God takes hold of and *possesses* Jesus. That's one of the reasons his family ends up thinking he's crazy. He's got the wild Spirit of God running loose inside him. To paraphrase an old and famous saying: *Jesus has a tiger in his tank.*

You want to know what that Tiger will do? Want to know what happens when you get too close to God, when you get touched by the power of God's Spirit? You don't sit still and enjoy the view, you don't lay down and take a nap, you don't bask in the glory of what great thing has just happened to you. You go immediately to wild work. To work for God is to be thrown directly into the path of those who would oppose God. And so Mark tells us that Jesus was immediately *driven* into the wilderness by the Spirit of God. He didn't get lost. He didn't just happen to wander across the wilderness border by mistake because his compass was broken. He didn't take a campfire holiday. He was *driven* by the Spirit into the wilderness for the specific purpose of engaging Satan in hand-to-hand spiritual and physical combat.

And you think he's in trouble *out there*? The wilderness will prove to be the *least* of his problems. You think things are bad when he's within striking range of the devil and wild beasts? It's when he gets into the *civilized towns* with the *religious* people who go to synagogue every Sabbath and church every Sunday that he *really* gets into trouble. *That's when things really get wild.* That's when he gets into the kind of danger that will threaten his life. The wilderness looks like a first-century Disneyland compared to his hometown, the synagogue, the Temple, and the religious leaders in charge of them. If you want to know what happens when God gets on the loose and gets into you, take a look at what happened to Jesus. When God gets into you, you get into trouble, because God *drives* you until you're running wild in a world hell-bent on religiously remaining its same, tame, shameful self.

So, looking at Jesus, let's see if we can figure out what it means for us that God has broken down the buffer zone of the heavens, torn the dividing wall of the Temple curtain, and fired out into human life. God on the loose, from the perspective of the leaders in Palestine, is a scary thing.

That's because leaders lead. Leading means getting people from here to there. The only way you do that is by keeping people in line, keeping order. That's what religion is about essentially, after all: keeping people in line, keeping the spiritual order, getting people from over here to over there. I know you say, "Well, that's not right, that's not all religion is." But look at it. There's a goal, right? What's the goal? To get to heaven. Everybody comes to faith because they'd like ultimately to go to heaven. Maybe not right now, not today, but when the time comes you don't want to go to oblivion; you don't want to go to hell; you want to go to heaven. Am I right? And you have religious leaders to help you get there. Am I right? And how do the leaders lead? By telling you what to do *now* so you can be right with God *then*. Am I right?

What they're doing is getting you ordered, getting you to do the right thing, getting you to stand in the right line. What they're doing is trying to tame the wild force that wants to run free and loose inside you and through you. Don't stand over there where all the gambling and prostitution is going on. Stand over here where there are nice people who go to church every Sunday and give their money to the church and to each other. Don't stand over there where there are people living the wrong way sexually, or where there are people suffering and dying from sexual diseases. Stand over here where people are spiritually clean and morally straight. Don't stand over there with people who cheat and steal. Stand over here where everybody acts nice. Don't stand over there with people who break the laws that make all of us safe and keep all of us doing the right thing before God and each other. Stand over here with those of us who will do what is necessary, lock up whoever we find necessary, to put the law first. Nobody is above the law, right? We were made to obey the law; the law wasn't made to support and obey us. Leaders get you to heaven by getting you to toe this religious party line. That's what the leaders in Mark's time did; it's what the leaders in our time do. And if somebody comes along and starts saying and doing different, then somebody's got to find a way to stop them.

Well, in Mark's Gospel, *Jesus* is the one who touches and holds lepers. *Jesus* is the one who parties with cheating tax collectors and stealing sinners. *Jesus* is the one who lets a woman the church fathers thought was a prostitute stroke and anoint him *at a party* in a *leper's* house. *Jesus* is the one who broke the Sabbath laws right in front of the people who had been obeying the Sabbath laws all their lives. *Jesus* is the one who told them that whoever said that nobody was above the law was wrong, that *everybody* was above the law, because the law was made to serve humans, humans weren't made to serve the law. So when the law hurts humans, humans ought to make it their duty to break it down, tear it up, rip it apart the way God ripped the heavens and shredded the Temple curtain.

This is what the world, the religious, spiritual, social, and political world looks like when Jesus sets God loose in it. It's a wild world out of religious, regulatory control, a world on the edge of time, a world that thinks the reign of God might break in at any moment, a world so sure that God is right around the corner that it stops thinking about standing in line and starts *lining* up the ways, all the ways the people in the world can think of to help each other. It's a world that cares more about purifying those who are sinners than *being* pure and separate *from* sinners. It's a world that cares more about touching and holding those who have dirtied themselves or have been dirtied by the situations of their lives than it cares about sweeping their churches and lives clean of anybody who's made mistakes. It's a world that would willingly and willfully break laws and customs that segregate people from each other, break laws that send people into unjust wars, break laws that allow the powerful and wealthy to have more opportunity in life than the weak and poor. It's a world that would look very much like Mark's world of Jesus walking around possessed by the power of the Spirit of God. In such a world you either go with the man and help him create the holy chaos he's creating or you find a way to do everything you can to stop him so you can get your people back in line.

I offer it as a choice in just that way as I speak before you this morning because, today, you, we are the leaders, aren't we? That means that the God that Jesus sets loose wants to devour the traditions we may hold sacred, that make us holy, that keep us set apart, that help us keep our people in line. You want to be holy, don't you? You want to be pure, don't you? You want to be set apart, don't you? I know you want to be a self who is righteous before others, don't you? That makes us . . . just like the scribes and chief priests and Pharisees. That's all they wanted. They didn't dislike Jesus personally. This was business. Religious business. What they wanted was to keep people in line and to get Jesus back in line with them. To have the holy over here, the unholy over there, with a buffer zone of Temple, synagogues, churches, deacons, elders, priests, trustees, senior choirs, usher boards, and apostles in between them, separating them, so as to keep them from mixing, for fear that the unholy folk might contaminate and mess up the holy folk. They never figured, *like Jesus evidently figured*, that the opposite might happen, that the holy folk might contaminate the unholy folk, that the pure might touch and cleanse the impure, that the people of the law might help the lawless see why the law had been established in the first place, not to hurt but to help, not primarily to stop us from doing stuff *to* each other, but to start us doing things *for* each other. But Jesus did. In his crazy classroom of convoluted kingdom calculus, uncleanness plus uncleanness didn't add up to even greater uncleanness, it added up to wholeness. That's why when Jesus touched the leper, he didn't *get* leprosy, but the leprosy *got* transformed. That's why when Jesus sat down with tax collectors and sinners he didn't *get taken*, he *took* them with him on his journey to Jerusalem as disciples. That's why when Jesus let that woman with the shaky reputation soothe and salve him, he didn't *lose* his way, he helped her *find* her way to faith. That's why when Jesus broke the Sabbath laws in order to feed the hungry and heal the sick, he didn't end up on the *wrong side* of God, he ended up showing his people the *right side* of the law they'd forgotten, the side that serves God's people and doesn't make God's people bow down and worship it. That's what it looks like when God breaks loose.

But we might as well admit it. We don't *really* want a wild God on the loose. Not in our world. Certainly not in our churches. Not really. Especially not in church where we want everything just so. We really want a domesticated God, a charismatic but captivated cat, a holy but humbled hound dog. We want the power that God and God's reign represent, but we want that power domesticated, working for us. We want it on a leash. Our leash.

But Jesus' story of baptism suggests that this is not how God works. When God gets hold of us God drives us to where *God* wants us to go, to what *God* wants us to do, not where we'd rather be, or what we'd rather not do. God got into John the Baptist and *drove* him. He went around mouthing off at kings and soldiers and high priests. God got into Jesus' disciples and *drove* them.

They went around proclaiming the reign of God was at hand, hunting down people possessed with demons, touching and healing people with impure diseases, teaching people who didn't want to be taught in inner-city schools nobody wanted to get near. God got into Jesus and *drove* him. He went around cleansing the Temple that was supposed to be the pinnacle of religious cleanliness and spiritual purity in the land. That's what happens when God *drives* you. You start doing all that kind of crazy stuff that gets you into all kinds of crazy circumstances. When God gets on the loose inside you, you start to do things that turn your world upside down and inside out.

We go crazy if somebody changes the format of the Sunday bulletin. Imagine what would happen if someone touched by God on the loose tried to change the very way our church does church, or tried to make our church reach out to problem people and impure issues that we think ought to stay outside the life and concern of the church. Just imagine if people stopped doing all the traditional things in all the traditional ways, stopped standing in religious line and started lining up to make the kinds of moves necessary to transform their churches and the neighborhoods surrounding those churches in leper-touching, prostitute-protecting, sinner-sitting, tax-collector carousing kinds of ways. Imagine what would happen if people were so possessed by the power of God's Holy Spirit that they stopped caring as much for how pure and holy they looked and started getting down into the dirt and mud and muck of the world that messes up so many of God's people and started cleaning that world up. Too many of us treat heaven as if it's a cotillion and we've got to look spiritually gorgeous if we're going to get in. So we spend all our earthly time in church like it's a beauty salon, touching up our faith, washing our hands of the wrong kinds of people, perfuming ourselves so we won't be tainted by the smell of a disintegrating world, making over and reshaping our faces until we cover over concern for those unfortunate misfits struggling in the world around us. But when God is on the loose, God's Spirit *drives* you out of the church and into the unknown, into the wilderness, where staying clean is not an option, because, like Jesus, you've been driven into a down and dirty fight for God's people.

But that's the good news! There's good news whenever boundaries are broken down, buffers are ripped apart, dividing lines are shredded, and people are set free to reach out to others and set them free too. The good news in this story about God breaking free into Jesus and Jesus breaking free into our world is that we can tap into that boundary-breaking power to change the world in which we live. This is the kind of Tiger that it's *good* to have on the loose, running free and unfettered. This is the Tiger that protects you from the destructiveness of this world and gives you the power to stop this world from being so destructive to others. Recognize that God is loose in your life. Remember that God is loose in your church. Work with the God who is loose in your world. Do everything in your power to run after God and run loose yourself with the transforming power of God's Holy Spirit powering every-thing you do and bringing change to every situation you meet. That way when people talk about you to other people, they *won't* say, "He's a nice man." They *won't* say, "She's a good church worker." They *won't* say, "He's real religious." They won't *even* say, "She's a good Christian." They'll say something else instead. Something wild. Something crazy. Something dangerous. Something like "She's got a tiger in her tank!"

View Three: *Metanoeite*!
Gary W. Charles

She dashed into my study and assured me that she did not need much of my time. I was preparing for the frenzy of the week before Christmas and time was at a premium. I was the first research stop for her religion paper. Her assignment was to interview a group of religious leaders from different Chris-tian denominations, comparing and contrasting their theological positions. Though she asked for little of my time, I soon realized that each question she asked could take several hours to answer properly—for some scholars, a life-time. She wanted to know: "How does your denomination understand God?" "Who is Jesus for you?" "Does your church believe in a heaven and hell?"

Then, she pinned me down with the toughest question by far. She asked, "What is the central message of your faith?" I rambled a bit, giving her an accept-able answer, one that would pass muster before any examining body of main-stream theologians, but her question lingered long after our conversation ended.

Before she left, I queried her with my own set of questions. I learned, not to my surprise, that the church had largely been "missing-in-action" from her life. She saw herself as "religious" but not necessarily in a "Christian sort of way," and most certainly, not in a churchgoing way. The church in her mind's eye was a group of well-heeled hypocrites, too quick to judge and too ready to hold people to every letter of the law. I did not agree with her; neither did I disagree. I know the church well enough not to pretend there was no truth to her observations.

I never saw this young student again, never read her account of our interview, and have often wished for one more shot at her last question. What I would like to say to her has everything to do with the first words Jesus speaks when he begins his public ministry in Mark. Still dripping wet from the Jordan, Jesus says, "Repent, and believe in the gospel." Since, as Brian suggests, God is on the loose in the person of Jesus, then it makes perfect sense not just for characters in Mark's story, but for all people to "repent, and believe in the gospel." For with God on the loose in Jesus, things are going to change. This is not a distant hope for which we can pray; it is a present reality for which we must brace ourselves. With God on the loose, walls of ignorance will tumble, iron curtains of segregation will rip open from top to bottom in the world, in the church, and in us. That is how I would begin my answer to the young student.

The language Mark uses for our response to a God on the loose is "repent" (*Metanoeite!*). *Metanoeite* is a Greek verb that is plural in number, present in tense, active in voice, and imperative in mood. *Metanoeite* is not a quiet whisper from Jesus to a close friend; it's a booming voice from a bullhorn directed to anyone within earshot. The present tense and imperative mood of this Greek verb gives *Metanoeite* a recurring urgency, something that is always the *kairos*—the right time, the pregnant moment—to do or to do *again*.

Unfortunately, "repent" in English is a crippled word. It limps around most churches today, handicapped by misuse and overuse. A tired, old, church word. In the church's past the cry of "Repent!" evoked scary images of wild-eyed preachers thumping their Bibles and haranguing all sinners in sight. Today, in mainstream churches, it sounds anachronistic, petty, and useless; it is now blunt and dull. It has been pushed to the church's theological edge where it still retains its traditional harsh and severe sound, posing an ominous threat to "change your ways!" before the heavenly storm, brewing overhead, showers its judgment upon you.

That is not the *Metanoeite* we meet in Mark. Spoken from the mouth of Jesus, *Metanoeite* has an enticing charm to it. After his baptism, and having survived the temptations in the desert, Jesus arrives in Galilee to announce that God's reign is within breathing distance: "*Metanoiete*. Believe the gospel!" (1:15). In other words, "Turn around to take hold of something better than what you have now." Without question, *Metanoeite* carries with it the notion that we have some changing to do, some new directions to move; its primary orientation, though, is toward God's future rather than our past.

In Mark, *Metanoeite* is an imperative invitation—to trust in a future made possible by the grace of God. It is an invitation that means we are not stuck forever living in ways that knock the breath out of us. With God on the loose in the person of Jesus, we can find a new way to live that is literally a breath of fresh air.[25] This is far closer to Jesus' intent in Mark's Gospel when he

---

25. *Pneuma* is the Greek word for wind and is used in the New Testament to describe the Holy Spirit of God.

shouts *"Metanoeite"* than a pronouncement of personal doom. When repentance is made to sound like a trip to the principal's office or swigging a large dose of cod-liver oil, it betrays the very nature of the gospel in which Jesus calls us to believe.

In Anne Tyler's novel *Saint Maybe*, the main character, Ian Bedloe, feels he has caused his brother's death. Overcome by grief, he cannot sleep and this living nightmare consumes all his waking hours. Tyler writes:

> It was after seven on a dismal January evening, and most places had closed. One window, though, glowed yellow—a wide expanse of plate glass with CHURCH OF THE SECOND CHANCE arching across it in block letters. Ian couldn't see inside because the paper shade was lowered. He walked on by. Behind him a hymn began. . . . He missed most of the words, but the voices were strong and joyful. . . . He paused at the intersection, the arches of his sneakers teetering on the curb. He peered at the DON'T WALK sign for a moment. Then he turned and headed back to the church.[26]

Jesus says, *"Metanoeite."* Why? Because in Jesus, God makes it possible for us to repent. Ian in Tyler's *Saint Maybe* and you and I can start again and then again; our sinfulness does not finally get the best of us. That's the gospel, the good news, the glad tidings toward which Jesus invites us to stop, turn, and hold onto for dear life. Our sin does not finally blot out the future that God has in store for us. Things do not have to stay the way they are. In fact, to follow Jesus means that things *cannot* stay the way they are. Just ask Peter, James, Andrew, Levi, and John—the first five disciples—none of whom had applied for the job. Just ask Peter's mother-in-law, whose fever cooled with Jesus' soothing touch, or the leper whose life was no longer defined by his disease after his meeting with Jesus. Just ask those who lowered the paralytic through the roof, or the man whose withered hand caught more of Jesus' attention than obeying 4,352 Sabbath regulations!

Not all hear *Metanoeite* as good news. They insist that things need to stay just the way they are. And they spend every ounce of energy making sure that things do. After all, who needs to repent when everything is just fine? In Mark, those who most oppose repentance are not the secular humanists, but the religious leaders from the Jerusalem Temple. They are not interested in "turning around" but making sure that life moves forward in the same direction. "If it was good enough for Moses . . . " If it was good enough for David . . ." You get the idea.

---

26. Anne Tyler, *Saint Maybe* (New York: Alfred A. Knopf, 1991), 115.

Throughout Mark's Gospel, the religious leaders are so dead set on maintaining the "religious status quo" that they lose sight of the One for whom life is maintained. Just ask the paralytic who is lowered into a theological firestorm in which the religious leaders are too busy objecting to Jesus forgiving the paralytic's sins to notice that the paralyzed guy is now walking out the door. "Only God can forgive sins" is their party line. "Only God can restore life in such a fundamental way." Jesus agrees. "God *is* here, NOW, so *Metanoeite!*"

If God is on the loose in Jesus, then *Metanoeite* is a message for everyone. Every old way of living is going to change, every wall of resistance to God's future is going to fall, including the most formidable wall of sin. That is why Jesus not only instructs the paralytic to pick up his bed and walk but also tells him, "Your sins are forgiven." In these four words, Jesus announces what every human being, including the most strident religious leader, needs to know: Sin is real. Sin too often gets the best of us and makes us less than what God intends for our lives. Jesus asks his followers to believe that when a paralytic stood upright in Capernaum, the wall of sin started to crumble. And on the third day, when God's grace overcame even the sinful tyranny of the cross, the wall of sin collapsed.

Since the word *Metanoeite* is in the present tense in the Greek, it carries with it the idea of continuous action. You don't repent just once and be done with it. I wish all our fresh starts would result in totally changed people. We know better. No sooner are New Year's resolutions made than they are broken. No sooner do we promise to be a kinder and gentler nation then we act in ways that betray that kindness and gentleness. No sooner do we paint the church as a place of high moral virtue than another minister or priest is arrested for an immoral act while the church closes its doors to human need on its doorstep.

If you and I repent, only to need to repent again, why bother repenting in the first place? Why keep trying to head in a direction toward which our feet just don't want to go? One day a belligerent young man stormed up to Mahatma Gandhi. "You have no integrity," the young man charged. "Last week I heard you say one thing, today you are saying something entirely different. How can you justify such vacillation?" With his characteristic quietness, Gandhi paused and said, "It is quite simple. I have learned something since last week." A part of the good news announced by Jesus is that repentance is a continuous action.

Metanoeite is a plural verb in the Greek. Over the years, this verb has been downsized in English into a strictly singular affair. Surely, a person's decision to follow Jesus or not *is* deeply personal, but *Metanoeite* is a plural, imperative invitation that extends beyond one's personal decision. Most often addressed to the established religious powers who diabolically resist change and to disciples who keep turning full circle, never quite figuring out how to follow Jesus, the call to *Metanoeite* is a plural call.

As a plural imperative verb in Mark, *Metanoeite* speaks forcefully to disciples, religious leaders, and the crowd; and through Mark, it speaks forcefully to the church. Mark refuses to reduce *Metanoeite* to a privatized response to the invitation of Jesus—"Just me and Jesus." Mark will have none of that. "Believing the gospel" is a group effort. Christian life is not a solitary experience, but one lived in community. *Metanoeite* is a call to disciples of Jesus in every age, not simply to a singular disciple.

The congregation I serve dates back to the 18th century. Now predominantly white, our worship had many more blacks in attendance three centuries ago. They were not necessarily there by choice; they were slaves and were seated in the balcony. They listened as my predecessors in the Meeting House pulpit quoted Scripture to endorse the divine economy of their "condition." Later preachers quoted Scripture to women in the 19th and early 20th centuries to remind them of the subservient and nurturing role God intended for them in his divine economy. For a theological tradition that had long advocated a Christian engagement with civil authorities, a remarkable silence came upon our Presbyterian pulpit prior to the Civil War. The religious leaders of the day decided that the church had no business addressing such secular matters of slavery; the church trafficked only in eternal affairs.

The religious leaders and the disciples in Mark's Gospel look pathetic and tragic, until compared with too many chapters in the history of the church. The church in every age should rejoice then in how Mark begins and ends his Gospel. He begins with a plural, imperative invitation to all willing disciples to *Metanoeite*. And remarkably, the Gospel ends when in Mark 16:7 the messenger at the empty tomb says to the women: "Go tell the disciples and Peter that he goes ahead of you to Galilee." The last time readers saw Peter in Mark's Gospel, he had crumpled into a pile of his own sin, while the rest of the disciples, at least the male disciples, had taken an early bus out of Jerusalem (14:50, 66–72). So the Gospel ends with an invitation from the risen Jesus for those who had betrayed, denied, and fled him in his greatest need to return to Galilee. It ends with an implied invitation for them to *Metanoeite*.

I wish that student would come dashing into my office one more time and ask again, "What is the central message of your faith?" The message, I would tell her, is a gift. The gift is the call to *Metanoeite*, which, simply put, means the freedom to change and embrace God's future, because God *is* on the loose and, in Jesus, gives us the chance to begin again.

2

A "Real" Family Reunion
Mark 3:7–35

View One: From Text to Sermon
Brian K. Blount

J. S. Winstead was an esteemed member of the church I once pastored. A retired school principal, he was used to getting quickly to the point. His only child, Carolyn, recounted the time she had traveled from her Atlanta home back to Newport News, Virginia, to visit her parents, unaccompanied by her three children—Winstead's three grandchildren. Upon exiting her car, she found him already on the front porch; he had been eagerly anticipating the arrival. He was not, however, completely satisfied with the fact that the car surrendered but a single occupant. "Where," he asked, "are my people?"

According to one manner of interpreting a key phrase in Mark 3:20, Jesus had come home.[1] According to Mark's interpretation of what happened when he arrived, there is some question as to the whereabouts and, more important, the identity of "his people." The narrative that stretches from 3:7 to 3:35 delivers a rather definitive answer. The people who populate Jesus' ancestral and national lineage are not his true kin; "his people," his real family, are constituted by behavior, not blood. The members of that family could come from anywhere, could be anyone. Those who attend to Jesus' proclamation about the imminent reign of God and govern their lives according to its transformative, countercultural mandates (see Chapter One exegesis) forge his faith family stock.

The gestation begins with the legion of people who swarm to Jesus by the sea.[2] In the opening summary passage, 3:7–12, Mark builds on Jesus'

---

1. Because of the ambiguity in the Greek, the translations "he came into the house" and "he came home" are of equal merit. See Hooker, *Mark*, 115.
2. Within the space of two verses (3:7–8), Mark twice describes a "great multitude."

boundary-breaking ministry in 1:1–3:6, and in 3:13–35 he prepares the reader for the continuation and consequences of similar behavior. The people mob Jesus in desperate pursuit of his revolutionary abilities to transfigure physical (illness) and spiritual (sin, possession) maladies.[3] They are equally attracted to his groundbreaking critique of religious laws (holiness and purity) that had become tactics of social exclusion. Mark makes this point by his renewed appeal to the language of touch that was so important in the story of the leper (1:40–45). Jesus' touch of the impure man signaled an acceptance the priestly Torah interpretations had denied. Now, Mark declares, people beaten, broken, and impure by disease are reclaiming their standing in God's community by touching Jesus (3:10). Other transformative touches will follow. At 5:27–31 a woman suffering the brokenness, impurity, and exclusion brought on by twelve years of bleeding touches him. At 6:56, 7:33, and 8:22, people of various physical limitations touch him. At 10:13, he touches children. Instead of dirtying Jesus, their touch transforms and makes them whole. Not only are they wholly cured; *prior to the cure*, they are symbolically accepted into the movement of God's imminent reign and the community forming in expectation of it.

The makeup of the mass by the sea is as conspicuous as the touch of the people who constitute it. These people are from everywhere. Mark had already made the point at 1:45 that, because of the healed leper's preaching, crowds flock to Jesus from all over. He clarifies that claim now with geographical specificity. The designations "from Galilee" (3:7) and "from Judea, Jerusalem" (3:8) are not surprising. But then the evangelist extends his narrative reach. There are others in the melee from Idumea, and beyond the Jordan, and around Tyre and Sidon (3:8). These designations open up dramatically the constituency of this congregation. Idumea starts the break; it was a region of non-Jews until the Hasmonean John Hyrcanus (134–104 B.C.E.) forced the faith and its physical mark of circumcision on them. "Beyond the Jordan" probably refers to the Upper Jordan and the Greek territories of the Decapolis (see 5:1–20; Matt. 4:15, 25). Although Jews did live in Tyre and Sidon, those place names designated foreign locales that never were a part of Israel proper.[4] What is the point? Joel Marcus has argued that "Mark may also wish to suggest that people from predominately Gentile areas are beginning to be attracted to Jesus; the six place-names represent an increasing sociological distance from Judaism."[5] Jesus' people, in other

---

3. The desperation is depicted in 3:9 (when Jesus directs the disciples "to have a boat ready for him because of the crowd, so that they would not crush him") and 3:10 (when those with disease "pressed upon him").

4. Blount, *Go Preach!* 260–1.

5. Marcus, *Mark 1–8*, 260.

words, come increasingly from beyond the boundaries of Jewish space; they flock to him, not because of who he is, but because of their faith in what he can do. The communal ground is shifting toward the impure and unholy, even toward the Gentiles. We know the movement is in the direction God desires because even the demons recognize its instigator as God's son (3:11) and therefore the representation of God's earthly intent.

Still, emulation of Jesus' effort would have attracted bitter opposition, particularly in the time Mark was writing.[6] As Mark penned his Jesus story, Jerusalem was under siege. Vespasian's (and later his son Titus's) legions had intervened in response to a Jewish war effort aimed at removing Gentile presence from the land. The popular, patriotic position was to join forces with this zealous move to reclaim political independence, presumably so that God's people could once again offer singular devotion to their Lord. Jews who accommodated Gentile interests, by moderating their feelings of hostility or attempting to find avenues of conciliatory compromise with the Romans, were considered traitors by many. Radical revolutionaries like the *Sicarii*, or "dagger men," assassinated not only Gentiles, but also Jews considered allies with them and/or their interests.[7] No doubt Mark, whose narrative focus directed his community to follow the lead of its Lord and allow *anyone* into its faith family, was on dangerous ground. Mark may well foreshadow this threat by the way he plays out Judas's name. While many scholars believe the description "Iscariot" refers to the place from which he hailed,[8] others suggest a more formidable implication. Marcus argues that Iscariot is "similar to the name of the revolutionary party the Sicarii at whose hands the Markan Christians may have suffered."[9] If he is right, it could well be that Mark has a dual narrative purpose here. Not only does Judas personify Jesus' suffering; the faith community following in Jesus' universally welcoming footsteps could also anticipate suffering (13:9–13).[10]

Jesus' construction of his discipleship corps at 3:13–19 picks up immediately on the theme that communal membership is no longer based on blood and ethnicity. The new community of disciples, while based on the symbolism of Israel's historical family of faith and nationality, counters its culture of exclusion by reconfiguring its identity into one with universal parameters.

Internal reconfiguration comes first. Mark begins on familiar metaphorical

---

6. Cf. Blount, *Go Preach!* 55–76.

7. On the *Sicarii,* see Myers, *Binding the Strong Man,* 59–60.

8. Hooker, *Mark,* 113.

9. Marcus, *Mark 1–8,* 269.

10. In fact, it is notable that at 13:9–13 Jesus' declaration that the Gospel must be taken to all nations is framed as a warning of the community's suffering. Suffering and universalistic preaching go together.

ground: mountains are climbed (3:13), people are called (3:13), leaders are commissioned (3:14–15). The imagery is clearly Mosaic due to Mark's designation of "the" mountain. Given that Mark has not previously mentioned any mountains in his Gospel account, "a" mountain would have made better narrative sense. The evangelist, though, is trying to make a narrative point; "the" mountain conjures the mental picture of Sinai in the hearer-reader's mind. As Marcus points out, in the Septuagint the phrase "to go up the mountain," occurs twenty-four times; eighteen of them are in the Pentateuch, and most of them refer to Moses.[11] A particularly significant parallel to Mark 3:13–19 is the ascent at Exodus 24:1–4, where "Moses ascends Sinai in the company of a group of priests and elders and sets up pillars symbolizing the twelve tribes."[12] Jesus has appropriated the old imagery in the interests of creating a new communal model.

In an effort to populate this prototype, Jesus extends a call. The call terminology Mark chooses indicates his understanding of the invitation as a radically transformative one. First, Mark meticulously choreographs the crowd's movement; instead of just saying they "go" to Jesus, he stipulates that they "go *away*" to him. As was the case with the disciples at 1:16–20, the implication is that former lives (or, at the very least, former possessions and ways of life) must be left behind.[13] Something wholly new is happening. Second, he chooses his "call" word (*proskaleomai*) carefully. As Marcus notes, "Both the middle voice of *proskaleitai* ('called to himself') and the pleonastic *autos* ('himself') emphasize Jesus' power of choice, which mirrors the sovereign electing power of God in the Old Testament (see e.g. Deut 7:6–8; Isa 41:8–10); in Isa 45:4 significantly, divine election is accompanied by a renaming, as in Mark."[14]

Mark then exploits the term in a very revealing manner. With the exception of 15:44 (when Pilate summons the centurion to confirm Jesus' death), Mark consistently makes Jesus the verb's subject. In each case, Jesus subjects the person or people called to a circumstance that overturns the routine of first-century, Palestinian, Jewish life. At 3:23, he gathers his followers in order to tell them a parable that will ultimately claim his status as God's true representative and simultaneously mark the institutionalized scribal leadership as God's enemies (3:28–30). At 6:7, he commissions his twelve leaders to the same kind of healing, exorcising, and teaching ministry that he himself

11. Marcus, *Mark 1–8*, 266.
12. Ibid. See also Hooker, *Mark*, 111.
13. Marcus, *Mark 1–8*, 266.
14. Ibid.

has used to transform the community's understanding of God's work in and intent for the world. When he gathers his group at 10:42, it is to share the controversial premise that leadership is service. At 12:43, he overturns common reason and sense by declaring that an impoverished widow's pittance was the greatest of the Temple contributions.

The most dramatic scenes occur in chapters 7 and 8. At 7:14, Jesus summons listeners so that he might submit the idea that no food on the outside going into a person could make that person unclean. That offbeat observation leads to Mark's outrageous declaration that Jesus had proclaimed clean all foods, and therefore all the peoples (i.e., Gentiles) who consumed a previously considered profane diet (7:19). Mark had already laid the groundwork for this shocking revelation in the 3:23 call narrative, contending that the crowd into which Jesus served that subpoena was composed of people from everywhere. As if to reinforce just this point, at 8:1 Jesus gathers his gang around the goal of feeding an apparently Gentile crowd. And, at 8:34, in what is one of his strongest and most provocative declarations of discipleship, Jesus invites both his disciples and a larger crowd to receive his pronouncement that *anyone* can be his disciple—all he or she has to do is take up the cross and follow him. Every time Jesus calls his followers, Mark contends, expectations are overturned, while opportunities for change and, most provocatively, opportunities for membership are opened up.

Clearly, the opportunity in this text is that a gathering of people from everywhere now has the opportunity to become part of the new thing that God is doing. No wonder, then, that Mark's narrative description deploys the clever idiom of Genesis. Out of the larger grouping that he gathers on the summit, Jesus "makes" (*epoiōsen*) twelve (3:14, 16). The verb has strong ties to Genesis 1 events in which God "made" creation.[15] Mark also conspicuously employs the verb in his description of Jesus' miracles.[16] "The dual emphasis of the verb . . . allows a reader to access the constitution of the discipleship community as a creative act on a par with Jesus' miracles, exorcisms, and boundary crossing behaviors."[17]

The boundary-breaking component of the act gathers its intensity from Mark's testimony that Jesus singled out twelve of his followers.[18] The count reminds readers of the Mosaic segmentation of Israel into twelve tribes. Jesus,

---

15. Ibid., 262, 267.
16. Mark 5:19–20; 7:37; 9:39; 10:51; 11:28–9, 33; see also 1:3, 17; 10:6.
17. Blount, *Go Preach!* 102.
18. So significant is the number twelve at 3:14 that Mark repeats the same detail at 3:16. Though the Greek gives reason to suspect this verse as a later scribal interpolation, it is more likely a product of Markan repetition, a long-acknowledged literary trait of the evangelist. Thus the declaration of the "making"

up on "the" mountain, apportions what is apparently a reconfigured Israel into the same symbolic units.[19] As Myers has argued, it seems likely that such an act would have been viewed as a hostile reproach to the presently configured Israel by representatives of those instituted to manage it (i.e., the scribes who had come down from Jerusalem): "But the political character of this discourse would not have been lost upon Mark's Palestinian audience: Jesus, having repudiated the authority of the priestly/scribal order, now forms a kind of vanguard 'revolutionary committee,' a 'government in exile'! The community of resistance has been formed."[20]

As if to reinforce this point of reinterpreted identity, Jesus renames three of the twelve who will become his closest advisers, which, Myers observes, "functions as a literary fiction, connoting Jesus' consolidation of his alternative community."[21] Jesus consolidates them for a particular two-pronged purpose. It is notable that one of their tasks will be to emulate his preaching, the same controversial, boundary-breaking acts of exorcising, healing, and authoritative teaching (6:7–13, 30) that have already made him infamous (3:6). No doubt, this is why he forewarns them that such activity can be likened to picking up a cross (8:34); it will guarantee trouble (13:9–13).

And yet such preaching activity grows naturally from being in his company and being with his agenda. That is the other reason for their institution; they are to be "with him." Contrast that designation with the way Mark uses a traditional Greek idiom to describe Jesus' family as those "from beside him" at 3:21. Here Mark is taking yet another none-too-subtle swipe at traditional thinking; Jesus' family is composed of those who choose to be *with* him, *around* him (3:32), and to follow his mandates, not those who come *from* his bloodline. The evangelist is setting up the final move of the narrative section; Jesus' *family*, and by inference (since he is God's son), God's family, is not limited to those with the traditional national and ethnic ties of Israel.

Indeed, those with the more traditional ties, because of their allegiance to

frames, and therefore highlights, Jesus' motive for singling out these twelve. The reference to "apostles" (3:14), however, seems to be a later insertion attempting to match Luke 6:13. See Bruce Metzger, *A Textual Commentary on the Greek New Testament* (Stuttgart: Biblia-Druck GmbH, 1975); Marcus, *Mark 1–8,* 263.

19. See D. E. Nineham, *The Gospel of St. Mark* (London: Penguin Books, 1969), 118; Tolbert, *Sowing the Gospel,* 143; Hooker, *Mark,* 111. Interestingly, the Qumran community, which established itself as a counter to the institutionalized Judaism of the time, was ruled by a council of twelve. See also Myers, *Binding the Strong Man,* 164: "By reenacting a 'new Sinai' covenant on the mountain, Jesus is attacking the ideological foundation of the dominant order. He chooses (*epoiēsen*) a new leadership, a word that is used in the LXX to refer to the *appointing* of priests (1 Kgs 12:31; 13:33; 2 Chr 2:18) and Moses and Aaron (1 Sm 12:6 . . .)."

20. Myers, *Binding the Strong Man,* 163.
21. Ibid.

those ties, find themselves at odds with Jesus and in danger of thereby exclud-
ing themselves from the company of Israel as he is reconstituting it. His blood
relations, the ones from beside him at 3:21, who are specified as his mother and
brothers at 3:31, seek to seize him out of his ministry.[22] They are convinced that
he has gone mad, the Greek *exestē* ironically suggesting demon possession.[23]
Thus Jesus, the ultimate exorcist whom the demons fear because they know his
true identity as God's son, is thought by his own family to be possessed by
demons. It is a charge that Jesus' official opponents, the scribes who have come
down from Jerusalem, will escalate into a verdict of satanic collusion (3:22).
Even here, Mark implies that the reason for the difficulty lies in Jesus' transformative, boundary-breaking preaching endeavors. In what must have been a
delicious play on sound, Jesus, the one whom the scribes had diagnosed as
chronically unlawful (not *exestin*, 2:24, 26; 3:4),[24] was feared by his family to
have gone crazy (*exestē*). The reason for the allegation is bound up in the comparative sound; Jesus' craziness is that he continues to defy a legal system any
competent observer must know would destroy him to protect and sustain itself.

Before Mark finishes this portrait of familial dysfunction, he heightens the
treachery of Jesus' kin by allying it with the hostility of Jesus' official opponents. Their attempts to seize him play right into the hands of the scribes from
Jerusalem who claim to corroborate their diagnosis of madness; the man has
been taken over by the Lord of Demons.[25] Apparently conceding the point that
Jesus was able to perform mighty works that transformed the physical and
spiritual situation of many people, the scribes turned to the politics of spin.
Their job, it appears, was to interpret the events in such a way that great power
would be attributed to great evil. Jesus' legacy could remain intact. Indeed,
they needed it intact in order to turn it against him. And what better expert
witness to their appraisal of the situation than Jesus' own family?

It is at this point that Jesus calls the crowd and unleashes for the first time the
teaching weapon Mark describes as a parable. The alleged lunatic reasonably
explains that the fruits of his actions belie the source of his power. His miracles
oust demons from their human hosts; Satan would never charge one of his own
minions to such a task. A power working at such cross-purposes would soon

---

22. See Marcus (*Mark 1–8*, 279), who notes that the family's act of trying to seize Jesus foreshadows
the later attempts by the authorities to detain him. The evangelist uses the same arresting vocabulary
(12:12; 14:1, 44–5).

23. Hooker, *Mark*, 115.

24. See also 6:18; 10:2; 12:14.

25. Marcus notes, "It is also interesting that, cross-culturally, people accused of being demon-possessed
are often those who, like Jesus in our passage, are at variance with their nuclear families" (Marcus, *Mark
1–8*, 271).

fall. Satan was smart enough to know that. Satan wouldn't do that. Jesus, there-fore, must be operating at the behest of another power: God's power.

Given the level of animosity between Jesus and the authorities, one wouldn't expect them to be persuaded. Perhaps, however, there might have been some narrative hope for Jesus' family. Mark squelches it immediately. Still intent on taking hold of him and talking him out of his insane ministry, they send mes-sengers to call him out (3:31). Note Mark's choice of vocabulary. Jesus, who calls disciples and sends them out as preaching emissaries, is here called for by messengers himself. He wants to preach; his family, following the failed attempts of the scribes, want to stop him. That intention places them both geo-graphically and symbolically outside the new family Jesus is in the process of creating. A crowd, presumably made up of followers from everywhere (3:7–12), sits around (with) Jesus, while his family stands fitfully outside. The crowd has access to his teaching and his power; his family is ignored. Indeed, were he to go to his family, accede to their wishes, he could not continue his ministry. His choice is clear. No doubt, the difficult choice Mark's readers must make should be just as clear. They must choose God's path as Jesus has out-lined and modeled it, even though that choice might necessarily mean leaving family and family expectations behind (1:16–20; 10:28–31).

For Mark, the belief that the community of God was a closed one was one of the expectations to be left behind. As Jesus here rejects the call of his fam-ily and declares a new family of those who are "with him," he also defines the entry requirements for this new clan. Anyone (3:35) is welcome. There is only one restriction, and it has nothing to do with purity, holiness, or ethnicity. One only had to do the will of God as Jesus, God's son, lived and taught it. No doubt these were welcoming words to the gathering that Mark had earlier described as not only coming from Judea and Jerusalem, but from beyond the Jordan, as far as Tyre and Sidon. Jesus has not only reconfigured the makeup of his own Israelite family (which would be boundary breaking enough); he has reenvisioned the makeup of the family of Israel.

View Two: "Then He Went Home" (Mark 3:31–35)
Brian K. Blount

[Introduction: This sermon was preached for the occasion of the 2001 Blount family reunion in Smithfield, Virginia.]

When I sat down at my computer to write this sermon, I honestly didn't know what to do. I've written sermons for all kinds of worship occasions, but I've never written a sermon for a family reunion. I'll tell you what I finally did. I thought back to when I was little. My mom and dad would tell me that if I was scared or lost or hurt or, as in this case, didn't know what to do, that I should think about Jesus. So, that's what I did. I wondered whether Jesus ever preached a family reunion sermon. The more I thought about it, though, the more I began to worry. Jesus is probably the last person on the planet you'd want to go to in order to get some advice about preaching at a family reunion. In fact, the more I read the more I realized that Jesus is probably the last person you'd even want to *invite* to a family reunion. Knowing what I know now, if I were the person in charge of making up the mailing labels, sending out the newsletters, and crafting the T-shirts and hats, I'd let Jesus' mailing label fall accidentally into the trash. I'd send Jesus' newsletter to some unknown occupant in some unrecognizable residency. I'd white out all the family logos on Jesus' shirt. I'd hang Jesus' hat on somebody else's hook. Why? Because once Jesus got to the family reunion there is absolutely no telling what he would do.

Know what I found him doing? Think about THIS family man. First thing he does is call disciples (1:16–20). That's good for us; we get disciples to lead the church. That's good for Jesus; he gets disciples to spread God's Word. Think, though, about what it means for the families of those men who drop everything to follow Jesus' charismatic call. In Jesus' first-century world a family was completely dependent on the male provider of the household. In an extended family, the sons would work together to help the father keep the family going until the father died and the sons took his place. Women didn't work; single-parent families for the most part didn't exist. Generally, a man somewhere was protector and provider. It was a man's world and there had to be a man around somewhere to care for the people, his people, in it.

Now Jesus comes along and takes such men away. Simon and Andrew fished to provide food and sustenance for their families. To whom do their families turn now that Jesus has made them fishers of people instead? People fishing has never been a very high-paying job, then or now. You don't earn enough to send money back home to your folks when you're fishing for people. The job is 24/7 and you only seem to get paid in leftover loaves (6:42; 8:8). James and John were their father's partners in the family fishing business, but when Jesus calls they drop Zebedee like a net full of spoiled fish and leave him alone in the boat and adrift as family provider (1:20). Twenty-one centuries later we might feel nice and cozy about this story of men leaving everything to follow Jesus. Think how you'd feel if you were a wife or a father or a son or a daughter and your "man" said, "I can't be with you anymore. I've got to leave everything. I've got to leave you. I've got to follow a man I just met." You think you'd be inviting *that* man to any of your family reunions?

I don't think so! You can't even talk about the kind of stuff he's doing at a dysfunctional family reunion. How are you going to go to a man like that to get advice about preaching at a real, caring family reunion?

I'm caught in this tough place now, though, because I'm thinking, "Where else can I go? I'm preaching about family to a Christian family. Shouldn't I start by talking about God's family? That means it makes sense, then, to start with God's son, right?"

So, I decided to preach on Jesus' theory about family anyway. We hear all this political talk today about strengthening the family, about theories on the family, about preserving the integrity of the family. I figured, maybe it will be good for us to learn a little bit about what God's son thinks about family.

This is what I found. Jesus takes old families and recycles them into a new family. That's why his family sayings and actions seem so odd. For him family reunion isn't about celebrating the past. It isn't about partying and picnicking over who we were and who we are. It's about forging possibilities for who we might be. Jesus is about the business of creating the kind of family he believes God wants. So he shakes *up* the family *that is* until he shakes *out* the kind of family that *ought to be*.

He starts with his national, ethnic, and religious family of Israel. He does here just what he does everywhere else—the unexpected. He withdraws from everyone and takes his disciples with him. He goes up on a mountain, he appoints twelve, and then he gives them names (3:13–19). Does this sound familiar to you? Know anybody else who did this? Moses. You remember Moses, the father of the people of Israel as a national and political entity. Moses went up on a mountain. Moses separated the people into twelve tribes (see Exod 24:1–4). Moses' actions with God ultimately gave this band of slaves the name Israel. Now, Jesus sets about doing it all over again. He sets about re-creating the family of God that Moses had already created.

See the trouble he causes. It's like going into someone's meticulously decorated house and rearranging all of the furniture right in front of their eyes. I don't like it when people sit in my special chair; no way I'm going to let them rearrange my office or my special room. I can't even imagine the uproar if you came in and starting moving my wife's furniture around. It would be worse in a church. People don't want other people sitting in their pews. Imagine if they came in on a Sunday morning and their pew on the left aisle was now over there, on the right, and the pulpit was in the back of the church instead of the front. Do you understand what I'm talking about here? Jesus was symbolically rearranging Israel right in front of the eyes of the priests and scribes.

Just two and a half chapters into his Markan ministry and he's moving around and messing with all his people's sacred furniture.

Moses crafted a people for a reason. They were to be a lamp to the nations. By the light of Israel's faith and obedience, the people of the world were supposed to find their way to God. Now Jesus is implying that all that Mosaic effort didn't work out as well as it should have. So, he's going to restructure things. He's going to run a "reorg" on an entire people.

We get a sense of what he thought Israel had failed to do by what he teaches his new people to do. He calls them, orders them, fashions them, and renames them so they will have the power to preach the nearness of God's future reign. The presence of that future reign is so powerful that it is already transforming the present time with such force that demons will be exorcised, illnesses will be cured, and ignorance will be enlightened. Just as Jesus exorcised, healed, and taught in a way that transformed human lives, so the people who will populate Jesus' new family are called to go out and change the world, to transform it so that those who are possessed by evil, those who are overwhelmed by disease, those who are haunted by their inability to know God and to know each other, will be changed when they realize that the power of God's reign to make change is right within their grasp.

You want to know why a family is united and then reunited? Jesus believes that it is for the purpose of conquering evil wherever it is found, bringing wholeness wherever there is brokenness, teaching wherever there is someone who needs to learn. Jesus crafts a family not for celebration, not for warm hugs and cute kisses, but for dangerous discipleship and terrible, tremendous transformation. Family units become change units, family love becomes love for justice and hope, family reunion becomes the time of gathering to plot the strategy for changing the world around them. That's why Jesus called them up to the mountain for this, their first Jesus family reunion. Not for the spectacular view or the fresh air. Not for the camaraderie or the food. Not for seeing someone they hadn't seen in such a long time. Jesus calls them to plot the plan for changing their world by their exorcising, healing, and teaching power. You want to know what Jesus would do at a family reunion? Well, here it is. And it's trouble. It's about teaching a family to trouble a world with the power of God's reign until the world and that reign start to resemble each other in the same way that a son resembles his father and a daughter resembles her mother.

When I went asking Jesus about something nice to say at a family reunion, this story about a new family with a new commission for changing a world that did not want to be changed is what I found.

I kept reading. I was thinking that sooner or later things would start to chill out. This text, after all, does include a story about Jesus and his family. When the Son of God finishes stirring up trouble on that mountaintop, he comes down to the valley and the story seems to take a turn for the better. Mark says it simply: "Then he went home" (3:19 NRSV). See, that's family-reunion kind of language right there. "Then he went home." Right away I started thinking warm reunion thoughts. I remembered how I always felt when I was away from home in college or in seminary or in graduate school or on a trip. As the time of my journey drew to a close, I'd think about home. Whether it was my mother and father as it used to be, or my wife and children as it now is, thoughts of going home are always good thoughts. No matter what trouble you're in, my mom and dad had always said, you know you can always come home.

I figure the same thing must have been the case for Jesus. Already he has done so much, changed so much, offended so many, challenged so often those in high places, that Mark proclaims that the leaders of the people take counsel together against him to plot a strategy to destroy him (3:6). Knowing all of that as Jesus does, you'd think he'd lay low for a while. But no, instead of laying low, he went up high, to a mountaintop, and did more of the same kind of troubling thing. Now, though, it should be different. Now, he's going home. He's coming down from the mutiny on the mountain to peace in the valley. He's coming home. Surely, there is a word for a family reunion right here.

Seems to be. Jesus is as famous as Shaquille O'Neal. He's the Big Preacher, the quotable preacher, the human healer. Ain't no demon strong enough to keep him from scoring points for God with his teaching. Ain't no human authority figure big enough to keep him from presenting the authority of God's reign by the way he lives his life. People are coming to him from everywhere to be touched, taught, and transformed. There are so many gathered around him that he can't even find room to eat. Tiger Woods doesn't know this kind of popularity. Michael Jordan never soared this high. This is Jesus. He's only been preaching a few narrative days and already it seems the whole world of Palestine knows his name. This is the man, the great man, who is coming home. Surely, he'll find some adulation, peace, and comfort here.

It's not to be, of course. The scribal and priestly leaders have too much at stake. They follow him, track him down to his Nazareth lair and lean on him with all the weight of the Jerusalem Temple. They agree. He's a great man. Yes, a very great man. No one, certainly not they, can deny that he can do the powerful things that he does. Don't deny it. Don't doubt it. They know they can't turn the crowd, his hometown crowd, his family crowd against him by arguing that he's a fake. They know the real thing when they see it. They are the religious authorities, after all; they're authorized to recognize true power when it dawns. In Jesus they see raw, true power cutting like lightning through the night.

So what do they figure to do? They figure to use Jesus' power against him. They say, yes, Jesus is strong, but he has the strength of Satan, not God, backing him up (3:22). You ever see anything other than the demonic cause the kind of change Jesus causes? Of course you haven't. God doesn't mess around in human history; God stays out of our way. It's the demonic that keeps trying to change things around in our part of the creation town. So, since Jesus is the one doing all this changing, that must mean that Jesus is demonic. It's by the prince of demons that he does things like cast out demons. So if you side with him, if you believe in him, if you follow him, then you find yourself following the demonic too.

That's where Jesus catches them and teaches us about his purpose on earth (3:23–30). He says, "Listen to what they're saying. They say that I cast out demons. That's right. That's how I use my power. Now, they agree and you see that that's how I use my power. I cast out the demonic. I track it, hunt it down, and kill it. Now, if I work for Satan, how could I work well if I use all my power to destroy everything that Satan does? It doesn't make any sense. What does make sense is that the coming of my power means the end of satanic rule on this earth. Satan is the strong man, the dictator who has ruled your world with impunity for centuries. I am the thief in the night who has come into the strong man's house to plunder it. But before I can take what is his, I must tie him up, bind him. Every exorcism, every healing, every teaching that I do is one more link in the chain that locks him down. And you know what else, if you're fighting against me, since I'm fighting for God, then it's you, you who are the ones fighting on Satan's side. I don't care how many robes you dress up in, how religiously you go to church, how many times a day you get down on your knees to pray, if you're fighting me, you're fighting God, and for that you will pay a heavy, heavy price. My commission is to change this world so that it looks more like the reign of God that is even now, in my person and ministry, breaking in. If you get in my way you obstruct the very way of God."

Jesus, folks, is in a fight. And since the people he's fighting with are the ones who have all the power in their land, it's already clear, even this early in his ministry, that it's going to be a fight to his death. It's good that he's home now. Good that he's in a place where he can get some family support. No matter how much trouble you're in, Jesus, you can always go home.

And yet, that's where, surprisingly, it gets even worse. This family reunion turns sour before it even gets a chance to kick in. With all the crowds pressing in on him, with the powers-that-be coming down hard on him, his flesh and blood, his relatives, his mother and brothers and kinfolk find their way through the masses and attempt to lay hands on him (3:31–2).

Let me clarify. This isn't the *good* kind of laying on of hands—the kind where people celebrate somebody's calling to be a minister or deacon or elder. This is the bad kind, the one where you lay your hand upside somebody's head. The translations of the Greek are confused at this point. The King James Version says, when his "friends" heard that he was home they went out to seize him, for they were saying he is out of his mind (3:21). These weren't his friends. These were his family. The New Revised Standard Version recognizes that and says, when his "family" heard that he was home. But then it tries to make the story easier to swallow, too. That version then goes on to say that people, some people, other people than his family were saying that he'd lost his mind. The Greek actually says, his *family* tried to lay their hands on him, tried to get to him and seize him, because *they, his family*, thought he'd lost his mind. That's what Jesus gets when he goes home. His own people think he's crazy.

Why? What's he done to make them think he's crazy? It's not because he does all this preaching about the coming of God's reign. Well, you have to admit, it's a little bit unusual, this preaching about the end-time thing. But it's not crazy. John the Baptist preached the same thing; people didn't think he was crazy—they just thought he was dangerous. It's not because he heals and exorcises. There were other people who supposedly had the power to heal and exorcise in Jesus' time, and none of them were thought to be crazy. Why would you think someone with such gifts was crazy anyway? Healing and teaching, those are good things. So why? Why does his own family think he's crazy when he comes home looking for some family reunion? Did he not pay his registration fee on time? What?

I'll tell you why they think he's crazy. Because he's doing the kinds of things that shake up his world and therefore get the people who are powerful in his world angry with him. And then he creates a new family to help him do this kind of transformative work. Then, he and that new family keep acting up even when they know the scribes and Pharisees and Herodians and chief priests are planning to destroy him. Any sane person would stop doing what they were doing, would lay low for a while, would stop trying to change the world until the world changed a little bit. But not Jesus. He thinks he's working for God and that God works overtime and even into the time when people get mad at him. So, even at a family reunion, he's still working this theme of God's coming reign and still talking about changing people and changing the world. He won't let up. That's why his family wants to let him know that they think he's lost his mind.

That is why his family is outside calling for him (3:31). They send an emissary, a little newsletter note that says, "Look, J, we're out here having a little family reunion. Won't you come join us? We want to see you. Don't want to alter your plans or anything. Just want to reunite for a while. Come on out with your mother and brothers and celebrate with us for a while. Just let us talk for a moment or two."

But Jesus didn't do what a good son would do. He didn't get up and say, "Wait a minute, disciples and friends, my mom and my brothers are outside. I'll be right back." Instead, he says, "Who are my mother and my brothers? I'll tell you who. My *real* mother is *not* the one who gave me birth. My *real* brothers and sisters are *not* the ones who grew up around me. You. The ones here sitting with me, who are willing to give up everything to do the will of God, to change this world so that it looks like God's reign, to do right and make right wherever there is wrong. *You* are my mother and brothers and sisters. *You* are the ones I want to be in reunion with when I come into the reign of my God" (3:33–35).

See, that's it, right there. Jesus has transformed family from a cadre of people joined by blood into a force bound to the commission of championing the transformative reality of God's reign. Family is *not* about blood. Family is *not* about kinship. Family is about the reign of God coming and the world of humanity changing so that it can meet that reign in a right relationship when it gets here. That's why families unite and reunite for Jesus—so they can gather their collective strength, support one another, love one another, empower one another so that wherever the strong man rears his ugly, vicious, venomous head in this world, they will have the collective power and inclination to bind him up and tear him and his forces down.

View Three: Inside, Looking Out
Gary W. Charles

Home at last. No more mountain climbing, ducking into tents, bonding with the boys. No more daily specials at the village diner. No more long lines of admirers awaiting an autograph. Finally, a few minutes of peace and quiet. A hearty meal. A good glass of wine. A long, hot bath followed by a good night's sleep. By the close of Mark 3, Jesus is home at last.

Jesus is home, but he is not alone, at least not for long. No sooner does he put the first bite in his mouth than the doorbell chimes, the phone rings, the fax sounds, the pager vibrates. People will not leave Jesus alone (3:19–20). Mark says they come from north, south, east, and west (3:8). And, more important than their points of origin, Mark—in two asides—tells us about who will soon show up at Jesus' front door—his family and an entourage from the Jerusalem headquarters (3:21–2).

His family will not arrive holding a bunch of balloons or waving a makeshift banner saying, "Welcome Home, Son!" They will show up wearing hoods so no one can see their embarrassed faces, so they can make their "intervention." Jesus' family is not puzzled by his reputation, or quizzical about all he has said; they know the problem. Their "little Jesus" has lost his mind; he's mad and something has to be done (3:21). That's what families do when there is a problem in the family, or a problem child; they take care of it.

Though the family is convinced that Jesus is certifiably crazy, the boys from headquarters say the matter is much worse. They announce that no, Jesus has not lost his mind; what he's lost is his soul! He's demon-possessed and by Satan himself (3:22)! What a homecoming! Not only does Jesus miss a good home-cooked meal and some longed-for serenity; the sacred squad from Jerusalem also arrives on the scene and calls him "Satan"!

Jesus soon makes their twisted logic seem ridiculous. To even charge him with such an idea, Jesus remarks, is an assault on the life-giving Spirit of God. Jesus does *not* say that a person who blasphemes (a charge the sacred squad will later level against him) against the Spirit of God will not be forgiven. He *does* say that such a sin can never know forgiveness, because forgiveness requires some level of self-awareness and confession. One who sins and refuses to acknowledge that sin or the power of God's grace to forgive sin will never experience forgiveness (3:28–30).

After a brief battle over who's really Satan, Jesus' family arrives. Early on, Mark tells us that they are heading home to "seize" (*kratēsai*) Jesus (3:21).[26] Ched Myers makes the following assessment: "We might well be sympathetic with their intent to silence Jesus; for surely to them it was lunacy for a marked man to continue to provoke the highest authorities in the land. He was courting disaster, and they wished to protect him—as well as their family reputation. Such is the real anxiety of those related to political dissidents."[27] Myers has gone soft on Jesus' family. Mark, however, is not nearly so kind. It is tempting to picture Mary and his brothers storming into the house, asking the crowd for a few minutes alone with Jesus. You can imagine the conversation that would follow behind those closed doors. The trouble is that you *would* have to picture that scene and imagine that conversation, because, in Mark's story, events do not happen that way and that conversation never occurs. The family of Jesus never steps inside.

---

26. The verb *krateō* is also used in conjunction with Jesus' arrest (14:1, 44, 46, 49).
27. Myers, *Binding the Strong Man*, 168.

As a boy, I cringed whenever my brother found me outside and with a glee-ful smirk announced, "Mom wants to see you inside, *NOW!*" Jesus' own flesh and blood do not storm into the house. They wait outside. They will not dis-honor themselves by stepping into the house of this lunatic. They will not pro-fane themselves by associating with those who are inside. So, they ask Jesus to step outside.

Jesus surely grew up reciting the commandments. He knew the words "Honor thy father and mother." We expect Jesus to excuse himself, walk out-side, and face the family music. Instead, when Jesus is told that his mother and brothers are waiting for him outside, he asks those inside the house, "Who are my mother and my brothers?" (3:32–33).

That should be an easy enough question to answer. "Jesus, your mother and brothers are outside and they want to see you *NOW!*" Wrong. Without wait-ing for a response, Jesus looks around and answers his own question: "Here are my mother and my brothers. Whoever does the will of God is my brother and sister and mother" (3:34–35 NRSV). As Brian says in his exegesis, "Here Mark is taking yet another none-too-subtle swipe at traditional thinking; Jesus' family is composed of those who choose to be *with* him, *around* him (3:32), and to follow his mandates, not those who come *from* his blood line."

Mark's point is not to be missed. Jesus comes home only to redefine fam-ily. Why? What possible good could Mark serve by telling a story in which Jesus did not honor his biological family? Walter Wink argues that "Jesus was so consistently disparaging because the family in dominator societies is so deeply embedded in patriarchy and is a major inhibitor of change. It is in fam-ilies where most women and children are battered and abused. . . . The goal [of Jesus] is not the eradication of the family, but its transformation into a non-patriarchal partnership of mutuality and love."[28] Whatever the reason for its inclusion, then, this story in Mark means that tracing our family roots will now require more than genealogical skills.[29] We will never be "kin" to Jesus, says Mark, by standing on the outside looking in. The sole requirement of kin-ship is faithful discipleship. "Whoever does the will of God is my sister and mother and brothers" (3:35).

Mark must have known that when you stand on the outside looking in, Jesus *does* look crazy or possessed. Looking at Jesus from the outside, it only makes sense to "seize" him before he makes a fool of himself or a fool of us. From the

---

28. Walter Wink, *The Powers That Be: Theology for a New Millennium* (New York: Doubleday, 1999), 78–79.

29. Note that Mark, unlike Matthew and Luke, has no interest in tracing Jesus' blood lines back to any-one (Matt. 1:1–17; Luke 3:23–38).

outside looking in, Jesus seems to have no respect for tradition. He claims authority that belongs to God alone, and the Jerusalem authorities have every right, and even a moral responsibility, to silence him (3:6). From the outside looking in, Jesus seems like someone who has no family values, for whom his immediate biological family arrives just in time to restore him to his right mind.

From the outside looking in, Jesus seems insane, and the thought of following him, maddening. He asks us to open our borders, but we know what terror can happen when we do not restrict and narrowly determine who we keep in and who we keep out. He asks that we pray for peace when we know there is no balm that can soothe the Israeli and Palestinian abscess. From the outside looking in, Jesus eats with all the wrong people. He takes tours to parts of town where tourism is always down. He forgives before people repent; he calls people before they apply for the position; he extends himself on a cross while every follower is out of sight. From the outside looking in, Jesus will be the ruination of the church, for what church can open its arms as wide as Jesus did and still survive morally?

Mark says that Jesus simply cannot be understood from the outside looking in, nor can Christian discipleship. The Jesus we meet in Mark is fond of the plural imperative verbs: *akouete*[30] (listen, pay attention) and *blepete*[31] (look, see, take notice). To come inside is to *akouete* and *blepete*. From the inside with Jesus, looking out, the world looks much different. From the inside looking out, washing hands and honoring Sabbath law are important, but healing the sick and exorcising the demonic are more important. From the inside looking out, obeying your father and mother is important, but extending the family beyond blood or nationality or ethnicity is far more important. From the inside looking out, Jesus redefines power, restructures success, and reorders the religious life.

From the inside looking out, prayer is not an action of religious desperation, as if to say "all we can do now is pray." Prayer is confidence in the power of God despite the very real powers that seek to contravene the will of God (3:6). "When we pray," contends Wink, "we are not sending a letter to a celestial White House, where it is sorted among piles of others. We are engaged, rather, in an act of co-creation, in which one little sector of the universe rises up and becomes translucent, incandescent, a vibratory center of power that radiates the power of the universe."[32]

From the inside looking out, kinship is defined less by bloodlines than love

---

30. Mark 4:3, 24. See also 9:7.
31. Mark 4:24; 8:15; 12:38; 13:5, 9, 23, 33.
32. Wink, *Powers That Be*, 186.

lines. A few years back, the congregation I served elected Tom as a deacon. From the outside looking in, it must have appeared as an act of Christian sentimentality. Tom lugged a large oxygen tank around with him, for though young in age, his lungs were old due to a rare degenerative disease. A deacon is not an honorary office in our congregation, and from the outside looking in, Tom's election must have looked pitiful—elect the disabled person to show how magnanimous and enlightened we are.

From the inside looking out, Tom's election was obvious. While others slept, Tom wrote notes to shut-ins. While others spent their days on the job, Tom would call hospital patients or first-time visitors. While others traveled on vacation, Tom would visit people less ill than himself. While others were too busy to voice a political concern, Tom made sure that his representatives always heard from at least one citizen on issues of shelter, drug rehabilitation, and hunger. Tom lived as a brother of Jesus and died as a child of God.

From the inside looking out, anyone who seeks to do the will of God is welcome in the family of Jesus—the church. While my denomination fights about who belongs in the church and among its leadership, Jesus says, "Come on in. Anyone is welcome and all who do the will of God are my kin." From the inside looking out, Jesus sets the church free from gatekeeping; God will do that (3:29). Our business is obeying the summons of *akouete* and *blepete*, so we never close the door of possibility on those seeking God's grace and who are ready to come inside.

Tragically, institutions intended for the common good—the biological family and the religious community—do not fare well in Mark's Gospel. Their power has become too narrow, their focus too ingrown, and their compassion too restrictive. The Jesus we meet in Mark is met full-force by these family and religious powers who seek to silence him. He would not be silenced, though, even finally by a cross. Jesus "was not intent on putting a new patch on an old garment, or new wine in old skins (Mark 2:21–22). He was not a reformer, bringing alternative, better readings of the law. Nor was he a revolutionary, attempting to replace one oppressive power with another (Mark 12:13–17). He went beyond revolution. What Jesus envisioned was a world transformed, where both people and Powers are in harmony with the Ultimate and committed to the general welfare."[33]

Mark 3:7–35 tells the story of what happened when the religious authorities and the family of Jesus viewed him only from the outside looking in. Beyond this narrative note, Mark asks denominations, congregations, as well as individual Christians, "Where are *you* standing?"

---

33. Ibid., 81.

3

By the Beautiful Sea
Mark 4:1–41

View One: From Text to Sermon
Gary W. Charles

*T*he phrase "by the sea" conjures up almost universally delightful images. Whether it be the serenity of a quiet walk "by the sea," or a tranquil stroll "by the sea," or a cruise "by sea" to tropical islands, modern images of the sea are typically tame and inviting and are frequently romantic. They easily lull us into associating the sea with a sense of tranquility.

Not so for Mark.

For Mark, the "sea" (*thalassa*) is a metaphor for the demonic and apocalyptic chaos that confronts Jesus, terrorizes his disciples, and thus threatens the future of the gospel. Nowhere is this Markan metaphor used more frequently and effectively than in Mark 4. Unfortunately, in their rush to analyze the parables and interpret the perplexing sayings of Jesus, scholars often neglect how Mark uses *thalassa* as an apocalyptic metaphor to frame this chapter.[1] In Mark, the sea is not the locus for romantic cruises on aquamarine waters, but for demon-filled waters that threaten to leave widows behind whenever their loved ones set sail in pursuit of their livelihood. The sea, then, for Mark is far more than a geographical notation; it is where discipleship is challenged, where boundaries are impassable, where life always hangs in the balance, and where evil lurks as a formidable foe.[2]

---

1. Note John's use of the "sea" in Revelation 21:1 ("the sea was no more," *hē thalassa ouk estin eti*) as a metaphor for the elimination of the final boundary obstructing the advent of the new heaven and new earth.

2. According to Sharyn Dowd, "The Markan usage of *thalassa* conforms to the practice of the LXX, which translates the Hebrew *yam* with the Greek *thalassa* (cf. Num 34:11; Josh 12:3; 13:27). This enables Mark's narrator to evoke the ancient Near Eastern myth of the divine warrior who battles and finally conquers the forces of chaos represented by 'the sea,' or a sea-dwelling monster or dragon" (Dowd, *Reading Mark*, 52).

Typical of Mark's repetitive, oral-aural style, in 4:1 he uses the word *thalassa* three times. Then, in 4:41, the last verse of the chapter, Mark uses *thalassa* again to complete the literary and theological frame. In between, Mark loads this chapter with teachings from Jesus that at first seem oblivious to the setting "by the sea." And yet, within this apocalyptic frame, Mark alerts his readers to the eschatological and apocalyptic importance of the land-based teachings of Jesus that will follow. "He climbed into a boat on the sea" (4:1) is more than an incidental geographical notation for Mark and his readers. It is a narrative red flag for them to "pay attention" (*akouete*, 4:3; *akouetō*, 4:9) to the words of Jesus in parables, allegory, and parabolic sayings.

With the sea looming as an implied apocalyptic danger from the first verse of chapter 4, Mark makes this implied peril explicit with his first of two parabolic stories of the sea. The initial parabolic sea story accents themes introduced throughout chapter 4 and, at the same time, provides an oral-literary transition to the risks awaiting those venturesome enough to cross to the other side of the *thalassa*.[3] In addition to its apocalyptic function, the sea serves throughout this Gospel as a boundary marker between Jews and Gentiles.[4] In Mark, when Jesus with his disciples cross to "the other side of the sea" (4:35) they move beyond the safe harbor of existing Pharisaic and scribal interpretations of Torah and the resulting traditions, rituals, and belief systems that logically followed.[5]

Beginning in 4:35, Mark narrates several sea crossings of Jesus with his disciples.[6] While these sea crossings serve to increase the narrative tension within the story, they serve mainly to prompt Mark's readers to see Jesus as one who will break down the most fundamental boundaries dividing humanity. It is not surprising to Mark's readers that the first four disciples are called into service while Jesus is passing "by the sea" (1:16). In 2:13, Jesus calls another disciple, Levi, while traveling "by the sea." Readers soon learn that the first five Jewish disciples are not only called "by the sea," but are led by Jesus to cross the "sea" (both a literal and metaphorical boundary) into pagan lands where their circumscribed Jewish lives are thrown into ethnic and religious chaos.

---

3. See 10:46–52 as another example of a transitional parabolic story.

4. So Dowd's claim that, in Mark 4:35–41, "the Son of God delivers both Jews and gentiles from the oppression of the Destroyer" (Dowd, *Reading Mark*, 55).

5. Richard Horsley warns against interpreting such movement as a break from Judaism per se: "Far from abandoning or breaking with the 'Jewish Law,' Jesus is insisting upon the most fundamental commandments in the Israelite tradition as the basis of societal life. He is doing this, however, in direct rejection of the great tradition of Jerusalem represented by the scribes and Pharisees, whether in their 'tradition of the elders' or the written law codes that they hold authoritative" (Horsley, *Hearing the Whole Story,* 176).

6. Mark 5:21; 6:45; 8:13.

Throughout Mark 4, Jesus and the disciples, though "on the sea," are still situated well within Jewish territory. The setting is ominous and foreboding but still familiar. They have not yet crossed over "to the other side of the sea" (5:1). With the sea as a silent but threatening backdrop, Jesus teaches the high cost and yet extraordinary blessing of trusting in the coming reign of God. Mark peppers these verses, spiced with apocalyptic urgency, with the imperatives *akouete* (plural noun—pay attention, listen, or understand) and *blepete* (plural noun—take notice, look, or look out.).[7] Through these admonitions, the Markan Jesus not only addresses his disciples in the boat "on the sea" and the crowd standing "by the sea," but also the Markan community caught up in the chaotic last days of the second Temple and readers in any age who have eyes to see and ears to hear and faith to follow.

Sitting in a boat on the sea, Jesus teaches the crowd and his disciples "in parables" (4:2). Mark does not explain the meaning of the Greek term *parabolē* to his readers, but many scholars have written extensively about the function of Jesus' parabolic teaching. Though lacking any scholarly consensus, Sharyn Dowd speaks for much of the current Markan scholarship on the parables:

> The author of Mark uses the term *parabolē* in a way that is consistent with the understanding of the term in the Greek rhetorical tradition. By contrast with the historical example story, the parable is understood by Aristotle to be realistic fiction—a story that might have happened, but did not happen. This distinguishes it from a fable, which could not have happened.[8]

Prior to telling his first parable, Jesus insists that everyone "pay attention" *(akouete*, 4:3). Jesus then tells a simple story of a sower who casts seed on mostly unreceptive land. The parable is hardly spellbinding and does not seem to merit Jesus' command to *akouete*. The surprise ending comes when some seed lands on receptive soil and produces a harvest beyond the wildest reach of any farmer's imagination.

By this point in Mark's Gospel, readers have a context from which to hear this parable. They have seen examples of the first result of seed scattering—birdseed plucked from the earth. They have observed healings, exorcisms, and astute rabbinic debates of Jesus, only for religious rulers and even his own

---

7. Mark 4:3, 24 (see also 4:9, 12). Mark will return to the themes of paying attention and listening in chapters 13 (vv. 5, 7, 9, 23, 33) and 14 (vv. 58, 64), when the stakes are much higher than an impending sea squall.

8. Dowd, *Reading Mark*, 38.

family to reject Jesus as a threat to religious authority or as a public embarrassment. Readers know that the ones best positioned to appreciate the authority of Jesus are precisely those who contest it the most; thus the hardpan opposition to the will of God.[9] The remaining rocky, thorny, and good soil leaves readers wondering who will fill which roles as Mark's story unfolds. Mostly, though, the surprise ending to this parable leads readers to expect a surge of faithful discipleship before the Gospel closes—a harvest of apocalyptic proportions.

Next, Mark shifts the focus from public teaching by Jesus to a behind-the-scenes conversation between Jesus and his disciples. The disciples flash their backstage passes and demand insider information, asking Jesus to make sense of this parable. In typical Markan irony, Jesus responds to the disciples' request for "insider" information with a parabolic saying. While assuring them that they alone have been given mysterious knowledge of the reign of God, Jesus does not explain the nature of this reign. Instead, he assures his disciples that they know more than those on the "outside" (*exō*) to whom everything comes in the form of parables and whose hearts are hardened.

In 4:12, Mark revisits earlier themes in the Gospel—looking, listening, and turning. This time, those cast in opposition to Jesus are precisely those who do not perceive while looking, do not understand while listening, and do not seek forgiveness by turning their lives to align with the will of God. By the repetition of the verbs *akouō*, *blepō*, and *epistrephō* (turn back, turn around), Mark leads his readers to understand that true disciples, the good earth, yield a remarkable harvest. Not only do they look, they also perceive. Not only do they listen, they also understand. Not only do they turn once, they turn again and again, away from the sin that promises to drown their faith.[10]

In 4:10–12, though, the Twelve do not act like "insiders." They ask Jesus to explain the fairly straightforward parable that he has just told. Mark's readers are also on the inside. Through this "insider" exchange between Jesus and the disciples, Mark leads his readers to begin to wonder about the capacities of the Twelve. At this point, readers start to question the disciples' capacity to heed Jesus' demand: "Pay attention to what you hear" (v. 24). Readers then know what the other "insiders," the disciples, do not know. As Brian has

---

9. This opposition is crystallized in the tragic foreshadowing of 3:6: "The Pharisees went out and immediately conspired with the Herodians against him, how to destroy him."

10. Dowd insists that Mark 4:10–12 is consistent with Isaiah 6:8–11 and 40:1–2 to the effect God keeps people unrepentant until they have paid a price for their sin and rebellion (Dowd, *Reading Mark*, 46–47). While that may be true, Mark is less interested in this theological nuance than in demonstrating that these "privileged insiders" are actually *exō*, on the "outside," as we learn in 4:35–41 when they do not perceive, hear, or repent.

noted, "It is one thing to have been given the secret that Jesus represents the power of God's kingdom in his preaching ministry, quite another to comprehend what that representation means for how one must live one's life."[11]

The allegorical interpretation of the parable of the Sower points out the challenges before disciples/readers. Jesus warns that three sowing scenarios lead to failure: seed sown "on the path" (4:4, 15); seed sown on "rocky ground" (4:5–6, 16–17); and seed sown "among thorns" (4:7, 18–19). Seed sown on the path represents those who will never accept God's Word because of the powerful force of Satan/evil opposing it. Seed sown on rocky ground represents those who will accept God's Word briefly, only to reject it under conditions of trial and persecution. Seed sown among thorns represents those who will accept God's Word enthusiastically but will set it aside under conditions of affluence. Some others, however, will not fail, but produce a harvest of faith (seed sown on "good soil," 4:8, 20). In this allegorical interpretation, as Sharyn Dowd notes, "The Markan Jesus is not warning the disciples to be good soil; rather, he is warning them (and the overhearing audience) that even as the reign of God takes root and flourishes in some quarters, it will provoke opposition, persecution and seduction from the forces of evil. It is the nature of the reign of God to provoke opposition; it cannot be otherwise."[12]

Jesus follows the allegorical interpretation of his parable with a flourish of apocalyptic and eschatological images. He announces that in God's reign no one will be kept "in the dark" but will be brought into the light of the gospel (4:22); lamps will not be hidden under beds but will shine openly to root out all demonic darkness (4:21). Also, in God's reign, faithful lives will be "measured" (4:24) from generous to overflowing (like the great harvest of 4:8, 20). "In the apocalyptic texts found in the caves near Qumran, the image of the 'measure' is used in contexts about having or not having knowledge or spiritual insights."[13] Finally, in God's reign, the secrets of God's purpose will be broadcast far and wide so that no one will be "outside" (*exō*). All will be "insiders." "There is nothing hidden, except to be disclosed; nor is anything secret, except to come to light" (4:22).

This teaching chapter continues with two additional parables of Jesus (4:26–29, the parable of the Seed Growing Secretly; 4:30–32, the parable of the Mustard Seed), each adding something about the coming reign of God. In the parable of the Seed Growing Secretly, Jesus speaks of the mystery of

11. Blount, *Go Preach!* 118.
12. Dowd, *Reading Mark*, 50.
13. Ibid., 48.

how the earth produces a harvest from scattered seed and does so "automat-
ically" (*automatē*), even while the sower sleeps. Reminiscent of Isaiah
55:10–11, disciples/readers are left with a sense that the future of God's reign
will depend less on their efforts than on the mysterious and yet trustworthy
ways of God. Consistent with the apocalyptic tenor of this teaching chapter,
Sharyn Dowd adds, "Although the growth is gradual and automatic in the
parable, the time of the harvest comes with jolting suddenness—'immediately.' The suddenness of the end will be reemphasized in the later apocalyptic discourse, Mark 13."[14]

The next parable, the parable of the Mustard Seed, provides another
prism into the imminent reign of God. Though as simple as the prior two
parables (and the shortest of all three), this parable is filled with prophetic,
eschatological, and apocalyptic themes. Echoing the parable of the cedar in
Ezekiel 17 and the eschatological prophecy of Ezekiel 17:22–24 in particular, this parable closes with a vision of an expanse in which all may dwell
and find refuge, a place where no one is an outsider and no secret survives
the light of exposure. In Mark, however, the expanse is not a mighty cedar
but a mustard shrub, large enough to host all who seek its shelter. As Dowd
notes, "The cumulative effect of the three seed parables is encouragement
to hearers who may feel that God's reign is losing more ground than it is
gaining."[15]

As chapter 4 comes to a close, readers know that the Twelve are specially poised to follow Jesus. The "riddle" of the parable has been interpreted only to them (and the readers); they have had a private audience
with Jesus, and they have heard two additional parables that unpack parts
of the mystery of God's coming reign. The disciples have learned of the
power of trusting in God's hidden purpose and what God can make possible even with faith the size of a mustard seed. As the disciples push out to
sea (4:35–6), readers are left with a certain envy of the Twelve who, for no
obvious reason, are extended an intimate relationship with Jesus. However,
by the time the boat docks on "the other side of the sea" (5:1), their envy
will change into startled disbelief that God's reign can be furthered through
this confused crew.

The calming of the sea story begins simply enough. Jesus ends his lecture,
packs up his notes, gets comfortably situated in the boat, and suggests to the
disciples, "Let's go to the other side of the sea" (4:35). By this point, the disciples have learned enough to trust someone who suggests that they "cross

14. Ibid., 42.
15. Ibid., 43.

over" into Gentile territory.[16] And, to their credit, they set their oars in the water without protest and head "to the other side of the sea."

Though silent from the beginning of chapter 4, the sea roars as Jesus and his disciples push away from shore (4:37). The demonic forces that reside in the sea's underbelly stir the waters and wind into a *lailaps* ("sea squall" or "whirlwind"), echoing the apocalyptic encounter between God and Job (Job 38:1). As the sea turns violent, the classroom education of the Twelve is put to the test. And they fail miserably. Jesus does not criticize the disciples for fearing a storm; evidently, this was a storm that would frighten any seagoer. Rather, he faults his disciples for thinking the demonic forces of the sea were more powerful than he (4:40).

Those given "the secret of the reign of God" (v. 11) know less about their companion sleeping in the stern than Jonah's shipmates knew about their Hebrew passenger (Jonah 1:7–10). The parables called for trust in God's good and mysterious purpose, yet the disciples exchange panic for trust. They cannot see how God or God's agent can sleep through such a storm. The parables called for confidence that God is bringing about a reign in which all will know security and safety. The disciples, though, are sure of only one thing: their boat is sinking (4:38). In chapter 1, Mark tells of Jesus exorcising a demon from a man (1:29); now, using the same language, Jesus exorcises the sea of its demonic forces (4:39).[17] Then, Jesus "rebukes" the demonic in the disciples whose faith is revealed to be even smaller than that of a mustard seed (4:40). This is no miracle story. It is an exorcism story packed inside a parabolic story. The story closes with the stark Markan irony that, while the demonic sea "pays attention" to Jesus, those seemingly "on the inside" do not yet understand who he is (4:41). The story asks, "Who is really asleep in the boat?" and "Who really needs to wake up?"

Readers leave this chapter with a keen appreciation of the demonic forces active in nature and at work even in the closest associates of Jesus. Using the

---

16. Regarding the residual meaning of "crossing over," Lamar Williamson notes, "In its present setting in the Gospel of Mark . . . the story addresses a community of believers in Jesus Christ who, in the guise of the disciples, are challenged to trust Jesus more. They may also be challenged to 'cross over' to the Gentile mission, despite the turmoil this movement stirred up in the early church, for this unit lies between Jesus' ministry on the west bank of the Sea of Galilee and his first mighty work in pagan territory" (Williamson, *Mark,* 101).

17. Dowd points out that "the defeat of the sea monsters, originally a creation motif, later became an apocalyptic image of God's final victory. In Daniel 7 'one like a son of man (human being)' comes with the clouds and receives authority from the Ancient of Days to replace the beasts from the sea as the ruler of the universe. . . . The deliverance of the elect by the defeat of the sea in the original exodus story became the model for the deliverance from Babylonian bondage in Isaiah and for ultimate deliverance from the powers of evil in later apocalyptic thought" (Dowd, *Reading Mark,* 52).

"sea" as an apocalyptic metaphor, Mark prepares his readers for what will happen "on the other side of the sea," not by offering shining examples of faith and discipleship but by pointing to a weary boat dweller who can sleep through apocalyptic chaos and calm it by command. Readers start the chapter identifying with, and even envying, the disciples. By the chapter's end, readers cast their sights solely on the One whose identity continues to elude the disciples but not the readers.[18] Clearly Mark 4:41 leaves readers wondering if the disciples will ever understand Jesus and faithfully follow him. Mark has led his readers to ask, "If those closest to Jesus cannot understand, then who can?"

View Two: "No More the Sea" (Mark 4:35–41; Rev. 21:1) Gary W. Charles

[Introduction: There are seasons in a congregation's life when tragedy prevails. The winter and spring of 2000 was such a year for the congregation that I serve. Most of the tragedies were quiet ones, personal, familial, and vocational. They were not the tragedies that stop life in its tracks but the haunting ones that leave you numb and push you to make sense of what you believe about God. When this text from Mark's Gospel, coupled with the affirmation from the book of Revelation, appeared in the New Common Lectionary, I realized that it offered me a much-needed pastoral and prophetic word to speak to my congregation. It also offered a refreshing word of promise to me, a pastor wearied by watching the suffering of those he loves.]

For years, religious literalists and Enlightenment liberals have battled over this story from Mark. Literalists say, "It's a factual, miracle story. It records just what happened, exactly as the reporter called it into the wire service." Liberals say, "It's religious fiction, a simple parable of an embattled church trying to stay faithful in stormy times." Literalists respond, "It's not a parable; it's history. It happened." Liberals retort, "Did not." Literalists counter,

---

18. So Horsley argues against reading Mark's Gospel as a treatise on discipleship: "If we take the Gospel whole . . . attending to the story of the twelve disciples as they are actually portrayed, it is difficult to find anything but unmitigated faithlessness and failure from the middle of the story to the end. Mark's Gospel must be about something other than discipleship" (Horsley, *Hearing the Whole Story*, 97). Horsley misses Mark's intent, however, by failing to differentiate between the disciples of Jesus, who do indeed fail miserably in Mark, and the future discipleship of those who hear or read the "whole" Gospel. By including readers as "insiders" with the disciples in chapter 4, Mark calls his readers to "pay attention" to how they hear and to make more faithful choices than their first-century colleagues. Thus, with considerable storytelling skill, Mark's Gospel is very much about discipleship.

"Did too." "Did not." "Did too." While the theological bickering continues, poor Mark must shake his head and weep.

Mark tells this story, and another like it two chapters later, because it is true. He leaves its factual merit to the curiosities of the Jesus Seminar or to the conservative guardians of Christianity. What Mark refuses to leave open for debate is the truth of the story he tells.

The obvious characters in this story are Jesus and the disciples, but Mark adds another character often missed as this story unfolds: the sea. For all you romantics who view the sea as the site for an afternoon sail, with a book of poetry in one hand and a jug of wine in the other, this story will soon disappoint you. For here, as in most of the biblical witness, the sea is a site not for romance but for terror, not for serenity but for chaos. People whose livelihood meant going out to sea knew that the next trip always held within it the potential to be their last.

In ancient Babylon, they told a story about the creation of the world when the god Marduk slew the dragon Tiamat, whose name means "the sea." Throughout much of Scripture, the sea is more than a physical locale; it is where chaos and the demonic reside. In *Revelation*, Eugene Boring talks about how John uses the concept of "the sea": "Throughout Revelation, 'sea' represents the chaotic power of un-creation, anti-creation, the abyss-mal depth from which the dragon arises to torment the earth."[19] It's no accident that the formative story of Israel's freedom is when God defeats the torrents of the Red *Sea* for the people to pass to safety.

The psalmist especially knows about the sea. In Psalm 69 we hear the cry, "Save me, O God, for the waters have come up to my neck" (Ps. 69:1 NRSV); "Do not let me sink; deliver me from those who hate me from the deep waters. Do not let the floodwaters engulf me or the depth swallow me up" (Ps. 69:14–15). In Psalm 89 we hear the affirmation, "You are mighty, O LORD, and your faithfulness surrounds you. You rule over the surging *sea*; when its waters mount up, you still them" (Ps. 89: 8–9). In Psalm 93, we are warned, "The *seas* have lifted up, O LORD, the *seas* have lifted up their voice; the *seas* have lifted up their pounding waves. Mightier than the thunder of the great waters, mightier than the breakers of the sea—the LORD on high is mighty" (Ps. 93: 3–4).

Perhaps the most familiar psalm about the sea is Psalm 46, in which we hear, "God is our refuge and strength, a very present help in trouble. Therefore we will not fear, though the earth should change, though the mountains

---

19. M. Eugene Boring, *Revelation* (Interpretation; Louisville, Ky.: Westminster/John Knox Press, 1989), 216.

shake in the heart of the *sea*; though its waters roar and foam, though the mountains tremble with its tumult (Ps. 46:1–3 NRSV)." Echoing in the background of Mark's story, we also hear Psalm 44: "Rouse yourself! Why do you sleep, O Lord? Awake, do not cast us off forever! . . . Rise up, come to our help. Redeem us for the sake of your steadfast love" (Ps. 44:23, 26 NRSV). The psalmist knows about the sea.

John of Patmos, stranded on an island, jailed on all sides by water, also knows about the sea. In his "revelation" about the end time, John declares, "Then I saw a new heaven and a new earth; for the first heaven and the first earth had passed away, and there was *no more the sea*" (Rev. 21:1, my italics).

As Mark preaches his Gospel, just before he tells us about the storm at sea, we learn that Jesus spoke parables to the crowd and "explained everything in private to his disciples" (4:33–34 NRSV). In the storm-tossed boat, then, the disciples had every reason to let Jesus sleep, to hold hands in a prayer circle and chant the chorus of Psalm 65: "By awesome deeds you answer us with deliverance, O God of our salvation; you are the hope of all the ends of the earth and of the farthest *seas*. . . . You silence the roaring of the *seas*, the roaring of their waves" (Ps. 65: 5, 7 NRSV, my italics)." Instead, they panic, wake Jesus, and shout, "How can you sleep in a time like this?!" Despite all they have experienced and been taught, the disciples still know little about Jesus; but they know a lot about the sea.

So do you and I. If you have ever watched a loved one make that slow slide into death, you know about the sea. You know the flood of emotions that turns clear thinking into a dense fog. You wonder what life was like when everything was calm and normal. You either eat too little or you can't pass a pantry without grabbing something else to stuff in your mouth. People treat you like you are diseased. They look away as they pay their respects, leave their casseroles, and keep at more-than-arm's length, as if dying and death were contagious. You are lost at sea and, like the disciples, you scream, "God, I'm sinking. Don't you care?"

If you have ever said good-bye to a job you love, you know about the sea. The future may be coated with every flavor of promise, but the undertow of the past pulls at you with a nearly irresistible force. You know the old job. You've got a tempo and a routine and a well-worn path. You know the people there sometimes better than your own family. In contrast, you know so little about what lies ahead. Are you skilled enough? Will you have the energy it takes to do everything for the first time again? You stare into the future as if it were an angry sea and you scream, "God, I'm sinking! Don't you care?"

You know about the sea if, by society's measure, you are too old, if you keep hitting a glass ceiling while hearing lame excuses about being "not right for the job" from potential employers, half your age and with a quarter of your experience. You know about the sea if you are stuck between doing what you know is right and what you have been told to do, and having no doubt what will happen if you refuse to do it. You know about the sea if you dread going home to artificial silence where the love is gone and you're just going through the motions. As the sea roars, like the disciples, you panic inside and shout to the heavens, "God, I'm sinking. Don't you care?"

The church also knows about the sea. Once there was a time when anyone who was anybody went to church on Sunday mornings. They went to Sunday school, and their children sang in the choirs and went to summer camps, and their youth met for food and fellowship on Sunday night. Now, as national membership declines and giving decreases, fingers point and panic sets in, resulting in meanness and narrow thinking. Good people want to know what is happening; the storm is inside the boat, and we shake our fists and cry, "God, we're sinking. Don't you care?"

In Mark's story, faced with the terror of a roaring sea, the disciples imitate the captain of Jonah's ship (Jonah 1:6). They shake the one soul who could possibly sleep through such chaos and they shout, "How can you sleep in a time like this?" And you can almost see Mark smile when, in his typical irony, he describes the response of Jesus: "Did I tell anybody to wake me up? Before we set sail, I explained everything about God and faith to you. What did you not understand?" In this story, Mark asks us: "Who is really asleep in the boat?" and "Who really needs to wake up?"

Then, in another twist of Mark's irony, Jesus rebukes the sea. He casts out the demons that stir it into a storm. But instead of breaking out into a song of celebration, the disciples scratch their heads and wonder, "Who is this guy and how'd he do that?" Sadly enough, disciples today still expend far too much academic and spiritual energy asking and debating the same two questions.

In his vision of the end time, John of Patmos paints a richly textured picture. In it, we hear of a replacement heaven and earth that will overwhelm all the dirt and defects and disasters of life as we know it. He then tacks on the little phrase, "And no more the sea" (Rev. 21:1). In the Gospel story, Mark preaches about a life in Christ in which the sea no longer holds the final word for us, no longer consumes unsuspecting sailors, no longer tosses the innocent and guilty alike into a helpless abyss. The disciples in Mark's Gospel never understand Jesus and never fully grasp the life he is promising them. They are far too immersed in explaining how Jesus calmed the sea to rejoice that, by God's grace, somehow, he did. And what of us? And what of us terrified by an angry sea?

I would suggest that the best explanation of Mark's sea story comes from a German monk who wrote nearly five hundred years ago. Thrown out of the church and fearful for his life, hiding in a dank castle amid a sea of uncertainty that threatened to ruin him, Martin Luther wrote, "And though this world, with devils filled, Should threaten to undo us, We will not fear, for God hath willed His truth to triumph through us. The prince of darkness grim, We tremble not for him; His rage we can endure, For lo! His doom is sure, One little word shall fell him."[20] No more the sea. God does not sleep. No more the sea. God hears us. No more the sea. God cares about us. No more the sea. God loves us. No more the sea. God leads us beside the still waters. No more the sea. "He is not here. He is risen. He is going ahead of you." Trust, then, in this world and in the world to come—there is no more the sea.

View Three: Dead Calm
Brian K. Blount

When it is all over, Mark records these words: *kai egeneto galēnē megalē* (4:39). Most Bibles translate the words literally and, I might add, correctly: "and there was a *great* calm." But there is something about a *great* calm that is noticeably disquieting, particularly if it occurs on the heels of a thunderous, explosive squall. Anyone who has sat through a lightning storm on a hot, humid August afternoon in the South can tell you how loud the tempest can be and, equally, how markedly mute everything seems in those first precious moments just after the monster has exhausted its last breath. There is something almost disconcerting about a stillness that strikes out the life of a whirlwind and leaves the air flush with silence. There is something almost homicidal about it, something that demands poetic interpretation, something that says, "While adjectives like *great* are sound, they are not sufficient." Translated once, they must be interpreted again. They must give more than grammatical fact; they must relay truth. And that is why I think the translators of the New Revised Standard Version got it right. They didn't settle for the correct word, they reached for the right one, the one that represented the reality that Mark most likely wanted to convey. When it was all over, when Jesus had exorcised the demonic fury of the wind and wave, what followed was a *dead* calm. It was so great that it sucked the life out of chaos and restored order. Jesus' kind of order. *That* is what was so frightening.

---

20. Martin Luther, "A Mighty Fortress Is Our God," *Hymnal* (Louisville, Ky.: Westminster/John Knox Press, 1990), no. 260.

Think about the most forbidding horror movie you've ever seen. Good horror movies ratchet up the terror with each ensuing sequence of the script. Something ominous has just occurred. The thing was so shocking that it took your breath away. Then the screen went quiet. Deadly quiet. A dead calm has a life all its own. There's something eerie in the moments when the background music stops playing, when the sound of cluttering conversation gets canceled, when the actors stop moving and are hardly breathing, when the movie theater itself becomes deathly quiet. You're thinking that the pure power of this moment is so palpable you can feel it pound against you. It's the quiet that gets you, that haunts you, because it is pregnant with all kinds of precarious possibilities. You in your seats and the characters in their roles have just survived some horrible scare, some theatrical storm played out with frightening efficiency, and the calm makes you think that what's coming, what's lying in wait out there in the future, will certainly resemble what has just horrified you in the past. *Only it will be worse.* That's why you are sitting on the edge of your seat. That's why, even though one horror sequence has just finished and you made it through unscathed, your nerves are tingling with anxious anticipation. That's why the quiet has unnerved you. The calm has a disturbing deadness to it. And that deadness frightens you. As it should.

By the time Jesus chastises his disciples in Mark 4:40, we are so mesmerized by nature's fury and Jesus' ability to control it that we risk missing how Mark sequences the script. It is for this reason that when we interpret this text we typically do as I have done and continue to do. We focus on the church as a storm-tossed boat that comes to the realization of good news. Jesus is in the boat with us, still present as our risen Lord, still empowered with the ability to quiet the storms that seek to drown us. Perhaps, though, there is another window onto this text. A window that looks not back at the scary storm but forward into the calamitous calm. The frighteningly *dead* calm.

Jesus opens his rebuke of the disciples with a telling question: "Why are you afraid?" (*ti deiloi este*; 4:40). The verb is in the present tense. "Why," he asks them, "*are* you afraid?" The language certainly has the potential to mean something like "Why *were* you afraid of the storm when you knew I was in the boat with you?" But if it has the potential to mean something it does *not* literally say, certainly it also has the potential to mean something that it *does* say: "Why are you *now* afraid?" Why indeed? If we translate the present tense Greek verb into a present English tense, then we are driven toward the possibility that they are afraid not so much of the storm, which after all has now ended, but what may happen next in the dead calm after the storm. Perhaps, like the observant aficionado of the good horror movie, they are already anticipating that the calm isn't the finish of a bad storm just ended but the prelude to a bad one just beginning. Only this storm will be worse; it will be of Jesus' and not nature's engineering.

It sounds ludicrous, of course. Why should they be afraid of the calm present and future when they've just been delivered from this great storm? It hardly seems to make sense. Hardly, until one attends to the evangelist's overall narrative script. First, there is the big picture. Mark is an apocalyptic text oriented forward, toward the future reign of God anticipated there and represented in the present through Jesus' preaching ministry. Mark builds on the past, but Jesus is always pointing his disciples toward the future reign of God. Such an emphasis would support a reading of the text that saw the fear stemming from what was going to happen based on the inexplicable and unpredictable actions of the One who was dozing during duress.

The start of Mark 5 will confirm this suspicion as a "storm" stirs in Gerasa (5:1–20). This one is land based. A man possessed by a legion of demons has run amok through the countryside all his life, disrupting and disturbing (5:3–5). When Jesus steps onto his side of the lake, predictably, the demoniac's first act is to direct his fury Jesus' way (5:6–7). As with the chaotic wind and wave, though, Jesus calms the storm inside the man by casting out the demonic frenzy and fomenting a great and apparently deadly calm. Mark 5:15 is telling: "They came to Jesus and saw the demoniac sitting there, clothed and in his right mind (calm), the very man who had had the legion; *and they were afraid*." "Why are you afraid?" Jesus might have wanted to ask them. He didn't have time; by 5:17 they are begging the perpetrator of this peace to leave their neighborhood and take his dead calm with him. Like the disciples on the boat, they are not afraid of the storm, not now, now that it's over. They're afraid of the calm that has come in its wake and of what might follow at the hand of this meddling medic.

I am reminded this time of a different kind of movie, the Western. Westerns tend be violent, as apparently the real West itself was, so they rarely make good comparative copy for a Jesus story. Nonetheless, since I'm already perched out on a limb looking into this text from what some might perceive to be a slightly cracked window, I might as well slip on out as far as I can to the edge. I'm thinking here about those Westerns in which a town full of peaceful folk is being harassed by local thugs. One of my favorites is Clint Eastwood's *High Plains Drifter.* The locals don't have the gunfighting expertise to out-duel the thugs, so they hire a gunslinger to do it for them. Even though the hiring is protective, the locals are afraid. They don't know whether the drifting gunslinger might want more than money. Perhaps in the end he's just another thug looking for control too. In the end, he does what they want. He cleans up their town. But once they realize that he intends to clean up *their* thuggery too, they become afraid. He expects something from them. He expects the truth. He expects repentance and justice. The calm he gives them is even more frightening than the thuggery they've learned to live with, partly because they *had* learned to live with it but mostly because he expects them to use the calm as an opportunity to confess their sins and make recompense for their wrongs. This was no cheap calm; it was a calm attached to a cause.

So is Jesus'. That's why, after he has calmed the thuggery of nature, the disciples become afraid. They know, like the people of Gerasa know, that this calm comes with a cost. He expects them to make use of it. And that's where things get really dicey. In this particular Markan case, as Jesus is asking, "Why are you afraid?" we readers ought to be asking, "What does Jesus want from this calm that could make people so afraid?"

I'd say it has everything to do with the boundary crossing that Mark signals when he says that Jesus wants to cross to the "other side." Gary refers to it in his exegesis. If Mark is writing to a community of Jewish believers in the Messiahship of Jesus, and this community is struggling already with a heavy influx of Gentiles into their midst, and struggling about the possibility of inviting and even seeking more Gentiles to join them, then the tensions that erupt in any multiethnic situation would certainly be expected here. This would especially be the case at a time like the Jewish war against Rome, when ethnic passions on both sides were heating up and Jews and Gentiles were at each other's proverbial throats. In answer to the zealous belief that God was about to exorcise all Gentile presence and influence from Palestine, Mark offered a controversial, alternative answer. Not only did God not desire the expulsion of Gentiles from Israelite land, God intended that Gentiles would become full participants in God's expansive coming reign. That is why Jesus' ministry, as the presentation of that future reign in the present, crosses back and forth figuratively, as well as literally, between Jewish and Gentile territory, as he does in this particular text. The narrative presentation of squalls and storms surrounding such activity was no doubt as "true" for Mark's time of ministry as it was for Jesus' actual trip across the sea. In this case, it's not the storm that is frightening. The fear comes when Jesus answers the storm with his actions, when he exorcises its power of ethnic separation by embodying in his ministry a seeking out of, a crossing over into, Gentile land. This boundary-breaking reality is where the calm carries them. Jesus' actions kill the separatism and open up the possibility of a peaceful, rule-of-God kind of ethnic coexistence, the future possibility of which must be made a present reality. That, I think, is why they are afraid. They are afraid of what his miracle of calm represents for them and their ministries.

Jesus' question to his disciples is still a relevant question for the contemporary church. "Why *are* you afraid? Do you still not have faith to engage the world with boundary-breaking behavior now that I've calmed the storm for you?" Let's face it. As Gary says, the church may well be marginalized by our secular culture today, but it is not a storm-tossed boat fearful for its physical existence. It is not persecuted. For the most part, it is not poor. The church in the United States is a calm institution that has found safe harbor in a storm-tossed world. Many boundaries abound in our world, some of them cutting divisive swaths through the church itself. But they do not threaten our existence. So we learn to live with them. They do not make us afraid, at least not afraid enough to explore more powerful ways to trespass and therefore overcome them. To do so would be to upset the deadly calm to which we've become accustomed. We are content in our racially and ethnically segregated sanctuaries. We are calm in our financially stable, recently renovated or rebuilt structures. It is only when someone clarifies for us that the calm was not supposed to be a safe haven in which to dock but a launching pad from which to fire out our boundary-breaking emulation of Jesus' Markan ministry that we become afraid. Such a clarification demands change and action, dangerous action. We aren't afraid of the storms. We are afraid of just what will be asked of us if some somnolent Savior comes along and reminds us that we've been given the calm we have as a gift, so that out of it we may give of our corporate selves to a world locked into division and the disturbance that comes from it. Our task is to cross over and to carry people with us back and forth, back and forth, no matter how uncomfortable and how frightening that feels, until the boundaries that separate us erode and ultimately disappear. At the close of Mark 4, Jesus is about to take his calmed disciples onto Gerasene soil to begin that difficult process in Mark's Gospel. No doubt the living Christ is beckoning us calmed-down American Christians onto foreign (ethnic, racial, economic, political, class, etc.) soil today for the same reason. The very engagement of such a trespassing act will cause stress; it is as frightening a proposition now as it was then. But that is apparently why the power of God's future reign rules in the present, so that those who are its conduits might hop off their boats onto foreign soil and seek out ways to further establish this great, deadly, infectious, and redemptive calm.

4

What's in a Name?
Mark 5:1–6:6

View One: From Text to Sermon
Gary W. Charles

*S*ales clerks are fond of looking at my credit card and then informing me that I have three first names—Gary, Wayne, and Charles. Actually, I have many more names than that. In the neighborhood where I grew up, I had several names. Due to an early battle with weight, the less delicate neighbors called me "The Rotund One." Based on my complexion and hair color, the older kids often called me "Red." This name has followed me into my adult years on mission trips to Mexico. There, the children in the village we visit each year call me "El Rojo." Since my ordination in 1980, people often address me as "Pastor." My children call me "Dad." On good days, my wife calls me one of several endearing names. My mom most often called me "Gary Wayne."

What's in a name anyway? What does it matter how people address you? It can matter a lot. Should Arafat be called a terrorist or a freedom fighter? Should the occupied West Bank be called Palestine or Israel? Names matter, and how we use names matters. Names can diminish and demean people—"queer," "nigger," "wop," "the Rotund One"—or they can point to promise and possibility in people—"lover," "visionary," "Samaritan," "friend." Mark 5:1–6:6 closes with a list of names that people called Jesus: "carpenter," "son of Mary," "brother of James and Joses and Judas and Simon." Notice that no one calls him by his given name, "Jesus," which, in its Hebrew origin, means "one who saves." Not one of the names on the list begins to capture Jesus' real identity. For Mark, then, what's in a name? Everything.

Just as *thalassa* ("sea") framed Mark 4, so in 5:1–6:6 Mark frames a series of stories with an ironic use of names. The first name we meet is Gerasa (5:1). To those unacquainted with the geography and ethnography of first-century

Palestine, Gerasa is just another unfamiliar name. For Jesus and company, as well as for Mark's readers, Gerasa is on the other side of the lake. More important, it is on the other side of the religious tracks.

Fresh out of the boat, Jesus is met by a Gerasene demoniac (5:2). The situation for this demon-possessed man has deteriorated over time. Once he could be restrained for his own good, but now the demon within has grown stronger than any means of bondage (5:3–5). The man howls like a wild animal (5:5), and we later learn that he lives naked among the tombs (5:15). There is no longer a way to distinguish the demoniac from the demon.

In Mark's story, the demoniac remains unnamed, but his demon has a name. With a note of Markan tragic irony, the demoniac bows before Jesus and begs Jesus not to torture him (5:7)—as if there were torture worse than being inflicted by the demons. As the demon pleads with Jesus, he addresses Jesus as "Son of the Most High God." He calls Jesus by his true name and then Jesus asks for his name. The demon's name is Legion (5:9), from the Latin word for a large Roman military unit. The political overtones in the demon's name are another case of Markan irony, especially as we watch where the Legion marches. Richard Horsley argues persuasively that "not only [is] the demon's name symbolic, indicating that the Roman army is the cause of the possessed man's violent and destructive behavior, but the man also is symbolic of the whole society that is possessed by the demonic imperial violence."[1] Mark describes the demon named Legion to a church that is inescapably aware of the omnipresent force of Rome and thus a church always tempted to accommodate the Gospel to dominant powers or to locate ultimate power in Legions.[2]

Like Jacob seeking the name of the angel he wrestles at Jabbok (Gen. 32), here Jesus demands the name of demons possessing this man.[3] Ironically, in this story, only the Legion know the real name of Jesus and address him as "Son of the Most High." The Legion beg (*parakaleō*) "the Son of the Most High God" to grant their request to remain in the area (5:10). Jesus agrees,

---

1. Horsley, *Hearing the Whole Story,* 140.

2. Ched Myers offers the following socioliterary interpretation: "Given the odds against political liberation from the might of Rome, the disciple/reader was bound to be incredulous. Mark thus reassures the audience in no uncertain terms that the healed man was none other than 'the very man who had been oppressed by the legion' (5:15). . . . Mark's narrative strategy . . . represents Jesus' inaugural challenge to the powers. Put in military terminology, they signal the decisive breach in the defenses of the symbolic fortress of Roman Palestine. The political and ideological authority of both the scribal establishment and the Roman military garrison—the two central elements within the colonial condominium—have been repudiated" (Myers, *Binding the Strong Man,* 194).

3. On the significance of names in the Bible, see Paul J. Achtemeier et al., eds., *Harper's Bible Dictionary* (San Francisco: Harper & Row, 1985), 682–84.

and the Legion enter a local herd of swine (5:11–13).[4] Like the mighty armies of Pharaoh (Exod. 14:48), the unclean spirits and the unclean swine are soon engulfed by the unclean sea.[5] Richard Horsley suggests that Mark challenges the church/readers to trust in One whose power is greater than that of Roman imperial rule.[6]

In a comic echo of Luke's Christmas story, in which shepherds (*hoi poimenes*) announce the glad tidings (Luke 2:17–18), so in Mark the swineherds (*hoi boskontes*) rush to town to announce (*apangellō*) what had happened. Mark does not say that they left to announce the arrival of the "Son of the Most High God," the restoration of the demoniac to sanity, or the glad tidings of the death of a Legion of demons. Rather, the swineherds run to announce that their own livelihood has just taken a nosedive off the cliff.

Like the shepherds in the fields in Luke's Christmas story (Luke 2:15), the people of Gerasa come to see what has happened (5:14). They come to see swine swimming to their death, the demoniac without his demon, and a Jew called Jesus. The swineherds and the people do not marvel at the wonder of the healing of a man once possessed. Instead, the swineherds tell the townspeople about the financial repercussions of the demoniac's healing. "The loss of pork they might have sold to the Roman quartermasters does not incline the citizens of Gerasa to respond favorably to Jesus' presence. Like the disciples in the boat, they are afraid (*ephobēthēsan*—4:41; 5:15)."[7]

When the townspeople arrive on the scene, they take a hard look at the man whose howl had haunted their nights and whose strength had tested their chains. As they look at the former demoniac, the townspeople see something amazing, something they never thought they would see—a sane man who is clean-shaven and demon-free (5:15). Their reaction is equally amazing; they do not celebrate the good fortune of a man who has known none. They do not throw a party for one who was lost but now is found (Luke 15). Rather, they are afraid (5:15).[8]

---

4. Mary Ann Tolbert notes the potential effect of such a scene on its ancient audience: "As oral performance, rhetorical works of all genres aimed to persuade by *entertaining*. To please the hearers, to entertain them, was the sine qua non of persuasive speaking and writing. Plato called rhetoric 'amusement' (*phuchuxagogia*), and the desire to entertain was at one with the desire to influence the audience. . . . [T]he narrative relish of the herd of swine hurling themselves over the cliff in the healing of the demoniac (5:1–20), or the increasingly nitwit responses of the disciples throughout the Gospel may serve the purpose of entertainment as well as moral instruction, for that combination is a special grace of Hellenistic rhetoric" (Tolbert, *Sowing the Gospel,* 46).

5. See the discussion of the word *thalassa* in View One of chapter 3.

6. Horsley, *Hearing the Whole Story,* 147.

7. Dowd, *Reading Mark,* 55.

8. Don Juel captures part of the reason for the fear of the townspeople, but he misses the political-economic threat posed by Jesus in this story. The story may not say explicitly that the townspeople "were

Even more amazing, the Gerasene townspeople and swineherds ask Jesus to leave (5:17). Earlier the demonic Legion begged (*parakaleō*) Jesus not to send them away from the region (5:10); now the demonic townspeople beg (*parakaleō*) Jesus to leave that same place. Faced with living sane amid the townspeople's insane lack of faith in the One who brought about his restoration, the nameless, Gerasene, Gentile grave dweller begs (*parakaleō*) Jesus to let him leave with him and the disciples (5:18). Jesus denies his request (5:19).

Recalling the story of the healing of Naaman (2 Kgs. 5:1–19), Jesus tells the man that his vocation is to succeed where the swineherds failed (5:19). His vocation is to stay at home and announce (*apangellō*) the goodness of the Lord God of Israel, which has been made known in Gentile country upon the visit of the "Son of the Most High God." As Dowd notes, "The good news for this tormented specimen of humanity is not that he is accepted just as he is, but that he is transformed into the person his Creator intended for him to be, no longer distorted by powers that are alien to his created self."[9] As the story continues, not only does the first Gentile disciple "announce" what has happened in Gerasa; he also goes throughout the Decapolis preaching (*kērussō*), bearing a personal witness to the mercy of the Lord.[10] In the allegorical interpretation of the parable of the Sower, Jesus says that those who are of the good earth "hear the word and accept it and bear fruit, thirty and sixty and a hundredfold" (4:20 NRSV). In this anonymous, once-possessed man from the wrong side of the tracks, readers catch a glimpse of the reign of God that Jesus is initiating.

Despite the enthusiastic witness of the now sane Gerasene, Mark tempers any enthusiasm that the Gospel has become contagious as he describes the reception of this man's preaching. The crowds do not overcome fear or come to faith. They react in the same way as the frightened townspeople; they are simply amazed (5:20). A similar response awaits Jesus when he returns to the other side of the sea (6:6).

---

scandalized by the magnitude of their financial loss" (Juel, *Gospel of Mark*, 112). However, Mark emphasizes the role of the swineherds and repeats the story of the swine to emphasize that the Gerasenes find the presence of Jesus in their lives far too costly. With this significant omission noted, Juel is right when he observes about Mark 5:1–20: "Jesus threatens the stability of their carefully structured world, as he has for those whose everyday life is defined by the Law of Moses. And so they urge him to leave" 112).

9. Dowd, *Reading Mark*, 55.

10. As Lamar Williamson explains, "The distinction between 'tell' and 'proclaim' or 'preach' discloses two nuances in the text. Verse 19 underscores the intimate, personal nature of the witness the man was asked to bear while verse 20 points to its broad public dissemination. But the two are synonymous. Surely the simple telling of 'how much the Lord has done for you, and how he has had mercy on you' is a powerful proclamation of the gospel. And surely the most effective preaching is done by those who can, and from time to time do, simply tell how much Jesus has done for them" (Williamson, *Mark*, 107).

Even as the inhabitants of Gerasa ask Jesus to leave (5:14), a "great crowd" greets Jesus as he crosses the sea and lands on Jewish soil (5:21). While in the Decapolis, Jesus was met by swineherds and townspeople and a demoniac, none of whom were named. Back in Jewish country, Jesus is met by one with both a name and title: Jairus, the leader of the synagogue (*archisunagōgŏs*, 5:22). While historians dispute the precise status of the *archisunagōgŏs*,[11] Mark gives him the status of the only named character in chapter 5, other than a Legion, a pack of demons. In stark contrast to the townspeople in Gerasa who beg (*parakaleō*, 5:17) Jesus to leave, Jairus begs (*parakaleō*, 5:23) Jesus to lay hands upon his daughter so that she might be saved (*sōzō*, "heal" or "save") and live.[12] Jesus respects the request and follows Jairus; the "great crowd" follows too (5:24).

While on the way, Mark interrupts the story of Jairus and his dying daughter with a story that involves another request for the healing of a woman. Mark does not give his readers the name of Jairus's daughter or this ailing woman. All he tells us is that both of their situations are desperate—one terminal and the other chronic. The anonymous woman has suffered from a flow of blood for as long as the anonymous daughter of Jairus has lived (5:25). Donald Juel remarks:

> The woman is the starkest possible contrast to Jairus, a male and a synagogue official. In addition to her lower status as a woman, she is suffering from a social disease as well as a physical malady and cannot even enter the synagogue. Thus she cannot identify herself to Jesus and ask for help—she would be driven off if discovered—but must try to conceal her problem if she is to get close enough to touch him.[13]

---

11. Horsley differs from many current Markan scholars who see the intercalation of Jairus and his daughter (5:21–24, 35–43) with the hemorrhaging woman (5:25–34) as a contrast between the powerful and the powerless. Rather, he contends that Jairus was simply a leader of a local Galilean village assembly—i.e., a community leader not necessarily wealthy or powerful (Horsley, *Hearing the Whole Story*, 221). While I think Horsley seriously understates the significance of this Markan contrast, he does accurately note that "both women are villagers and, while the younger is still in the household of her father, both are in desperate condition, their life ebbing or having ebbed away" (221).

12. The NRSV of Mark 5:23 reads "so that she may be *made well*." While this is an adequate rendering of *sōzō*, it fails to capture Mark's repetition of this verb throughout chapter 5, thereby reducing the request simply to one for physical healing. As Williamson notes, "the Greek verb (*sōzō*) translated 'make well' in this passage (vv. 23, 28, 34) is usually translated 'save' in the New Testament. In the present passage it retains a nuance of more than physical wholeness" (Williamson, *Mark*, 110).

13. Juel, *Mark*, 115.

Though different in fundamental ways from the powerful Jairus, the hemorrhaging woman resembles Jairus in her willingness to defy all social and religious barriers to seek out Jesus.[14]

And, like the friends who find a way to lower the paralytic to Jesus in Mark 2:3–4, the nameless, ritually impure woman finds her way to Jesus. She approaches him from behind to touch his garment in the faith that if she does, she will "be saved" (5:27–28). "Immediately" she recognizes that her long years of blood loss are over (5:29), and "immediately" Jesus recognizes that he has been touched by a person of faith (5:30). "The woman touched him [Jesus] with absolute faith that she would be saved; that faith was the crucial factor," writes Mary Ann Tolbert. *"Faith, then, is the prerequisite for healing for the Gospel of Mark, not its result.* One does not have faith *because* one was healed; one has faith *so that* one can be healed. The miracles in Mark are not intended as signs to induce belief; they are, instead, the visible tangible fruits of faith."[15]

Readers aware of Jewish ritual law know that the woman has defiled Jesus with her touch. Leviticus 5:19–30 is clear that vaginal bleeding renders a woman unclean. Yet, remarkably, as Juel notes, "Jesus is not defiled by her touch; she is cleansed."[16] In this story, Jesus and a nameless, ritually impure woman recognize the power of faith, while Jesus' disciples remain unaware of what has happened in their midst (5:31). So when Jesus stops and asks who touched him, the disciples point out the obvious, having missed the miraculous. They dismiss Jesus' question as laughable since, as Mark told us in 5:21, Jesus is surrounded by a "great crowd." Readers sample another example of Markan irony as disciples belittle Jesus for asking such a stupid question, evidently having forgotten the power of the One who both calms the sea (4:35–41) and restores to wholeness those who are demon possessed (5:1–20).

After she is healed of her disease, the once hemorrhaging woman does not slip out of the crowd as inconspicuously as she slipped in. When Jesus turns

14. As Pheme Perkins explains, "her flow of blood poses the danger of ritual impurity for anyone who comes into contact with her (Lev. 15:19–33). . . . [T]he woman's condition has made her 'impure.' Therefore, she must overcome social and ritual boundaries to approach and touch Jesus" (Pheme Perkins, "The Gospel of Mark," *New Interpreter's Bible* 8:587).

15. Tolbert, *Sowing the Gospel*, 169. Cf. Dowd: "In the Markan narrative it is often made clear that the people who come to Jesus seeking miraculous help do so because of his reputation as a miracle worker . . . There is a direct connection between the reputation of the healer and the faith of those seeking healing. They believe that Jesus can heal them because they have heard about his healing others. It is in this sense that miracles, or rather reports about miracles, do lead to faith in the Gospel of Mark" (Dowd, *Reading Mark*, 61).

16. Juel, *Mark*, 115.

to see who has touched him, she responds like most biblical characters who encounter the Divine. She is filled with fear and trembling, and yet her faith overcomes her fear as she tells her story to Jesus (5:33).[17] Jesus addresses her with the same affection that Jairus addresses his child. Jesus calls her "daughter" (5:34). Bruce Malina and Richard Rohrbaugh argue that, by addressing the woman as a family member, Jesus demonstrates that the social ostracism caused by her disease has been overcome.[18] In this healing, then, Jesus has torn down yet another boundary separating the religiously pure from the impure. Moreover, Myers makes a persuasive argument that when the woman is given the name "daughter," Jesus gives her a status greater than the unnamed daughter of a synagogue leader and even of his male disciples, who are "without faith" (4:40).[19] Jesus tells this newly named daughter to go in peace and know that she is well (*sōzō*, 5:34). While her "wellness" includes a longed-for return to physical health, it also includes a return to both social and religious acceptability.

As Jesus is addressing this new daughter, news comes from Jairus's house that his daughter is dead. The messenger with this news suggests that the teacher need no longer be bothered since Jairus's child has died (5:35). These messengers would know that Jesus would be ritually defiled should he touch the corpse (Num. 19:11–21). As the once nameless woman confronted her fear to face Jesus, so now Jesus tells Jairus that he must not concede to his fear but live in faith (5:36).[20] So too, later in the Gospel, Mark's disciples will be asked to overcome fear with faith as Jesus is crucified in Jerusalem. Foreshadowing the company that Jesus will take upon a mountain in Mark 9:2 and with him into the Garden of Gethsemane in 14:32–33, Jesus leaves the crowd and heads to the house of mourning with only Peter, James, and John and the child's parents (5:37).[21] There he witnesses what one often finds in the time

---

17. On the relationship between faith and fear, Tolbert writes: "Faith is not solely the domain of the strong, the powerful, and the confident, but even the weak, the lowly, and the cowardly can respond with faith that drives out fear and thus saves" (Tolbert, *Sowing the Gospel*, 169).

18. Bruce J. Malina and Richard L. Rohrbaugh, *A Social-Science Commentary on the Synoptic Gospels* (Minneapolis: Fortress, 1992), 209–10.

19. Myers, *Binding the Strong Man*, 202.

20. Williamson offers a poignant interpretation of this Markan scene between Jesus and the grief-stricken father. Jesus' " 'Fear not,' so characteristic of appearances of God in the Old Testament (e.g., the theophanies in Gen. 15:1; 21:17; 26:24; 46:3), represents here as well the divine intervention to save and to give life. Not even after death is it too late to hope. . . . Beside an open casket or at the moment of our own death we are invited to respond to the words *Talitha, cumi* not with a historical question about a past event but with a thrill of anticipation" (Williamson, *Mark*, 111).

21. Perkins argues that the limitation of witnesses echoes Elijah's taking the widow's son apart to his own chamber in 1 Kings 17 and Elisha and his servant's going into the room alone to restore life to the Shunammite woman's son in 2 Kings 4 (Perkins, "The Gospel of Mark," 589).

of death—especially a premature death—confusion and weeping (5:38). He encounters the official *shomer*s (watchers) who, in Jewish ritual, stay with a body from death until burial.

At Jairus's house, Jesus asks a question that makes complete sense to Mark's readers, but again sounds ridiculous to the characters in the story. As the risen Jesus asks Mary in the garden in John's Gospel (John 20:15), here the earthly Jesus asks this group, "Why all this commotion and crying?" To make matters worse, he tells them that the child is asleep, not dead (5:29). The mourners turn from tears to laughter at such an assertion, but Jesus, like a storm out of control, exorcises (*ekballō*) these demonic doubters from the house (5:40). Jesus and his select company enter the girl's room, and he finally does what Jairus had earlier asked him to do. Jesus takes the hand of Jairus's daughter and in Aramaic tells her to get up (5:41). Jesus does not become impure; rather, the dead daughter of Jairus lives (5:42). Asking the absurd, and again foreshadowing the trip down the mountain after his transfiguration, Jesus then tells them that no one should know what has happened. Finally, he instructs the family to give the girl something to eat, which is perhaps Mark's way to remind his readers that ghosts do not dine and that the transforming reality of the reign of God is not illusory (5:43).[22] Like the daughter who touched Jesus in the streets (5:27–29), by the power of Jesus' touch the daughter of Jairus is saved.

Tolbert provides a valuable summary to Mark 5:

> These three healings . . . depict miraculous results when the word is accepted in faith rather than fear. . . . Furthermore, that a man whose home is in the Greek cities of the Decapolis (5:20), a poor woman (5:26), and a leader of a Jewish synagogue (5:22) should all prove themselves to be good earth with faith capable of producing fruit indicates the universal nature of the kingdom of God. Whether Greek or Jew, male or female, powerful or weak, all can be part of God's ground if faith is their response to hearing the word.[23]

In the next scene, the testimony to the power of faith in Jesus is cut short as Mark invites readers back home with Jesus. Surrounded by the familiar,

---

22. Ched Myers stresses the reversal of social fortune implied in this story: "As far as Mark's Jesus is concerned, the social order represented by the synagogue ruler's Judaism is on the verge of collapse. The statusless woman had suffered twelve years of destitution at the hands of the purity system and its 'doctors'; yet she still took initiative in her struggle for liberation. The object lesson can only be that if Judaism wishes to 'be saved and live' (5:23), it must embrace the 'faith' of the kingdom: a new social order with equal status for all" (Myers, *Binding the Strong Man*, 202–3).

23. Tolbert, *Sowing the Gospel*, 170–71.

in his hometown synagogue on the Sabbath, Jesus is not embraced by faith but harangued by a list of insufficient names (6:3). "Isn't this Mary's boy?" "Where does a carpenter get the wisdom to say the things he says and the power to heal?" "Isn't this the brother of Simon and James and Jude and Joses? And aren't those his sisters?" The demon in Gentile Gerasa recognizes Jesus as the "Son of the Most High God," but at home fellow Jews see in Jesus no more than someone's son or brother, no more than a child from a blue-collar family acting as if he were upper class. "The people of Nazareth are like the seed that fell beside the path; they never take root," says Dowd. "Their opinions about who Jesus is stand in their way."[24] So, rather than praising the virtue of this hometown son, the crowd is scandalized (*skandalizō*) by Jesus, reacting much as the Gentile crowd in the Decapolis does to the glad tidings of the healed demoniac.[25] After a string of remarkable exorcisms and healings, Mark sounds a dissonant note when he remarks that the power of Jesus is rendered virtually impotent at home (6:5). As Perkins notes, "Since the miracles in the previous chapter emphasize the importance of faith in those who approach Jesus for healing, the conclusion that Jesus is unable to work many miracles in Nazareth is hardly surprising."[26] In 6:1–6 Mark again leaves his readers with no doubt about the importance of faith as the fertile soil of the mighty acts of God. For, as Dowd contends, "Merely recognizing that Jesus has power is not faith. Faith is confidence in the saving power of God manifest in the ministry of Jesus."[27]

In 5:34, Jesus was amazed by the faith of the hemorrhaging daughter. At the opening of chapter 6, Jesus is amazed by the lack of faith of those in his own hometown (6:6). In 5:1–6:6, Mark shows that faith in Jesus brings restoration and transformation. And he smashes the most formidable borders—between Jew and Gentile, between the powerful (Jairus) and the powerless (the hemorrhaging woman), between male (the demoniac, Jairus and the Twelve) and female (the two daughters), and even between the familial and the familiar (the synagogue in Nazareth). Williamson offers an important corrective to how this pericope is sometimes read:

---

24. Dowd, *Reading Mark*, 60.
25. See Mark 14:29, when Peter promises that he will not be "scandalized" by Jesus' impending death. According to Myers, "the name that Jesus was making for himself scandalized the neighborhood, upset the status quo (6:4). Without their cooperative faith (6:6)—that is to say, their openness to a new order—Jesus can accomplish none of the 'mighty works' (6:5, *oudemian dunamin*) that have aroused the hometown crowd's suspicion" (Myers, *Binding the Strong Man*, 212).
26. Perkins, "Gospel of Mark," 592.
27. Dowd, *Reading Mark*, 60.

The point is not that Jesus is impotent without our faith, for he did some-times work wonders without reference to faith. On the other hand, the point is that the unbelief of Jesus' own people had a restrictive, dampening effect on his work in their midst. It also marked the end of his work there. Rather than stay to argue with his own people, or to try to convince them by fur-ther mighty works, Jesus moved on.[28]

The importance of names is explicit in this 5:1–6:6: Gerasene, demoniac, Legion, swineherds, Jairus, daughter, disciple. As this chapter closes, Mark leaves readers with the unspoken question, "By what name will you call Jesus?" To the townspeople in Geresa, Jesus is an unwelcome intruder who threatens their economic security and challenges the religious status quo. To the disciples and the professional mourners in Jairus's home, Jesus is an embarrassment and a walking conundrum. To the hometown crowd that remembers when Jesus hammered his first nail, Jesus is nothing more than a local boy whose head has swollen. But, to those whose human need has lev-eled all economic walls and torn down all social and religious boundaries— to the demoniac, the unnamed woman, to Jairus and his unnamed daughter—Jesus is the Son of the Most High God, the very One who brings salvation and shalom to broken lives. There is no secret, then, about the name that the faithful will call Jesus.

So, what's in a name anyway? For Mark, everything.

View Two: "A Witness to the Resurrection" (Mark 5:1–20)
Gary W. Charles

[Introduction: While on vacation in August 2001, I got a call from a good friend who is a member of the church I serve. He apologized for calling me while I was on vacation and then explained the reason for the call. I hung up the phone and wept. For over twenty years, Doug and Judy Feaver had watched the demon of schizophrenia strip their youngest son, Steven, and them of any semblance of a normal life. The Feavers became experts in traversing the elaborate maze of mental-health services in America. They watched as the mentally ill and substance abusers were treated with little differentiation and increasingly ignored or undertreated by federal, state, and local agencies.

Steven was a scary schizophrenic. When he was off his medications, some-thing bad inevitably happened, and when he was on them, he often felt

---

28. Williamson, *Mark*, 115.

depressed. So, Steven would not stay on any one medication for long. The experts, who were sometimes quite caring, were helpless in "binding this strong man." After an August automobile accident that was his fault and would have resulted in his losing his driver's license, Steven decided that he would have the last word about his condition. He hanged himself.

I asked Doug and Judy for permission to speak openly in my sermon about Steven's suicide and his years of losing the battle with mental illness. The Feavers were gracious enough to give me their permission with the prayer that a focus on the plight of the mentally ill in America would be helpful. As I prepared to preach at Steven's memorial service, I thought immediately of Mark's treatment of the Gerasene demoniac. I also thought about the theme of how Jesus cares and redeems the lives of the nameless needy in Mark 5:1–6:6. Too often preachers see funerals and memorial services as occasions to skirt the truth about the Gospel, a person's life, and society's failings. As a result, funerals and memorials often contribute to our society's denial of death and minimize the radical promise of the resurrection.

I am grateful to Doug and Judy, who held me to a higher standard. Pre-ceding my sermon are the remarkable comments of a grieving father about his beloved and almost always deeply troubled son.]

Doug Feaver Remembers His Son, Steven

There's an old saying that memorial services are really for the living, not the dead. Judy and Chris and Steven's grandparents and aunt and uncle and cousins and I are truly blessed today by your presence and by the kindness so many of you have shown. Steven would be both pleased that you are here and irritated that he is once again the center of a lot of unwanted adult attention.

Very few of you knew Steven personally. He lived in a different world than most of us, and his friends were also from that world. He met his girlfriend about a decade ago when they were both patients in a psychiatric ward. She cannot be here today because she is again in a psychiatric ward and very ill. His closest friend and sometime roommate, recently released from a hospital, is also not well enough to be here.

Judy and I have been trying to remember the times when Steven was happy. He would have loved the weather today because it is beastly hot and humid. We would be sweltering were he in charge, because he would have turned off the air conditioning.

He loved the ocean. The first time he encountered it was at Virginia Beach, at the age of about six, and he could have stayed there forever, darting in and out of the waves.

He loved to play soccer and, later, basketball. He was good at both, for a short guy, because he was so competitive. Even when he was in the deepest fog, he could provide a complete analysis of all the NBA teams and a rational explanation of why the Wizards will never get there.

We went to a meaningless Wizards game late last season. The Wizards led most of the way and took a healthy lead into the fourth quarter. Steven turned to me then and informed me with great assurance that the game was lost, that the Wizards would fold and Tracy McGrady would simply win it for Orlando all by himself. That is exactly what happened. Steven was very pleased when his prediction came true.

And he loved to play bridge. He could force his sometimes deranged mind to crystallize on how best to defeat that little slam contract, then defeat it, then rejoice in the triumph, then descend minutes later into total irrationality.

It became clear when he was in junior high that he was troubled. To say that he experimented with drugs and alcohol would be to put the most sympathetic light on the matter. By the time he was a young adult, the trouble had become diagnosed as schizophrenia, with its delusions and hallucinations and the unsilenceable voices that command.

Medications do not control schizophrenia that well in all people, and the antipsychotic drugs can have unpleasant side effects. Steven hated them, and as soon he could escape the constant monitoring of a hospital, he would stop taking them. He preferred his own medication, marijuana, which the mental health professionals told him time and again interfered with the effectiveness of the antipsychotic drugs.

There are two schools of thought on the subject: that the illegal substances can cause the mental illness or that the mental illness can cause the individual to self-medicate with illegal substances. This has become a doctrinal debate with strong adherents for both positions within the mental health profession and the righteous antidrug/criminal justice types. Neither answer works in real time. There is one known fact about this chicken-egg question: about half of all diagnosed schizophrenics also have substance abuse issues.

When Steven got sick enough—when he decompensated, as the mental health people would say—he would do something outrageous or threatening. His parents or the police or a frightened neighbor would intervene, and he would be involuntarily hospitalized or jailed. We lost count of the number of times that happened.

In recent months, Steven actually appeared to be doing better, to be settling down. He was in a new apartment that he liked. He was on a new drug regimen that he appeared to be tolerating. He had made friends with a neighbor, and he was delighted when the neighbor strung balloons on a shared balcony to celebrate his thirty-seventh birthday, in June.

In July he got his driver's license back. It had been suspended for six months under Virginia law because of his conviction on a marijuana possession charge. The return of the driver's license meant he could return to his part-time delivery job.

Saturday afternoon he was involved in a minor traffic accident. He was charged with failure to maintain control and, more important, with possession of marijuana. That would mean another court appearance, another six months' suspension, and another six months without work. His body was found Sunday morning by the neighbor who had strung the balloons.

The pain and anger that we sometimes felt as parents and family is nothing like the pain Steven felt, something I had to tell myself often. One of his former counselors, the wonderful Rhonda, reminded me Monday that "Steven never quit trying." He also never quit trying to define the world in his own terms, but his touch was incendiary. He burned every bridge, including his last one.

In the early 1980s, Steven had not yet displayed the classic signs of schizophrenia. But troubles beyond normal adolescent difficulties were beginning to be obvious, even to this denying parent. I was ranting to my own father in my typical way about how, by God, that child was going to obey me and start walking a straight line or I would toss him to the world.

Dad was failing badly, sliding into his own dementia. But he sat straight up, turned to me, and said sternly and with great clarity, "Doug, I don't understand everything that is going on with Steven. But you must not give up on him."

And Judy and I did not, although we were certainly tempted from time to time. And I am confident—it is the core of my strengthening faith—that God has not given up on him either.

I hope Steven has been assigned to the Wizards reclamation project.

Sermon: "A Witness to the Resurrection"

On Sunday afternoon, after Doug called to tell me about the tragic death of Steven, I got in the car, prayed for Steven, prayed for Doug and Judy and Chris and all the family, prayed for the wisdom to say anything of comfort, and then, out of the blue, the story of the Gerasene demoniac came to mind. This story is not even remotely a traditional text for memorial services, but I am convinced that is the right text for this service.

"No one could restrain him any more, even with a chain for he had often been restrained with shackles and chains, but the chains he wrenched apart, and the shackles he broke in pieces; and no one had the strength to subdue him. Night and day among the tombs and on the mountains he was always howling and bruising himself with stones" (5:3–5 NRSV). I would ask you if Mark's description of the possessed demoniac does not describe the Steven Feavers of the land? For years Steven traveled in lands unknown to most of us, at times visiting in a land for which the terrain is more familiar, but most often, he lived in lands in which sanity had little meaning and even less lasting power. In those lands, violence was a norm that even included violence against his own self. Trained caregivers, loving parents, brother, grandparents and friends tried to counsel him, to treat him, at times even to detain him; but "no one had the strength to subdue him."

The same demons that possessed Steven Feaver also possess thousands of others in America today. Some of the possessed live functional lives through the aid of medication and therapy, but many find functional lives an elusive finish line that they rarely cross. So far, I have belabored the obvious, for after all, mental illness is not new to this century or to this country. Mark tells this story, though, to do anything but belabor the obvious. Note the reaction of the crowd when the Gerasene demoniac is finally made whole. Rather than throwing a ticker-tape parade, the community is leery and then becomes angry that this man's healing has placed a financial burden on those who are not ill (5:14–16). As they watch livestock options take a plunge over the cliff and into the sea (5:13), the crowd suggests that this Jewish healer take his medicine and return home (5:17).

On Sunday afternoon, after Doug called and I had said my prayers and started to think about this haunting story from Mark's Gospel, my emotions evolved from sorrow to anger. Since then, my anger has only grown more intense. In one sense, Steven's suicide was his final statement that no one was going to bind this "strong man." But in another sense, Steven's was an "assisted suicide" by you and me and a society that has decided it cannot afford the financial burden of responsibly caring for the mentally ill, especially the adult mentally ill.

I know. I know. I can already hear the objections. Whenever such statements are made in public discourse, a similar litany of excuses follows: "It's nearly impossible to treat schizophrenia successfully" or "Why should I have to pay exorbitant costs of providing treatment for someone who often only exacerbates her disease by doing drugs?" or "Well, Gary, as a society, we simply can't help everyone, and as the Bible says, 'The Lord helps those who help themselves.'" Say what we will, excuse what we may, but you and I can no more wash the blood of Steven's death from our hands than Pilate could wash the blood of Jesus from his hands.

Currently, in our society, while we debate how to spend our $300 in federal tax rebates, we are sending the mentally ill in America to the streets or to prisons or to apartment basements with a rope. In the process, we are the ones bound by the chains of the status quo. We are the ones who refuse to imagine and then to implement a better way to care for those wrestling with the demons of mental illness. Instead, we express our condolences at Steven's death almost as if it were an inevitability, rather than a judgment on the land for the reprehensible way we provide for "the least of these our sisters and brothers."

If you think I am going a bit overboard here, especially at a memorial service intended to bring peace to grieving parents, family, and friends, then I respectfully suggest that you are wrong. For what Doug and Judy know, as well as any two adults can, is that there is never any peace without justice. And there will never be peace for the Stevens and the families of the Stevens of our world until our society sees mental illness as something more than a stubborn, financial black hole that we bemoan but largely ignore.

If you read on to the end of Mark's Gospel, you will see Jesus heal the infirm, send demons on their devilish ways, and calm troubled seas. You'd expect a celebration, a Fourth of July display of jubilation, but the celebration never begins. No one ever uncorks the champagne and laughs with uncontrollable glee. Even the healing of a wild man, who lived among the tombs and howled like a wolf and could not be bound, does not result in a community chorus of praise. Instead, Jesus goes to his grave with most people thinking that the rich and powerful, those most vested in maintaining the status quo, finally "bound the strong man."

Sometimes though, "most people" are wrong. Early last Sunday morning, "strong man" Steven Feaver met more than his match. He met a Lord whose death was also the result of people who had too much invested to change, who dared not let themselves move beyond fear to faith. He met a Friend who was thought weak and ridiculous by the ones who had bound him. He met a Judge who happens also to be a Lover, who, in Steven, has restored one more broken soul and carried him into a land where violence has no place and misery has no company.

As the hours ahead pass by for the family, at first like molasses, only soon to return to their normal ebb and flow, I pray that the One true "strong man" will give Doug and Judy and Chris, and all who loved Steven, a glimpse of that cherished land, near—but still far away—so that they may find the peace that throughout much of Steven's life escaped them as well.

As for us, may we express our sympathy to the family, as well we should, but may we do more, much more for every Steven who deserves a safe home and a real hope, too often denied. May God show us that the vision and will to do so is empowered by the One in whose name we all are saved, the one true "Strong Man."

View Three: Responding to Madness
Brian K. Blount

I am struck by the madness that this section of Mark depicts. As I read it and reread it, as I ponder Gary's exegetical reflections about it, I get the eerie feeling that haunts me when I read a Stephen King novel. The horror builds so fast and with such devastating consequence that sometimes the movement is almost strangely comic. It is like finding out that the intelligence behind a massive invasion of the planet is located not in the humanoid creatures that fly the attacking spaceships but in the fungus that creeps across their bodies like a communicable disease.[29] All of a sudden, the wonder of interstellar encounter becomes a kind of bizarre spray-and-wash germ warfare. It is as odd as depicting Jesus' combat with the dazzling demonic forces who would rule heaven and earth in terms of a preposterous pork stampede. But that is precisely what Mark gives us. And, as it turns out, the premature soaking of all that potential ham, sausage, and bacon in the sea is the least exasperating of all the mad moments that preoccupy the evangelist's narrative intent. As I read and reflect, I count (presently, at least!) four.

1. There is the madness of unreasonable reason. The section is lit up by its manifestation at the end of the long opening set. Just after Jesus heals the Gerasene demoniac and the amazed people rush away to tell all that they have seen, an impressed but nonetheless dubious crowd returns with an anxious request. They would like Jesus to leave. You'll remember that no one else had ever been able to tame this wild man because of the savage spirit that possessed him. Apparently the dirty grunt job had been handed over to professionals with chains and locks; they had failed. The man and his possession were too strong. Jesus doesn't come looking to do some spectacular work. He doesn't need the prestige. He doesn't ask to be paid. He just sees a job to be done and he does it. That was his style. Where people were in need he addressed them and their concern. He only asked to be seen as the pointer to God's rule that he was.

The Gerasenes saw him as the road to trouble. So they did what any good

---

29. See Stephen King, *Dreamcatcher* (New York: Pocket Books, 2001).

board would do with a high-profile employee who doesn't make the cut: they asked him to submit his resignation. The petition is sadly comic; essentially, they are firing him for doing too good a job. That is what is so unreasonable. But that is also precisely Mark's point. Illogic had become the operational ground for living in this first-century world. That is because in this world it made sense to harbor a possessed man in a possessed state so long as you could keep him from harming others or destroying himself. As long as you could maintain equilibrium, keep up the status quo, even a destructive status quo, you were doing well. Jesus disrupted all of that. His healing created a situation that demanded change in the way the Gerasenes lived their lives. Now, someone would have to account for the well-being of the formerly possessed man. Now, someone would have to sweat out the paperwork of creative accounting to balance out ledgers that had suffered a severe economic loss in the demise of an entire herd of swine. Now, someone would have to answer for the fact that a powerful Legion, the representation of a Roman army and thus Roman rule, had fallen prey to the prowling power of a resistant God who, through Jesus, claimed a contrary right of rule over this people and their land. All this disruption to the status quo would be noticed and, the Gerasenes knew, would have to be accounted for and explained.

Their lack of reason, given these circumstances, therefore seemed quite reasonable indeed. An excellent, contemporary corollary to the predicament of the Gerasenes was described in a sermon by the Reverend Otis Moss. Moss recognizes the seductive allure even a destructive status quo has upon a populace. People recognize that transformation not only brings change; it also demands responsible, responsive behavior. Often, it exacts a costly price. It may therefore seem more reasonable to maintain and manage a present horror than to chance the risks that come from seeking and implementing change. Moss takes reverent delight in the perplexing predicament of the Gerasenes. While their demoniac was mad, and therefore a chronic cause for extreme societal anxiety, they were fine. It was only after he was healed, and logically no longer a threat, that they became mad. Why?

> I see a black and white parallel here. As long as we were struggling in the cotton fields of Tennessee, Georgia, Alabama, and Mississippi with our cotton sacks across our shoulders and to our sides, picking cotton and having our fingers burning from stinging cotton worms that would hide under the cotton leaves; as long as we were barefoot, actually and symbolically, laughing when we were not tickled . . . America was satisfied. . . . But one

day America saw us marching to the voting booth, sitting down at lunch counters, and all of America became afraid.[30]

It is only after black people were "healed" of their imposed madness, after they knew who they were and went about the business of pursuing a societal recognition of equality based on this rehabilitated state of awareness, that American society, like Legion's, became afraid. American society had learned to live with and manage the horror of inequality; it wasn't yet ready for the sacrifices change would mandate. The unreasonable clinging to the status quo therefore had the most "rational" of foundations. It is a state of affairs the Gerasenes knew well.

2. There is the madness of losing hope. I have a daughter. I can imagine the anguish that prompted Jairus to seek out even the most outrageous form of alternative medicine. Even a quack with the queer reputation of having just been kicked out of a town for a controversial pig treatment would have been an attractive source of possible power. When you're losing hope, when your little boat on the Galilean sea is sinking, when your precious daughter is dying, the madness of the moment can drive you anywhere, to anyone. It drove Jairus, the upstanding Jew with a stellar background in the corporate faith, to this rogue rambler whose charisma attracted every hopeless fool with an infirmity, but whose penchant for troublemaking had convinced his fellow authority figures (the scribes) that he was working for the devil (3:22). Only a man mad with the specter of an unthinkable loss could sell out his standing, his religious reputation, and his communal soul, in so public a way.

Such a man would be elated when the miracle worker consented to his request. Focused only on himself and the task he had set at Jesus' hand, he would no doubt have been highly agitated when Jesus stopped to converse with that no-name woman on the side of the road. The madness would surely have turned to hostility and anger—at Jesus, and at the woman—when word came while Jesus was still engrossed in conversation that his cherished daughter had died. Here is where reason, reasonable reason, should have overwhelmed the man and put an end to his quest. But Jesus challenges Jairus to forget reason, to descend into the madness that motivates his ministry and believe that there was still hope. Jesus asks him to go on, to ignore the word of death, and lock onto his word of life. They were laughing at Jairus's house when Jesus made this same mad case before the mourners who had gathered

---

30. Otis Moss Jr., "Going from Disgrace to Dignity," in *Preaching the Gospel* (ed. Henry J. Young; Philadelphia: Fortress Press, 1976), 52–53. Though Moss's sermon is on the Lukan version of the same account (Luke 8:26–35), the thematic point he makes applies equally well to Mark's presentation.

to help Jairus come to terms with the tragic loss of his daughter. Like Abraham and Sarah, who could not believe that God could give a child to people of such an ancient age, Jairus's friends mocked Jesus' pretension that he could transform this situation. Some things were so bad that no one could do anything about them. People simply had to take them and endure. The laughter was a form of contagious madness; the laughter was their metaphor for giving up. It is this madness that Jairus's friends, in their reason and logic, invited him to share. They had come to grieve with him. All he had to do was give up his belief in Jesus' ability to change this situation and receive their comfort. This is the magnetism of madness. There are crucial moments in life when it looks right. Jesus offers the alternative. "Despite what you see," he tells Jairus, "do not fear. Believe!" (5:36). Fear multiplies madness. Belief captures the energy of that madness and bends it back toward hope.

3. There is the madness of seeking salvation, of wanting to be "saved." I had been working in the pastorate for maybe six months when it happened. I had my first professional experience with a "saved" Christian. I was planning an Easter sunrise service that would include a wide variety of denominations. It would take place at sunrise on Easter morning down by the shore of the Hampton Bay in Virginia. This particular day I was visiting the pastor at a large, well-known church in the city. It was a fruitful ministry; the church boasted several thousand members.

On my way to his office I encountered the church receptionist. She was very polite, very receptive. She was very good at her job. She told me pleasantly that the pastor's counseling session had run a little late but that he would be with me momentarily. She then asked if I'd mind taking a seat. I didn't, so I sat down in a waiting area already occupied by another woman. Right away, in a church of thousands, she knew that I was not a member. Impressive. She asked me why I was there. After I told her, after I explained that I'm a minister, she looked at me doubtfully and asked with a straight and rather demanding face, "Are you saved?" I choked a bit. I was caught off guard. While I gathered myself, she asked again, "Are you saved?" I said, I'm a minister, ma'am," thinking this would satisfy her curiosity. But now that I'd given the wrong answer she came at me again. "Are you saved?" I told her, "Ma'am, I grew up in the church. I've known I've been a Christian for as long as I've been alive. And now I've accepted what I believe is God's call"—at this point she interrupted by asking yet again, "Are you saved?"—and I finished, rather aggravated, "at the Presbyterian Church down the street." A mournful frown on her face, she didn't ask anymore. Evidently the mere mention of Presbyterianism assured her that I most certainly was not saved. So now she went into evangelism mode.

As she talked it became clear to me that in her mind to be saved meant to be an active member of God's church—which is to say, her church. Not just that local one, but the denomination of which it was a part. In her mind Christianity had become a kind of caste system. There were those who were saved, who belonged to the right church and held the right beliefs about God and Jesus espoused by that church—which, of course, I was now being taught. There were those like myself, who saw partially, who saw people, but they looked like trees walking (8:24), who needed the proper push from their naive start in some baby faith like Presbyterianism and needed someone's final healing touch. Whether we realized it or not, we were spiritually dying. Then, there were those completely outside the church, for whom there is only damnation.

I talked to her for maybe ten minutes before the receptionist called and told me the pastor was ready. I left her, sitting there, saved, pitying me, as I hauled my unsaved, deutero-Christian carcass into her pastor's study. She still haunts me, that lady, because I couldn't convince her she was wrong. She knew her Bible. I mean, she was a walking Bible content exam. For every point I made, she had a potent counterpoint. And then, as I reflected on Gary's exegesis and sermon, she came back and haunted me again. Perhaps, had I been thinking of these texts, I could have told her what Mark appears to be telling his Christian community. Following Jesus isn't as much a matter of being saved as it is a matter of being placed in service. It is not being saved from life that matters, but one's willingness to be placed in all the rigors, tremors, turmoils, and trials of life. The woman with the twelve-year issue of blood is saved by a faith that pushed her from the safety of ignominy and exclusion and pushed her into an encounter with Jesus that was unacceptable and unlawful by all the purity and holiness standards of the people. She risked a great deal in reaching out in her broken state to seek wholeness from this man whom she had never met. Her faith, her belief, pushed her toward a salvation that was not a static, safe place from all harm but was an active engagement with the world around her and the people who inhabited it in such a way that she demanded and received transformation. Jairus's little girl was saved by the same dogged determination of her father. Here was a man who risked the loss of his societal standing, a respected leader of the synagogue, a colleague no doubt of the very scribes who were even now plotting ways to destroy this Jesus. And yet his despair and his budding faith in the power of this man drove him to the mad belief that he could save his daughter. For Jairus, too, salvation was not about a safe space; it was the end result of a engaged, mad encounter with unreasonable hope in the midst of overwhelming risk.

4. There is finally simply madness. On the morning of September 11, a date so infamous in the lexicon of American thought that it needs no appendage of year, I had just arrived in my campus office on Stockton Street in quiet, peaceful, safe Princeton. I was going through my morning routine. I had dropped off my children at their respective schools. I had arranged my papers in the order in which I would attack them that day. School would be starting soon; much of my attention was focused on the lectures for the opening weeks. My e-mail was open and I was just about finished with the final pieces when I heard the small alarm bell on my computer. I'd just received another e-mail. Months ago, I had signed up with the CNN Web site. Whenever there was breaking news, they would send an e-mail alert so that I would be in touch with breaking events all over the globe. This one was less than fifty miles away. The quick message line entry said that a plane had struck the World Trade Center. There was a link. I clicked on it.

When the picture of the first trade center building to be hit came up on the screen, I felt my lips twist into an involuntary gesture of disgust. My first thought was some lost pilot had been flying a small private plane somewhere he should not have been and had accidentally hit the building. I closed the Web browser and went back to work. Minutes later, my younger brother called. A director for NBC News, he often lets me know when news is breaking. "It looks like neither an accident nor a small plane," he warned. Moments later he said, "Another one just hit. It can't be a mistake now. Another one just hit. They planned it so it would hit on live TV."

By the time the buildings themselves began to collapse around the trapped civilians and heroic police and firefighters, I was at home, myself watching live while death paraded the streets of lower Manhattan and mocked the public airwaves of an entire planet. I don't know how to describe what that felt like. All of us who were conscious on September 11 must have our own take on it, our own measure of disbelief and hurt. It was madness. Pure and simple madness. And it struck so quickly, so unexpectedly, in the midst of everyday routine. That is why the perpetrators got away with it. They did it while we were going through our routines of living, doing the things we always do, not expecting evil to be lurking just around the bend of our next daily turn. It must be like being a fisherman, and getting off your boat like you do every day, and being met this day by a man possessed by a Legion of madness. Jesus stepped off the boat, like I stepped into my office, like men and women stepped into those twin towers, like other men and women stepped onto those planes. Madness was standing there, awaiting a challenge, awaiting the destruction of hope with its cold, calculated plans of destruction.

Maybe Mark saw something like September 11 long ago in that first-century world when Jesus stepped onto Gerasene soil and Legion accosted him. Maybe Mark's message from the telling of that encounter is that evil will endure. It will accost. It will destroy. But we must believe that there is a stronger power. Despite the devastation you see, despite the loss you endure, despite the evil at hand, believe that there is a stronger power. God's power, the power of God's coming rule, circulating through Jesus, percolating in your own faith and God's transformative action upon that faith. Don't seek a safe, saved place to hide out from the power of such madness and evil. You can't do it even if you try. Engage it as Jesus engaged Legion. Believe as Jairus and the woman with the twelve-year bleeding believed. In a world that sees what our eyes see, it is unreasonable to believe that our faith and the actions that stem from that faith can make a difference. But that is the kind of madness to which this section of Mark's Gospel calls us. It is the madness of faith.

5

It Started Off So Well
Mark 6:7–56

View One: From Text to Sermon
Gary W. Charles

*T*alk about a match made in heaven. This church was poised for growth and willing to call a pastor fresh from seminary. In short order, pews that had been sparsely filled began to become crowded, and members who had tended to long-standing internal battles began to tend to new opportunities for mission. Although I made my share of first-church ministry mistakes, grace abounded. Equipped with a superb theological education and a loving and responsive congregation, I felt like God had taken off the shackles and set me free. When I accepted another call, I left knowing that I had achieved much of what God had given me to do.

Twenty years later, I was invited to return to the church where my ministry began, to speak at the annual homecoming and to celebrate my twentieth year of ordained ministry. Over the years, my theology and ministry practices have evolved, and in recent years I have participated in a national advocacy effort to encourage the church to be more inclusive. I wrote an article for The *Washington Post* that advocated welcoming Christians of diverse sexual expressions as ordained church leaders in the Presbyterian Church (U.S.A.). Soon after the article was published, I received a letter from the governing body of my first church withdrawing their homecoming invitation. Perhaps my achievements were not as noteworthy as I had thought. Perhaps the recision of the invitation was a not-so-gentle reminder that measuring one's achievements as a disciple is not so simple and has little to do with discipleship.

Talk about a match made in heaven—Jesus and his first twelve disciples. They watch in amazement as Jesus cures lepers, casts out demons, and brings a young girl to life. As they line up to be commissioned as "apostles," the Twelve can hardly wait to set out on their first mission trip. Jesus' austere charge to them does not slow them down at all. So off they go, two by two, without so much as a phone card, with no ATM machine for miles around, and no hotel reservation. That is how this chapter *opens*. As it *closes*, the crowd clamors for more healing and hope from Jesus. Between this frame of adulation and success for the ministry of Jesus, Mark strings together a series of stories that range from the bizarre to the miraculous to the disturbing. For as 6:7–56 *opens*, Mark leads his readers to hope for great things from the band of Twelve chosen by Jesus. Yet, as the chapter *closes*, readers no longer suffer from such a naive and optimistic assessment of the disciples and no longer believe that the reign of God will arrive on the heels of these Twelve. Despite their initial success in 6:7–13, by 6:56 the disciples will have proven themselves oblivious to the source of their success.

As chapter 6 opens, Jesus leaves his hometown due to a lack of faith there (6:5–7). He takes the Twelve with him and commissions them with the authority to go into neighboring towns and villages to minister in his name (6:7). The Twelve go forth in pairs, partly for protection, but most likely, for Mark, to remind readers of the importance of a witness in Mosaic law (Deut. 17:6). Jesus tells his disciples to carry only minimal provisions and to trust in the hospitality of the receiving communities (6:8–11). As Israel was instructed not to store up manna and quail in the wilderness but to trust in the daily provision of their God (Exod. 16), so this "new" Israel is sent into mission with similar instructions. In addition to drawing parallels between this mission journey and the wilderness tradition, Richard Horsley relates the mission of the Twelve to the early prophetic tradition in Israel. He writes that the "commissioning of the twelve to preach and exorcize in village communities cannot help but remind those familiar with Israelite tradition of Elijah's commissioning of Elisha and his working with and through the scores of prophets."[1] Just as Jonah was called to preach repentance to the city of Nineveh and not simply to individual Ninevite citizens (Jonah 1:2), so the disciples are to go into the communities of Galilee and preach repentance to entire towns (6:12).

Jesus equips the Twelve with authority (6:7) and instructions for how to deal with those unreceptive to the power of the gospel. Jesus tells his disciples to "shake off the dust" from their feet whenever they are not gladly received in a community (6:11 NRSV). "Shaking off the dust," Lamar Williamson writes, was "the gesture . . . used by pious Jews of that time when they returned to Israel from a Gentile land to symbolize separation from any

---

1. Horsley, *Hearing the Whole Story,* 248.

clinging remnant of ritual defilement. It was a formal disavowal of fellowship which at the same time warned the unreceptive village of the danger they incurred in rejecting these messengers."[2] The disciples were sent out to embody the goodness of Jesus but not to linger if ministry in his name was not gladly embraced.

In contrast with the close of the preceding pericope ("And he could do no deed of power there," 6:5 NRSV), Mark ends this pericope on a sanguine note about the future mission of Jesus and his newly empowered disciples: "They cast out many demons, and anointed with oil many who were sick and cured them" (6:13 NRSV). After such a rousing success, readers anticipate that the next scene will find the Twelve enthusiastically recounting their first mission tour *in detail*. Instead, Mark inserts an ominous sentence for those who would follow Jesus: "King Herod heard of it, for Jesus' name had become known" (6:14 NRSV). Without any warning, Mark shifts from the exultant disciples to the appalling story of the execution of John the Baptist. The story foreshadows what will happen to the One whose name "had become known"[3] and, by implication, to those who follow him. Thus, the beheading of John the Baptist follows on the heels of a remarkably successful mission trip and alerts careful readers to the potential cost of discipleship.

Unlike most of Mark's narrative prior to Jerusalem, the story of the arrest and death of John the Baptist (6:14–29) is detailed and long. In this tale, Mark suggests that John the Baptist and, by inference, Jesus, are numbered among those like Elijah and the non-Temple prophets who were persecuted by the governing power and yet whose lives were redeemed by God.[4] As the story unfolds, readers hear overtones of Jezebel[5] in the strident voice of Herodias, who is incensed by John the Baptist and seizes this opportunity to silence his moral judgment (6:17–20). This gruesome tale of a head-on-a-platter also functions proleptically in Mark's Gospel to caution those who would take on

---

2. Williamson, *Mark*, 120.

3. While Williamson, regrettably, nearly excuses any culpability by Herod and later Pilate for the deaths of John and Jesus, he does expose an important Markan political parallel: "Both rulers [Herod and Pilate] are favorably impressed by the Jewish religious figures whose lives they therefore would prefer to spare; both wish to please the crowd by a gesture of magnanimity; both are manipulated to carry out the deadly hostility of a third party; both, though seemingly in charge, become unwilling actors in a drama beyond their control" (Williamson, *Mark*, 123).

4. So Horsley: "Twice in the story [of John's beheading by Herod] Mark refers to the impression that Jesus was making on the people: 'Jesus' name had become known. Some were saying "John the Baptist has been raised from the dead; and for this reason these powers are at work in him." But others said, "It is Elijah." And others said, "It is a prophet, like one of the prophets of old"' (6:14–15; cf. 8:28). In these passages Mark indicates that people who had heard of Jesus had fairly vivid memories from their cultural tradition of Israelite prophets, Elijah in particular" (Horsley, *Hearing the Whole Story*, 235).

5. 1 Kings 18:4, 13; 19:1–2; 21:1–16.

Jesus' mission to be prepared not only for the joy of casting out the demonic but also for being cast aside by the demonic in power.[6]

Scholars have long debated the apparently conflicting account of the death of John as told by Mark with the account of Josephus, who in his *Antiquities* (18 5.2) wrote that John was imprisoned and executed in the fortress of Machaerus.[7] As scholars debate the historical validity of Mark's account of the death of John, Mark's point is largely missed. Why does Mark include this bizarre tale in his Gospel? To readers dazzled by the disciples' stunning feats accounted in 6:7–13, this tale warns against the temptation to be corrupted by "achievements" in Christian ministry and alerts disciples to trust in the One whom even Herod cannot bind. Trust in Jesus, says Mark, rather than in the enchanting, enticing, and often deadly lure of power in whatever form it is lodged.[8] Mark ends this gruesome tale with the burial of John by his disciples.[9]

By the time of the transitional sentence in 6:30—"the apostles gathered around Jesus, and told him all they had done and taught"—Mark's readers cannot hear their report with undaunted enthusiasm. In fact, readers *never* hear their report in Mark's Gospel. Jesus plans for a leisurely retreat with the Twelve to debrief them following their mission trip far from the exhausting demands of discipleship, but the demanding crowd will not cooperate (6:31). Readers do not hear about their achievements; instead, Mark focuses on the demands of a needy crowd and the compassion of Jesus. Though unable to find time to eat himself, Jesus feeds the demand of this crowd.

As Jesus looks out upon the crowd, Mark informs his readers that Jesus was moved with compassion (6:34). "Compassion" in common English usage does not capture the force of the Greek middle passive verb (*esplanchnisthē*), which connotes guts, bowels, and vital organs. "Though a middle passive verb, *splanchnizomai* identifies a profoundly intense emotional response that

---

6. Ched Meyers argues persuasively that the beheading of John relates to the disciples' mission: "The point of the identification of Jesus and John is this: the political destiny of those who proclaim repentance and a new order is always the same. Now we can understand why the John story has been inserted into the narrative of the apostles' mission: insofar as they inherit this mission, they inherit its destiny. This is expressly articulated first in 8:34, then again in 13:9–11, but it is already here implied by the structure of intercalation in the last generative seam" (Myers, *Binding the Strong Man,* 217).

7. See Taylor, *Gospel according to St. Mark,* 312.

8. Mary Ann Tolbert draws a suggestive parallel between Herod and the seed sown among thorns (4:18–19): "Like the rich man, Herod is very sorry about what he is asked to do; also like the rich man, Herod is prevented from acting on his better instincts by his concern for other things—in this case, his reputation and word—before his guests. . . . Herod values his position, his reputation, and his oath more highly than what he has been hearing gladly" (Tolbert, *Sowing the Gospel,* 158).

9. Sharyn Dowd notes the irony anticipated in John's burial: "John's headless body is claimed by his disciples and laid in a tomb. When Jesus' time for burial comes, however, his disciples will be nowhere to be found" (Dowd, *Reading Mark,* 67).

viscerally propels one feeling compassion into action on behalf of others."[10]
The compassion that Jesus feels for the crowd is more than a casual and gentle sentiment that eventually passes with time. Drawing again on the Hebrew
prophetic tradition, especially that of Ezekiel 34, Mark explains that Jesus had
compassion on the crowd because they were like a sheep without a shepherd.
Such pastoral and emotive language may tempt modern readers to miss the
stark religiopolitical intent in Mark's Greek. In Ezekiel 34, the prophet tells a
parable that challenges a system in which the ruling class acts more like
wolves than shepherds. By having "compassion" on the crowd, who are like
sheep without a shepherd, Jesus addresses more than a personal and spiritual
dilemma. He condemns social and religious practices that contribute to the
misery of those in the greatest need.

By drawing on memories of Numbers 27:16ff. and the Elisha miracle cycle,
Mark infuses the biblical concept of "compassion" with its full boundary-
breaking potential. Fred Lyon, a doctoral candidate at Union Theological
Seminary and the Presbyterian School of Education, contends that the *compassionate* act of Jesus is an economic border crossing: "Here, economics
characterized by such standard operating procedures as hands-off laissez
faire, bean-counting quid pro quo, or cut-throat hostile takeovers are foregone
in favor of gracious beneficence in his enactment of overhauling the status
quo of the fundamental structure of human power in his day, namely, patron-
client relations."[11] In recounting the feeding of the five thousand, Mark
presses his readers to see the compassion of Jesus not merely as a matter of
temperament but also as a discipleship orientation. Disciples of Jesus are
called to break down all barriers—religious, social, economic, political—
between human need and God's liberating mercy.[12]

In the story of the hemorrhaging woman, the disciples belabor the obvious
by reminding Jesus that he is standing amid a huge crowd (5:31). They do the
same again in this story as they remind Jesus that they are in an *erēmos*, or
"deserted place," and thus have no easy access to food.[13] They do not understand that to follow Jesus is to extend his compassion beyond every bound-

---

10. On page 1 of an unpublished paper by Fred Lyon: *"Splanchnizomai* and the Correspondence between Compassion and the Coming Reign of God."
11. On page 10 of an unpublished paper by Fred Lyon: "The Course of Compassion: A Curricular Analysis of *Splanchnizomai* in Jesus' Teaching."
12. So Myers: "The only 'miracle' here is the triumph of the economics of sharing within a community of consumption over against the economics of autonomous consumption in the anonymous marketplace" (Myers, *Binding the Strong Man*, 206).
13. Mark, *erēmos* is a term that moves beyond the geographical as it recalls the wilderness wanderings and the prophetic vision of a coming day when life would flourish in the desert. See Mark 1:3–4; 1:12–14; 1:35; 1:45.

ary, trusting that God will provide resources for such radical discipleship
(6:37a). To disciples stuck in a consumer paradigm, Jesus insists that they
look beyond the most obvious options—either letting the people go to buy
what they need *or* spending an exorbitant sum for food to feed the crowd
themselves. Jesus asks the Twelve to look not at what they lack but at what
they already have: five loaves and two fish (6:38). Jesus then asks his first disciples to trust in God's power set loose despite finite resources and unequal
distribution.

In the actions that follow, Mark prepares his readers both for a Passover
feast to be celebrated later in Jerusalem (14:12–31) and for an eschatological
feast that will be celebrated in the reign of God (14:25). In addition, throughout this feeding narrative, Mark recalls themes from a time when Israel was
hungering in the desert, demanding to be fed, and was provided with manna
from God that did not keep for leftovers but was enough for the need at hand
(Exod. 16).

A subtlety of Mark's telling of the feeding of the five thousand is revealed
when, in 6:39, Jesus instructs the disciples to seat the crowd "on the green
grass" (*epi tō chlōrō chortō*). Twice Mark has reminded his readers of the setting for this story—in a desert (6:31, 35)—and yet here Mark emphasizes not
only that they sit on *grass* but on *green grass*. Reverberations of the coming
eschatological reign of God (Ps. 23; Isa. 40), when the desert will blossom
and the famished will feast, echo from this verse. So with the phrase—"on the
green grass"—Mark signals his readers that this is no ordinary desert and that
this will be no ordinary meal.

Prior to noting that people were to sit on *green grass* in a *desert*, Mark tells
his disciples to seat the crowd in large groups (6:39). With the crowd awaiting a meal in the desert, Mark both echoes the manna and quail in the wilderness and anticipates the messianic feast at the end time, thus preparing readers
for what will happen next. All eat their fill, but Mark does not indicate how.
His emphasis is twofold: all eat and are filled despite a situation of extreme
scarcity, and twelve basketfuls remain.[14] In the desert, compassion propels
Jesus to confront the human face of need before him and to trust in the super-
abundance of God's mercy.

While it looks back to the wilderness wanderings of Israel and ahead to the
messianic feast, this first feeding story in Mark points more immediately to
the last supper that Jesus will share with the Twelve in Jerusalem (14:12–31).

---

14. Dowd notes the significance of the twelve baskets of leftovers: "Not only is the hunger of the crowd
satisfied, but also the leftovers fill twelve large baskets (*kophinos*) typically used by Jews for carrying
loads. . . . The number twelve further reinforces the Jewish cultural setting" (Dowd, *Reading Mark*, 69).

After looking up to heaven, Jesus breaks bread in the desert amid thousands of onlookers and then gives the loaves to the disciples to distribute (6:41). Mark will later use identical language when Jesus blesses and distributes bread to his disciples in an upper room in Jerusalem (14:22).[15] Along with preparing readers for the coming Passover feast, Mark prepares readers to reevaluate the disciples who do not understand the miracle in the desert any more than they will recognize the true identity of Jesus in 6:47–52 or when he sits next to them at the Passover feast (14:17–26).

With his favorite word—*euthus* (immediately, at once)—Mark shifts the scene from the desert to the sea (6:45). Jesus compels his disciples to get in the boat and cross over to Bethsaida by themselves. After they set sail, Jesus dismisses the crowd, having addressed its most pressing need, and then goes up a mountain to pray (6:45–46). On three occasions in this sea story, Mark emphasizes the spatial distance between the disciples and Jesus, building suspense for this dangerous crossing and leaving readers wondering how these disciples will fare alone at sea.

An epiphany story follows, with its characteristic appearance of the divine, subsequent fear, and common expressions, such as "It is I," "Have no fear," and "pass by." Williamson ties this story to its Hebrew antecedents:

> It is reminiscent of Old Testament manifestations of God ("theophanies," e.g., Gen. 3; 15; 17; 18; 28; Exod. 3; 19; Josh. 5; I Sam. 3; Isa. 6) in which the divine presence is sometimes at first unrecognized and often inspires awesome fear. The words "It is I" represent the basic revelation of God in the theophany at the burning bush (Exod. 3:14) and in the Johannine discourses of Jesus (John 8:24, 28, 58; 13:19; 18:4–6). "Fear not" is a characteristic reassurance in theophanies (Gen. 15:1) and in divine revelation through angels.[16]

Consistent with Old Testament themes found throughout his Gospel, Mark tells this epiphany story to reveal something about Jesus, something already known by the readers since Mark 1:1 but still not clearly perceived by the disciples.

A phrase in this story that perplexes readers and scholars is: "And he intended to pass them by." Here it is critical to recall the Old Testament theophanies at the root of this story. In Exodus 33 and in 1 Kings 19, God will "pass by" first Moses and then Elijah to reassure these chosen leaders that God is present amid their terror. Later, Mark will explicitly introduce

---

15. See Taylor, *Gospel according to St. Mark*, 324.
16. Williamson, *Mark*, 130–31.

this Hebrew duo (9:2–8). Here readers familiar with the Hebrew biblical tradition will see the action of Jesus not as an attempt to ignore the disciples' plight but, metaphorically, as the saving presence of God. "As in 4:35–41," Dowd writes, "the Markan Jesus again demonstrates his superiority over the hostile sea power by striding across the sea, an activity attributed to God in Job 9:8 and Isa 43:16. His intent was to walk ahead of them—to lead them, like a good shepherd, to their destination (cf. Exod 33:2, 12–17; Ps 23:2b; Isa 40:11d)."[17] Once again, readers of Mark see Jesus as One who has compassion not only for an anonymous crowd but even for obdurate followers.

The disciples fare worse in this story than in the prior feeding narrative or even in the first calming of the sea in Mark 4:35–41. They see Jesus not as a divine savior but as a terrifying apparition (6:49). The winds calm, but Mark says nothing about the abatement of their fear. They are astounded by the events at hand, because, according to Mark, "they did not understand about the loaves" (6:52 NRSV). Here, the ecstasy of 6:7–13 sours as readers see the disciples for who they are—the seed sown on rocky ground—those who accept the Word immediately, endure for a time, but fall away when tribulation or persecution comes (4:16–17). After the second sea journey, the disciples' hearts are not alive with faith and trust in the One who calms storms but hardened to the secrets they were once promised (4:11).

There is little scholarly consensus about the haunting phrase "but their hearts were hardened."[18] Mary Ann Tolbert argues that the hardening of the disciples' hearts is a literary device, alien to modern literature but already anticipated in the Hellenistic literary world from which Mark borrows. Therefore, when Mark announces, "their hearts were hardened," he includes the disciples with the Pharisees and Herodians who are also described as harboring hardened hearts (3:5–6). For Tolbert, Mark offers little rationale for the hardening of the disciples' hearts; the rationale is left for readers to discern as they view other responses to the ministry of Jesus.[19]

New Testament scholar Donald Juel argues just the opposite. He argues that, since the verb "hardened" (*pepōrōmenē*) is in the divine passive, then God is the implied subject. If God hardened the disciples' hearts, Juel contends, then the disciples cannot be held culpable for their fear and unfaithfulness.

17. Dowd, *Reading Mark*, 69.
18. See Gary's discussion of this concept in chapter 3, View One.
19. For an extended discussion on *hē kardia pepōrōmenē*, see Tolbert, *Sowing the Gospel*, 198–200.

He goes on to argue that the disciples cannot be "foils" for readers, for if God would abandon the disciples to their blindness and hardened hearts, why wouldn't God do the same for those not nearly as close to Jesus?[20] Juel's argument, though, assumes character development, a literary practice common to modern literature but missing in Mark.[21] Juel also underestimates the critical role the Twelve play in challenging readers to make a more faithful response to the ministry of Jesus than did their religious ancestors. Thus, the Twelve have their hearts hardened less as a preemptive strike by God and more as a de facto statement of what kind of soil they are: rocky ground.

Scared disciples mistake the seaborne Jesus for a ghost, but once the waters are calmed and the boat has moored, the crowd makes no such mistake. Mark says that "immediately they recognized him" (6:54). They recognize him principally as a healer, but at least they recognize him as such. People flock from the marketplace, from villages, and from cities to touch Jesus and to be touched by his transformative presence. All those who touched Jesus "were healed," says the NRSV (6:56). Mark's Greek, though, is not nearly so general or reductive. The NJB gets it right when it translates *esōzonto* as "were saved." Though the verb *sōzō* can mean "heal" or "become whole," typically Mark uses this saving language to signal something more than the restoration of personal health (3:4; 5:23; 8:35, 10:52; 13:13, 20; 15:30, 31). Jesus' saving activity occurs *before* his death as a sign of God's inbreaking reign.[22] Access to this reign and its saving reality is no longer restricted to one nation or ethnic group but, according to Mark 6:56, is now open to everyone (*hosoi*, 6:56), even to Gentiles, women, and the ritually impure (7:26).

Mark says that "immediately they recognized him." Earlier, the ministry of Jesus had caught the attention of Herod. Now there is no hiding for Jesus or his disciples, in Jewish or Gentile territory. He is known far and wide. He is known by Herod, and he is known by anonymous crowds. Ironically, he is not fully known by the ones best prepared and equipped to bear witness to him, even though it started off so well.

---

20. Juel, *Gospel of Mark*, 185–87.
21. "The illustrative characters of ancient literature are static, monolithic figures who do not grow or develop psychologically. They have fundamentally the same characteristics at the end as at the beginning. They may, of course, change state, from good fortune to bad, from unknown to known, or from insider to outsider, for example, but such shifts are always implicit in the actions or principles the characters are illustrating" (Tolbert, *Sowing the Gospel*, 77).
22. For a sociocultural reading of Mark's saving language, see Blount, *Go Preach!* 134–36.

View Two: "Disciples' Medley: A Sermon in Four Parts"
Gary W. Charles

[Introduction: The narrative flow of Mark 6:7–56 suggested the form for this sermon. While the overarching theme of discipleship runs through Mark 6, the stories have a life of their own and can easily appear unrelated. This sermon tries to honor the narrative flow, capture some of the Markan ironic transitions, and present the readers with a sense of urgency about the faithfulness of their discipleship. Even as a medley is a mixture of things not usually placed together, in these texts Mark's picture of Jesus and the Twelve is a "medley" of mismatched company and misunderstanding. As descendants of the disciples, Mark's readers are left to ask themselves: How can ours be a more faithful medley?

The sermon was delivered in four parts, with each part sandwiched between music and/or prayers. First, Mark 6:7–13 was read, followed by the preaching of "A Rousing Success." This part of the sermon ends with a sense of enthusiasm that perhaps Jesus has also given us sufficient power for faithful Christian living and achievement. After this, the congregation sang "Kum Ba Yah," a song that many Christian youth or campers have sung in a time of religious enthusiasm. Second, Mark 6:14a was read, followed by "A Chilling Aside." After this, we read Mark 6:30–44 (the feeding of the five thousand). I followed this with "A Day in the Life," which concluded with an intercessory prayer. After the offering and the offertory, I preached "A Miracle Missed," which was followed by the first verse of the spiritual, "I Want Jesus to Walk with Me," sung by a soprano soloist. The spiritual captures both the irony of the Twelve who do not recognize Jesus who is walking beside them on the sea and the longing for disciples today not to miss the presence of the living Lord.]

Part 1: A Rousing Success
Mark 6:7–13

"What a trip. No suitcase. No hair dryer. No cell phone. No travelers' checks and no ATM card. No reservations. No valet parking and no spa. Not even a briefcase or a carry-on bag for the pills and perfume and all the little necessities.

"But who cares? It will still be the trip of a lifetime. For Jesus has given us all we need. We will be the talk of the town. Demons will dance their last jig before us. The lame will walk. The blind will see. Wherever people are broken, we'll fix them."

The disciples were right. It was quite a trip. Mark sums it up: "So [the disciples] went out and proclaimed that all should repent. They cast out many

demons, and anointed with oil many who were sick and cured them"
(6:12–13 NRSV).

Can you imagine what it would be like to go on that trip, to be given such
authority by Jesus? Can you imagine moving from being just ordinary religious folk to becoming celebrities, basking in the spiritual spotlight? You
would pray and people would listen. You would interpret Scripture and people would hang on to your every word. Your pews would be filled and your
church coffers would overflow. Peter Jennings and Connie Chung and Dan
Rather would call you for an exclusive interview about your life with Jesus.

I won't try to speak for you, but sign me up for that trip. Who needs the worship wars and budget battles and theological swordplay of the church today?
Who needs the grieving fields and the unanswered prayers? Who needs the
relentless Bible combat that leaves the church weak and worn? Who needs a
society that continues to push disciples behind the curtain of anyone's attention?
Who can help envying the twelve disciples for reveling in their rousing success?

I'll make you this bet: You and I would also follow Jesus if he would just
give us the same authority, the same vote of confidence that he gave his disciples that day.

Now, let me ask you this: What if he already has? It starts off so well. . . .

Part 2: A Chilling Aside
Mark 6:14a

Once upon a time, there was a party that no one would ever forget. No sooner
did glasses empty than they were filled. When the feast was finished, desserts
that dazzled the eyes were set out. Every key player in the kingdom was in attendance, and the most beautiful women in the land danced to delight the king.

One person, though, heard only the sounds of the party. He was in the
king's prison, kept safe at the king's command. This man had captured the
king's curiosity and respect. Even though the king was often perplexed by
what this man had to say, he knew the man to be a man of God. So the king
feared the man, even though the king held him a captive.

Everything changed at the party. When King Herod had had too much to
drink and was too much aroused to think clearly, all his fine promises of security to John the Baptist vanished before the movements of an exquisite belly
dancer. The executioner burst into the prison cell and emerged with John's
head on a platter. Herod's promises to John expired upon the enticements of
beauty and the stupidity of drunken oaths.

Before telling us about the beheading of John, Mark writes that the disciples "cast out many demons, and anointed with oil many who were sick and

cured them" (6:13 NRSV). Then, Mark writes: *"King Herod heard of it; for Jesus' name had become known"* (6:14, my italics).

One lesson disciples simply do not want to learn is that, when they follow Jesus, the end of the road will more likely be a platter or a cross than a spotlight or a toast. One lesson disciples find the hardest to learn is that, while it is enticing to be on a first-name basis with Herod, the results are almost always deadly.

Part 3: A Day in the Life
Mark 6:30–44

I carried all kinds of crazy and grandiose ideas with me into seminary. I figured that upon graduation, I would spend most days in holy encounters. I would invite members to stop by who would want to learn about the theological issues raised at the Council of Chalcedon. At the hospital, doctors would pull me aside to ask my advice on how to care for the "whole" patient. At City Hall, I would advocate on behalf of the powerless, and the powerful would be persuaded by my rhetoric.

When I finished seminary, I entered an altogether different world. I would spend hours preparing a sermon, only to look out from the pulpit and see a couple of tulip farmers with heads nodding and jaws agape, victims of an occasional spousal elbow. I would visit the hospital religiously, but whenever the doctor arrived I was invited to leave the room. I led an effort to open a soup kitchen in the neighborhood surrounding our church, only to have it shut down on a legal technicality when the city heard the neighbors' hue and cry.

I know exactly what the disciples must have thought at the end of a long day, and at the end of a long series of days, when Jesus said, "Feed them yourselves" (6:37). "Feed them yourselves?" Come on Jesus, you can't be serious. You want more from us? We've already made five trips to three different hospitals this week, written the bulletin for the memorial service, stopped by the nursing home, prepared for four committee meetings, consoled a confused teen, and calmed down an irritated adult. We've opened the city council meeting with prayer and tried to convince council members that a new low-income medical clinic in the neighborhood should have a prayer. You want more from us? We've already been at church for meetings three nights after work this week, driven the van to pick up the shut-ins for worship, and planned to take a week of annual leave to lead the youth on a mission work camp. And, now, Jesus, you want us to do what?

The disciples return exhilarated and exhausted from the rousing success of their first mission tour. They are ready to give their Powerpoint presentation on "How to be a successful disciple." But Jesus defers their report due to a demanding crowd, for *he* knows what they have yet to figure out. He knows that the disciples' report can wait but that human need cannot.

Mark says, "Jesus saw a great crowd and he had compassion on them." At least, that is how the New Revised Standard Version translates the Greek. But that doesn't even come close to the language Mark uses. Mark says that Jesus had his guts ripped wide open in concern for the crowd. Jesus would not settle for the disciples' lame, "it's after hours" excuse, as if ministry is from 9 to 5 or on Sunday mornings and human need will wait until disciples are well rested and church budgets are bulging and the local community thinks our mission efforts are heroic.

Whatever it means to follow Jesus, it means listening to him shout across the lake of time: "Feed them yourselves!" "Cross the boundary of consumptive consumerism." "Tear your hearts wide open on behalf of those whom most people simply ignore." Jesus delays the report on "How to be a successful disciple" because their presentation is just a few slides short. To disciples fresh off a standing-room-only mission performance, Jesus says, "Don't think your job is to shine in the sun. Your job is to follow me with open hearts and minds and wills and guts and respond to the cacophony of human need around you. And, by the way, don't go home until you do!"

Sometimes you and I actually do figure out how to minister in his name, but for all the many times that we don't, Mark tells the rest of this story. He speaks of a day when the disciples did not shine but their Lord did. A day when there was *green* grass growing in the *desert*, a day when there was too little food but it was somehow more than enough. A day when the Lord broke bread and blessed it and gave it to his disciples, who then gave it to every single person who hungered.

"Feed them yourselves." It sounds like an impossible imperative to disciples too tired to see any practical solutions to the problem. Maybe, though, "feed them yourselves" is a remarkable indicative made possible by a Lord who seeks followers who never find compassion inconvenient.

Part 4: A Miracle Missed
Mark 6:45–52

This story begins when Jesus tells his disciples to set sail without him, so he can go up the mountain to pray. But most modern readers are not too interested in how Mark begins this story. They want to talk about why Jesus did not sink into the sea. What's the scientific explanation behind this puzzling phenomenon? Was Jesus standing on a sandbar? Had the boat crept close to land in the night leaving Jesus only to wade in the shallow shoals?

Many modern disciples, though, insist that the *most* important thing in this story is that Jesus walked on water, and if you don't believe that then you don't believe the truth of the Bible. I happen to think that Mark would be saddened by both views.

Mark tells his second sea storm story in three chapters, less to stress that Jesus is a miracle worker and more to stress how often his disciples miss the miraculous intent of God. As the story closes, Mark does not say, "They were utterly astounded because Jesus had walked on water." He says that "they were utterly astounded, for they did not understand about the loaves, but their hearts were hardened" (6:51–52 NRSV). Were their hearts hardened as some sort of pre-emptive strike by God, therefore excusing them for thinking Jesus a ghost? Or were their hearts hardened by God because they refused to see discipleship for what it is—living, day after day, trusting in the miraculous possibility of God in the face of the harshest exhibits to the contrary, trusting that if God can make a desert green, then God can resurrect whatever is dying in us and in the world.

Richard Lischer writes, "The act of trusting is itself a replenishing activity, like loving or farming or writing. You can't hold back your best for another occasion. If you give of yourself fully, there will always be more to give. Trusting makes for greater trust, not disillusionment or timidity."[23] The miracle in this story from Mark, then, is not a positive one about profound trust in God that leads to faithful discipleship; the miracle is not so much that Jesus walks on water but that the disciples cannot see him for who he is and therefore cannot see themselves for who God calls them to be. And, most tragically, the disciples cannot see a world just waiting for them to speak a word of hope from their transforming Lord.

Maybe Mark was wrong to paint such an unflattering picture of our Lord's chosen disciples. Matthew and Luke seem to think Mark was wrong. Or maybe Mark believed that knowing the truth about our own kin might be precisely what disciples need to compose a more faithful and trusting medley.

Time alone will tell.

View Three: The Grass Is Always Greener
Brian K. Blount

I have never spent much time in a desert. I have been on a big sand dune at Kitty Hawk, North Carolina. Maybe that's close. Probably not. But there is a

---

23. Richard Lischer, *Open Secrets: A Spiritual Journey through a Country Church* (New York: Doubleday, 2001), 162.

lot of sand, and it takes some effort to cross it. With the sun driving down flashes of burning light and waves of searing heat in the dog days of an August summer, it can get pretty toasty. I imagine that if you expanded that national park with its rolling hills of cascading sand into a bleak, white ocean, it would be a dangerous place. I imagine that then it would be rather forbidding. As it is, you can hear the sounds of cars, see little water fountains strategically placed, and look across a road to a shopping center ice cream shop as you wipe the sweat from your brow with a colorful, Nags Head embroidered wristband.

The Greek term that Mark uses for "desert" doesn't have to mean this kind of sand-swept, sun-drenched landscape. It can also mean "wilderness." Though bleak enough, the Middle Eastern wilderness need not conjure up the image of an expansive Sahara. Still, I have been to Israel; I have seen its "desert" places. I wouldn't want to get caught out there without my water bottle or four-wheel drive either. Any way you think of it, the desert landscape is a forbidding, hostile place that neither solicits nor tolerates visitation for long. They are lonely, expansive, and clear spaces, which is why, perhaps for a while, Jesus sought to use one such desert place as a staging ground for his teaching about the coming rule of God. Out in the wilderness, he wouldn't have to worry about his voice competing with the sounds of the marketplace, or the sight line of his listeners being blocked by the silhouettes of houses and huts, or the attention of his present and potential disciples being distracted by the sights and sounds of town or village life. Out here Jesus had a captive audience.

He did not, however, have much else. And that would have been all right as long as he let them go with enough time to find their way to more hospitable landscape, shelter, and food. Jesus, though, apparently teaches with the same disregard for time as an indefatigable professor whose mouth keeps motoring on well past the appointed hour of class dismissal. It could be that it happens accidentally. It could be that this divine but absentminded educator forgot the time. I don't think so. In the Gospel of Mark, Jesus always seems to know what is going on around him. He is so aware, in fact, that he even reads the thoughts of those in conversation with him. It is unlikely that such an attentive mind would miss the signs of a setting sun and a wearying crowd. I therefore think he planned it. I think he kept them late intentionally in order to make a point.

As Gary noted in his discussion about the reverberations from Isaiah 40 and Psalm 23, there is something wrong about a desert place that has green grass upon which a crowd can sit. The green grass in the desert is a prelude to point out the potent power of God in barren moments of human living. Just as green grass can sprout up in a story about a desert, so will the power of God rain down onto lives withering in the midst of an often-hostile human landscape. Jesus' point is this: where a people of faith are concerned, the grass is greener . . . in the desert. Why? Because in the desert you know that any nourishment you find will save your life. Because in the desert you know that finding nourishment will be miraculous, such providence must come from God. There is no mistaking human capability for cultivation in a place where human ability will simply fail. Even on that massive sand dune in Kitty Hawk, if I had seen blankets of green grass, I would have known that something other than the skill of a proficient botanist was at work. I would have seen God. Lost on a vast desert with no sign of food or water for vast distances, a vision of grass would not have raised thoughts of lying out in the sun on a cushion of summer comfort; it would have suggested water beneath, and life above.

Of course, the point of Mark's story goes beyond the fact that in this desert place there is no food. There is also, apparently, no real belief in the power of God's rule manifesting itself in Jesus. The disciples are troubled because there is clearly not enough on hand to feed such a massive group. They also seem worried about taking money out of the treasury to foot the catering bill. Who knows if they even have enough? Who caters in the desert anyway? No doubt, they are also worried about how things will look if Jesus' attentive audience turns into a hungry, unruly mob. It is not just their reputations but perhaps even their lives that are at stake. There is one reasonable thing to do: send the people away so they can fend for themselves. Quickly. Jesus, however, won't cooperate. You can almost feel the frustration of Jesus' followers when their Lord orders them to give the people something to eat. They don't have anything! Even after scrounging around the desert floor, all they find are five loaves and two fishes. But, as Gary points out, Jesus wants them to see what they have, not what they don't have. He wants them to see green grass in the desert.

But these aren't a green-grass-seeing-in-the-desert-kind of people, these disciples. Even after Jesus miraculously feeds the multitude himself, even after they see him walk on the water, they still don't believe in the power sprouting (green) forth in their (desert) midst. Their hearts, Mark tells us, are hardened. It takes a lot of work, I think, to get your hearts so hard that they miss the beauty of seeing things like green grass in a desert, or seven pieces of food multiplied for thousands of hungry people, or a man walking on the surface of the water. I imagine that kind of hardness takes a lot of practice. It is like exercise, only it works against you rather than for you. A person hardens his body by doing the right thing. The more he pushes it, the more his muscles respond. They harden. Humans glory in hard bodies. They waste away in hard hearts. But they accomplish those hard hearts in the same way. The more they exercise disbelief, the more their doubt responds. It hardens. And their hearts stiffen with it. The disciples practice the ritual of disbelief on a daily, uninterrupted schedule in Mark. That is why they miss the magic of this moment; it is why they can't fathom what Jesus is doing with the bread and fish and why, when their own desert moments come, they wither and fail (14:50, 66–72). They can't see that they have been offered something miraculous; they have been given a power that they are as yet unequipped to use.

I would imagine that the opposite must also apply. Exercising one's faith must surely harden it in the same way that exercising doubt hardens one's heart. Perhaps that is the message Mark wants his readers to learn from the failure of Jesus' disciples. Even when you are trapped in a desert, exercise your belief in God's green grass. Look for it. Cultivate it. Act on it. Grow with it. Perhaps in the end that is how the intractable wildernesses like hunger will be transformed. Instead of fretting about what we don't have, we act on and multiply the resources that we do have. Perhaps for Mark, that is how we, like Jesus, can act with and for God.

The possibility is there in the story about the disciples even though they themselves cannot see it. As Gary points out, Mark 6 is a warning text. Jesus' act of sending out the Twelve frames the story of John the Baptist's beheading for a reason. Mark wants his readers to understand that the way of discipleship is a costly one; what happens to John may well be the future for one who follows in his God-directed footsteps. John's story is a dark harbinger of things to come for Jesus and any who would go with him. Even here, though, even in this desertlike narrative landscape, there is hope. We can see it if we concentrate on what we have instead of fretting about the life John the Baptist no longer has. If John's story shows the cost of discipleship, it also shows that God will not be stopped.

I am reminded of James Bond. Ian Fleming's master spy extricated himself from some of the most unlikely imprisonments throughout the course of his mythical career. There is one movie scene that I remember in particular. Cornered on a motorcycle, a brick wall to his back, a hovering helicopter, complete with machine-gun toting enemies to his front, he seemed to have run out of options. The female spy on the motorcycle with him lamented her assessment of the situation, from her vantage point behind him, with a single word: "Trapped." Bond's reply was equally succinct. "Never." And the derring-do commenced.

The circumstances surrounding John's death in relationship to the disciples' ministry is Mark's narrative way of saying *trapped*. God's answer, too, is *never*. God always has a way out. God always has a plan for the establishment of God's rule in human history. Stop John the Baptist, and Jesus will take his place. Stop Jesus, and the disciples were being prepared to take his place. That is why, no doubt, Mark makes a point of narrating their successful execution of exorcisms, healings, and authoritative preaching about the coming rule of God. The disciples, of course, stop themselves time and time again with their well-honed hardness of heart. And the forces arrayed against the plan of God as established in Jesus' preaching ministry trap them in disarray by the time the Gospel story comes to a close. Even then, though, even with the entire narrative in utter chaos at the close of the story at 16:8, God has a way out. God's *never* still resounds. Once readers come to understand the meaning behind the close of the book (see our comments on Mark 16:1–8 in the Introduction and in chapter 12), they also realize that, even in this desert of discipleship, God still has the power to raise up green grass.

6

No Dogs Allowed
Mark 7:1–8:21

View One: From Text to Sermon
Brian K. Blount

We are the chosen ones. The clean and pure ones. The ones with a soul. The ones God left in charge. That is why, although the majority of us love animals, we tend to keep them in their place. According to popular tradition, dogs are humankind's best friend. But they don't go everywhere we go. Restaurants. Hospitals. Workplaces. Churches. They stay outside. They're dogs. Unclean. Often unkempt. Always *unhuman*. There are times and places where they simply are not allowed. A supposition of Homo sapiens superiority guides our thinking in such matters. It is the same supposition that triggers the emotional recoil many of my students experience when they confront Jesus' controversial conversation with the Syrophoenician woman. He calls her a dog (7:27).

According to Mark, Jesus is God's son (1:1, 11; 9:7; 15:39). He has come to set the stage for God's imminent reign (1:15). Additionally, he has been commissioned to populate the community of that reign. Who's in? Who's not? He has the power to make the call. It appears that he has called this woman "out." By implication, the Gentile people she and her possessed daughter represent would have been evicted with her. In the holiest of all possible holy places, the reign of God, it has to be the rule that there are no dogs allowed. Amazingly enough, though, that is precisely the "rule" Mark intends to overturn with his narration of this troubling event.

Many scholars believe that Jesus' historical ministry was directed primarily toward the Jews.[1] Matthew certainly thinks so (Matt. 10:6; 15:24). Mark,

---

1. Joachim Jeremias, *Jesus' Promise to the Nations* (London: SCM Press, 1953); C. K. Barrett, "The Gentile Mission as an Eschatological Phenomenon," in *Eschatology and the New Testament* (ed. W. Hulitt Gloer; Peabody, Mass.: Hendrickson Publishers, 1988), 65–75.

too, for the most part describes a Jesus whose preaching power is deployed to the particular benefit of the people of Israel. Despite the fact that Jesus apparently did believe God's reign would one day encompass Gentiles (13:10; 14:9), miraculous encounters like the one that took place on behalf of the Gerasene demoniac (5:1–20) seem much more the exception than the rule.

Mark, though, is a master of presentation. He figured out how to tell the historical story in such a way that its "facts" about a ministry restricted to the Jews agreed with the contrary "truth" of a universally oriented reign of God. It happened like this. Mark wrote his Jesus story with the assistance of traditional sources: stories about Jesus' ministry. These stories were handed down from generation to generation as illustrations of the Lord's love and power. Principally used in the worship services of faith communities, they ultimately became the primary oral documentation for the Gospel writers. These stories traveled from person to person, community to community, individually, as small units about isolated events. There was a miracle story about Jairus, a healing report of a woman afflicted with bleeding for twelve years, an account of Jesus feeding a multitude of hungry people, and so on. All of these and similar pericopae were available to Mark when he set about his task.

Unfortunately, they were not dated. The storytellers had been more concerned about what Jesus had done than they had been about when he had actually done it. Like old family snapshots collected in a shoe box, the accounts were filled with names and faces but not stamped with dates and times. As Mark sought to shape this mélange of information into a story, he had to make a choice about how to order it. Since he couldn't do it chronologically (according to the time in which the events happened), he did it theologically. He ordered the stories about Jesus' life in such a way that, when they were put together, they explained God's ultimate intent for sending him into human history. That is why Mark took originally discrete stories about Jesus teaching Gentiles and including Gentiles in God's reign, and collected them in one place: 7:1–8:21.

The result was, in a word, miraculous; he manufactured a Gentile mission. By making such creative use of what were most likely isolated, exceptional interactions with Gentiles, Mark presented the "facts" about Jesus preaching primarily to Israel in such a way that they pointed to the alternative "truth" about God's reign: It was open and available to *anyone*. Each of the distinctive units in the section (7:1–5, 6–13, 14–23, 24–30, 31–37; 8:1–9, 10–13, 14–21) plays a role in maintaining and expanding this boundary-breaking thought.

The critical setup occurs in the first five verses. Mark hints at the significance of the section by opening with an introduction of the Pharisees and scribes who have come down from Jerusalem (7:1–5). Verse 3:22 was the only other time Mark unveiled such a formal description of the representatives of institutional Israel. At that time, Mark argued that Israel was being reconstituted in a most revolutionary, countercultural way.² Jesus' declaration that *anyone* who did the will of God could be a member of his, and therefore God's, family theoretically opened up the membership rolls to Gentiles (3:35). Behavior, not blood or nationality, was key. What that verse implied, this one makes explicit. Given what is at stake, it is not surprising that Jerusalem sends out reinforcements.

It is interesting that the challenge at this point goes not to Jesus but to his disciples. Jesus' behavior goes unquestioned. At both the open (7:2) and close (7:5) of the section, the leaders want to know why the *disciples* are eating bread with defiled (*koinos*) hands. Two conclusions can be reached from this observation. First, one may suppose that Jesus has settled down. Most likely, however, is that his disciples have now become as much a boundary-breaking nuisance as Jesus himself. As such, they have become models for Mark's readers. This is the second point. The question, hostility directed at Jesus' followers, betrays a later historical animosity between Mark's readers and the pharisaic/scribal leaders who opposed the continuing efforts of those readers to conduct the power of God's reign through their Jesus preaching. Thus Mark's story operates on two levels. On the surface he is recounting Jesus' earthly ministry; just beneath the surface, however, he is chronicling the consequences that have befallen a community of believers who, four decades later, have taken up the mantle of that ministry.

The matter of purity, represented in this case by hand-washing, was a pertinent issue for both Jesus' and Mark's time. The scribes and Pharisees are not, however, obsessing over matters of hygiene and physical dirt. They are concerned instead about the ritual laws that govern dietary rules and regulations. As New Testament scholar Roger Booth explains, "Mark shows by his description in vv. 2–4 of the Jews' cultic purification, with specific reference to handwashing, that he intends the question at verse 5 to be understood in a cultic sense."³

The cultic description of appropriate behavior is somewhat cryptic and therefore difficult to understand.⁴ Most likely, according to Mark, the scribes

2. See chapter 2, View One.
3. Roger Booth, *Jesus and the Laws of Purity: Tradition History and Legal History in Mark 7* (Sheffield: JSOT Press, 1986), 119.
4. Note, for example, the great deal of consternation over whether the term *pugmē* (7:3) should be translated "with a fistful of water," "up to the wrist," or "cupping the hand." See Hooker, *Gospel according to Saint Mark*, 175; Marcus, *Mark 1–8*, 441.

and Pharisees intended to say that the Pharisees and all the Jews wash with cupped hands before they eat any bread.[5] It is not only the manner of the washing that causes concern; just as troubling, there is no external corroboration that *all* the Jews washed their hands before eating bread. The ritual mandate seemed much more likely to have been applied to a specific category of Jews, like the Pharisees, and perhaps even a specific, more particularly observant group within the Pharisees (perhaps a group called the *Haberim*.)[6] It was certainly not the case that laypeople, who were perpetually unclean by ritual standards because of their work on the land, were held to such rigorous ritual standards.

While there are protracted discussions about the purity rules (the ways in which impurity could travel as contagion by touch) and the manner of cleansing that impurity, Joel Marcus's lucid discussion of the matter seems more accurate. He appeals to the Jewish *Epistle of Aristeas*, which argues that it was the custom of *all the Jews* to wash their hands in the sea in the course of their prayers to God.[7] If they washed their hands before prayer, and if they prayed before eating, he argues that it was also certainly the case that they washed before eating: "Although handwashing was not universal, therefore, it was widespread and was probably a 'boundary marker' by which Jews both identified themselves and were identified by outsiders as being set apart from their neighbors."[8] That's the critical point. Whatever else the ritual signified, it demonstrated that Jews were different, that they were set apart. It was, in Marcus's words, a "boundary marker." As the immersion of vessels in 7:4 was established by biblical mandate (Lev. 11:32; 15:12), that practice no doubt provided such a line of ethnic and religious demarcation as well. On this cultic basis, outsiders (Gentiles) could be easily identified—and excluded. By not observing the tradition, Jesus' Jewish disciples were blurring the lines and thereby making it easier for those outsiders to find their way in. Thus the accusatory question: "Why do your disciples not live according to the tradition of the elders?" (7:5 NRSV).

It is significant that the scribes and Pharisees appeal to tradition and not to the law. Of course, according to the Pharisees, this tradition was law. Unlike other Jewish factions—such as the Sadducees, who protested that only the written Torah should be observed—the Pharisees argued that an oral tradition

---

5. Hooker, *Mark*, 175. Hooker argues that the practice saves water.
6. Booth, *Jesus and the Laws of Purity,* 192–203. Booth believes that this subgroup of the Pharisees, the *Haberim*, wanted to expand the view of purity even where it was not recognized by Law. They could do so through oral interpretation of the written Law.
7. Marcus, *Mark 1–8*, 441.
8. Ibid.

had been passed from Moses to the elders on Sinai and continued through an unbroken historical chain to them. This oral law, given its source, was as inviolate as the written one. Its great attribute was its flexibility; it could be adapted situationally to changing circumstances in greatly altered times. "By no means did the Pharisees intend to make fulfillment of the law more difficult," argues Helmut Koester; "their interpretation in fact wanted to make fulfillment possible—for the sake of the rule of God!"[9]

There was, however, an equally great liability, for such a flexible tradition was also open to manipulation. This appears to be Mark's point. He foreshadows his concern by the vocabulary he chooses to describe the oral tradition: *paradosis* (7:3, 5, 8, 9, 13). As Marcus points out, its cognate verb (*paradidōmi*) becomes a technical term that signals not only the handing down of tradition, but also the handing over (or "betrayal") of John the Baptist (1:14), Jesus (3:19; 9:31; 10:33; 14:10–11, 18–21, 41–2; 15:1, 10, 15), and Jesus' followers (13:9–12) because of their understanding of God's reign.[10] The tradition by which the Pharisees live, in this case symbolized by ritual purity, becomes the mechanism through which the leaders of institutional Judaism terrorize Jesus, his followers and, later, Mark and his readers.

This opening section not only foreshadows the horror that will occur because Jesus and his disciples unrepentantly detour their ministries around traditional ritual routes, but also conjures up the image of universalism toward which they are traveling. It does so by highlighting the word "bread." Missing the point entirely, the RSV and NRSV offer rather tepid translations of the key phrases in 7:2 and 7:5, to the effect that the disciples were "eating" with unclean hands. Mark, however, clearly points out in both cases that they were "eating *bread*." Why highlight such an innocuous menu (twice!) unless its identity has something to say? For Mark, bread makes its point by the narrative company he directs it to keep; it is always associated with the imagery of boundary breaking. At 2:26, it is a narrative accomplice to Jesus' challenge to traditional Sabbath understanding. At 3:20, Mark makes the awkward statement that the crowd around Jesus is so large that he and his disciples can't eat bread. That reference stands smack in the middle of a scene where Jesus reconstitutes Israel as a people based not on blood or nationality, but on obedience to the will of God. *Anyone* could belong! At 6:8, Jesus tells his disciples not to carry bread as he commissions them to the same transformative preaching ministry as his own. At 6:37, 38, 41, and 44, the term is used over and over again in the story where Jesus feeds five thousand people in Jewish

---

9. Helmut Koester, *Introduction to the New Testament* (Berlin: Walter DeGruyter, 1982), 242.
10. Marcus, *Mark 1–8*, 442.

territory. That presentation is balanced by an equally prolific use of the term in Mark 8 (vv. 4, 5, 6, 14, 16, 17, 19), where Jesus feeds four thousand people on Gentile soil and must then immediately fight with the Pharisees over his authority to do such a thing.

He also makes available to the Gentiles the bread he gives to the people of Israel. Nowhere is that point made clearer than when Jesus compares the healing of the Syrophoenician woman's daughter to the sharing of the children's bread with Gentile dogs. Bread, in other words, is a boundary-breaking symbol. No wonder it shows up so noticeably here at 7:5, when the scribes and Pharisees who have come down from Jerusalem attack Jesus for ignoring traditions that keep the boundary between the two ethnicities intact. The term doesn't occur again in Mark until 14:22, when Jesus likens it to his broken body at his last Passover meal with his disciples. Could it be that, even there, the boundary-breaking line of thought is continued? Throughout the Gospel, broken and eaten bread symbolizes the openness of God's imminent reign to all people; Jesus' body is broken because he doggedly maintains that openness over against institutionalized opposition (3:6).[11]

Having set up the reader so carefully, Mark can move fast now with his telling of the tale. In the ensuing controversy unit of 7:6–13, Jesus immediately calls upon Isaiah for support. Verses 6b–7 rely on the Septuagint's Greek translation of Isaiah 29:13. Early on, the prophet recognized the tendency of humans to set up their traditions as binding, heavenly doctrines. At 7:8–9, and then at 7:13, Mark interprets this to mean that the institutionalized leaders of Israel place their traditions (like the hand-washing ritual described in 7:1–5) in a higher priority than God's law. In other words, Mark is alleging that the scribes and Pharisees who have come down from Jerusalem place a higher premium on their own oral traditions than they do on God's written commands. That is what this section is all about. That is why Mark calls them hypocrites (7:6).

In classical Greek, the term "hypocrite" originally designated an actor in a play.[12] Mark gives the definition a noxious twist; the scribes and Pharisees who have come down from Jerusalem spouting their oral traditions are only pretending (playacting) to obey God's law. They are really crafting and following their own. Even worse, by cloaking their self-interest within the framework of the traditions of the elders, they appear (as good actors always do) to be standing for God, even when they are really building platforms of interpretative power for themselves. Mark 7:8 makes this clear: "You abandon the commandment of God and hold to human tradition."

---

11. See the exegetical comments on Mark 1:1–3:6 in chapter 1, View One.
12. Marcus, *Mark 1–8*, 444.

To bring the case home, Mark calls on the lawgiver himself, Moses. He appeals to the specific case of the commandment to honor one's parents (7:9–13).[13] Interpreting it from an economic angle, he implies that in order to comply with the command, a child must give financial assistance to parents in fiscal need. That is the Torah! The elders, however, have countered that written law with their own oral tradition ("But you say," 7:11). According to tradition, when a child makes the vow, "Corban," that is, "gift to God," the financial property designated in the vow could now be used only for religious purposes. While the person who owned the property could retain the right to its use, he could not surrender it to anyone else, even a parent in financial need. A child who did not want to help his parents would therefore have a legal way to avoid giving the assistance that the law of Moses demanded. In this way Jesus argues that, while appearing to be law-abiding, the leaders have positioned their own human traditions above God's laws. And that, by implication, is precisely what Jesus argues they have done in 7:1–5, when they mandate the ritual washing of hands in such a way that it makes a visible distinction between Gentiles and Jews. Observing the traditional boundaries of their own devising, they refuse to accept God's boundary-breaking intent that blood and nationality no longer define membership in the people of God (3:31–35).[14]

In the teaching unit to follow (7:14–29), Jesus not only makes it clear that human tradition has been wrongly opposed to, and favored over, God's law; he specifies the particular concern to be the traditional principle that governs the makeup of God's people. Holding to the ritual dietary traditions opposes God's intent to open the doors of God's rule to *anyone* who would choose to participate in it. That is why Jesus calls (*proskaleomai*) the crowd (7:14); he wants to share this ground-breaking thought with them.[15] He gets to the point immediately. Using the vitriolic vocabulary of his opponents[16] he explains at 7:15 that impurity, "commonness," does not come from dirty hands or from

---

13. Exodus 20:12; Deuteronomy 5:16.

14. Scholars point out that there are several problems with the way Mark has devised the argument. Marcus points out: "The sort of abuse mentioned here is specifically forbidden in the third century by the Mishnah, which says that the imperative to honor parents overrules any vow (m. Ned. 9:1)" (Marcus, *Mark 1–8*, 445). Likewise Hooker: "The example hardly fits the argument . . . since the inviolability of an oath is affirmed in the Torah itself (Num. 30.2; Deut. 23.21–3), and the question is therefore not one of law versus tradition at all, but rather of the relative weight to be given to different parts of the law" (Hooker, *Mark*, 177). Despite these problems, it is clear that Mark is using the example to fit in with the case he has set up in 7:1–5, where human tradition is opposed to God's law.

15. Mark uses the language of "call" to signal moments of boundary-breaking teaching. See the discussion of *proskaleomai* in chapter 1, View One.

16. Jesus uses the verb form *koinoō* ("make unclean," 7:15, 18, 20, 23) to match the earlier adjectival form, *koinos* (7:2, 5).

putting the wrong (impure) kind of thing (food) inside one's body. In other words, the tradition of the elders was incorrect; the purity laws about washing and food discrimination and preparation are more about their customs than they are about God's intent. This is very dangerous stuff!

It is so dangerous that Jesus refrains from explaining the comment until he is behind closed doors with his disciples (7:17). Appealing to the kind of vice lists that were common in the early church later in the first century, Mark's Jesus declares that the moral turpitude that flows out of a person is much more egregious than any possible contamination that might occur on account of the kind of food going into a person (7:18–23). Indeed, given the fact that the list of moral offenses was much more like the kind of categorizations that occurred well after Jesus' death, scholars acknowledge that here Mark is editorializing upon Jesus' statements. The message in this case is for his church. He wants his readers, composed of both Gentiles and Jews, to know that food laws no longer determine relationship with God's reign; it is not what one eats but how one lives that matters (3:35).[17]

Mark brings that point clearly home with the shocking editorialization in 7:19b that Jesus has authoritatively cleansed all foods.[18] The man who used his authority as Lord of the Sabbath to shake up the traditional seventh-day observance (2:28) now uses that same sonship authority to challenge their interpretation of the Levitical code (Lev. 11:47). Make no mistake, there is more than food being served up here. By cleansing all foods, Jesus once again deposes a major barrier that separated Jews and Gentiles. Not only did Jews operate in a visibly different manner than Gentiles before eating (the dietary washing traditions), they also consumed a different diet. Certain foods were considered unclean; because Gentiles ate them, they, too, were considered unclean by association. According to Mark, Jesus was now wiping out that distinction and thereby shattering the boundary it had imposed. If Jews could eat any kind of food without becoming unclean, that meant that when Gentiles ate those foods they were no longer defiled by them. The bottom line? Jews and Gentiles could now eat together.

Mark climaxes his case with what appears to be a turning-point moment in Jesus' life that becomes a narrative teaching point for Jesus' disciples. Jesus heads up to Tyre in an effort to secure some rest (7:24). Already, there are

---

17. So Booth: "The Gentile Christians of the early church demonstrate in the dispute and explanations their concern to justify, by words of Jesus, their complete freedom from the Jewish food laws" (Booth, *Jesus and the Laws of Purity*, 219).

18. The Matthean parallel to this text (Matt. 15:1–20) not only downplays Jesus' statement at 7:15 about things coming out of a person being more unclean than the food going in (Matt. 15:11); it omits the radical 7:19b explanation altogether.

boundary-breaking implications. First, although Jews did live in Tyre, the place name is symbolic of non-Jewish space.[19] The man who has just opened up to Gentiles the possibility of membership in the reign of God is now going to operate the power of that reign in Gentile territory. Second, as Marcus points out, three of the four places where Jesus tries to hide (5:19–20; 7:24, 36–37) have to do with Gentiles, and the fourth (1:40–45) has to do with Jesus transgressing the purity laws. "This combination of the motifs of Gentiles and inability to hide is probably not coincidental; Jesus' glory cannot remain a secret for the same reason that the good news will not stay permanently bottled up within Israel."[20]

That's when the woman comes on the scene. Clearly, by the way Mark describes her with one of his patented two-step progressions, she is not Jewish. She is a Greek (meaning Gentile), and a Syrophoenician by birth (meaning Gentile). There are also parallels here with other women—Jewish women—whom Jesus assists. The fact that this woman's daughter is ill reminds us of Jairus's daughter who was also ill (5:21–24, 35–43). Like this woman, Jairus sought out Jesus' help. There is yet another Jewish "daughter" in narrative parallel with this woman. When Jesus tells the woman with the twelve-year hemmorhage, "Daughter, your faith has saved you," he speaks to her courageous—and what should have been defiling—touch of his garment (5:25–34). So at 7:24–30, an unclean Gentile woman, like the Jewish one, comes before Jesus and falls down at his feet (5:33). She subsequently asks Jesus to save her daughter from an unclean spirit.

Assaulting the pervasive boundaries drawn around purity regulations, Mark now unleashes some of his most potent boundary-breaking language. When Jesus responds to the Syrophoenician woman's request, he says that the children must first be satisfied (7:27). The language of satisfaction (*chortazō*) is suggestive; Mark only uses this verb here and in the parallel stories where first a Jewish crowd of five thousand (6:42) and then a Gentile crowd of four thousand (8:4, 8) are fed bread in the desert. Interestingly enough, here at 7:27 Jesus describes his healing power, metaphorically, as the children's "bread." Thus, given the aforementioned association between "bread" and boundary breaking, it seems that Mark once again asserts Jesus' boundary-breaking, eschatological power to feed the hunger of both Jews and Gentiles.

Here, of course, things get dicey. Even though the terms in the first part of 7:27 are suggestive of universalist themes, Jesus uses them to set up what

---

19. See chapter 2, View One.
20. Marcus, *Mark 1–8*, 467.

appears to be an exclusivistic, boundary-confirming statement. "Let the children first be satisfied," he clarifies, because "it is not right to take the children's bread and throw it to the dogs." Student recoil starts here.[21] Clearly, Jesus intends to say that it is not right to take the eschatological power of God's dawning reign and give it to unclean, defiled Gentiles. But these are the very Gentiles Jesus has included at 7:1–23! His calling them dogs here seems to contradict his earlier openness and conform to the exclusionary perspective shaped by the traditions of the elders, the very traditions he has spent so much religious capital debunking.

Why is Jesus now apparently upholding the very intolerance he has just ravaged? There are two primary explanations. One, Jesus was reflecting his own traditional understanding that his historical ministry was directed primarily toward Israel. In that case, his ministry objectives would have been in sync with the traditional sense of separation between Jew and Gentile. Although the hostile epithet of dogs is clearly harsh, it would have matched the manner in which Jews of the period thought of the uncleanliness of their Gentile neighbors. Indeed, it is noteworthy that in the woman's reply she accepts the moniker before she initiates her rebuttal. Two, Jesus was using this moment as a teaching opportunity for disciples who still found it difficult to move with him all the way in his boundary-breaking efforts. Believing that he had found someone who would respond in the proper way, he allowed himself to be shamed so that he could show the shame of an attitude that considered Gentiles prohibitively unclean. As Ched Myers argues, "This drama represents another example of status-equalization. Jesus allows himself to be 'shamed' (becoming 'least') in order to include this pagan woman in the new community of the kingdom; so too Judaism will have to suffer the indignity of redefining its group boundaries (collective honor) in order to realize that Gentiles are now welcomed as equals."[22] In other words, Jesus expected her to rise to the occasion; and she did.

Some of both perspectives is likely to have been a part of what happened in the actual encounter between Jesus and the woman. Jesus did perceive his ministry as oriented toward the Jews, but he also perceived an eschatological opening up of that ministry. Jesus also employed creative teaching techniques for his disciples, so it is not unthinkable that he could have done so here. Clearly, there are other cases where Mark believes Jesus knows the thoughts

---

21. While some argue that Jesus' use of the diminuitive in the Greek suggests that he was speaking affectionately (i.e., "pups"), the overwhelming evidence suggests that even in the diminuitive form the term was highly negative. Dogs, even little ones, in the Jewish tradition were considered unclean (see 1 Sam. 17:43; Isa. 56:10–11).

22. Myers, *Binding the Strong Man,* 204.

of those with whom he is conversationally engaged and uses that knowledge to his teaching advantage (2:1–12; 9:14–29). Perhaps he uses this ability here.

Whatever the case may be, it is the woman's response that Jesus does, and therefore we should, find remarkable. She agrees with the recognized status of Gentiles in the eyes of Judaism of the time. And yet, appealing to the same universal understanding of God that Jesus himself teaches, she declares that, although a dog may be unclean and therefore lower than even a child in the household, it still exists within the household. It is still a part of God's communal creation. She has taken Jesus' metaphor and reoriented it. Jews, considering dogs unclean, did not usually entertain them inside the house. Gentiles, however, would domesticate the animals and bring them in. In her Gentile worldview, it was therefore possible to be a dog and yet still be within the larger physical confines of family space. As such, a dog would have access to the leftover bread that falls from the children's table. Amazingly enough, in the two parallel feeding stories of Jews first and then Gentiles, there was an abundance of leftover bread. The Syrophoenician woman wonders why this "bread" cannot be used to feed her and her people's hunger (7:28).

When Jesus agrees (7:29–30), the implicit boundary-breaking movement of Mark's Gospel takes explicit form. Jesus grants her request because of the power of her argument. It is an argument that not only recognizes the difference between Jew and Gentile, but also breaches that separation by suggesting that Gentiles, too, should receive the power of God's healing reign. As if narratively to reinforce the point, Jesus moves immediately from this scene to the Gentile region of the Decapolis, where he will repeatedly touch a broken Gentile in an effort to heal him (7:31–38).

The bread feeding of the four thousand satisfied Gentiles climaxes the section (8:1–9). Again, Mark makes it clear by his recall of critical vocabulary from the previous bread feeding of five thousand satisfied Jews (6:30–44) that he wants this latter miracle to be thought of in parallel with the earlier one. What the Syrophoenician woman wanted, Jesus accomplishes; he shares the bread of God's reign with his people and with hers. Even more interesting is that only in the feeding of the four thousand Gentiles does Jesus demonstrate concern that this hungry people not faint "on the way" (*en tē hodō*, 8:3). Starting at 8:27, Mark uses this phrase as a technical formula for discipleship (9:33, 34; 10:32, 52). Nor is it immaterial that the earliest Christian movement was known as "The Way" (Acts 9:2; 19:9, 23; 22:4; 24:14, 22). By placing this suggestive language here in this context, Mark is foreshadowing the ripping down of the boundary between Jew and Gentile that many scholars think eventually happened in his own mixed-faith community.

The two passages that conclude this section (Mark 8:10–13, 14–21) both

continue the bread imagery and the hostile response of the institutional leaders to Jesus' boundary-breaking activity. Mark talks about the one loaf that
the disciples brought with them in their boat journey (8:14) in a way that suggests the symbolism of a single, mixed fellowship of believers. Counterposed
to that is the dangerous, divisive leaven of the Pharisees and Herod.[23] Their
leaven is to shore up boundaries that protect human tradition instead of God's
intent. It is for this reason that right to the end of this section, they find themselves at odds with Jesus and his eschatologically authorized efforts. Just as
the people of Israel faithlessly demanded a sign from Moses right after he'd
just demonstrated the Exodus power of God (Exod. 17:1–7), so now the Pharisees seek a sign at 8:10–13. In so doing, as Marcus points out, they have
learned nothing from either their own history or from Jesus' powerful present:
"In seeking a sign despite the existence of previous signs, the Markan Pharisees undermine their own legitimacy not only through their illogic but also
through their demonstration that they are the spiritual heirs of the disobedient
wilderness generations, who rejected Moses by demanding signs even after
they had seen astounding ones in Egypt and on the Red Sea."[24] They are disobedient because they defiantly use their traditions to rule out a people God
wants to bring in.

View Two: "Makes Me Wanna Holler"
(Mark 8:24–30; Matt. 15:21–28)
Brian K. Blount

*[Introduction: In May 1995, the senior class of Princeton Theological Semi-
nary invited me to preach at the baccalaureate service on the day before its
graduation. I prepared this message for them.]*

Let me tell you about my parents, Edward and Doris. When I was growing
up, my two brothers and I thought they were omnipotent. I can remember
being in church, and my mother working with the Missionary Circle and my
dad sitting on the deacon's bench and my brothers and me thinking, "Well,
we're all by our lonesome in the pew now. We can do whatever we please.

---

23. As Marcus explains, "'Leaven,' then, can be more or less synonymous with 'leavened bread' (see
Lev 7:13), as in the common phrase 'to eat leaven.' . . . This equation probably carries over to our passage,
where the leaven of the Pharisees and of Herod is contrasted with the bread Jesus has miraculously provided" (Marcus, *Mark 1–8*, 510).

24. Ibid., 503.

Laugh a little, move around a little, play a little. Our parents can't get up in the middle of the service and come over and tell us to quiet down. It'd be too embarrassing for them."

But, you see, they had this power that reached out across vast distances, a power that enabled them to transform situations without actually having to move over to those situations. They had this look. This dark pall would come over their eyes as they heard our gleeful disrespect for the worship, and all they had to do was do that look. The look God used to give parents the moment a child was born, the look that says, "I don't have to come over there, I can stand right here in the *Now* and make you know that, in the not too distant *Not Yet*, you're gonna pay." That's what we biblical scholars call eschatological power. That kind of countenance makes three little boys sit up straight, quiet down, and start praising the Lord.

I found out, though, as I got older and life got more complex, that there were other powers. Other great powers. And they didn't always wield their strength to help make a person stronger and better. When I went to the eighth grade I left my segregated elementary school and entered the world of integration. My cosmos was transformed. And so was my concept of power and who thought they really manipulated it. My brothers and I had done remarkably well in our segregated environment. But now my parents were being told, "Things are going to change. Those boys aren't going to be so smart when they start being compared to those white children."

My first year, my grades taught the doubters a lesson. But my next year I learned a lesson of my own. There are principalities and powers over which your best effort and your most sincere determination have no control. In my first advanced, college preparatory course, world history, in my first six weeks, despite all the effort I'd put in, I received a D. Just a hair trigger above failure. News of it spread. And it spread fast. I don't know how it spread because I was so embarrassed that I hadn't told a soul. But everywhere I went, everyone knew. I remember one teacher telling me, "I wouldn't want to be at your house when this report card gets opened up."

My world history teacher also taught advanced English and advanced chemistry. Anybody on a college track was going through her, one way or another. That meant that every black child that went through her on their way up to college went down in their grades. My older brother, who would graduate at the top of his university classes in physics and chemistry, barely passed her chemistry class even though he gave the class a maximum effort. My parents knew what was going on. They understood the message that was being sent. But they didn't, as omnipotent as I'd once thought they were, have the power to transform the situation. The school considered her a tough teacher.

The school understood why the best black students struggled in her classes but no others; she was tougher than any other teacher. The school maintained that she needed to be in a position to work with every black child headed for college because she would teach them how much they needed to work to survive in college. She didn't fail me or my brother.

But I knew later on what I didn't know then. That was never her intention. She wanted to destroy something more precious than a report card or a summer that would have to be spent in summer school making up for failed credits. She wanted to destroy something in our spirit, our self-confidence. She wanted us to believe what we'd been hearing. That we weren't good enough. That no matter how hard we worked, we'd never have the capacity to compete with the best and brightest college-bound white students. And she wanted us to infect my younger brother with that fear so that by the time he got to her he'd already know. I couldn't get out of that class; I couldn't get around her; she stood across the horizon of my college track like a sentry, the way many others like her stand guard at the portals of opportunity even today. And my parents didn't have the power to stop her. I had to take it. And take it. I remember how every time I handed her my report card to have a grade entered on it and took back a D it made me want to shake my fist in her face and holler.

I learned from the power of my parents' determination that year. No, they weren't omnipotent. But they did still have a power. No matter what was happening *Now* they had the power to see into the realm of the *Not Yet*. And it was to that *Not Yet* that they focused my vision. They taught me that, even though the way she treated me, oppressed me, made me want to holler against the wind and scream out my fury, I ought to channel it in other ways. Not extinguish it, but feed off it. Not to silence the scream, but to holler in another way. To make my life the kind of scream that would make people like her, and the people and the institutions that created them and used them, see that despite them, and even because of them, I could muster the power to transform the picture of life they wanted to paint for me and people like me. What that teacher did to me, what people and institutions like her continue to do to people every day, in every place in this country, makes me wanna holler still. I figure a person can't stop hollering until the world, weary of the sound, weary of the challenge, takes notice and transforms. As a matter of fact, I think that is exactly the kind of thing that Syrophoenician woman was thinking as she walked up before Jesus and his disciples. Her effort was for Mark a symbol, an example of how a screaming life can transform an oppressive life situation.

Now this is the historical situation that confronted her, a situation that she thought, given the condition of her possessed daughter, was supremely unfair and oppressive. The gift of divine power that was incarnate in the man Jesus was cordoned off so that her people were unable to avail themselves of its transformative benefits. Jesus, she'd heard and was about to hear again from Jesus himself, was sent only to the Jews. Her people, no matter how possessed and oppressed they were *Now*, would have to wait until some unforeseen, uncalculated *Not Yet* to receive the kind of spiritual, physical, and social deliverance he represented.

Consider Mark's presentation of Jesus in this passage. Jesus' statement, the one where he says he isn't supposed to help her, the one where he compares Gentiles to dogs (7:27), is so inflammatory and so clear that the conclusion is certain. Jesus felt that he was sent only to the Jews. Even this Gentile woman who has just been supremely insulted agrees (7:28). She contests neither Jesus' harsh remark nor the reality it conveys. As one commentator puts it, "She accepts the analogy and its implications, only pointing out that when the children are fed, the dogs also get some small benefit incidentally."[25]

But there is an opening that allows for a transformative possibility. At 13:10 and 14:9, we have two statements by Jesus which suggest that the gospel about him will be preached to all the world, to all peoples. At 10:45 and at 14:24 Jesus proclaims that his life of service was not on behalf of some people, but on behalf of the many, suggesting that his concern crosses national and ethnic boundaries. It appears then that, while Jesus did historically focus his mission efforts on his own people, he ultimately believed that his mission and message would incorporate the Gentiles as well. And even as Mark is recording his *Now* of Jesus' limited ministry, he seizes upon this universal possibility of the *Not Yet* and looks for a point and place of transformation. A place where the turn from one people to all people was made. A place where somebody's scream for transformation turned Jesus around in his Palestinian tracks and turned around the very destiny of his gospel message. He looked, I think, to this Syrophoenician woman.

There is no doubt that Mark sees Jesus' confrontation with her as a transformative moment. When Jesus leaves her, having granted her request, *he doesn't go back home; he doesn't return to his own people*; he goes directly to the Decapolis, a network of ten Greek cities, and engages his liberating, healing ministry there (7:31). A turn, a transformation has occurred. And the pivot point is the narrative holler of this Syrophoenician woman.

I imagine when Jesus told her he was specifically sent not to help her daughter but to help his own people *she must have wanted to shake her fists in his face and holler.* And in her own way that is exactly what she does. *She*

---

25. D. E. Nineham, *The Gospel of St. Mark* (London: Penguin Books, 1969), 199.

stands there toe to toe with somebody she thought had the ability to control cosmic and demonic forces, and she challenges what he is saying. Here's power! The power of a woman so determined to see her daughter's life transformed that she would dare challenge the very system of salvation. Maybe in the *Not Yet,* maybe somewhere in the not-too-distant future the power that Jesus represented would be represented on behalf of her people. But she couldn't wait for the *Not Yet.* Her daughter needed Jesus' power now. And so she acted now!

In Matthew's Gospel the story is even more detailed (Matt. 15:21–28). We know that Mark has a tendency to shorten all the stories, to make them more compact, so it's nice to have Matthew's longer versions to open up the accounts some. Matthew describes how the woman came crying out to Jesus, "Have mercy on me, Lord, Son of David; my daughter is tormented by a demon" (Matt. 15:22 NRSV). But Jesus just ignores her (Matt. 15:23a). Ignores her! You don't think she was ready to holler? Then, to make matters worse, Jesus' disciples say, "Send her away, Jesus, for she is crying after us, disturbing us. Make her stop whining and go away" (Matt. 15:23b). And Jesus backs them up! He turns to her and says, "Lady"—and this was the line that Mark couldn't get out of his mind or his narrative account—"I wasn't sent to help your people. I wasn't sent to help your daughter" (Matt. 15:24). And then, Matthew says, she got down on her knees in front of Jesus and begged for his help (Matt. 15:25). She must have been thinking, "I hear all these great things about you, I hear how powerful you are, how compassionate you are, how you make the impossible possible, how you turn night into day, how you bring life up out of the grave. If you turn away from me I am without hope. Please help me." But that's when Jesus says that thing about not throwing his salvific power to the dogs. Can't help you and your people, who are like dogs (Matt. 15:26). It's at that point that you figure, this woman's got to break. I know his disciples must have been thinking, now, now she's got to break. Now she's got to shut up and leave us alone.

Scholars have long wondered why Mark and Matthew kept this story in their Gospel accounts because it tends to make Jesus look like he didn't want to help her. I think they kept it in, particularly Mark, because she is exactly what Jesus is, a transformer. Because she doesn't break apart. She breaks back bad on Jesus. She does to Jesus what Jesus does to the Pharisees and Sadducees. She takes his response, stands up to what that response means, and then turns the response upside down and inside out. "Sure, Jesus, I don't care if the food is *meant* for the children, that doesn't mean that your loving, gracious Abba God wants everybody and everything else to go starving. That can't be what you're saying, Jesus, is it?" (Mark 7:28; Matt. 15:27). And Jesus marveled, evidently as much at her guts and determination to say it as for what she'd said. And when Jesus celebrates her remark to him, her standing up to him, I think Mark thinks he was maybe smiling inside and saying, "Yeah, this is what I want. This is what I've been looking for. What a contrast to the sheep who follow me." I think this was the message Mark wanted his sheep, his flock, to get. Yeah, this woman's attitude is what Jesus celebrates. Not the people like the disciples, who never really seem to understand what he is doing or have the determination and the courage to do what he is doing.

Look at Mark's portrait of the disciples. He is getting progressively tired of their obtuseness as the story unfolds. At 4:45 he laments when he sees them frightened over a storm, even though he is in the boat with them, because they have no faith. At 6:52, when they are again terrified because of a storm in their lives, Mark laments that their hard hearts prevent them from understanding Jesus' real identity and power. At 8:18, Jesus himself wonders so greatly at their lack of faith, courage, and understanding that he asks them if their hearts are hardened. And we know that after every moment when he explains that he must suffer and die, their fear throws them into disarray and they simply cannot understand it (8:31–9:2; 9:30–37; 10:32–45). Yes, Mark likes the fact that they follow Jesus; but it's a lame, sheepish kind of following that he apparently dislikes. We get this constant narration of the twelve men grazing along behind Jesus, rambling around, getting lost half the time, the other half not quite knowing exactly where they are, what they are doing, or what they are doing it for. No wonder Jesus told the parable of the Lost Sheep (Matt. 12:9–14; 15:24; cf. Mark 14:7). That's who Mark thought was following him. Lost Sheep. Wandering. Grazing. Baa, baa, baa.

So, when he celebrates, he celebrates the example of someone who is not a follower, not one of the flock. She walks into Mark's story out of left field in a striking way, as striking as a picture of a wolf cutting a swath of turmoil through a flock of once content, once comfortable, once calm, flaxen sheep. A she-wolf of determination to create transformation. When she challenges Jesus he doesn't get angry. Instead, it's almost as if he smiles proudly at what she does. His response to her acerbic, surprising, bold, ravenous remark is in Matthew, "Great is your faith" (Matt. 15:28). Mark doesn't call it faith. He defines it as nerve. Nowhere has Jesus seen somebody so desperate for transforming someone else's world that she would have the nerve this woman has. "Look, you sheep," Mark appears to be telling his readers, "here's a wolf. She's what I think Jesus wants you to be like."

You know, I can see those sheepish disciples with Jesus wondering what to do when they hear this woman, this Syrophoenician woman, yelling after them. And I can hear them tell Jesus, "That woman is yelling after us, maybe you'd better go and shut her up, because it isn't right, doesn't look right to have a man of your stature going around having strange women hollering after him. Especially strange Gentile women. Let's not diversify our discipleship cause with somebody like her." In fact, I think Mark knew that, in his community, diversity was probably one of the top ten words folk didn't want to hear. But this Syrophoenician woman doesn't care what they want to hear; she's determined that Jesus will hear her.

When I think of her situation I think of an athletic shoe commercial by the actor Dennis Hopper. You sports fans will remember it. Hopper is dressed up as a deranged referee rifling through the locker of pro football player Bruce Smith. He finally stumbles on what he's been looking for. Smith's athletic shoes. And as he holds up one of those shoes, madly sniffing in the aroma, we see pictures of Bruce Smith crushing opponents on the football field. And then Dennis Hopper turns to the camera and says, "You know what Bruce would do if he saw me messing with his shoes?" Before he tells us we get another picture of Bruce Smith crushing some hapless player. The camera then shifts back to Dennis Hopper, who is now shuddering down to his knocking knees, as he says, "Bad things, man. Ba-a-a-d things."

Now it may seem odd that in a Reformed pantheon of such luminaries as John Calvin and Karl Barth I would find anything worth quoting from a rogue actor like Dennis Hopper, but for Mark I think this fits quite nicely. This is the maverick kind of thing that I think appeals to Mark. You gotta imagine Jesus walking along with his twelve sheep, coming up on this she-wolf, and when those twelve turn and see her, see the ravenous look in her eyes, see the fury in her spirit and the gut and determination in the way she gets up and comes over to them, you can almost hear those twelve shuddering sheep bleating out, "Bad things, Jesus. Ba-a-a-d things."

Every sheep pen needs this kind of bad thing, this kind of Syrophoenician wolf every now and then. She's not so much an eat-'em-up kind of wolf as she is a shake-'em-up kind of wolf. She doesn't devour flesh. She devours complacency. She consumes the tendency to follow without understanding. She annihilates the tendency to try to understand without believing. She obliterates the timid desire to hide behind safe tradition. She demolishes the tendency to get caught up in the commonplace of ritual and habit and think that religious or academic routine is the same thing as faith. In fact, you know, she isn't so much a carnivore as she is a "routinivore." She isn't so much a carnivore as she is a "do it the way we've always done it 'ivore." She isn't so much a carnivore as she is an "I'm gonna go with the flow, vote with everybody else, stand with everybody else even if where they're standing troubles me, 'ivore." She isn't so much a carnivore as she is an "I'm gonna sit here and be silent even though I know I ought to stand up and holler but I'm afraid people won't want to hear what I have to say 'ivore." She eats up doubts and fears; she devours that sheepish tendency we have to say, "Well, somebody powerful told me to shut up so I'm gonna go over and blend in with the flock and shut up before I get sheared."

Remember, Jesus himself, the Good Shepherd, was a wolf of sorts. From the eyes of the leaders of his people in Palestine he wasn't a sheepish follower who did what he was told when he didn't think he was being told what was right. He wasn't a sheepish follower who observed the traditions he was given when he knew those traditions were damaging to God's cause and God's people. The religious leaders in Palestine felt they were shepherds of God's flock, too. But Jesus wasn't following. He said to them what this woman was saying to him: "If this is the way the kingdom road is going, I'm heading for an off ramp. I'm not following. I don't care if the priests who follow in Aaron's and Moses' footsteps are doing the driving. No, I'm driving another route, even if I have to pave the road myself. I'm raising a contrary voice. The cries of my people make me want to holler out for a different direction, where the Sabbath doesn't stop healing, where the temple doesn't stop believing, where the Romans don't stop freedom, where Satan doesn't stop liberation, where the systems that bind don't hold God's people. I hear their cries, I see their struggles, and I see that their leaders are shepherding them in the wrong direction.

"And it makes me wanna holler."

There's nothing so wrong about being a sheep. I guess most of us are. I know I am much of the time. But when life threatens you, when circumstances oppress you or people you love or the people whom God loves the way they oppressed that woman, you need to become a wolf. You don't go to church quietly, you don't listen to sermons and advice quietly, you don't go into seminary quietly and go out just as quietly, you don't take over a church and run it like a quiet professional administrator, only looking at the bottom lines of money and membership. You howl against the night and the people who impose it. You raise your voice. You holler like that woman until your voice and the actions that accompany it change your world. That's why every sheepfold, if you ask me, if you ask Mark, needs a wolf every now and then, needs somebody like this boundary-breaking, shut-up refusing, bold, back-talking, change-demanding, transform-tripping Syrophoenician woman.

You're going out to do ministry in a world that is very much like the world faced by that Syrophoenician woman, a world like the one Jesus faced, a world about which Mark wrote. It's the kind of world Marvin Gaye sang about in his song titled "Inner City Blues," where he sang, "It makes me wanna holler." There are many voices in this world unfairly silenced, many lives oppressively trampled, many hopes brutally decimated. I know you know about this world because I've been reading your papers these last three years. In our course just this semester on the reign of God, many of you have written passionately about the fiefdoms of humankind. One paper spoke of black males who not only have a life expectancy that is ten years shorter than that of their white counterparts, but who also have the highest rate of infant mortality in this country. They are being decimated on both ends of the life cycle. One in twenty-one of them will die before they reach adulthood. Fifty percent of them under the age of twenty-one are unemployed. And while they make up only 6 percent of the U.S. population, they make up half the population of male prisoners in the penal system.

Doesn't that make somebody wanna holler?

Another paper told me that there is this community where you've worked and lived in field education that is so troubled by drugs, violence, abuse, and hopelessness that it seems as if it is, like that Syrophoenician woman's daughter, possessed.

Doesn't that make somebody wanna holler?

Another paper told me how brutally women are treated in our society, in the world, and even—and sometimes especially—in the church.

Doesn't that make somebody wanna holler?

Your papers have told me about the struggles of the homeless, about the plight of the impoverished, and the inability and sometimes the contracted lack of desire on the part of our governments to create transformation that truly transforms for those in society who truly need change the most.

Doesn't that make somebody wanna holler?

I read in the public newspapers where the governor of the state of New Jersey has declared, after talking to two or three, maybe five or six of her citizens, that all us black males are out playing pregnancy games, and I figure she figures she can say it and get away with it nowadays because the president of her primary state university has already told her and the world that black folk are so intellectually inferior that maybe they won't even know they're enduring a class-action insult. That makes me wanna holler!

But I'm also wondering, where are the hollering wolves? I know where the sheep are. I can count on them being where I always expect them to be because, as sheep usually are, they're fenced in. I can go to any green pasture on any Sunday morning at 11 A.M. (maybe 10 A.M. if they graze early in the summer, maybe 9:30 and 11:00 A.M. if they have so many sheep crammed into the pen that they need to graze twice on a Sunday) and see the flock gathered. What I'm hollering for nowadays are a few wolves who'll run into the flock and drive the sheep out of the pasture onto the rocky terrain where people are socially and politically and economically suffering, struggling and dying with the terrible holler of transformation rising up from their prophetic throats. I'm hollering with my heart in my hands to see the passion in your work here in this seminary translate into passionate pocket moments of the reign of God that resist the destructive trends out there.

I remember this revival service my home church had once when I was growing up. Those services were always pretty powerful emotionally and spiritually. I remember one night when we had this especially powerful preacher. And even though I was only eleven or twelve years old, I still remember him as probably the best preacher I have ever heard. Outside the sanctuary on this hot August night a frightening, dog-days-of-summer electrical storm was erupting. We could hear the thunder roar as he whipped the congregation into a spiritual frenzy that became a storm all its own when the choir got up to sing. About halfway through the invitational hymn the lights flashed out and darkness swallowed us. The electric organ was gone, but the choir didn't stop. Neither did the organist. She slid across the organ bench and down the big drop to the lower piano stool and caught up with the choir and led them like a shepherd through a valley of darkness right on time. I remember how that smooth move fired up an already explosive congregation. There in the darkness I heard more noise in worship than I had ever heard before in my life. Screams, shouts, and the constant echoing of that name, "Jesus! Jesus! Jesus!"

I suspect that the darkness allowed some of the quieter folk the freedom to shout in a way they ordinarily wouldn't have shouted in the light of the religious day. But they were shouting now. It was loud now. If I pause for a second I can still hear the fury and see the lightning flash. The one thing I always had against those revivals, though, even as a young child, was that the people who engineered and participated in those loud, raucous worship services could be awfully quiet when they walked out of the church and walked into the screams cluttering up the audio tracks of the world. Seemed like the allegedly agitated screaming in church was really a form of comfortable quiet because it didn't agitate the kind of screaming that needed to be heard in places like those integrating schools.

That night that service provoked in me one of the angriest nightmares I have ever had. I couldn't get the service out of my mind. I couldn't get out of my mind the name of Jesus that kept being shouted over and over and over and over again in the darkness. And the next thing I knew I was shouting myself in the darkness of my bedroom. There were people all around me, like in the sanctuary, and they were all focused in on me, shouting, yelling, screaming, I don't know what. It was just that they kept yelling. Wouldn't stop yelling. And the next thing I knew I was yelling back. I kept yelling back until I heard this calm voice calling my name instead of Jesus'. "Brian, Brian," my mother was saying. "It's just a dream."

But dreams are so real to children. And this one, she could tell, wouldn't let go. That's when she offered up what she knew would be a calming remedy. "Think about Jesus," she said. "Just think about Jesus. That will calm you down. Just think about Jesus." I felt my mother's calming embrace, I listened to her soothing voice, I looked in the darkness for her gentle expression, and I wanted to say, but I couldn't quite form the words, because I didn't know how it would sound to her, but I was thinking, "You know, it's precisely because I am thinking about Jesus that this nightmare is happening to me." I found out that night what I've been finding out ever since. Thinking about Jesus will mess you up! Thinking about Jesus will quiet the shouts of hallelujah and the joyous, saved acclamations in sanctuaries of worship and raise the decibel level of the cries of protest and the whispers of agony outside the sanctuaries until the sound slashes our saved souls and shatters our salvific slumber.

Jesus, I've found, won't let you rest in peace. His reputation, his power, his mission call out to you the way they called out to that Syrophoenician woman. When your world is turned upside down, his very being hollers out to you. He won't let you graze in the fold quietly, he won't let you slumber in the sanctuary indefinitely, he won't let you contemplate the power of being immersed in the Spirit without challenging you to use that power in the physical terrors of the world around you. The way his reputation and power pulled that tormented woman out of her home, from the bedside of her daughter, to holler for his help, to holler for his transformative power, to become a hollering instrument of that transformation herself, so does who and what he is call out to us. Thinking about him makes you sensitive to noise. You hear people crying around you. To think about him makes you vulnerable to hope. You believe things you never would have dared dream of believing before.

I think that's why Mark kept this story of this Syrophoenician woman in his Gospel. He wanted us to holler for transformation the way that woman hollered for the transformation of her daughter's life situation, even when all the signals say that you ought to shut up, give up, and go home. If that woman could stand up to Jesus, I think Jesus was telling us, we ought to be able to stand up to anybody else or anything else on this planet. "You want change?" he seems to be telling the woman. "You're gonna have to fight for it. You're gonna have to raise your voice."

That's what I think a good seminary teaches people to do. To holler. Think

about our master plan. We start you hollering from the moment we put you in
OT101 and NT101 and CH101 and TH101 and General Ministries. I've heard
seminary students in my own day and your day holler about the situations that
confront them in seminary. I hope your voices will really howl once you go
forth from this place and confront the situations that confront our people,
God's people. 'Cause there's a seminary out there where you're gonna learn
lessons about faith and doubt, victory and defeat, God and Satan, that we
could never teach you in here.

Sometimes people tell me that we live in a time without prophecy. Perhaps
we do. But perhaps if we can't have prophets, maybe we can have
Syrophoenician women, perhaps we can have people like yourselves who,
like that woman, hear the cries of people around her so acutely that she is willing to stand up to anybody and any power and demand transformation.

Isaiah, you know, had this vision. It's an eschatological vision. It's about
the wolf lying down with the lamb in peace and tranquility (Isa. 11:6). That's
Isaiah's *Not Yet* vision. New Testament writers like Mark appreciated that
Not Yet vision and all, but they also wanted to drag pieces of that *Not Yet* into
the *Now*. I think this Syrophoenician woman represents for Mark what it
would look like if that *Not Yet* vision of the wolf and the lamb was dragged
into the *Now*. It's still a good vision. Because in the *Now* the wolf sure would
make that lamb mighty nervous. In the *Now* the wolf sure would keep that
lamb sorely agitated. In the *Now* the panting, salivating wolf sure would keep
that perspiring little lamb thinking about what he could do and ought to do
to urgently bring God's *Not Yet* future a little closer to present reality. In the
Now, when the wolf lies down with the lamb, you're gonna hear a little bit
more than some quiet bleating; you're gonna hear some hollering for transformation.

What's it gonna take to make you wanna holler? And when it happens,
what are you going to do about it? Or perhaps a better thing to ask is, what
are you going to be about it? Don't be sheepish. Be Syrophoenician, like
a wolf.

View Three: Take Time to Be Holy
Gary W. Charles

Recently, my wife and I had the "privilege" of lugging a year's worth of
"necessities" up to my son's dorm room, whereupon we were banished to the
lobby. I couldn't help overhearing a recurring exchange between incoming
parents and their college students. A parent would ask, "Tell me about your

roommate." After spending maybe ten minutes with their new roommate, the student would bemoan, "Oh, we have nothing in common."

In Mark 7, the Pharisees rip into Jesus: "Why do your disciples forget that they have nothing in common with Gentiles? Why in the world do they eat with unclean hands, like those common people?" (7:5). Jews washed their hands before meals, ritually, religiously (7:4). As Brian notes in his exegesis, "Whatever else the ritual signified, it demonstrated that Jews were different, that they were set apart." In the Hebrew language, that's what holiness is all about—being set apart from the unclean, from the common.

Twice in the early verses of chapter 7, Mark uses the Greek word *koinos*, or "common." The marketplace Greek of Jesus' day was called *koinē,* or the common person's Greek. Intellectuals looked down upon *koinē* as slang or "common," in the least complimentary sense of the word. The Pharisees come to Jesus and want to know why his disciples are not *holy*, why they eat like vulgar folk, like "those people."

As a child in the South, I learned that *those people* was most often a euphemism for African Americans. The message was clear: "You and *those people* do not belong together on this earth, for they are common and you are not." As a youth, I often heard my peers—scared and confused about their own sexuality, much less about anyone else's—say, "I've got nothing in common with *those people*." This time the euphemism was for gay and lesbian persons, and it was never said politely. The message could not be missed: "We do not belong with *those people*, because they are common and we are not."

In the debate of Mark 7:1–23, the scribes and Pharisees hammer Jesus for forgetting that he and his disciples have nothing in common with Gentiles. I like to mock Pharisees as much as the next Christian, but the trouble is they have a point. We will never understand the conflict between Jesus and the Jerusalem authorities until we grasp that this debate was not a religious version of Trivial Pursuit. Jesus was a Jew defying his own tradition. His parents had no doubt taught him better than to act as if tradition didn't matter. Tradition is integral to the self-understanding of a people or a person. Tradition gave Jews identity and stability through centuries of instability and affronts to their identity.

Aside from this first-century quarrel between Jews, I happen to like tradition myself. I like for things to remain the same. I like the dinner table to have four Charleses around it, not three, not two. I like holiday rituals to remain unchanged. I like to see familiar faces come out of church offices and see the same people sitting in the same pews. I like to sing hymns that I have loved since childhood. I like for people and places and family traditions to remain the way they have always been.

In her book *Dakota*, Kathleen Norris praises the traditions of the prairie, a life she has learned since leaving her manic Manhattan existence to lead a far more placid life on the plains. She describes her new home in ways that make me want to travel there, yet she is not an uncritical immigrant. She writes:

> The land does not change, or does so only slowly; maybe Dakotans emulate the land in that respect. The danger is that in so doing they can lose an important aspect of their humanity. In forsaking the ability to change, they diminish their capacity for hope. We don't need change. What we need, as my friend suggested, is to turn back the clock to the ways things were twenty years ago, when the town was booming and the world made sense. There was nothing that couldn't be judged by the values we all shared. But she may find, as Gatsby did, that disconnecting from change does not recapture the past. It loses the future.[26]

God help followers of Jesus whenever we try to disconnect ourselves from change; when we act as if we must do things only as the church did them yesterday; when we spend so much time deciding who's in and who's out of the church, who's clean and who's unclean, that we lose sight of God's future for the church. In Mark, as Jesus debates with his religious kin, he does not toss his tradition into the wastebasket and forget the richness of his heritage, nor does he try to change things just to shake up those in power.

In Mark 7 Jesus is *not* challenging the value of his own tradition; he is challenging the value of a religious tradition that has lost its moorings. In Mark, the Pharisees do not care if the disciples' hands are clean, as was the original ritual intent of this tradition. Brian writes, "The matter of purity, represented in this case by hand-washing, was a pertinent issue for both Jesus' and Mark's time. The scribes and Pharisees are not, however, obsessing over matters of hygiene and physical dirt. They are concerned instead about the ritual laws that govern dietary rules and regulations."[27] In other words, obsessing over clean hands was a way to keep up religious appearances and remain separate from the *koinos* people, the Gentiles. Lamar Williamson says it another way: "By emphasizing the secondary place of human traditions and the primary place of the commandment of God, this text calls us beyond arguments over what is old and what is new to a concern for what is vital."[28]

---

26. Kathleen Norris, *Dakota: A Spiritual Biography* (New York: Mariner Books, 2001), 63–64.
27. See View One earlier.
28. Williamson, *Mark*, 136.

As a Presbyterian, I am indebted to my tradition, to church women and men who have gone before me, many of whom have shaped my values and taught me about the wide expanse of God's grace. I stand proudly within the Reformed tradition and gladly claim much of its theological wisdom as my own. But I worry as I see a growing theological rigidity in Christian denominations in America. While many in our society feel religion to be superfluous to their lives or just plain silly, many churches and Christians seem hell-bent on proving them right. We engage in ugly church debates about who's holy and who's common, confident that some folk are common but we are not.

Just a few verses earlier in his Gospel, Mark recounts the amazing story of Jesus' feeding thousands of people with less than enough food (6:30–44). Instead of celebrating the expansive generosity of God with Jesus and his disciples, the Pharisees cannot see beyond their narrow theological categories; pathetically, they call Jesus on the carpet because his disciples do not wash their hands before coming to the table. Within their theological tradition, they were 100 percent right, but according to Mark, they were also dead wrong. As Brian observes in his exegesis, "By cloaking their self-interest within the framework of the traditions of the elders, they appear (as good actors always do) to be standing for God, even when they are really building platforms of interpretative power for themselves." While appearing to be the keepers of tradition, the scribes and Pharisees defile it by using it as a weapon to cordon off God's grace for the well washed.

Mark tells this story to defy such an abuse of tradition, to end any notion that *holiness* means "we have nothing in common with *those people*." Mark has absolutely no patience with a tradition that boasts, "We have nothing in common with *those people*, for they are common (*koinos*) and we are not." Mark has a great interest in warning the emerging church not to replicate the religiously sanctioned segregation advocated by those from headquarters in Jerusalem.

Luke, who writes some years later, makes Mark's point even more explicitly. Peter, who has known since a boy what food to eat and what food to leave alone, has an illuminating food dream. He sees a banquet of forbidden foods set before him (Acts 10:9–16). He rightly objects that he cannot eat such common, unclean food (Acts 10:14). He then hears this response from God: "Don't call what I make clean, unclean or common" (Acts 10:15).

Two years ago, while doing research for a book on the church in the twenty-first century, I visited some congregations exploding with vitality; but sadly, I also visited far too many that resembled museums or family chapels. It was if they were crouching behind a tradition that no longer had any breath, a frozen form of old thoughts and beliefs. In interviews in these congregations, I heard people say, "We want to grow" while, in the same breath, they communicated, "But we don't want anything to change." They would claim, "Our church is open to all people" and then say in the same sentence, "But *those people* would be much more comfortable worshiping with their own kind." As Brian preaches so eloquently in his sermon, "It made me wanna holler!"

Why? Because in Christ, *you and I are one kind*. In Christ, we are made *holy* so we can share everything in common, because nothing is unclean; all has been made clean. In Christ, you and I are made *holy* through the love of a God who yearns for us to spend more time breaking down walls that divide people than laying new brick to keep the *common* folk out.

Mark loves to follow a good debate with a good story, and he does so again here. After his disciples are chastised for defying tradition by eating with *common* hands like *common* people, Jesus heads into *common* country (7:24). He travels to the other side of the tracks, to Gentile country, where no self-respecting believer would ever go. Once there, a *common* woman asks him a favor. He gives the right answer according to tradition: "God's blessings are intended for God's children, the Jews." But the *common* woman will not settle for the traditional answer. As Brian argues so powerfully in his sermon, this *common* woman "hollers" above the din of traditional views of Gentiles and gender and power. She's a wolf who howls for justice, not another one of Jesus' many lost sheep. This Syrophoenician woman hollers with such force that she even teaches Jesus a thing or two about being *holy*.

The old hymn implores, "Take time to be holy." That's a dangerous occupation in Mark's Gospel. To be *holy* means we've got to reevaluate what is important and who is important. To be *holy*, in the way Christ makes us *holy*, will open the church, open us, to *those people*. For in Christ, the streets we walk and the roads on which we drive are filled with *those people* with whom you and I have everything in common—everything that finally matters.

In *Operating Instructions*, Anne Lamott, a recovering alcoholic and drug addict, tells about her first year of recovery. It is a story worth repeating:

> When Sam was six days old, I took him to my little church in Marin City, the church where I've been hanging out for four years now. . . . I got in the habit of stopping by the church on Sundays but staying in the back, in this tense, lurky way, and leaving before the service was over because I didn't want people to touch me, or hug me, or try to make me feel better about myself. After I got sober and started to feel okay about myself, I could stay to the end and get hugged. . . . Anyway, the first Sunday after Sam's birth, I kind of limped in . . . and everyone was staring joyfully and almost brokenheartedly at us because they loved us so much. I walked, like a ship

about to go down, to a seat in the back. But the pastor said, Whoa, whoa, not so fast—you come up here and introduce him to his new family. So I limped up to the little communion table in the front of the half circle of folding chairs where we sit, and I turned to face everyone. The pain and joy were just overwhelming. I tried to stammer, "This is my son," but my lip was trembling, my whole face was trembling, and everyone was crying. When I'd first started coming to the church, I couldn't even stand up for half the songs because I'd be so sick from cocaine and alcohol that my head would be spinning, but these people were so confused that they'd thought I was a child of God. Now they've seen me sober for three years, and they saw me through my pregnancy. . . . Toward the end of my pregnancy, people were stuffing money into my pockets, even though a lot of them live on welfare and tiny pensions. They'd sidle up to me, slip a twenty into the pocket of my sweater, and dart away.[29]

Though the members of Lamott's small church in Marin City may not be what the hymnwriter had in mind when he wrote "Take Time to Be Holy," they are exactly what Jesus had in mind. For they have in large measure what Jesus gives to any church willing to ask for it. They have the wisdom to know what is important and who is important and how to make even *those people*, like alcohol-sodden and drug-laced Anne, know that, in the eyes of God, they are important. You can almost hear Mark applauding, and you can certainly see Jesus smiling. What a difference it made that one church did not worry about how it might look if they welcomed a *koinos* person, one of *those people*. What a difference it made that one church took time to be holy.

---

29. Anne Lamott, *Operating Instructions: A Journal of My Son's First Year* (New York: Fawcett Columbine, 1993), 26–28.

7

One Cross Fits All
Mark 8:22–9:13

View One: From Text to Sermon
Gary W. Charles

I do not wear jewelry. I have nothing against jewelry and do not object to those who wear it. I just don't wear jewelry. Now that my college-student son has added a stylish piercing to his look, I stand alone in my family in this peculiarity of fashion. On second thought, though, to say that I have nothing against jewelry is not altogether accurate. I do have a visceral disdain for one particular type of jewelry. I cannot abide cross or crucifix necklaces. This is not a Protestant or Catholic reaction to such necklaces; it is far more fundamental.

I find something tragically ironic whenever I listen to a jewelry salesperson describe the fine points of a "cross" necklace. I am convinced that if consumers had even half an idea of the meaning of the cross, the value of and interest in such jewelry would plummet. Most likely, if people knew the real meaning of the cross, they would tear the necklace from their necks and toss it into the sea.

What I want to know is how a biblical bull's-eye has been transformed into a sanitized chic trend in fashion. How has the public horror of a crucifixion been reduced to a public fashion statement by both the religious and nonreligious? This consumer craze reinforces my belief that we can sell anything in the West. If a cross can be made fashionable and to fit every neck, it cannot be long before crowds will clamor for a 14-carat necklace with a noose or a syringe or an electric chair.

The irony of the cross as jewelry intersects directly with Mark's irony in 8:22–9:13, for it is in these verses that Jesus makes his first mention of the cross. The disciples are not enthralled with what Jesus has to tell them; they are too fascinated with reflective glory spilling off the Son of Man to take seriously the rough-hewn way of discipleship. As a result, Mark tells us that those best prepared to follow Jesus are as impaired in vision as the blind man from Bethsaida after Jesus first spits in his eyes (8:22–26). It is only after a second touch by Jesus that the blind man sees clearly. By now, Mark's readers wonder how many times Jesus will have to "spit in the eyes" of the Twelve before they will see more than "trees walking around" (8:24).[1] With images of Isaiah's salvation oracles (Isa. 29:18; 35:5; 61:1), Mark signals to his readers that as Jesus restores sight to the blind man, the promise of salvation has come and the ancient dreams of the exiles have been fulfilled. The readers have known this about Jesus since 1:1, but after miracles, exorcisms, and incredible acts of love, the Twelve still see only "trees walking around."

The story of the healing of the blind man in Bethsaida is found only in Mark. Some speculate that a two-step healing process did not fit the image of a mighty Messiah, and so Luke and Matthew omitted this story. Others argue that the two-step process testifies to the power of Jesus to heal even the most debilitating forms of blindness. Tolbert argues that this story reflects "the hardening of opposition, not the weakening of Jesus."[2] Whatever its origins, in this distinctive healing story, Mark revisits some of his favorite theological themes.

Like the leper in 1:40, the frightened crowd in the Decapolis in 5:17, the prestigious Jairus in 5:23, and the crowd assisting the deaf man in 7:32, the blind man from Bethsaida now begs (*parakaleō*) Jesus for help. In each case, even when the crowd pleads for Jesus to leave the Decapolis, there is an undeniable desperation present in the request. Mark repeatedly reminds his readers that dealing with Jesus is not a casual encounter and, therefore, that discipleship can never be a casual affair.

Mark mentions the touch of Jesus three times in this brief story (8:22, 23, 25). This is a visceral story through which Mark intends to evoke a similar reaction in his readers. To touch or be touched by Jesus is not to experience incremental changes in life; it is to have your life transformed. As with the leper in 1:41, the encounter between Jesus and the hemorrhaging woman in 5:30–31, and the crowds who surrounded him in 6:56, here, through the touch of Jesus, salvation arrives, walls collapse, and boundaries are crossed. The blind man sees at the end of the story, but do the Twelve?[3]

---

1. So Mary Ann Tolbert: "As the story of Jesus' rejection by his hometown and consequent inability to accomplish mighty works (6:1–6) makes clear, miracles in the Gospel are not signs to induce faith in unbelievers; they are, instead, the fruits of faith. Since faith is the prerequisite of miracle, as the disciples manifest deeper degrees of unfaith, Jesus encounters greater difficulty in performing mighty works" (Tolbert, *Sowing the Gospel,* 180).

2. Ibid., 187.

3. Vincent Taylor sees hope for the disciples in this passage: "Anxious for the sake of his readers to insist that blindness prevented the disciples from receiving the sign of the loaves, he wished none the less to sound a note of hope. The blind could be made to see . . . [and now] saw all things clearly. So did the

The next story sounds strangely familiar to Mark's readers. Just as the residents of Jesus' hometown speculated about Jesus' identity (6:3), so now Jesus raises the question himself, while "on the way."[4] Blount draws the parallel between Deuteronomy's description of Israel as a people "on the way" and Mark's depiction of those who follow Jesus to the reign of God (Deut. 1:33; 8:2; 9:12, 16; 11:28; 13:5; 25:18; 31:29).[5] "On the way" the disciples give the word-on-the-street speculation about Jesus' identity. Earlier in Mark, Herod's speculation about Jesus proved not only wrong but deadly for John the Baptist. Certainly, the readers hope, the disciples of Jesus will not make a similar mistake. At first, readers are relieved when Peter confesses Jesus to be the Messiah (*ho Christos*), the first time a human has made such a positive identification of Jesus in Mark's story. It looks as though the disciples, or at least Peter, see clearly at last.

Jesus responds to Peter's "confession" by using the same command (*epitimaō*) with which Jesus had earlier silenced (*epitemaō*) the demons and the demonic sea (1:25; 3:12; 4:39). So also at 8:30, Jesus silences Peter just when readers are celebrating that one disciple finally knows the identity of the One he is following. Peter is silenced, but Jesus speaks openly about "the way" before him. Peter cannot know the essence of his confession until and unless he follows Jesus faithfully on "the way." But Peter finds "the way" that Jesus describes to be repulsive and repugnant (8:32). Peter's confession evidently assumed that the promised *Messiah* would incite revolution and inflict suffering, not experience suffering. "Of what possible good could a dead Messiah be?" asks Douglas R. A. Hare.[6]

Invoking images from the book of Daniel, and recalling the political and religious unrest of Israel under the rule of Antiochus Epiphanes IV, Mark's Jesus declares that "it is necessary" that he suffer and die at the hands of those who should be the doorkeepers of freedom (8:31).[7] Some scholars argue that

---

disciples and so would Mark's readers" (Taylor, *Gospel according to St. Mark,* 370. See also Juel, *Mark,* 74–76. Unfortunately, both Taylor and Juel miss the intent of Mark's narrative, as the following pericope will confirm. For even in a moment of ecstatic clarity (see 9:2–9), the disciples still do not see.

4. Regarding the phrase "on the way," Ched Myers writes, "This is the way that Isaiah through John announced in the wilderness; the kingdom lies *on,* not *beside* it (4:4, 15; cf. 10:46). The disciples must take no sustenance for this way (6:8), for Jesus will sustain them upon it (8:3). In this section this metaphor figures centrally, occurring near the beginning of each of the three cycles (8:27; 9:33f; 10:32). It is also the site of the section's two contrasting call stories: the nondiscipleship of the rich man (10:17) and the discipleship of the blind beggar (10:52). And it will shortly be revealed as the way that leads to Jerusalem" (Myers, *Binding the Strong Man,* 241). A brief history of interpretation may be found in Blount, *Go Preach!* 127.

5. Blount, *Go Preach!* 127.

6. Douglas R. A. Hare, *Mark* (Louisville, Ky.: Westminster John Knox Press, 1996), 99.

7. Juel notes the scandal of such a prediction in the context of first-century Judaism: "There is no evidence that Jews believed the Messiah would suffer and die. In fact, there is every reason to believe that

dei ("it is necessary") means that all descriptors that follow imply the blue-print of God. Both Blount and Myers make convincing cases for an alterna-tive, sociopolitical reading of *dei*. Myers asks:

> Why is this "necessary"? Is Mark betraying a "theological discourse of pre-destination," as Belo complains (1981: 156f.)? No; but he is challenging the accepted bounds of political discourse in the war of myths. According to the understanding of Peter, "Messiah" *necessarily* means royal triumph and the restoration of Israel's collective honor. Against this, Jesus argues that "Human One" *necessarily* means suffering. This is so because, as the advo-cate of true justice, the Human One as critic of the debt code and the Sab-bath *necessarily* comes into conflict with the "elders and chief priest and scribes" (8:31). In other words, "it is necessary" is not the discourse of fate or fatalism, but of political *inevitability*. It is in this sense that Jesus addresses his political vocation "openly." . . . Peter's fantasies of power must be censured by clear-eyed realism."[8]

Insisting on a political understanding of *ho Christos* ("the anointed one"), Peter has the audacity to rebuke (*epitimaō*) Jesus (8:32). Since Mark con-sistently uses *epitimaō* to describe Jesus casting out demons, the verb here suggests not only that Peter sees something demonic in Jesus but that he needs exorcising. "Peter appears to have fallen into the same trap as Jesus' relatives. He thinks that Jesus is insane and needs to be exorcised."[9] When Peter "silences" Jesus, not only does he suggest that Jesus needs to be exor-cised, he also implies that he is in a position superior to his master, that he can exorcise demons from Jesus. Williamson is right, then, when he says, "The issue is, who is in charge. To say 'Christ' to someone is to give up the right to define what 'Christ' means. . . . Peter tries to behave like a patron, not a disciple."[10]

Jesus' suffering and death would have disqualified him as a candidate for royal office. Mark's portrayal of religious and political expectations is accurate. Both the religious and political leaders think it absurd for anyone to claim that Jesus is the Messiah-King" (Juel, *Mark*, 102).

  8. Myers, *Binding the Strong Man*, 243–44. Appealing to the use of *dei* in Josephus and Appian, Brian Blount bolsters Myers's argument by making an important distinction between *inevitability* and *necessity*: "Inevitability and necessity have different nuances, both of which are caught up in Mark's use of 'it is necessary' here at 8:31. Jesus' preaching, because of the cultic and social boundary crossing that it represents, makes it inevitable that he will clash with those in power. Because they have power, more social and political power than Jesus at this point, the end result will necessarily be Jesus' suffering. The necessity, thus, operates from the perspective of the rulers who have no other option if they want to cur-tail Jesus' boundary-trespassing preaching. If he will not stop, they must destroy him" (Blount, *Go Preach!* 130).

  9. Perkins, "Gospel of Mark," 624.

  10. Williamson, *Mark*, 153.

Peter *tries* to rebuke Jesus, but Jesus *does* rebuke Peter.[11] Jesus will not be patronized by Peter as he explains that the proper position for disciples is not beside him (10:35–37) or guarding him (9:38), but "behind" him (8:33). "Disciples are not to guide, protect, or possess Jesus; they are to follow him."[12] Either Peter and the rest of the Twelve will follow this boundary-breaking Messiah on "the way" and embrace the inevitable suffering that will follow, or they will become "the Satan," ironically, a false title of which Jesus has already been accused (3:21–23).[13]

Lest Peter, the remaining disciples, or the clamoring crowd have any reason to misconstrue his identity, Jesus makes a strong public clarification: "If any want to become my followers, let them deny themselves and take up their cross and follow me" (8:34 NRSV). The repetitive "o" sounds of all three imperatives—*aparnēsasthō* ("deny"), *aratō* ("take up"), and *akoloutheitō* ("follow")—give readers an aural sense of imperative urgency.

While Mark frames this scene as a public call to discipleship, this lecture from Jesus has often been reduced to privatized instruction for personal piety. Such readings diminish the force of the mood of these verbs. In 8:34, Jesus redefines the ancient Hebraic concept of *messiah* through three complementary public imperatives. Jesus does not call disciples to deny something (as in the modern Western practice of Lent) but to deny the primacy of self. How? By taking up the cross. To "take up your cross" is not to endure stoically the burdens of life but rather to set oneself on the same trajectory of Jesus, thus to "follow me [Jesus]." As Sharyn Dowd notes, to deny self by taking up the cross "does not mean adopting a posture of a doormat by abandoning all sense of self. It does not mean giving up certain pleasures or desires. It means, rather, abandoning all claims to self-definition and accepting and asserting God's program for and God's claim upon one's life."[14]

While modern fashion has reduced and diminished the cross to a public fashion statement, such was hardly the case among Mark's readers. As Myers

---

11. In light of the escalating conflict, Richard Horsley writes, "Mark 8:27–33 is thus Peter's *confrontation* with Jesus more than Peter's 'confession,' which is only the opening salvo in the intensifying confrontation. . . . [I]f we survey all the other references to Peter in Mark, after the initial call and appointment of the twelve, every one portrays him as speaking stupidly or behaving faithlessly" (Horsley, *Hearing the Whole Story,* 92–93).

12. Ibid.

13. "The only ones in the text thus far who have been linked with Satan (3:22–30) are the scribal leaders. And their conflict with Jesus resulted because of their self-protecting refusal to accept the boundary transformations Jesus' preaching ministry anticipated. Peter's satanic identification here at 8:33 . . . bears the same kind of implication. Anyone who wishes to preserve the status quo, *even the status quo of messianic expectation,* cannot follow the Lord's way to the kingdom" (Blount, *Go Preach!* 132).

14. Dowd, *Reading Mark,* 89.

notes, "The 'cross' had only one connotation in the Roman empire: upon it dissidents were executed. . . . [T]he turn of phrase [take up your cross] could have no other meaning except as an invitation to share the consequences facing those who dared challenge the ultimate hegemony of Rome."[15] Nothing could have sounded less fashionable to the ears of Mark's readers than when Jesus compared discipleship to the public spectacle of the cross. With this horrific image, Jesus demands that those who would follow him move beyond the safe confines of private religious experience. To "take up your cross" is a call not to ascetic spiritual disciplines but to public ministry that confronts whatever powers prevent the saving work of God. Jesus has just told Peter that such a public ministry will inevitably lead to his suffering and death. Readers, then, are left with an unequivocal pronouncement about what it might mean to deny self, take up the cross, and follow Jesus.[16]

Jesus anticipates the jarring response to his imperative discipleship imagery by following it with a paradoxical saying in which the Twelve function as the antithesis to the saying. They are called to follow the gospel-giver selflessly; instead, they do so with an eye on profit. Jesus calls them to lose themselves for the sake of the gospel; the Twelve ask Jesus for special privileges—divine powers (6:1–7), privileged status (9:33–34), and a box seat in heavenly glory (10:35–45). Peter will later live out the tragic consequences of the first phrase of the paradoxical saying when he denies Jesus not once but three times (14:53–72). Judas will also keep company with Peter as he betrays Jesus for a small profit (14:10–11). For, as Myers comments, "Everyone, it seems, has their price. Except Jesus. On Golgotha, he will be reviled by his enemies for his commitment to 'save' others, but not his own life (15:32)."[17]

For Mark, following Jesus means delivering Jesus' transforming message not only within the safe confines of a religious institution but also to the brokers of power and the drawers of boundaries, both within and outside the church. The paradox of this Markan text is that we discover who we are not through introspective self-actualization but by discovering who Jesus is. Every time we seek to define the Messiah as a conveyor of private, spiritual blessings, we can hear our public, suffering Lord say, "Get behind me, Satan."

Mark's apocalyptic emphasis comes to the forefront in 8:38–9:1. Appropriating imagery from the apocalyptic courtroom myth in the book of Daniel

---

15. Myers, *Binding the Strong Man*, 246.

16. Blount notes the religiopolitical dimensions of Jesus' command to "take up your cross": "No doubt, since the Roman leadership desired the same socio-political stability coveted by the Israelite leadership, it would not have been too difficult for the scribal and high priestly leaders to convince the Romans that Jesus' boundary trespasses were as much a threat to them as to the traditions of Israel" (Blount, *Go Preach!* 133).

17. Myers, *Binding the Strong Man*, 247.

(Dan. 7:13–14), Mark emphasizes that following Jesus is not simply a pru-
dent choice among competing choices; it is the only choice that results in life,
despite suffering and death; and it is a choice with eternal consequences.[18]
While scholars have long debated whether 9:1 is out of place in Mark's
Gospel, both a literary and sociopolitical reading of this text favors its inclusion. Jesus has told the disciples/crowds/readers that he must suffer and die
and that they must be willing to follow at the expense of similar consequences. Mark 9:1 bridges the imperatives of Jesus with the lingering hope of
his disciples that maybe there is still a real profit to discipleship. Maybe disciples of Jesus will be spared not only suffering but also death.[19]

No sooner does Jesus expound the imperatives upon which discipleship
is founded, as well as the inevitable sacrifice and suffering that follow,
than he is transfigured (*metemorphōthē*, 9:2). Prior to his passion narrative
(14:12–15:47), Mark is largely uninterested in chronological detail. Yet he
begins this story by noting "six days later" (9:2 NRSV). Whatever its original
intent, "six days later" serves as a literary bridge from what was said "on the
way" to Caesarea Philippi to what will be seen and heard on the mountain.

Jesus takes the privileged yet theologically challenged trio—Peter, James,
and John—with him up a mountain (9:2), even as earlier he had taken only
these three disciples into the home of Jairus (5:37) and later will take only
these three into the Garden of Gethsemane (14:33). As Jesus and his disciples
climb the mountain, Mark's readers cannot miss the numerous allusions to
Moses on Mt. Sinai and need to wait only a few verses before Moses himself
arrives (9:4).[20] Elijah, though, will arrive first, reversing the chronology of

---

18. So Myers: "This mythic discourse functions to help us interpret the outcome of the story; it gives
us 'eyes to see' the apocalyptic moment of the cross as the 'glory of the Human One'. . . . [T]he disci-
ples/readers must choose which 'reality' we will trust: to be vindicated in the Danielic courtroom is to be
condemned in the Jewish/Roman one and vice versa. We either stand *with* Jesus, deny ourself and lose our
lives 'for his sake and the gospel's' (8:34f), or we stand 'ashamed' *before* him and the angels" (Myers,
Binding the Strong Man, 249).

19. Tolbert suggests a narrative function for 9:1: "Before Jesus, the kingdom is present in potential;
with Jesus, it is revealed with power. Jesus' saying to the crowds and disciples in Mark 9:1 functions perfectly well on the level of second degree narrative: 'Truly, I say to you, there are some standing here who
will not taste death before they see that the kingdom of God has come with power.' The character Jesus
speaking to other characters insists that some of them will not die before realizing that the kingdom has
already come in power. The audience, on the level of first degree narrative, affirms the truth of Jesus' saying, because it knows that Jesus himself has inaugurated that state" (Tolbert, *Sowing the Gospel*, 173).

20. Williamson summarizes the numinous elements in this pericope: "The cloud symbolizes the divine
presence (as in Exod. 13:21; 19:9, 16; 33:9; Num. 9:15). The voice from the cloud is that of God (as in
Exod. 24:15–25:1). The brightness of Jesus' garments evokes the light of the *Shekinah*, the divine pres-
ence perceived as radiance in the pillar of fire, on the mountain, in the sanctuary, and in apocalyptic visions.
That radiance was reflected in Moses when he came from talking with God on Sinai (Exod. 34:29)"
(Williamson, *Mark*, 158).

their appearances in the Old Testament.[21] Elijah's arrival reminds readers of the theophany that the prophet experienced on Mt. Horeb (1 Kgs. 19:9–12) during which he heard "a still, small voice." Arriving first on the mountain, Mark again emphasizes the important role that Elijah played in preparation for the coming Messiah.

This apocalyptic moment not only looks back to Sinai/Horeb but prepares readers to interpret the scene at hand and to look ahead to God's intended future. As Jesus is transfigured, his garments take on an unspoiled and unmistakable "whiteness" (9:4). The term *leukos* ("white") connects this story to other apocalyptic literature in which whiteness is symbolic for the clothing of faithful martyrs (e.g., Dan. 7:9–14; Rev. 3:5, 18; 4:4). In the previous passage, Jesus spoke about the "necessity" of his suffering and death; here he is portrayed in the heavenly garb of a martyr. Within Mark's narrative, the transfiguration of Jesus should provide the three disciples with definitive insight into Jesus. For Mark's readers, the transfiguration story offers little new information. Since 1:1 they have known that Jesus is the Son of God, and since the last story, they have known that the Messiah must suffer, die, and after three days, rise again.

Narratively, then, the benefit of the transfiguration of Jesus is principally for the three disciples.[22] While it is intended as an epiphany story for Peter, he experiences no epiphany when Jesus is transfigured before his eyes, only more misunderstanding and misconstrual of the man in white. Addressing Jesus not as Messiah (8:29) but as "rabbi" (9:5; cf. 11:21 and 14:45), Peter suggests that this mountaintop experience be extended. "The foolishness of Peter's response . . . [is] indicated by the narrator: 'For he did not know what to say, for they were exceedingly afraid' (9:6). Peter's inappropriate response to the incident stems from fear, the human trait that blocks out faith."[23]

While Peter is anxious to recapture the historic intimacy of the days when God "tabernacled" with Israel (9:5), Mark declares such an understanding of discipleship null and dull. For six verses, the emphasis in this story has been on the visual wonder of the transfigured Jesus. The divine response to Peter's inappropriate suggestion moves from eye to ear as God repeats the pronouncement made at Jesus' baptism (1:11; 9:7). The disciples are not to gawk at Jesus in his glory; they are to "listen (*akouete*) to him." The only literary problem is that Jesus hasn't said anything in this story. The divine

---

21. Dowd notes that this follows the order of Septuagint's translation of Malachi 3:22–24 (Dowd, *Reading Mark*, 90).

22. See Tolbert, *Sowing the Gospel*, 204–6.

23. Ibid.

imperative from the cloud, then, refers these disciples back to the prior words of Jesus in Caesarea Philippi, calling for lives that trust in the boundary-breaking power of the reign of God. Mark points his readers beyond the blindness of Peter toward the inbreaking reign of God present, not in a mute and shining Jesus, but present whenever disciples listen and respond in faith to the One through whom God is breaking into the world and in whom God is breaking down all barriers that obstruct that entry.[24] When the voice from heaven has spoken, Elijah and Moses are gone and Jesus is no longer trans-figured (9:8). The grand vision is over. Readers can only hope that by now these three dense disciples will hear distinctly and see more than "trees walking around" (8:24).

The trip down the mountain quickly proves otherwise in its comic irony. After witnessing Jesus in his martyred glory, the narrator announces this telling aside: "So they kept the matter to themselves, questioning what this rising from the dead could mean" (9:10 NRSV). This questioning comes from the same trio who accompanied Jesus into Jairus's house and witnessed the transformation of a young girl from death to life (5:37) and who have just seen Jesus in his martyred glory. To make matters worse, the disciples then ask about a scribal tradition that called for the return of Elijah as the forerunner to the Messiah. They have just seen Elijah on the mountain *alive* and talking with Jesus, and yet they ask their question as if Elijah has not yet returned. Even as Peter earlier did not understand how Jesus redefined the meaning of Messiah, so the disciples here do not understand that Elijah has come, first preaching and baptizing in the Jordan (1:3–8), then with his head on a platter at Herod's banquet (6:17–29), and now alive atop a mountain with Jesus and Moses. The fact the disciples never consider, even after the epiphany on the mountain, is that Elijah has come and was killed, as will be the One to whom he pointed, and any who follow him.

The disciples descend the mountain as if wearing a shiny cross, oblivious to the irony of such unsullied and fashionable discipleship. Mark 8:22–9:13 opens with a two-stage healing of a blind man by Jesus. The restoration of the blind man's sight by Jesus, though, was simple compared to the difficulty of getting the disciples to see the truth of what was before their very eyes. These verses open with a blind *man* and sadly close with blind *men*.

---

24. "The directive points back to Jesus' difficult message in 8:34–9:1, the one about discipleship that must be ready to endure the cross, that inevitably stands on the horizon of the preaching way. At the cli-mactic moment of the most starkly apocalyptic text in the narrative, then, the reader is directed toward the message of what it means to be a disciple who follows Jesus on the Lord's way" (Blount, *Go Preach!* 137).

View Two: "A Strange Interlude" (Mark 9:2–9)
Gary W. Charles

[Introduction: This sermon was preached on "Transfiguration Sunday" (the Sunday before Lent) at the Old Presbyterian Meeting House in Alexandria, Virginia. The congregation receives new members on each Transfiguration Sunday, and this sermon was an attempt both to listen to Mark's call to discipleship in this text and to tie it to the call of discipleship on this day.]

It's back again—just days before we will smudge foreheads with ashes and confess, if only for a moment, that we are dust and to dust we shall return. Tradition calls it the "Transfiguration Story" for lack of a better name. And it's back today like that dreaded uncle who always overstays his welcome; out in public one more time as it is every year on the Sunday before Lent. This fantastic tale interrupts Mark's gritty telling of Jesus' determined march to Jerusalem. It is a strange interlude, an odd tale that turns scholars a bright red trying to explain it away or taming it into some genteel moral lesson. But the tale is too wild to be tamed and too important to be explained away.

For the first eight chapters Mark peppers his story with a narrative urgency; things happen "immediately," "right away," "at once." Crowds swell, popularity soars, disputes heighten, and egos clash. For eight chapters, Mark hauls us on an express train to Jerusalem, pausing just long enough at each station for us to peek out the windows.

During seminary years, Jennell and I took one of those Freddie Laker, low-budget, eat-one-cheap-meal-a-day trips to Scotland to visit a college friend. We had one full day in London and decided that we would see everything the city had to offer in those twenty-four hours. We hit the Tower of London, the British Museum, Westminster Abbey, the Wax Museum, and we squeezed into St. Paul's Cathedral just seconds before the start of the final tour of the day. I was thrilled when I spotted a tiny, ancient woman who would be our docent. I thought, "At last, a chance to catch my breath." To my great dismay, she walked and talked faster than my feet or mind could manage.

Mark does much the same as he tells his Gospel at a frenetic pace, telling story after story of "the good news of Jesus Christ, the Son of God" (1:1 NRSV). In each story we almost always want more details than Mark offers. We want to know why Peter and John left their nets and what happened to their family business after they left. We want to know why Jesus healed the sick and then told those healed to keep it to themselves. We want more, but Mark gives us less. That is, until today. Until this astonishing tale. Until this strange interlude.

Surely if Mark should have kept any story short and sweet as he leads us to Jerusalem, it is this one. And, yet, instead, with this story Mark stops the train, invites us to get off, stretch our legs, and take a nice long look around. Some decline Mark's invitation and race on to the rest of the story, embarrassed to be found lingering in such incredible terrain. I say since the train is stopped and we're already off, why not take a look?

At first sight, what we see is plain enough. For the story begins with three simple words: "Six days later" (9:2a). That's a normal enough way to begin a story. "Six days later we got the results from the lab." "Six days later the package was leaning against the screen door." "Six days later" is a perfectly fine way to start a story. The only problem here is that, throughout, Mark seems remarkably uninterested in chronology, in the inevitable march of day after day. For Mark, the story of Jesus is typically not about that kind of *chronos* time, or "clock time," but about *kairos* time—time pregnant with possibility for great good or great evil. And yet this story begins with chronological specificity: "Six days later." But six days later than when?

The story continues: "Jesus took with him Peter and James and John, and led them up a high mountain apart, by themselves" (9:2b). Why take Peter and not Matthew, James and not Andrew? Why leave the other disciples down below? Hadn't they too left everything to follow Jesus? What mountain did they climb? Sinai? And why take a camping trip in the middle of a sprint to Jerusalem?

So far in this story Mark includes details that make no sense and omits details that it would only make sense to include. Then, without any word of warning Mark moves the story from black and white to color. You can almost hear Dorothy on her arrival in Oz whisper to Toto, "I don't think we're in Kansas anymore." Most English Bibles translate what happens next like this: "And [Jesus] was transfigured before them, and his clothes became dazzling white, such as no one on earth could bleach them" (9:2c–3). "Transfigured" is an English rendering of the Greek verb *metemorphōthē*, from which we get the word "metamorphosis." Written in the passive voice, Mark wants us to know that Jesus is no magician, doing tricks to dazzle this trio. No, for Mark, whatever happens "six days later" on an unnamed mountain happens by the hand of God alone. For Peter, James, and John, as well as for the readers of Mark's Gospel, the Jesus we know before the mountain—and the one we follow down the mountain—is, for this brief time, by God's hand, unmistakably transfigured.

If you think matters cannot get more bizarre, you're wrong. Next, two old mountain dwellers enter the story. Suddenly, out of nowhere, Elijah and then Moses appear (9:4). In one snapshot, Mark shows us religious history from the Ten Commandments to the prophetic tradition to the promised Messiah. On top of the mountain, we see the ultimate religious "Who's Who" reunion! At such a sight, Peter speaks the first sane words in the story. He says, "Isn't this great that we can all be here? I'll build a tent, Jesus; one for you, one for Elijah, and another for Moses" (9:5).

Just before climbing the mountain, Jesus had delivered a dreary sermon saying that he would be betrayed and die and that faithful discipleship inevitably involves suffering and tragedy and death (8:31–9:1). Atop the mountain, Peter says, "This is more like it. Give me ecstasy over suffering any day." Give me even half a choice and I'm with Peter. Just me and God's all-star religious lineup sipping tea far above the maddening cries below. After all, who wants to go below, where first-graders gun down classmates on playgrounds while political leaders grow hoarse from their bipartisan cowardice? Who wants to go below, where people pay top dollar to see gratuitous violence and sickening human behavior, degraded and at its lowest ebb? I'm with Peter. I like the metamorphosed Jesus—whiter than white, with no stain to remind him that he too is human, with no blood on him to remind him that Peter and the rest of us are also all too human.

But before Peter can drive in the first tent peg, the story continues. In case we did not get it already, Mark repeats a scene from the flatlands, from early in his Gospel when Jesus is baptized. A voice from a cloud above again announces, "This is my Son, the Beloved, listen to him!" (9:7 NRSV). The disciples look around and Moses is gone (9:8). Elijah has vanished as quickly as he had appeared and there stands Jesus all alone as the voice declares, "This is my Son, the Beloved; listen to him!" In one short phrase, Mark says that you and I won't find God by looking back or staying put.

Some look for God today by looking back to the days when everybody knew everybody else in church, when hymns were easier to sing and anthems always made your heart dance. Some look for God back in the days when children prayed in school and families sat around the dinner table for civil conversation and daily devotions. Some look for God back in the days when Sunday meant church and a delicious meal in the afternoon, followed by a leisurely walk and a restful nap.

Some are less nostalgic. They are quite content with the way things are. Like Peter, they try to hold on to moments of peace and serenity. Life is just fine the way it is. Why try something new in worship when what we do now works well? Why consider a new mission destination when we already know how to run efficient trips to Mexico and Appalachia? Why speak out on divisive issues when things are finally settled down around here? Why? Because you won't find God by looking back or staying put.

While walking down the mountain, Jesus speaks for the first time. He asks Peter, James, and John to keep a confidence, "to tell no one about what they had seen, until after the Son of Man had risen from the dead" (9:9 NRSV). You see, everyone wants a dazzling white magical Jesus who is like some untouchable and remote icon, a lucky charm, immune from the scars that come when good friends betray, trusted friends deny, and respected judges wash their hands of justice.

Mark stops their determined march to Jerusalem long enough to give us time to gaze upon a metamorphosed Jesus, to "ooh" and "aah" at the company he keeps and the clothes he wears and the acclaim he receives. And just when we start to be impressed by this strange interlude, Mark shows us the same old Jesus who walks down the mountain and climbs up a cross. Not many days later, people will go to the tomb to locate his remains (16:1–8). But, once again, we don't find Jesus by looking back or staying put.

I can't tell you where Jesus is leading this congregation, but I can tell you it is to someplace other than where we are now and someplace other than where we have ever been. It may involve occasional cozy moments atop a mountain or a solitary gaze upon rippling waves, but mostly it will involve crowded moments when there is more to do than time to do it, struggling moments when you tell others the good news about Jesus and they look at you as if you have a third eye in your forehead, truthful moments when you speak beyond the borders of your own self-interest and refuse to let stand the most comfortable lies.

Following the metamorphosed, crucified, and risen Jesus may involve crowded, struggling, and truthful moments, but it will always involve loving moments. Renegade preacher and writer Will Campbell tells the story of a wise old woman from his hometown in Mississippi. He writes, "Miss Velma Westbury used to say, 'If you just love the folks what's easy to love, that really ain't no love at all.' She said, 'If you love one, you have to love 'em all.' That is the radical message of Easter. That is the glad tidings of Christmas." Campbell adds, "Of course, some folks said Miss Velma was crazy."[25]

Some folks say Mark was crazy to include such a tale in his Gospel, a tale with a passing glimpse of the resurrection, a tale that dares us to hope beyond even the black hole of death, and so a tale in which we somehow find the courage, or more likely are given the courage, to come down the mountain, to go below where mobs scream and crosses wait and God's love does not yet rule in every heart. Maybe Mark was crazy to suggest that God's grace was

---

25. Will D. Campbell, *Soul among Lions: Musings of a Bootleg Preacher* (Louisville, Ky.: Westminster John Knox Press, 1999), 48.

enough for Jesus, was enough for Peter, James, and John, and is enough for us even on the other side of this strange interlude.

View Three: Spit Shine
Brian K. Blount

It's the spitting that gets to me. If I were somehow teleported back into time with my twenty-first-century sophistication and my doctorate in biblical studies intact, I could hang with Jesus on his colorful preaching tours out and about town. I'd cheer his touch of the leper and his reception of that bloody woman's embrace. I'd breathe a sigh of relief after hearing his interpretative challenge to the Sabbath. And, as someone whose ethnicity often singles me out even when I don't acknowledge it and no one else mentions it, I'd salute his efforts to bring sinners, tax collectors, and even Gentiles within the transformative grasp of God's coming rule. I'd be a one-man ovation celebrating his every boundary-breaking move. Whenever he put the holiness and purity codes back in their place and human beings up front in theirs, I'd shout out his name and affirm my allegiance.

I don't know about that spitting, though. You put your spit on someone and you might as well call them a dog. This ultimate show of disrespect has lived for centuries as one of the most provocative means of demonstrating one's disfavor and disgust. In our twenty-first-century society, it is so maligned an act that it brings as much disfavor on the person doing the spitting as that person had intended to shower (so to speak) on the person spit upon. It is an act so atrocious that many parents counsel their children that it should never be perpetrated in public for any reason (athletes notwithstanding). Maybe, then, that is the one purity regulation Jesus ought possibly to have kept in place. In fact, knowing what we now know about the communicative capability of saliva (the stuff conducts germs the way metal channels electricity), maybe on this occasion I might have encouraged Peter . . . you know . . . just maybe . . . with all necessary and due respect . . . to counsel our Lord that perhaps there was a better way to make his point and effect the blind man's cure than by using spit (8:23). Peter actually has enough nerve later on in the story to advise the Messiah about how he should be Messiah (8:32), so I figure he would be able to offer this much more cautious bit of advice without much of a problem. Surely a man who thought children (who would have no doubt much appreciated the coolness of Jesus' spitting) too messy to be in contact with the Lord would have been concerned with this somewhat juvenile breach of social etiquette.

The more I think about it, though, the more I think that perhaps this act, too, Jesus had carefully planned. Gary notices, quite appropriately, that there is an emphasis on touch in this section. Indeed, the power of touch, whether it be Jesus' touch of someone or someone's touch of Jesus, is on demonstrative display throughout Mark's Gospel. The touch is the mechanism that effects cures; it is also the hammer that smashes boundaries. Jesus touches people whom the purity and holiness laws say should be excluded from human community and interaction. By doing so, he reclaims them and champions an ethic of similar reclamation for anyone who would follow him and support his vision of God's coming rule.

First, there is the emphasis on the cure. The contemporary Christian hymn "He Touched Me" emphasizes the gesture's transformative power and hope. The provocative energy bottled up in Jesus explodes on contact; as walls fall, individual and communal wholeness rise up. But there is something controversial in this process of healing that is troublesome for the authority figures whose witness of the events ignites their acts of conspiracy and threat. For them, Jesus' actions are destructive; they disrupt traditions for living that had been in place for thousands of years. They threaten personal and social chaos. Maybe this is why Jesus, whose cures never before needed this kind of physical sharing to be effective, acts the way he does this time. In their blindness to his person and purpose, they cannot see that it is his activity that truly interprets God's original intent for the holiness and purity codes. Their interpretations of these codes had become legalistic measures that divide people from each other; they no longer brought them *together* before God. Jesus, therefore, in a gesture that is bound to conjure thoughts of impurity and incivility, spit as much on their improper and destructive enforcement of God's ancient traditions as he did on the man's infirmity. Ironically, by deploying the symbolism of impurity, he returned the ex-blind man to a status of cultic purity; mockingly, by wielding an unholy tool, he reclaimed for this once broken man God's full measure of wholeness. It is hard to believe that the spitting didn't make precisely the point Mark's Jesus intended it to make.[26]

Second, there is the emphasis on the one who is touched. Basketball, I am told, is as much a game of confidence as it is a game of endurance and skill. If one is a shooter one has to believe, no matter the situation, that one's shot is going to fall. A perceptive observer can tell when a player has reached that level of confidence. You can see it in the way he walks, the way she stares, the way he struts and nods as he backpedals away from another shot whose

---

26. On the impurity of saliva, see Numbers 12:14; Deuteronomy 25:9; Job 30:16; Isaiah 50:6.

only encounter on its journey through the hoop is the silky smooth touch of nylon cord. We say such a player is in a zone. We say such a player has the touch. We really mean that such a player has been touched by an assurance that whatever she throws up is coming down on target. Players don't develop that kind of confidence from salutary newspaper articles, crowds cheering their names, or even from the sometimes-comical superstitious rituals they observe before a game. They get it from knocking up against other players and from long hours in the sweat and rigor of practice. They don't *get* confidence; they *build* it. Then they go out on any given night and wield it.

Apparently, that's what Mark believes happens to Jesus and to many of the people who are transformed by him. Jesus knocks up against John the Baptist in that wilderness baptism; he is rewarded by the touch of God's Holy Spirit descending into him like a dove, driving him out into the desert (1:9–13), and from there into confrontation with human illness, doubt, ignorance, and rejection. The disciples knock up against Jesus; they are immediately touched by a call that compels their surrender of family, home, and occupation as they journey into a world of following that sees them heal, exorcise, and teach with Jesus' transformative power (1:16–20). Then there are those outsiders who knock up against Jesus in the danger and uncertainty of chaotic lives: lepers (1:40–45), tax collectors (2:14–15), the dead daughter of a distraught dad (5:21–24, 35–43), a bleeding Jewish woman (5:25–34), a grieving Gentile one (7:24–30), a blind Bartimaeus by the side of the road (10:46–52), and this spit-upon blind man begging him for help on the outskirts of the village Bethsaida (8:22–26). It is not just their contact with Jesus that makes a difference; it is, perhaps more importantly, their belief that such contact will make a difference. Unlike Jesus' own home folk whose disbelief in his authority deters and by some accounts even disables Jesus' abilities (6:1–6), these "touched" folk are Mark's narrative testimony to his readers that an honest encounter with Jesus will provide similar confidence and therefore similar transformative possibility. The message, in other words, is for us. We, too, can have the touch!

That, of course, brings me back to my concern about the spit that Jesus lathers up on the blind man as a part of his cure. This kind of touch is messy. People stoked up by their confidence in God's touch upon their lives will often perpetrate the kinds of boundary-breaking activity that wreaks havoc with long-established traditions that divide and oppress. Maybe that's why the spit is highlighted so dramatically in this story that acts as the prelude to the more important one that will follow. There, Jesus will offer up such a virulently messy vision of suffering Messiahship that a horrified Peter, acting as proxy for the other eleven disciples, will rebuke Jesus because of it (8:32). The disciples, though, miss the point. The brokenness and impurity that accompany Jesus' death are the inevitable results of a life ordered by God toward the goal of an integrated community of wholeness. By directing the disciples toward their own crosses, Jesus challenges them—and, through them, Mark's readers—to engage in similarly transformative, messy behavior.

That final point brings me to a recollection of my Aunt Didee's shoe shop. Set on a wharf hill that overlooked a peaceful river, it was one of a collection of storefronts that catered to our small town of Smithfield, Virginia. I remember the potbelly stove that heated it in winter, the high counter behind which my aunt greeted her customers, the smell of the shoe polish and shoe leather arranged all about, and the counsel of one of her workers who expounded on things most of the time mundane but sometimes metaphysical. Perhaps his discourse on the qualities of spit fit into both categories. Polish was good. A clean cloth and a broad brush were helpful. A strong but caring hand was a necessity. So was spit, he claimed, if you wanted to get a superior shine. Buff the polish up, mix the spit in, massage the leather all around, and by the time you finished, you'd be able to see your face in the shine. I loved the end; I was always, I must admit, somewhat repulsed by the means. I wondered whenever my mom took my shoes to my aunt's shop and they came back looking so bright and clean just how much of his spit was mixed into my shine. I loved the shine; I eventually got used to the spit.

I suppose that blind man at Bethsaida was a little bit like me. I can't believe he didn't flinch once or twice, or at least wonder what was going on when he heard Jesus spit. He must have figured something unusual was happening when the slobber touched his eyes. But then, *he saw*, and I imagine the mess of the miracle must have taken a backseat to the charm of the cure. Perhaps, for Jesus' disciples, it will always be like that. The messiness that comes with following Jesus' boundary-breaking ways will take a backseat to the transformations that shine in the world as a result. Perhaps, in the end, that is what Jesus' message about taking up the cross and following is all about. Through the spit of sacrifice and struggle, the glory of God's coming rule will shine. Rub it on.

8

Stay Close
Mark 9:14–10:52

View One: From Text to Sermon
Brian K. Blount

*F*or a five-year-old girl whose bicycle flight deck is an asphalt parking lot, the termination of training wheels is a big deal. I was ready to catapult her solo for the first time onto the clear oval track marked out by stationary cars to either side. But she was showing signs of aborting the launch. "I'll fall," she said. "You won't," I countered. "Trust me. You're ready to ride. You're ready to ride alone." I was certainly ready to discontinue my escort service running desperately at her side while she increasingly quickened her pace and built up her endurance. Doubled over, sweat pouring profusely down my face and across my body, clothes ruffled and dampened from the perspiration, muscles cramping, I'd look up in amazement when she'd say, "What are you waiting for, Dad? Let's go!" "I need a moment," I'd gasp. "I'm not tired," she'd come back. "You're sitting down," I'd point out. "Come on, let's go," she'd demand.

And so, on we'd go. As long as I was right beside her, hanging close, she was fine. There were times I didn't even have to hold the bike. She just wanted me there just in case she slipped. In case the front wheel caught a wayward piece of gravel, spit out its grip of the ground, and threw her off course and off balance. The last time that had happened I was right there. In what must have been no more than a half second of insecurity, I'd caught the handlebar with one hand, steadied the frame with the other, and righted her back on track. The heavy gasp and relieved smile were all the thanks I got. Or needed. That is why she was sure she needed me close.

What I had to do now, I realized, was find a way to make her feel my closeness even while I wasn't running alongside. I had to build a sense of trust in my presence even while she was riding twenty and thirty yards away. I had to instill a faith in her that even if she did fall, I'd come running to pick her up, and she'd get up and ride again. So we laid the bicycle down and had this little talk. "I'll run to the halfway point," I promised, "and then I'll stop. But I'll be able to see you and coach you no matter where you are on the track. And if you need me, I'll be right there. I won't be right beside you. But I'll be close."

In this text that moves from Mark 9:14 to 10:52, Jesus is dealing with a similarly skittish group of novices. He is preparing them to preach the reign of God with transformative power even when he is not right there walking beside them. He knows the time is coming when they will lose his physical presence completely. He must ready them to ride a hard path whose way to God is marked only by a cross. And he must ready them to do it without him. He knows they are afraid. He also knows that fear will render them powerless. And stupid. That's why he takes three separate moments to teach them. Believing that God will always be near, they need only stay close. Close to God's person. Close to God's design. Close to each other.

At the start, it's personal. Having just come down from a mountain high, Jesus finds his disciples locked in verbal combat with some scribes (9:14). After the crowd and the combatants see Jesus, they move their gaggle and their attention to him (9:15). The more they close in on him, though, the more distant Jesus feels from them. At the center of the storm is a man whose son has been held captive since his youth by a violent spirit. He believes that Jesus can help. "Had he not put some credence in the view that an omnipotent deity can intervene through a miracle worker, he would have stayed home."[1] But when the father calls Jesus by the title "teacher" (9:17), it is both an appropriate and a lamentable moment. In the Gospel of Mark, only outsiders or insiders, who act like outsiders because of their lack of faith or understanding, call Jesus "teacher."[2] He's looking Jesus in the eye, yet he's facing away.

Why wouldn't he be unsure? After all, his son's affliction is great, and Jesus' disciples have been unable to do the very thing Jesus has only recently empowered them to do (3:15; 6:7, 13). They can't exorcise the spirit; it has beaten them. The father wonders whether its longevity and leverage will beat Jesus too.

Despite this stage setting for yet another dramatic confrontation between Jesus and the demonic forces of the satanic strong man (3:21–27), Mark's emphasis is not on a cure or Jesus' ability to provide it. By now, even if the

---

1. Sharyn Echols Dowd, *Prayer, Power, and the Problem of Suffering: Mark 11:22–25 in the Context of Markan Theology* (Atlanta: Scholars Press, 1988), 109.
2. Mark 4:38; 5:35; 9:38; 10:17, 20, 35; 12:14, 19, 32; 13:1; 14:14.

disciples don't, the readers realize that Jesus has the power to transfigure any situation that confronts him. He has cured illness, fed thousands, calmed wind and wave, and even returned life to a dead little girl. Just as remarkably, only moments before this encounter in the valley, he underwent a spectacular metamorphosis up on a mountain (9:2–8). Readers realize who he is and what he can do. Mark no longer needs to highlight Jesus' messianic status. Even if that were his aim, how could a mere exorcism story outshine the fransfiguration? No, the point here lies elsewhere. Jesus' confrontation is less with an unclean spirit than it is with an "unbelieving generation" (9:19) that is singled out in the characterizations of a frantic father and dumbfounded disciples.

Even if the father speaks first, it is the disciples who come most powerfully into view. When Jesus comes preaching that the reign of God is at hand and that people should repent and *believe* (1:14–15), it is the disciples who fall in line and follow (1:16–20; 2:13–17; 10:28). They are the ones who believe. Apparently, though, like the father ("I believe; help my unbelief," 9:24), they do not yet believe the right way. Their belief is warped by unbelief (4:40; 8:17). In the same way that a cancer cell grows from a gross disruption of a healthy one and then turns on and tries to devour its sound siblings, so unbelief rises from the festering of a faith being sorely tested. Unchecked, it metastasizes into a generation of faithlessness. That is what Jesus senses in the people crowding about him. It is not only the man who isn't sure that Jesus can help him—and therefore couches his request in language like "if you can" (9:22–23)—that disturbs Jesus. It is not only the obstinacy of the scribal leaders who hound his every move, seeking a crack in his eschatological armor, that annoys him. What dismays him most is the faithlessness of his own followers. Their faith in what God is doing through Jesus' preaching of God's imminent reign does not translate into the realization of that reign's transformative power. At least not in this case. Not when the evil is this entrenched.

Interestingly enough, this critical concept of believing is used in verbal form only twice before this text. The first occurs at the signature statement of 1:15, where Jesus teaches that believing the good news is the proper response to the imminent presence of God's reign. The second plays a significant role in the scene that chronicles the death of Jairus's daughter at 5:35–43. There, too, Jesus is fighting to sustain belief in a people faced with what appears to be an intractable evil. Both the boy here and the girl there appear at one point to have been killed, the girl by her disease, the boy by the violent exit of the exorcised spirit. In both cases, Mark uses the language of resurrection (*egeirō, anistēmi*, 5:41–42; 9:27) to describe what happens after Jesus crosses the line of purity expectations and touches the "corpse" and revives it. In both cases, Jesus operates successfully despite the skepticism many of his onlookers exhibit. In both cases, Mark also gives his readers a hint as to what he means by "faith."

As becomes clear in one of the instructive texts that follows this one (9:38–41), faith for Mark is not synonymous with membership in the Markan church community. The disciples follow Jesus, but they don't always have faith. There are others who demonstrate faith and yet are not a part of Jesus' discipleship community. When Jesus tells Jairus to believe (5:36), Sharyn Dowd notes, "The call is not to become a disciple but to trust Jesus' power to help."[3] The woman with the twelve-year issue of blood is not a member of Jesus' community of followers and yet she, too, according to Jesus, demonstrates faith (5:34). Indeed, the disciples are disgruntled at 9:38–41 because someone is exorcising demonic spirits, the very thing they were just unable to do (9:18), without showing the courtesy of following "us" (9:38). The pronoun is critical. The fact that the disciples do not say that the unlicensed exorcist is not following "you" demonstrates the early church's concern that people who use Jesus' power should fold themselves into the church's communal camp. Jesus, however, sanctions the man's effort as one that demonstrates the connection between believing in the power of his name and using that power transformatively, whether or not one joins the club (9:39–41).

What does faith mean then? It does not mean to be a follower who accepts the confessional standard of the community.[4] Neither does it mean, argues Dowd, making a "positive assessment of someone's claim to speak and act for God."[5] It means, instead, a demonstration of the very thing that the woman with the twelve-year issue and the unlicensed exorcist demonstrated and the disciples here at 9:14–29 fail to demonstrate, as Dowd concludes: "Faith means confidence in the power of God to do the impossible on the behalf of the community."[6]

This is why Mark highlights Jesus' repetition of the man's halting request for help. His words, "if you are able" (9:22 NRSV), are the prototypical demonstration of doubt, the certification of his admitted "unbelief." When Jesus counters that everything is possible to the one who believes (9:23), "he challenges the child's father to share his faith."[7] Or as Sharyn Dowd puts it, "Everything is possible for God, and God will do the impossible for those who ask with confidence in God's power."[8] Faith, then, is the belief in a worldview

---

3. Dowd, *Prayer*, 95.
4. Ibid., 63.
5. Ibid., 95.
6. Ibid.
7. Hooker, *Gospel according to Saint Mark*, 224.
8. Dowd, *Prayer*, 96.

that asserts God's power to affect events in the world in ways that are impossible for humans.[9]

Dowd points out that while in pagan miracle stories faith is a consequence of the miracle, in Mark it is the necessary condition for the miracle. That certainly seems to be the gist of Jesus' statement in 9:23, or in the case of Bartimaeus (10:46–52) or the hemorrhaging woman (5:24–34). The faith that leads to the miracle subsequently appears to strengthen when God's divine power intervenes. It is precisely at this point that one needs to be careful. Mark is not saying that faith resides in the miraculous outcome; faith resides in God's *power* to *create* the miraculous outcome. Therefore, *even if there is ultimately no miracle*, God's power is not diminished. The person's worldview that God still has the power to intervene should remain intact. "Thus, the Markan Jesus' emphasis on faith seems to be a call for persistence in maintaining the community's worldview even in the face of unanswered prayer. When the requested miracle does not happen, the power of God is still not to be questioned."[10]

It is precisely at this point that the resurrection language ties this text together with the story of Jairus's daughter (5:21–24, 35–43). Ched Myers believes that both stories have major implications for doubtful disciples who are struggling with the possibility of resurrection. They may believe that it is possible in the theoretical sense, but can it really happen for Jesus? This event assures them, as it assures the father, that it is not a question of God's power; it is a question of a believer's faith. "But Jesus intervenes to 'raise up' the boy. What is the meaning of 'resurrection,' the disciples wondered? Is it not the exorcism of crippling unbelief, which renders us dead in life (9:22) rather than alive to our dying (8:35)?"[11] This is the meaning of the exorcism, to teach what the resurrection is all about. Not power. The power is a given. It is to teach about faith, which, unfortunately, is not a given.

The question is, "How does one obtain this kind of faith?" Jesus' answer is direct: by staying close to the power and reality of God through prayer (9:29).[12] Once again, in Mark's narrative there seems to be a pregnant play on words. Jesus is speaking to a possessed boy in the middle of a faithless

---

9. Jesus echoes this same belief in God's ability when he prays, "Abba, father, for you all things are possible" (14:36).

10. Dowd, *Prayer*, 110.

11. Myers, *Binding the Strong Man,* 255.

12. The emphasis on prayer in this text seems to be exclusively Markan. Matthew maintains a focus on faith in his recitation of the event and thus eliminates Mark's prayer references altogether (Matt. 17:14–20). Interestingly enough, Luke, known for his emphasis on prayer, omits the prayer emphasis here altogether (Luke 9:37–43). See Hooker, *Mark*, 225.

generation (*genea*, 9:19). Once in private conversation with his disciples, who compose a notable constituency in this faithlessness, Jesus explains that this kind (*genos*) of resistance to God can be driven out only by prayer (9:29). One wonders whether the similarity in sound would have made Mark's readers connect the kind of possession with the kind of generation in such a way that Jesus' words would have taken on an even more potent meaning. The kind of faithlessness that marks this generation can be driven out only by prayer!

Apparently, the disciples had everything else they needed for their preaching tour. They had the kind of faith that would allow them to do some healing, some authoritative teaching, and some exorcism (6:7–13, 30). But they did not have what it takes to counter such intractable resistance because their faith was not supported by the close connection with God that comes through prayer. Only *that* kind of faith could bring the changes the father and the faithless generation that accompanied him sought. The father demonstrates this "prayer" faith by positioning himself close to Jesus and seeking his help. Jesus, knowing that he will soon be physically taken from the disciples, as the following passion predictions of 9:31 and 10:33–34 demonstrate, teaches his disciples that they can similarly position themselves close to God and seek God's help through prayer.

In fact, almost every time the language of prayer occurs in Mark, it demonstrates the potency of such conversation with God for empowering transformation. Of the ten occurrences of the verb (*proseuchomai*) in Mark's Gospel,[13] half connect Jesus' prayer directly to God's power and in four others he teaches his disciples that their prayers can do the same. The only time the noun (*proseuchē*) is used outside of this text is 11:17, where Jesus proclaims that the Temple was to have been a house of prayer *for all the nations*. In other words, the Temple, through prayer, was to have been a generating station for the phenomenal kind of change represented by the destruction of the boundary that separated Jews and Gentiles from being one people before God.

This is why Mark connects his narration of the transfiguration (9:2–13) with the exorcism of 9:14–29. Using the two pieces together, Mark not only teaches the reality of God's divine power working through Jesus in human history, but also, and perhaps even more important, explains how *even amid faithlessness* humans might access that power in their often tragic daily lives. One can almost hear the combative conversation that Mark's writing engages. "Fine, Jesus was transfigured up on that mountaintop. Meanwhile, I'm down

---

13. Mark 1:35; 6:46; 11:24, 25; 12:40; 13:18; 14:32, 35, 38, 39. The only time the use of the verb does not connect with either Jesus or his disciples is 12:40, where Jesus chastises scribes for praying improperly.

here in the valley being persecuted from every side. How do I maintain belief in the reality and power of God's reign when the power of human and demonic forces seems to hold sway in human life and history?"

The answer is, "Stay close by staying in a mode of prayer!" At 11:22–25, the largest piece on prayer in Mark, the disciples are told by Jesus that anything the community of faith asks in prayer will be done for it. Here in this text Mark demonstrates that when the father prays to Jesus (9:24), Jesus delivers. Even against such improbable odds. The key is that the father, like the community in Mark 11, must *ask*. *That* is the definition of prayer. As Sharyn Dowd observes, "Jesus is empowered by God to render powerful assistance to human need, and the evangelist makes it clear that there can be no question about Jesus' willingness (1:40–41) or ability (9:22–23) to help. Jesus' power is available to those who ask for help. No one who asks fails to receive."[14]

Faith and prayer take visceral shape in the father's story when he cries out, "help my unbelief!" (9:24). Believing that Jesus can indeed change not only his son's condition but his perspective on Jesus' ability to engage it, he asks for Jesus' assistance. By Jesus' own reckoning, *that* is the definition of prayer (11:24). The father is prototypical of a person who has learned to pray. He does not depend on his own strength or merit, but realizes his weakness, acknowledges it, and yet appeals in spite of it to God's mercy. It is similar to Jesus himself who, in Gethsemane, while wrestling with God's plan, realizes that he cannot control his destiny but must submit himself and his mission to God's will (14:36).

Prayer, then, is coming close enough to God to ask for transformative assistance with the belief that God has the power to commute hopeless situations into hopeful ones, as God will do in transfiguring the cross into an apocalyptic victory. "To pray is to learn to believe in a transformation of self and world," notes Ched Myers, "which seems especially impossible—as in 'moving mountains' (11:23)."[15] The hope in Mark's text therefore pushes well beyond the yearning for an exorcism; Mark's ultimate hope is that the disciples and the generation they inhabit can evolve beyond their chronic faithlessness. They will do it only through prayer.

The two long sections that trail this one (9:30–10:31; 10:32–10:52) follow up on the importance of staying close to God through prayer. Twice (9:31; 10:33–34) Jesus warns his disciples that his time with them is rushing to what on the surface can be described only as a miserable end. Only a faithful people preoccupied with the power of prayer will be able to see the revolutionary

---

14. Dowd, *Prayer*, 1.
15. Myers, *Binding the Strong Man*, 255.

possibilities of prayer. Clearly demonstrating just how faithless and far from Jesus they remain, however, the disciples decode his remarks in the most moronic manner imaginable. Miraculously, Jesus transfigures even these less-than-stellar, simpleminded moments into opportunities for teaching. He not only tutors them about the importance of staying close to God through prayer, he also teaches them how they can stay close to, and therefore draw strength from, one another through service.

Jesus' predictions about his suffering and death emphasize his role as servant. In each of the two long sections, the punch line focuses on service. If anyone would be first, that one must be last of all and a servant of all (9:35b). The Son of Man also came not to be served but to serve and to give his life as a ransom for many (10:45). What does all this mean? Suffering is never necessary or helpful for its own sake. Suffering is valuable only when it is done in the process of service. Perhaps this is why Mark is at pains to close the final teaching statement in this section with the notation that Jesus' suffering can only be truly understood as an act of supreme service.

The way of the cross is therefore the way of servanthood. It is precisely this recognition, or lack thereof, that puts the disciples in such a bad light. The fact that they argue about greatness after each of Jesus' two predictions of his suffering (9:33–34; 10:35–45) demonstrates that they have missed the point entirely. Having recognized the necessity of suffering, they consider how the application of this necessity can raise their status before God. Suffering threatens to become the competitive standard against which true discipleship is measured. One cannot be a disciple without suffering. The more one suffers, the greater one's discipleship status becomes. Or, as Myers puts it: "If the 'way of the cross' is not religious asceticism or a pious approach to human anguish, but a concrete political choice of resistance to the powers, is it then to be identified solely with the heroism of martyrdom? And does this not immediately suggest a new elitism?"[16]

In their anxious self-interest the disciples erroneously connect the necessity of suffering with a malignant desire for status. "If I'm going to suffer, I might as well get something out of it," they seem to feel. New Testament scholar Anitra Kolenkow suggests that something ought to be status in the discipleship community that will translate, eschatologically, into status in God's coming reign.[17] Mark undercuts this distortion by connecting reward with ser-

---

16. Ibid., 257.
17. So Anitra Bingham Kolenkow ("Beyond Miracles, Suffering and Eschatology," *SBL Seminar Papers, 1973* [Chico, Calif.: Scholars Press, 1973], 161): "The problem . . . with saying that the disciples-opponents do not accept suffering is that Mark presents the disciples as accepting a demand for suffering.

vice. It is service, along with prayer, that builds up and strengthens the faith community, not suffering. Certainly not suffering for gain! At 9:41, Jesus declares that the one who serves the needs of those laboring in his name will receive reward. At 10:41, the reward of service is the status of being first. "Mark generally does not present suffering as an end in itself as in a way to gain power. Suffering is 'for me' or for the gospel or the word."[18] Suffering, therefore, becomes one form of service; service must be primary. This is why Mark uses two powerful antitheses in this set of texts. The first is in terms of the greatest versus the least, highlighted at 9:35b. Indeed, Jesus' own status is tied up not with earthly kingship, what humans might consider first, but with the sacrificing of his life and status for others. The second antithesis is expressed in terms of great versus servant. Mark 10:43 declares that whoever would be great among you must be your servant. This repeats the point of 9:36–37 that greatness develops out of service toward those of the low status in the community (e.g., children).[19] No wonder Jesus can declare that the Son of Man's primary task is one of service (10:45). Even Jesus' suffering is important only as a supreme measure of service.[20] Suffering is only the manner in which that service comes about. Jesus is not great because he suffers; his greatness lies in his service. The suffering is a means; the ministry to be imitated is the service.

Through service the members of the community stay close to each other just as they stay close to God and the soon-to-be-departed Jesus through prayer. Prayer and service, enlivened by faith, then, are the transformative tools at the believing community's disposal. This is the message Jesus is trying to teach them. The stakes are high; the transformative possibilities are huge. If they can manage to stay close! To God. And to each other.

The second of the disciples' seeking-for-power stories (10:35ff.) hinges on the issue of suffering as the basis for power. . . . Mark presents the disciples as acknowledging the necessity of suffering as a prerequisite for power."

18. Kolenkow, "Beyond Miracles," 161.

19. So D. E. Nineham, *The Gospel of St. Mark*, 252: "But in the Marcan version the point lies not in the *child's* attitude, but in the attitude of others *towards* him, the connexion presumably being that the true disciple achieves greatness not by holding great offices but by doing services to insignificant people such as the child."

20. See Hooker, *Mark*, 248. Hooker points out that readers should not be too quick to identify Jesus' suffering here with the Suffering Servant of Isaiah 53, noting that the connections between the texts are not as clear as one might think. First, the verb that Mark uses for serve (*diakoneō*, 10:45) is not used in the Greek translation of the OT in Isaiah or elsewhere. She goes on to point out that the lowly service Jesus speaks of has little thematic relationship with the honorable status of God's Deutero-Isaiah servant either. Second, Mark's choice of terminology for ransom (*lutron*) bears no relation to the Hebrew terminology used in Isaiah 53:10 which means "give an offering for sin" (*ean dōte peri harmatias*). See also Blount, *Go Preach!* 138–42.

View Two: "Stay Close" (Mark 9:14–29)
Brian K. Blount

[Introduction: In May 1994, the graduating class of Princeton Theological Seminary invited me to preach at their annual Senior Worship Service. I prepared this message for them. The service marked their final chapel celebration. I was subsequently invited to preach the sermon at the Memorial Drive Presbyterian Church in Houston, Texas.]

I remember the first time, when I was about five or six years old, that I walked unannounced through the closed door of my parents' bedroom and something other than sleeping was going on. My parents are very religious people, very devout. A child, even one so young, always wonders if a person's actions agree with a person's words. Do they do what they say, or do they only want you to do what they say, while they go on about the business of doing whatever they please? My dad, you see, has preached to me all my life, from day one, about having faith, about staying close to God in moments of difficulty. He told me once, "Brian, my back's been up against the wall many times, but God always makes a way out at just the right moment." It is the code by which he has lived his life. His back has seen the wall many times, but God has never allowed him to be crushed against it.

I was thinking about how his spirit matched his words when I went home from my Ph.D. program in Atlanta for a visit. My parents have never had a lot of money, so I've always worried about their financial health. It has been the financial wall that has most often attempted to break their spiritual backs. And so there I sat riding in the car with my father, the retired farmer, longshoreman, and meat packer of faith, and I asked him, "How are you doing?" He knew what I meant. It wasn't a question about physical health or spiritual metaphysics. Before he answered I could tell by the softness in his eyes that, yet again, the demands of life had backed him up against the wall. And when he didn't answer, I did. I said, "Seems like sometimes it never ends, doesn't it?" And then he said something I'd never expect a man of his faith to say. He said, "I think God doesn't intend for some people to have much of anything, much of any physical things." "But if you believe that," I said, "how do you keep on going? How do you keep believing? How do you keep thinking God will always make a way?"

And then he smiled and went on silently about his driving. And while he drove and smiled still, I thought, and I remembered. I remembered walking unannounced into that bedroom that first time. And there I saw them, the two of them, huddled, each against their respective sides of the bed, on their knees, their hands folded before their faces the way they were even then teaching me as a little child to fold mine before I slipped beneath the covers. Praying. Staying close. The reason the walls that break many men never broke and never will break him is that he stays close to a power that overwhelms the very powers that seek to overwhelm him. He was doing and has always done what he teaches me to do and live, to stay close to God even when circumstances and people try to convince you that you are far away.

It is the same message Jesus teaches his disciples in Mark 9:14–29. It is prayer that has the power to establish a close connection with God, that enables one who believes to perform miraculous transformations of the life conditions, the oppressive walls, that haunt so many of God's people. Or, as Ched Myers writes in his interpretation of this passage, "What is unbelief but the despair, dictated by the dominant powers that nothing can *really* change, a despair that renders revolutionary vision and practice impotent. The disciples are instructed to battle this impotence, this temptation to resignation, through prayer."[21] They are instructed to stay close.

And for those who don't know, Mark explains how they are to stay close. They are to depend on the kind of prayer exemplified by that possessed boy's father. Faith and prayer come to the father's story in the last part of his cry to Jesus, "help my unbelief!" (9:24). He asks for Jesus' assistance, and this is, by Jesus' own reckoning, the very definition of prayer (11:24). Now, on the surface those words may not seem very faithful, but this is precisely the kind of prayer faith that is necessary for receiving the power of God. The father is prototypical of a person who has learned to pray. He does not depend on his own righteous value before God, but realizes his problematic stance, acknowledges it, and yet still appeals to God's mercy. It's somewhat similar to Jesus himself who, wrestling with God's direction in Gethsemane, realizes that he cannot control his destiny but must submit himself and his mission to God's will (14:36). As one commentator writes, it is the person who realizes the inadequacy of his or her own faith, given the apparent impossibility of his or her situation, and yet continues to be entirely dependent on God, who has learned to pray.[22]

Prayer, then, is energized by faith, even, and perhaps especially, the recognition of the inadequacy of one's faith. And because of this, Mark knows that it is just as important that one understand from this story the meaning of faith. But before he tells us what faith is, Jesus shows us exactly what faith is not.

---

21. Myers, *Binding the Strong Man*, 255.
22. Eduard Schweizer, *The Good News according to Mark*, trans. Donald H. Madvig (Atlanta: John Knox Press, 1970), 190.

Faith is not following. Not even following Jesus. Not even following God. Why? Because following is never enough.

I remember sitting in a mission project board meeting at the church where I pastored, as one of the elders, furious at other elders in the church because none of them were helping him in his efforts, demanded, "All of you said when we began this clothing project, 'Willie, go on and lead, we'll follow.' Well," he growled, "you are following, but you're following from so far back that I can't see you."

No, faith is not the same thing as following. The disciples in our story are a case in point. Sure, it's obvious that they're following Jesus. But we all know what happens when crunch time comes, when Jesus has to carry that cross through the streets of Jerusalem. They're following, but they're following from so far back that Mark can't even squeeze them into the narrative frame of his story. And it is just as obvious that when it comes time to help that possessed little boy, these followers lack faith (9:17–19). We're like the disciples in many ways. We act like to be in, to belong to, to work for, to follow in membership in a church is to have faith.

I remember growing up hearing folk sing the songs like "I have decided to follow Jesus." Folk would be singing it like Jesus was right there in the choir loft with them. Oh yes, I'll follow Jesus. Singing that while you go your way, I'll follow Jesus. While you go the world's way, I'll follow Jesus. Singing about following Jesus all the way into hell and back as long as they're singing it in that comfortable, climate-controlled, pew-padded, spiritually sophisticated service of worship. But, come the next week, many of them weren't even willing to follow Jesus out to where misguided children were raising a ruckus in front of the corner Tastee Freeze, much less follow him to the foot of the cross.

Even in Mark's community, the requirement for belonging was not faith but "followership."[23] But following is obviously not enough. Look at the Gospel presentation. Followers don't believe enough to move mountains. Followers don't believe enough to cast out demons. Followers don't believe enough to stay afloat in stormy seas. Followers don't even believe enough to stand up when they are challenged in the gardens of oppression and evil and say, "Yes, I am with Jesus. Yes, I am a follower of Jesus." No, followers, yesterday and today, when times get tight and moments get tough, are too often following from so far back that it's hard for God, even with God's omni-

23. See Elizabeth Struthers Malbon, "Fallible Followers: Women and Men in the Gospel of Mark," in *In the Company of Jesus: Characters in Mark's Gospel* (Louisville, Ky.: Westminster John Knox Press, 2000), 41–69.

sciently divine 20/20 vision, to see them. Following, let me echo Mark one more time, is not faith. It will not energize efficacious prayer.

So what is the faith that will so energize our prayers? It is the kind of faith that believes God can do the impossible (9:23). This is the kind of faith the disciples did not have; this is why they failed in their exorcism attempt. They don't have the faith to resort to prayer because they don't believe that God is powerful enough to answer some prayers. This is why they fail. This is what Jesus implies in 9:29 when he says that this kind of demonic force cannot be driven out by anything but prayer. Their faithlessness is ultimately due to their prayerlessness. They don't stay close. Evidently, they resorted to everything *but* prayer. The only reason can be that prayer is dependent on faith, and it was this kind of faith that these followers of the Jesus community did not have. A person packing this kind of faith prayer has the force to perform potent, powerful, practically unbelievable transformations of possessed and oppressed human life and human lives. The disciples were offered this possibility of power but couldn't believe the possibilities and therefore lost the opportunity to transform that little boy's tragic life.

This happened because they didn't believe it, just like many modern followers don't believe it. Because we're reality-trained and even seminary-trained critics. The story just doesn't add up. The plot just doesn't pan out. The script is just too fantastic to believe. They can't possibly act this kind of transformation out. God has written a plot that no right-thinking, right-following disciple could possibly believe. These right-thinking, right-following disciples can't possibly transform the life of that possessed, we might even say oppressed, little boy.

We followers of faith are very often just like them today. I sometimes think that if God were a twenty-first-century author, the way God was a first-century author writing through someone like Jesus, we wouldn't believe the fantastic stories, the fantastic possibilities offered to us. If God were an author today, we wouldn't publish God. In fact, I think there are times when God does try to write the power of faith on human hearts today and we do indeed refuse to publish God. Why? Because God's plots are so twisted, so unlike life, so unbelievable. No one would believe the projection of power in the Gospels, in the Old Testament if it weren't written down as true. Some of us find it hard to believe it anyway. I know how it feels to send in a manuscript and have it turned back to you, rejected. Particularly a fiction one, especially when the comments suggest that the story could never happen this way, nothing could happen like this in real life. God would feel the same way with the kind of stuff God tries to get away with writing. Death being transformed into life, people being set free from oppressive powers, people being healed of infirmities that limit their potential, people being saved by a man who has the willingness and the power to sacrifice himself for others. What kind of schlock is that?

If God sent such a story to the denominational publishing houses of the twenty-first century, God had better include a self-addressed stamped envelope because we'd certainly be sending God's manuscript back. We'd tell God, go back and write it over. Nobody will believe this. Nobody will try to live this. Nobody has the power to transform the demons of inner-city death into municipal life. Nobody has the power to create avenues of communication between ethnic and racial groups that more and more converse through hateful actions. Nobody has the power to climb down into the depths of institutional oppressive evils in our communities, cities, and country and resurrect the hope for equality and change. Nobody's gonna follow all that.

People, too many Christian people and Christian leaders, have stopped trying because they know anybody who writes such a script doesn't know how to write. So our Christian leaders and our Christian folk turn to the kinds of things we think we can change. We talk about how to run our church, we talk about who ought to belong in our church, we talk about how to build new churches, we talk about how to convince more people to join our church, and we debate about what and how they ought to think and believe once they've joined, because, unbelievably, after all we've seen God do, this is all we believe we can do for God. So this is what we busy ourselves and our best minds with. Meanwhile, possessed little boys and girls are writhing in pain and hopelessness right before our genuflected feet. And when someone comes forward to demand, as Jesus does when he comes down from that mountain, that we use what we've learned to change what appears to be unchangeable outside the church, it appears to me that God finds too many followers hovering around pulpits and communion tables and not enough believers out in the muck and mud of human reality transforming the lives of those who stand with their backs against the wall.

Which will you be? Are you going to be a follower? Follow the line of graduation out the door of seminary and into the seclusion of righteous spirituality. Or are you going to stay close to God in the power of Mark's kind of prayer? You do that and I believe you will be compelled to stand against the walls, and furthermore, you'll have the power to transform these walls, to break them down, and indeed, to be transformed yourselves.

But transformed into what? Let me share something with you. I love to hear great singing, and I've heard some lately. Particularly, I've heard some powerful spirituals and been moved greatly by the music. But I always wonder when I hear spirituals sung in the wrong context. And these days that some-times means the church context. And I don't mean when they're sung in white churches by white choirs as some might suppose. I mean even when, and per-haps especially when, they're sung in middle-class African American churches. Long ago, author Zora Neal Hurston wrote that whenever the spir-itual is sung in a context other than that of the oppression out of which they arose, when the song is sung for artistic or even worship's sake, it's not really a spiritual that's being sung. And why? Because, as I argue in my own dis-sertation, the spiritual came to life and gave life in the context of hopeless struggle, like that of a father with a child whose possession will not go away. Once you take the song out of that context, it loses a great deal of its mean-ing and power. Indeed, we often change them, pacify them, domesticate them the way we do a dog we teach to lie down, go fetch and play dead. So I'm annoyed these days when I sit and hear a spiritual like "We Am Clim'in Jacob's Ladder," which I've heard several times now, where we modern Christians who think we know better the imagery of how to think, pray, and sing properly in Christ change the imagery of the slave lyrics the way we think they make better Christian sense and better peaceable impressions on the world. So, we change the ending to the song they sang in slavery. Now it goes like this: "We am clim'in Jacob's Ladder, every rung goes higher, higher, fol-lowers of the cross." I heard it sung just this way not too long ago in this very chapel. "*Followers* of the cross." The slaves weren't following; they were fighting, fighting for survival. Their ending was military. Their climbers were "*soldiers* of the cross."

I'm disturbed because even those illiterate slaves had a word for follower. They knew what followers were. They knew what following meant. If they had meant followers, they would have said followers. They didn't say it because they weren't singing about followers or following. They didn't need followers. They were praying for soldiers. Followers do just that; they follow, sometimes close, sometimes at a distance, depending on what the conditions of the following happen to be. Soldiers not only follow in ranks, they lead sometimes, sometimes they get wounded, sometimes they die, but they don't fall back unless their leader does. The slaves believed that if they were going to endure with hope in a hopeless situation, if they were going to call on God's power to threaten, challenge, and defeat oppressive power, they were going to have to help in that cause as soldiers of the cross.

I believe that today, given the massive problems that will face you as you leave this place in the cause of the Lord, given the insurmountable odds that loom before you, we don't need followers who will debate, counsel, and dis-cuss while children writhe and twist before our eyes. We need soldiers who gather phalanxes of militant troops willing to operate by any nonviolent, gospel-directed means necessary to change the conditions of our world. It's not so much what we do as that we do something, and that we do it with the attitude that we must act urgently. The little possessed boy in our Scripture had all the followers huddling around him that he could handle. The people and communities that are possessed in so many ways in our world today also have all the followers huddling in worship that they can handle. What they need more of are soldiers who stay close to the program of and the power behind the cross.

Watch the father. Despite his unbelief, he stays close to Jesus in a way that even Jesus' disciples do not. Because of his unbelief, he realizes that he needs Jesus' help, and he appeals for it, believing that Jesus can make a difference. And even after Jesus exorcises the boy, when it appears for a moment that the successful spiritual surgery has killed the patient, when the others think the child is dead (9:26), the father still apparently has not given up; there is no sense from him that Jesus has failed. This has major implications for the disciples who are struggling with the possibility of resurrection at this point. They may believe *it's possible* in the Jewish theoretical sense, but can it happen for Jesus? They don't seem to understand that it can. But this event assures them, as it assures the father, that it's not a question of God's power; it's a question of whether one has enough faith in that power. This is the meaning of the symbolic exorcism: to teach what the resurrection is all about. Not power. The power is a given. But faith. Which, unfortunately, is not.

If, then, this Scripture story does indeed have a message, a calling even, for you who are about to leave this place it is the calling to stay close to the power that comes from prayer by staying close to faith, the father's kind of faith. The kind of faith that believes that God can give you the power you need to face the social, political, and spiritual challenges you will certainly face.

But it is also the calling to stay close to the action. Prayer power not only enables, it involves the person who stays close to God through it. The kind of prayer Jesus talks about is as active as it is contemplative. It changes things. This is why you must stay close, to maintain the power to change things. And there is so very much that needs to be changed. Our church, and I don't mean just the Presbyterian Church, is a little like my great-grandmother was at ninety-six. A little old. A little tired. I remember the first time I ever saw a bottle of Geritol; it was in my great-grandmother's house. She was in her eighties at that point, and I remember asking her, "Jen, what do those things do for you?" And she smiled and said, "Baby, I've got an old body, but those Geritol pills make me feel like I've got new blood moving inside it." You know, don't you, that God intends you to be the Geritol that sweeps from this orifice of higher theological education into the bloodstream of the church? And let me tell you how much we need you.

We have a struggling church today not only in Presbyterianism but in every denomination. People stopped believing in us somewhere down the line, and I think it's because we stopped believing in ourselves. Like those disciples we became timid, unsure of ourselves, afraid to push ourselves like warriors into a battle for God's people and God's causes, because we're not soldiers any more, we've become strategic planners and tiptoeing followers. We don't engage; we talk about how others should engage. We develop committees and commissions and we plan, like those disciples, and all the while the possessed boys are groveling on the ground, the fathers are pleading, and Jesus comes down from the mountain and says, "My God, what is going on here, why are you, who have the power to help, talking and debating over here? Why aren't you out there using what I've already shown you?"

I'm not sure that there doesn't need to be a generational shift in the church where you, a new generation, can move into the church with vision and hope, with the eschatological fire of impatience that Jesus showed burning in your bellies to call us out of our sleepy spiritual and internal, in-house, overindulgent ecclesial self-concern, to be the Geritol in our lackluster blood that pumps up the church to the point of cardiac arrest, because that's where we should be and that's what I'm hoping you can begin to do for the church— instill it with a feverish capacity to engage the problems, to fight the battles, unashamed, unafraid, unwilling to stop at planning and willing to push your churches, presbyteries, conferences into a real belief that God's reign is coming imminently. And we need, not tomorrow, not when we get ourselves straight, not when the signs are feasible, not when all the people we don't want are out and all the ones we do want are in, not when we've had a chance to debate and strategize it through and through, but now, urgently, to move toward the children possessed in our own world and the fathers and mothers praying on their behalf to show and say, "Jesus sent me. I may not be able to do all he could do, but by God, I'll come out of my sanctuary and do what I can do in his name."

This is the image that Jesus and, to some extent, the father presents in the story. But not the disciples. In this school we've taught you about eschatology. For most of us that's a theological concept we've demythologized, demystified, and nullified for all practical purposes. It lives here (the head) but not here (the heart), not where it makes you move and push as if there is no tomorrow, as if we've got to make our push in the church, for the church, and even over the church if it won't get out of our mission way so that we can prepare our people, God's people, for the reality that is God's reign. That's why I think

Jesus was so frustrated. "How long am I to be with this generation that keeps on stumbling and bumbling about, doing things the way they've always been done, afraid to push with a fire in their spiritual bellies to change themselves and their world, acting like they've got all the time to argue and debate until I come down off the mountain?" he must have wondered.

"Stop waiting for me to come off the mountain, followers. Stop waiting for me to drop out of heaven, followers. I've told you what you must do, I've taught you how to do it, now stop debating about it and just do it."

But the disciples are neither close enough to Jesus' power nor close enough to the action to engage. Notice how they are having this little meeting about what they are supposed to be doing instead of doing it. They are, right here in this story, the first committee Christians. There is a boy writhing in pain right before them, and instead of using their gifts, they're off to the side having a meeting, trying to decide what to do, when Jesus has already taught them what to do. What they need to do is get back over there with the boy and start doing it.

I tell you, when I think about discipleship, about what it means to stay close to God's powerful presence through prayer and what that means for how we as soldiers engage the causes of God's struggling people, I think about playing intramural basketball here at Princeton Theological Seminary. Now anybody on my team will tell you that I'm not that great a basketball player, and I know one of the reasons why. I'm too timid. One of my student teammates used to tell me all summer how much the team needed my twenty points a game if it was going to be successful. I think I ended up supplying maybe 0.5 points a game. So that student teammate would tell me after every game, "You need to shoot more."

They say good shooters have neither conscience nor memory. They don't care that they miss a shot and they don't remember if their missed shot hurt the team effort any one time down the floor. They shoot again because it's what they do. But I'm timid because I have too much conscience and my memory has always been one of my stronger suits. I remember how embarrassed I can be when I shoot an air ball. I don't want people laughing at me, thinking I'm a poor player, which I am, but I don't want people thinking it. So I don't push myself to realize what capabilities I do have. I watch others push themselves. And I lean on their abilities because I'm scared I don't have what it takes, I'm scared I'll mess up, that I'll push to the point of no return and find out I don't have a return ticket home to safety. So I watch others score and struggle, while I run around on the edges of the action and counsel in my mind, think about whether I can do that, debate as to whether next time down I'm gonna try that too, and all the while I'm thinking and debating, while the game is going on now, my teammates need me, they don't need me to do more than I can do, they just need me to do what I can do. And I can't do that if I'm scared into committee rather than motivated into the fight.

I think this was why Jesus was so annoyed with his nine boys down in the valley. "There's a game going on, guys," he was saying. "Look at God's people hustling up and down the courts of misery, loss, oppression, disease, loneliness, and fear. I gave you the jump shot that can sink the power of sin. I gave you the spin move to wipe away the evil that hangs on to their spirits. I gave you the drive to push past those who would oppress my people as you cleared them out of the way to lead my people to the goal of hope. I gave you the ability to leap above the doubts and the fears so you could take all the chains that bind the hopes and aspirations of my people and dunk them into oblivion. So why, for God's sake, are you running up and down the court of this boy's suffering on the edge, away from the action, scared to engage? Stop worrying about how you might feel embarrassed if you can't do everything I can do! They don't need you to do everything I can do—they need you to do what you can do! Come over here, get out of the huddle of your thoughts! Get out of the huddle of your worship services, action plans, and strategy sessions, and take the ball! For God's sake, get in the game! Stay close to me, and I'll go with you into the game!"

It's the message, the powerful connection that transforms followers into soldiers.

But before I close I must come clean myself. You know, when I first heard about this invitation, my first inclination was to turn it down. Not because I'm not honored that you would ask me to preach at such an important occasion (which I am), but because I was a little afraid. Not of preaching, but of preaching in this academic context. I never preached in this chapel while I was a student, and when I returned, I honestly intended not to preach here as a professor. When I was a student it was because it always felt more like an academic exercise than a spiritual one because I felt, even then, that I was being graded. Now it's because I remember how my sermons in my community in Virginia sometimes got me into trouble, and junior professors already have all the trouble they can handle just by being junior professors. I worry about that kind of stuff all the time, it seems now. About how people perceive me. About whether I'm doing too much. Saying too much. About how far I have the resources to push myself beyond the confines of this sheltered seminary existence to work where I ought to be working in the world around it.

Used to be I was like you, sitting here, anticipating my graduation, on my way, fearless, to say anything, do anything I thought was necessary to bring about the kind of change I knew God wanted me to create. No matter what the consequences. The clerk of my presbytery disliked me, because from day one as pastor of my church, twenty-five years old, I'd say in open presbytery that our presbytery was hiding in a closet from the troubles plaguing our black Presbyterians and non-Presbyterian people, doing our little heavenly business while the commerce of hell was buying and selling the lives of black people wholesale, and I'd tell him and the presbytery over and over and over again as I pushed my church to live the mission it read about in the Scriptures. The mayor of our city wanted to jail me on occasion because I stood in city council meetings projecting economic revival plans for our black community that would empower a people she wanted to patronize.

But graduate school made me cautious because I needed to calm waves, not make them. Sometimes I'm cautious, scared still. Believe me, there will come a time when you start to worry in the same way. Worry about offending parishioners, threatening the budget, offending powerful people on the session, in the presbytery, on the deacon board, in the bishop's office, in the mayor's office, on the school board, on the chamber of commerce, in the PTA, and you start to think, you know, "I've got a family. I want to have friends. I want people to like me. I want to keep my job or secure it for a long time." So you can start to think, "Maybe I ought to do Christianity, do faith the way Brian Blount plays basketball, without risk, without doing anything that might push me to the point of no return." I'm here tonight, though, because I want to tell you, and remind myself: if that's what you've graduated to do, then maybe your presbytery can use you, maybe your bishop can use you, maybe your church can use you.

But I'm not so sure God can use you.

Appears to me, by then you're pretty much all used up. God needs soldiers, not used-up followers. God needs players who can give God twenty points every night. That's what finally came to me as I meditated on the decision to worship with you this evening. I thought about my father struggling and believing. I thought about those slaves singing and believing. In cotton fields, in cornfields, in tobacco fields, in fields of misery and hopelessness, and yet they sung the Lord's song in a foreign land. They stayed close to God, and that gave them faith and the faith gave them power. That's why they sang, "We am clim'in Jacob's ladder. We am clim'in' Jacob's ladder." God needs you on Jacob's ladder. Soldiers, yes, I said, soldiers of the cross.

View Three: Not One of Us
Gary W. Charles

The disciples of Jesus look dumb in Mark's Gospel. That statement may lack a certain religious tact and sound a bit harsh. To be kinder and gentler, then, the disciples of Jesus are *myopic* in Mark. One might object: "How can you say that, Gary? Didn't they see clearly enough to know how important Jesus was? After all, they left everything to follow him" (10:28). I would concede that point, if it were not for this exception: They "follow" one who is running first in the polls, not the second or third runner-up, nor the loser.

There is an annoying device on my office computer that rings like a muffled bell to remind me of an appointment. It tolls and is silent just long enough for me to forget about it; then it tolls again. By the third time, I know I'm already late for my meeting and I'm ready to throw this piece of advanced technology into the Potomac River. Why don't I just get up and move at the first toll or the second? I'm not altogether sure. Sometimes, it's because I think what I'm doing at that moment is more important than what I'm being called to do. Other times, I'm simply too tired to move on to another job.

In Mark's Gospel, there is a verbal bell that sounds three times trying to get the disciples' attention. It never succeeds. The first toll rings in 8:31–9:2, the second in 9:30–7, and the last in 10:32–45. In Mark 9, Jesus takes the Twelve aside and tells them what he wants no one else to know. He warns them that the road ahead leads to suffering and sacrifice, to Jerusalem—a geographical curse word for Mark, a place where prophets are spit upon, where evil prevails, and where the Son of Man will die.

In 9:31 (NRSV) Jesus warns: "The Son of Man is to be betrayed into human hands, and they will kill him, and three days after being killed, he will rise again." Twice now, Jesus has whispered this profound secret to his closest friends. In his exegesis, Brian writes, "Jesus is preparing them to preach the reign of God with transformative power even when he is not right there walking beside them. He knows the time is coming when they will lose his physical presence completely. He must ready them to ride a hard path whose way to God is marked only by a cross." After Jesus shares these dark and foreboding thoughts with the Twelve, what is their response? Mark tells us: "They did not understand what he was saying and were afraid to ask him" (9:32 NRSV). What's not to understand? And, if unclear, what makes them afraid to approach Jesus for answers?

Just when it seems Mark could not cast the disciples in a more disparaging light, it gets worse. Inside the house in Capernaum, Jesus asks them this conversation stopper: "What were you arguing about on the way?" (9:33). In Mark's narrative, Jesus has just shared his most confidential thoughts with his disciples for a second time, has shared a vision of the terror and hope ahead, and what do the disciples do? They debate which one among them is the greatest disciple. They press their togas and polish their sandals, so they will look good sitting at the head table for the heavenly banquet.

Not willing to give up on this less-than-inspired group, Jesus has yet another talk with the Twelve. To paraphrase Jesus in Mark, he says: "I'll tell you how to be great. Serve anyone and everyone in sight. People who push to the front of the line will find themselves catapulted to the rear. Those who never hope to see the front will suddenly be first in line" (9:35–37). Earlier, Jesus had told the Twelve that those who seek life will lose it (8:35); the same is true for status. You gain status in the sight of God, says Jesus, not by *debating* greatness but by serving others. The concept of faithful service to others is grasped primarily by women in Mark's Gospel, but repeatedly lost on this blind bunch of male followers.[24]

Even so, Jesus keeps trying to teach the Twelve. Recognizing that his pithy sayings have not made much difference to date, Jesus uses an old trick of the prophets. He moves a child to center stage and says, "Whoever welcomes one such child in my name welcomes me, and whoever welcomes me welcomes not me but the one who sent me" (9:37 NRSV). Given the low estimation of children of the day,[25] this enacted parable should have made perfect sense to the Twelve and surely did to Mark's readers.

Holding a child before him, Jesus talks to the Twelve about a category of existence. He speaks about those in society, no matter their age, who are always last in line and are valued the least by society. Jesus is not making a theological argument for the natal innocence of children, or that his disciples should seek such a state of innocence. Jesus is asking his disciples to extend their hands and hearts to those who often feel only the back of the hand and the hardness of the human heart. A "child" for Jesus is more akin to an outcast, a person we avoid intentionally, than to an infant whom church members coo over in a nursery.

Sounding like a twenty-first-century Mark, Will Campbell challenges the church to pay attention to this enacted parable of Jesus. About the homeless on our city streets, he writes:

> For the past few weeks, I've been out peddling books. . . . In every city I visited I inquired as to the number of people living on the streets. Then I asked how many churches, synagogues, and mosques there were. I was not too surprised to learn that in most cities there are about the same number of houseless people as there are congregations.
> Quite often when I make a speech to a church group . . . someone will

---

24. Peter's mother-in-law (1:31), the woman who anoints Jesus for burial (14:3–9), and the women who travel to the tomb with their spices (15:40–41; 16:1) exemplify Mark's positive orientation toward women disciples, though, as the Gospel closes, even the women fail to serve faithfully due to fear (16:8).

25. Myers, *Binding the Strong Man*, 266–71; Dowd, *Reading Mark*, 96–97.

say, "You complain a lot about the faithlessness of the steeples, but you never tell us what we can do to make the world better."

Well, how about this: Let every congregation adopt one person who lives on the streets. Ask no questions as to the worthiness of these people. Who among us *is* worthy? Just find them lodging, a job, friends—give them hope.

"But how would we afford it?"

The same way you afford your tall steeples, rich edifices, preachers' salaries, and all the rest. With tithes and offerings.[26]

Jesus pleads with his disciples to welcome "children" in the same way they have welcomed him into their lives. How then do the disciples respond? We have no idea; Mark is mute. Readers are left to consider that maybe Jesus has finally connected with the Twelve. Such a hope is dashed in the next scene.

Just after Jesus has both shown the disciples and twice told them that God's company includes those whom everyone else excludes, John comes running up to Jesus, sounding like a jealous schoolboy: "Teacher, we saw someone driving out demons in your name, and as he was *not one of us*, we tried to stop him" (9:38). *Not one of us*? Jesus was just holding a child before them, a living, breathing symbol in his society of *not one of us*. Jesus had just told them to welcome those who are *not one of us*.

There are few phrases in any language that are uglier than he was *not one of us*. The disciples discover someone who brings wholeness to broken lives, giving credit to Jesus for the healing. Do the disciples then come running to Jesus and say, "Hallelujah! The lame can walk. The blind can see. The possessed can think straight again"? No. They say, "Rabbi, we saw someone casting out demons in your name and we tried to stop him, because he was *not one of us*." What of the child being held by Jesus? Now, we know the disciples' response. Again, they don't get it.

Earlier in Mark 9, the Twelve could not heal a child, even though Jesus had given them the power to do so (9:14–29). Now, someone outside the inner circle casts out the demonic in Jesus' name and the disciples seek a divine restraining order. Jesus responds, "Do not stop him; for no one who does a deed of power in my name will be able soon afterward to speak evil of *me*" (9:29). Note the change in pronouns from *us* to *me*. Discipleship, in Mark, is not about people following *us*; it is about following the One who calls us. Jesus hears their report and shifts the pronoun back where it belongs: "Whoever then is not against *us* is for *us*" (9:40).

---

26. Campbell, *Soul among Lions,* 15–16.

After a short interlude, the bell tolls for the final time in Mark 10. Like a parent who won't rest until she's explained what lies ahead for her children, Jesus tells the Twelve for a third time that he will soon suffer and die and rise (10:32–34). This intimacy and pathos is immediately followed in Mark by a request from two disciples that sounds as familiar in the twenty-first century as it was in the first (10:35–37). "James and John step up, not to console him or to offer their support, but to ask a favor," observes Dowd. "It is as though they have heard and seen nothing since their vision of Jesus' glory on the mountain. The result is a grim comedy of boorish non sequitur that cannot have been lost on the Markan audience."[27]

Typical of Mark's love of repetition, the story of James and John echoes the earlier story in Mark 9 when the disciples were debating their greatness (9:33–37). Each story follows upon an intimate account of the suffering and sacrifice ahead for Jesus. In Mark 10, James and John are looking for what is due them. After all, there must some payoff for following Jesus.

Like the patient father of Luke 15:12, Jesus asks the Zebedee boys, "What is it you want me to do for you?" "Grant us to sit, one at your right hand and one at your left, in your glory," they answer (10:37 NRSV). Fast-forward to Mark 15 and his irony is almost too biting, because readers know that those who will be to the right and left of Jesus "in his glory" are two crucified thieves (15:27).

The irony in Mark 8–10 reaches a climax in this story of James and John. Despite Jesus' teaching to deny self (8:34) and his three predictions that he would suffer and die (8:31; 9:31; 10:33–34), James and John come looking for personal privilege and special status. And the other disciples fare no better! They are outraged by the behavior of their colleagues (10:41), but their outrage is a thinly veiled frustration that they had not bent Jesus' ear first.

In Mark, the glory of God is reserved for servants of God who are not looking to be well compensated for services rendered but who are willing to follow Christ even to the foot of the cross. In a recent public prayer meeting, I heard a prayer that sent a chill through me. "O God," the person prayed, "we know that you bless us with success and prosperity whenever we follow you." That is the prayer of James and John. I could almost hear Jesus respond: "Only peddlers of prosperity dish up such self-serving pablum; it is not to be so among you." Jesus asks James and John if they are able to be baptized with the baptism with which he will be baptized (10:38). They assure him: "We are able" (10:39). Mark's readers know better.

Mark closes this two-chapter account of failed discipleship with the story

---

27. Dowd, *Reading Mark*, 110.

of a blind beggar (10:46–52). Just as Jesus asked James and John, "What do you want me to do for you?" (10:36), he asks the same of Bartimaeus (10:51). James and John ask for status. Bartimaeus asks for sight. These two disciples, whom Jesus called to follow him in a prayerful, self-denying faith, cannot. Bartimaeus gains his sight but receives no such call from Jesus (10:52). Bartimaeus is told to go. Nevertheless, he follows Jesus "on the way"—Mark's shorthand for faithful, self-denying discipleship.[28]

In Mark's sharpest irony yet, this story ends at the entrance to Jerusalem. It is not only Jesus' specially selected disciples who will walk the haunting trail into Jerusalem; they will be joined by *not one of us*—Bartimaeus—once a blind man who now sees far better than the Twelve.

---

28. The language of "the way" begins as early as 1:2–3 in the conflation of Malachi 3:1 and Isaiah 40:3. As Myers notes, "Other texts function to introduce 'the way' as the central discipleship motif in the gospel" (Myers, *Binding the Strong Man*, 124). See also Mark 6:8; 8:3, 27; 9:33–34; 10:17, 32; 12:14.

9

So Who's in Charge around Here?
Mark 11:1–13:2

View One: From Text to Sermon
Gary W. Charles

*T*hey've made it to the big city and the adrenaline is running high. Each one is carrying a city map and a disposable camera in their Holy City Tours tote bags. All they need now are a few autographs and a copy of the glossy souvenir book of the Temple court, especially decorated for the High Holy Days. The bus driver insists that they not linger in the Temple, lest they miss the reenactment of Jesus' birth at noon, accompanied by a living nativity scene in Bethlehem. At the entrance to the Temple, they gladly drop in their "suggested donation" for the Scribal Benevolence Fund. Then, they queue up for a short film on "The Temple Today—Faith in Action." One of them turns to the next in line and says, "I can't believe we're here. Just pinch me."

The scene above is a composite caricature of contemporary tourist exploitation of religious sites in the Holy Land and a tongue-in-cheek portrait of the first trip to the Jerusalem Temple by the disciples in Mark's Gospel. The disciples have traveled through both Jewish and Gentile towns and villages, and now they have finally arrived at Zion, the Holy City of Jerusalem. They listen to Jesus inside the Temple, but it is as if they are wearing earmuffs. They watch Jesus toss out the moneychangers and rail against the abuses of the religious leadership, but they are too busy gazing upon the long, intricately designed robes of the scribes (12:38) to hear the intended warning. It only gets worse for this chosen elite when they walk outside the magnificently designed Jerusalem Temple and strain their necks, twisting in amazement at this architectural feat (13:1). Their amazement turns to puzzlement as Jesus tells them to look while they can, for "Not one stone will be left here" (13:2 NSRV).

Prior to Mark 11, Jesus and the religious authorities from Jerusalem clashed regularly. From as early as 3:6, Mark signals an impending epic battle to the death. This decisive battle for the religious imagination occurs in 11:1–13:2 as the Sanhedrin and their Roman partners line up in waves to spar with Jesus about issues of divine authority and scriptural interpretation. Inside the Temple, Jesus anticipates their verbal barrage by telling a parable whose point is hardly subtle (12:1–12). Meanwhile, the crowds, by their continued fascination, complicate the Temple leaders' intention to kill Jesus (11:18). Throughout 11:1–13:2, the disciples prove as unfruitful as the cursed fig tree (11:12–14, 20–25) and the leaders of the accursed Temple. By the time of Jesus' pronouncement in 13:2, readers know that the Temple will fall; they also know that Jesus is a "dead man walking." The only unknowns are the time and place of his execution.

The opening scene to 11:1–13:2 is as familiar to most readers as any text in Mark. Throughout church history, these verses have been domesticated into what is called "Palm Sunday" (11:1–11). This is an unfortunate misnomer, since there are no palms in Mark's Gospel, and the "sweet hosanna" that the church sings each year at the onset of Holy Week strips this text of its socio-political claim and diminishes its religious import. In fact, Mark spends more time describing the preparations for Jesus' entry to Jerusalem (11:1–7) than the entrance itself (11:8–10),[1] more time talking about a colt than talking about the intentions of the one who will ride it.[2]

As Jesus approaches Jerusalem, Mark addresses two levels of apocalyptic expectations. First, Mark addresses the crowd's anticipation of a coming Messiah by drawing on Old Testament prophetic and apocalyptic writings. For instance, in Zechariah 14:2–4, the battle for God's ultimate purpose is located on the Mount of Olives (Mark 11:1) and the common animal on which the messianic king would arrive is described in Zechariah 9:9 (Mark 11:2, 4, 5, 7). Though these scriptural allusions are obvious to readers acquainted with Hebrew Scripture, the way Mark employs these allusions is more satiric than historic. Myers explains: "Although this text also belongs to the liberation-of-Jerusalem tradition, it is expressly antimilitary in its tone. Jesus does *not* intend to fight for the Temple state, and the Mount of Olives will in fact be used for the purpose of judgment (13:3). This parade, then, is filled with conflicting signals, as if it intends to be a satire on military liberators."[3] Second,

---

1. As Vincent Taylor notes, "Strictly speaking, there is no Messianic entry; as in Lk. xix. 37–40, the story describes the rapturous exultation felt when the city comes in sight. When Jesus enters He is accompanied by His disciples only, and, when He has looked round at everything, He departs with the Twelve to Bethany" (Taylor, *Gospel according to St. Mark*, 452).

2. Mary Ann Tolbert writes: "More space in the episode [11:1–9] is actually devoted to securing the colt than to entering the city and the Temple. This conspicuous prediction-fulfillment interlude both validates Jesus' credentials as prophet and signals the increased importance of this role for Division Two as a whole" (Tolbert, *Sowing the Gospel*, 257).

3. Myers, *Binding the Strong Man*, 294.

as Jesus approaches and then enters Jerusalem, Mark addresses both Jewish and Christian apocalyptic expectations surrounding the Roman siege and fall of the Jerusalem Temple in 70 C.E.[4]

Mark brackets the procession of Jesus and his disciples toward Jerusalem with the words. "Those who went ahead and those who followed were shouting *(ekrazon)*" (11:9). In the previous scene, blind Bartimaeus was also "shouting" (10:47, 48). Both Bartimaeus and "those who went ahead and those who followed" shouted *(krazō)* for Jesus, identifying him as the Davidic messiah who would bring salvation to Israel and its people. Their shouts of "Hosanna" echo Psalm 118, the last Hallel psalm sung by pilgrims preparing to enter the Temple. Beginning then in 11:1, Mark sets up his readers for a clash of expectations. Will Jesus act as the obedient "son" of David and restore the lost fortunes of Israel? The crowd and disciples think so as they cheer, "Blessed is the one who comes in the name of the LORD. Blessed is the coming kingdom of our ancestor David" (11:9–10).[5]

When Jesus does not restore the Davidic kingdom, the adoring crowds shout *(krazō)*, "Crucify him!" and the disciples are nowhere to be seen (15:13–14). In Mark's Gospel, whatever kingdom Jesus is ushering in, it is not a restoration of the political privilege enjoyed by Israel during the reign of David, nor is it a confirmation of the accommodationist policies of the Sadducees, the revolutionary strategies of the Zealots, the reformist activities of the Pharisees, or the isolationist tendencies of the Essenes.

From 11:1 until 14:32–42 (Gethsemane), Mark parallels Jesus' first visit to Jerusalem and the Temple with the Jewish festival of Passover. Some scholars gloss over this parallel as either an historic observation or a narrative explanation for the timing of Jesus' arrival in the Holy City. Brian Blount suggests a more compelling thematic reason for this parallel: "Passover was celebrated as a remembrance of socio-political liberation. Jesus' entrance personifies the extension of God's kingdom power into the holy city at the time when the people were celebrating the historical extension of God's liberative power through the Exodus event. A new kind of liberation is about to take place."[6]

---

4. While scholars do not agree on whether Mark wrote before or after the fall of the Temple, most agree that he wrote in the decade either preceding or immediately following—between 60 and 80 C.E.

5. Sharyn Dowd discusses the clash of expectations of Jesus' entrance into Jerusalem: "The acclamation of the disciples in chiastic form (11:9b-10: hosanna, blessed, blessed, hosanna) is based partly on Ps 118:26. This psalm portrays a procession of thanksgiving to the Temple and emphasizes national sovereignty and defeat of Israel's enemies. In Mark, however, nationalism has been transmuted into world-transforming apocalyptic; the patriotic shout becomes a cry of welcome for the eschatological savior promised by Isaiah (33:22), whose coming inaugurates the inclusion of all the nations into the people of God (56:7)" (Dowd, *Reading Mark,* 118).

6. Blount, *Go Preach!* 144.

Blount then summarizes the conclusions of Paula Fredriksen as follows: "Jesus' [triumphal entry] near the archetypical festival of 'national' liberation (Passover) in the context of his mission ('The Kingdom of God is at hand!') would probably have been readily understood *by any Jew* as a statement the present order was about to cede to the Kingdom of God."[7]

In Mark, just as preparation to enter Jerusalem proved more dramatic than the actual entrance, so preparation for Jesus' first entrance into the Jerusalem Temple proves far more dramatic and noteworthy for Mark than the actual entrance. Unlike Matthew, Luke, or John, Mark describes a benign first entrance by Jesus into the Jerusalem halls of religious power. In 11:11, Jesus enters the Temple, looks around, leaves the Temple, and then leaves town. Despite the earlier plaintive cries of Bartimaeus and those shouting "Hosanna" on Jesus' entrance into Jerusalem, Mark's narrative insists that Jesus will "save" the people,[8] but not according to popular assumptions about the Davidic messiah. Jesus will not lead a revolt against Rome and will not restore the Temple again to its religious and political prominence. Despite establishing narrative expectations for a titanic conflict, Jesus' first visit into the Jerusalem Temple disappoints the traditional expectations for the role of Jesus and thus prepares his readers to see the messiahship of Jesus in a new way.[9]

Perhaps the most important intercalation[10] in Mark's Gospel is found in 11:12–19, a passage in which Jesus curses a fig tree, then castigates the abuses of the Temple leaders and merchants, and then is told by Peter that the fig tree has withered to its roots. Read out of context, when Jesus curses the fig tree for not producing fruit "out of season," readers are left in a quandary. Why would Jesus curse anything, much less a fruit tree for not producing fruit out of season? Read in context, however, it is one of the most powerful and condemning stories in the Gospel.

Building upon Old Testament images of the fig tree (Isa. 28:3–4; Jer. 8:13; Hos. 9:10, 16; Joel 1:7, 12; Mic 7:1), Mark uses this visual pronouncement

---

7. Ibid. See Paula Fredriksen, "Jesus and the Temple, Mark and the War," *SBL Seminar Papers, 1990* (SBL Abstracts and Seminar Papers 29; Atlanta: Scholars Press, 1990), 299.

8. The transliterated Hebrew term *hosanna* is a cry to God, meaning "save now" (e.g., 2 Kgs. 2:26; Ps. 12:2; 20:10; 28:9: 60:7; 98:1; 108:7).

9. So Myers: "Many have puzzled over this verse, complaining that it adds nothing to the narrative; but this is precisely its power—*nothing happens.* Mark has drawn the reader into traditional messianic symbolics, only to suddenly abort them. This prepares us for the shock when Jesus *does* 'intervene' in the Temple—not to restore, but to disrupt, its operations" (Myers, *Binding the Strong Man*, 297).

10. Intercalation is a favorite Markan literary technique in which he frames, or "sandwiches," one story within another, with the result that "the two related stories illuminate and enrich each other, commenting on and clarifying the meaning, one of the other" (David Rhoads and Donald Michie, *Mark as Story: An Introduction to the Narrative of a Gospel* [Philadelphia: Fortress Press, 1983], 51). See also Mark 3:20–35; 5:21–43; 14:53–72.

story to foreshadow what is to follow. Since the leadership of Israel is faithful only when it bears the fruit of righteousness, the Jerusalem Temple and
its leaders will soon be condemned like the fig tree—for not bearing fruit.
Even worse, once outside the Temple, Peter will see that the cursed fig tree
has died to its roots (11:21; cf. 4:6). Dowd explains, "It is legitimate for the
Markan Jesus to expect fruit on the fig tree (11:12–14) because his ministry
has inaugurated the reign of God, which was supposed to be characterized
by unlimited fruitfulness and abundance. The barrenness of the fig tree
reflects the faithlessness of the Temple leadership."[11] Peter and company do
not fully grasp the full import of this theological "sandwich," but Mark's
readers do. Even as it is only a matter of time before Jesus will die, so too it
is only a matter of time before this unfruitful institution and its leaders will
fall (12:1–12; 13:1–2).[12]

The second visit by Jesus to the Temple is not nearly so sedate. As soon as
he enters the Temple, Jesus "casts out" those transacting religious business there
(11:15–16). The verb Mark uses to describe the action by Jesus (*ekballō*) is the
same verb Mark uses whenever Jesus is casting out the demonic from people
or nature.[13] But, what is demonic about the customary transaction of Temple
business in preparation for Passover sacrifices? Reminding his readers of such
Old Testament allusions as Genesis 12:1–4a and, more specifically, Isaiah
49:6, Mark portrays the anger of Jesus not at commerce being conducted in
the Temple—a customary activity necessary to sustain a sacrificial system—
but at the exclusionary policies practiced within the Temple and by its leaders, practices that resulted in the Temple remaining a closed ethnic enclave.
The demonic in the Temple is the institutional boundary that assured the
Temple's ethnic particularity to the exclusion of Gentiles. Jesus condemns
such Temple practices because, as Brian Blount notes, "The house of Jewish
prayer must become a house of prayer for all the nations. This is the eschatological fruit the Temple-tree must bear. If it does not . . . it will, like the fig
tree, experience destruction."[14]

When Jesus curses the fig tree/Temple, he is pronouncing judgment on a
religious, economic, and political order that has lost its Abrahamic, Mosaic,

---

11. Dowd, *Reading Mark*, 119.
12. Tolbert adds this cogent interpretation: "Jesus' cursing of the tree is not a fretful attack on the seasonal cycles of nature but a symbolic cursing of all fruitless, faithless responses to human need. The narrator's explanation that it was not the season for figs (11:13) encourages the audience to perceive the
symbolic rather than the mundane character of Jesus' action, and the ominous finality of Jesus' words to
the tree, 'May no one ever eat fruit from you again,' suggests that time can, indeed, run out for fruitless
trees, prayerless Temples, and perhaps faithless disciples" (Tolbert, *Sowing the Gospel*, 193).
13. Mark 1:34, 39; 3:15, 22–23; 6:13; 7:26; 9:18, 28, 38. Cf. 12:8. See chapter 3, View One.
14. Blount, *Go Preach* 151.

and prophetic moorings. Both Horsley and Myers argue that Jesus' first words and actions in the Temple also reflect a critique of greed and exploitation by Temple leaders consonant with the prophecies of Malachi (Mal. 3:5, 8, 10) and Jeremiah (Jer. 7:4).[15] However, Blount and Marcus argue against such an economic explanation by focusing on Mark's language. They suggest that Mark's use of the word "bandit" (*lēstēs*, 11:17), instead of the more generic word "thief" (*kleptēs*), indicates that Jesus is condemning more than surreptitious avarice by Temple leaders.[16] They argue that this scene reflects the actions of the Zealots who had desecrated the Temple by 66–70 C.E., especially Eleazar, son of Simon. Thus Blount concludes, "The revolutionary false prophets . . . were using the Temple as a staging ground for revolutionary behavior that included the purification of the Temple, the place of *international* prayer, from Gentile presence. It is for this reason that God's intervention would result in Jerusalem's destruction rather than its restoration."[17]

As Jesus leaves the Temple for the second time (11:19), readers know that it is an institution slated for demolition. When Peter notices that the fig tree has withered to its roots (11:21), he confirms what Jesus has pronounced in the halls of power. Just as the unfruitful fig tree has withered to its roots, so too the unfruitful Temple will soon suffer the same fate. For the disciples of Jesus and for Mark's readers (living in the chaotic period just prior to or during the destruction of the Jerusalem Temple by the Romans in 70 C.E.), this prospect raised a religious question of existential urgency. If the center of religious life is no longer to be located in the Temple, then where? If no longer in a system of religious sacrifice, then in what?

In his sayings outside the Temple, Jesus anticipates the theological crisis created by the destruction of the Temple-state and its sacrificial system. If the Temple is destroyed and Temple sacrifice is no longer possible, how can believers practice a faith in God?[18] In the verses that follow, Jesus commends

---

15. Myers, *Binding the Strong Man*, 302–5; Richard A. Horsley, *Hearing the Whole Story*, 110.

16. Blount, *Go Preach!* 152–56; Joel Marcus, *The Way of the Lord: Christological Exegesis of the Old Testament in the Gospel of Mark* (Louisville, Ky.: Westminster/John Knox Press, 1992), 116–18. On the violent and political connotations of the term *lēstēs*, see Raymond Brown, *The Death of the Messiah: From Gethsemane to the Grave: A Commentary on the Passion Narratives in the Four Gospels* (New York: Doubleday, 1991), 971.

17. Blount, *Go Preach!* 154. Dowd adds, "The word *lestes* means not cheats, but muggers or pirates, who use their 'dens' not for robbing people, but for evading detection and punishment. This was Jeremiah's original complaint; the priest were relying on the supposed inviolability of the Temple to protect them from the consequences of their faithlessness" (Dowd, *Reading Mark*, 154).

18. Dowd discusses the essential role that the Temple played in ancient Judaism: "Like all ancient religions, Judaism had a tradition of understanding the Temple of the deity [as] the place where petitions were sure to be granted. Egyptian Temples, for example, had rooms in which holes in the walls represented the ears of the deity into which petitioners could speak their requests" (Dowd, *Reading Mark*, 120).

to his disciples the efficacy and possibility of a faithful life that is independent of the Temple. For Mark, "the Temple had been rejected as a failure long
before the Romans destroyed it, but because of its traditional role as the guar-
antor of the efficacy of prayer, the rejection of the Temple required a reasser-
tion of the importance of community prayer and the power available to it."[19]

Outside the Temple, Jesus assures his disciples of the power present to
them independent of the Temple-state in a life lived in faithful prayer
(11:22–25). In Mark, faith is the prerequisite for the miraculous, not the result
of miracles. Tolbert captures the essence of this Markan perspective on faith:
"Faith is the heartfelt conviction that something will be done *prior to* the
event, and, moreover, it is that conviction itself which assures the result. . . .
For Mark, the key to miracles, effective prayer, and divine forgiveness lies
within the human heart."[20] Since the Temple-state is slated for destruction, a
prayerful faith is imperative if this religious-political "mountain" is to be cast
into the sea (5:11–13).[21] "That is to say, faith entails political imagination, the
ability to envision a world that is not dominated by the powers [of the Temple-
state and Rome]," says Myers.[22]

On the third trip to the Temple (11:27f), Jesus is met by representatives of
the institutional "Trinity"—elders, chief priests, and scribes. Reminiscent of
earlier scenes in Mark 2:6–7, 16, 18, and 24 and 3:6 and 22, these religious
"authorities" challenge Jesus on the critical issues of divine authority and
scriptural interpretation. Who will speak for the future of the Temple—its current religious leaders, or an uncredentialed and itinerant interloper? From the
close of chapter 11 and throughout chapter 12, Mark presents his readers with
a fascinating chess match to settle these issues. This chess match is made all
the more enjoyable for readers because they know, in advance (1:1), who will
win. From the initial query about John the Baptist's authority (11:27–33) until
Jesus leaves the Temple for the last time (13:1), the Temple leaders are intent
on exposing Jesus as a messianic fraud, while Jesus is intent on exposing the
fraudulent piety and practices of his opponents.

As the parable of the Sower in 4:1–20 thematically informed the Markan
narrative through chapter 10, the parable of the Tenants (12:1–12) informs the
remainder of Mark's Gospel. In this parable, Jesus reframes the question of
authority raised in the earlier scene by telling a story about the abuse of author-

19. Ibid., 122.

20. Tolbert, *Sowing the Gospel*, 194.

21. Horsley elucidates the comparison: "In both his symbolic condemnation of the Romans in the
demon identified as 'Legion' and in his condemnation of the Temple, Mark portrays them as destroyed in
the Sea (5:1–20; 11:15–24)" (Horsley, *Hearing the Whole Story*, 101).

22. Myers, *Binding the Strong Man*, 305.

ity by those to whom it has been given. The parable is not subtle and the Temple leaders do not need a key to interpret its meaning (12:12). By telling this parable in the confines of the Jerusalem Temple, Jesus stares down those in power and throws down the gauntlet of religious imagination and authority.

The parable assumes that the authority of the Temple leaders is God-given. So, too, the parable critiques a long history of the Temple leaders abusing their divinely given authority. The parable pictures an authority that will soon end. It does not suggest that the religion of Israel is about to be usurped; it does maintain, however, that the religious authority of Israel's leaders is about to be taken from them.[23] Echoing Old Testament allusions from Genesis 11 (the tower of Babel) and Genesis 37 (the removal of Joseph by his brothers) as well as specific scriptural references—Isaiah 5:1–7 (the Song of the Vineyard) and Psalm 118:22–23 (the rejected stone)—this parable is replete with Markan irony and tragi-comedy.

As the story opens, the owner of a vineyard entrusts its care to a group of tenants (12:1). At the right time for fruit (unlike Jesus' expectation of the fig tree), the owner sends tenant after tenant to retrieve the fruit of the vineyard (12:2–5). Each tenant is treated with increasing violence. Some tenants return empty-handed to the owner, while others are beaten and killed. After establishing a pattern of disrespect, beatings, and killings, the story describes two absurd actions. First, the owner decides to send not a servant but his beloved son to retrieve the fruit (12:6). This decision strips the story of any verisimilitude, for why would an owner continue to send tenants in view of the violence done to them, and then his beloved son?

The second absurd action follows when the tenants decide to kill the owner's only son in order to inherit the vineyard themselves (12:7). Though some scholars do exegetical gymnastics to explain why this was a legitimate possibility, for Mark the action is intended to appear as ludicrous as the tenants' logic. The heir's death will not change the status of the tenants; it will still be the owner's property to do with what he wishes. The violent action and corrupt logic of the tenants points to the violent and exploitative means to which stewards will sometimes go to maintain their privilege, particularly the stewards/tenants of the Jerusalem Temple, that is, chief priests, Pharisees, Sadducees, and scribes. Spoken from the Temple pulpit, this parable is a verbal sword thrust by Jesus at those whose Temple platforms and policies defile

---

23. Horsley sounds an important warning: "There is no justification for taking the parable of the tenants to mean that 'the Jews' generally rejected Jesus so that the 'vineyard' is taken away from them and given to the 'Gentiles.' . . . Far from indicating some sort of break with 'Judaism' toward a mission to Gentiles and/or a newly formed community, Mark's story as a whole emphasizes the continuity between Jesus' ministry and the history and tradition of Israel" (Horsley, *Hearing the Whole Story*, 180).

the sacred trust that they have been given. The parable is not mysterious; it argues that unfaithful stewards of divinely given authority will have that authority taken from them. Lest the point of the parable possibly be missed, Mark quotes Psalm 118:22–23 to reiterate that the rejection of Jesus (the rightful heir and beloved Son) by the tenants (the Jerusalem authorities) will result in the collapse of these "wonderful stones" (13:1–2).

The Temple leaders assure readers that they are indeed the tenants in the parable by their reaction in 12:12. It comes as no narrative surprise, then, that the parable of the Tenants is followed by a series of challenges to the authority of Jesus by representative members of the Temple tenants—the Sanhedrin. In effect, what follows the parable of the Tenants is a second telling of the temptation story of Jesus from 1:12–13. The temptation now will occur not in the wilderness but in the very heart of religious power.

In the first challenge to the divine authority of Jesus (12:13–17), he is "tested" (*peirazō*, 12:15; cf.1:13) by a strange coalition of religious and political bedfellows. The challenge begins with Pharisees and Herodians falling over themselves with insincere praise of the truth-telling qualities of Jesus (12:14). Jesus responds to their duplicity by asking them why they are playing the role of Satan through their "testing" (1:13; 3:23; 4:10, 15; 8:33). The history of Christian interpretation of this text has most often missed Mark's literary intent. The Pharisees and the Herodians are not interested in debating the fine nuances of a believer's obligations to religious institution and state. They are interested in swaying public sentiment in their favor, so they can get rid of this dreamer and see what becomes of his dream (Gen. 37:20). So, they set a trap (*agreuō*, 12:13).

Jesus responds to this awkward alliance of Herodians and Pharisees by asking them to produce a denarius (12:15). He then answers them in a way that confounds his opponents and continues to confound interpreters of this text. "Give to God and give to Caesar their due" (12:17) has led some interpreters to see this as Jesus' instruction to pay to Caesar the dreaded head tax,[24] while others contend the exact opposite.[25] Mark's narrative intent is not to debate the sociopolitical obligations of believers. Mark has already told his readers that this is not a debate; it is a trap (*agreuō*, 12:13). This "trap" reveals for readers a growing wave of religious and political opposition mounting to discredit and ultimately destroy Jesus.

The next question to Jesus comes from the Sadducees, the aristocracy of Temple life (12:18–23). The Sadducees' reading of the Torah precluded any

---

24. For example, Williamson, *Mark*, 219.
25. For example, Myers, *Binding the Strong Man*, 312.

notion of the resurrection (12:18).[26] So, they set their trap by asking Jesus a question that assumes some notion of the resurrection. Like the Herodians and Pharisees in the prior episode, the Sadducees here are not looking for information. Since they do not believe in the resurrection, they would have no legitimate curiosity about an afterlife. The story, then, is an absurd trap. As Myers argues, "By a *reductio ad absurdum* it insists that Moses would not have prescribed the practice of levirate marriage if it was going to cause moral chaos in the afterlife."[27] By their willingness to use Scripture not for insight but as a debate weapon, the Sadducees' question testifies to the "withering" of faith within the Temple (11:21).

In his response (12:24–27), Jesus obliterates the boundaries of gender privilege as well as the privileges of the monied class, that is, the Sadducees.[28] Jesus insists that while the Sadducees "know" Scripture, they do not "understand" Scripture. Jesus responds to their reading of Torah with his own reading of Torah, in particular, the story of the burning bush (Exod. 3). Elizabeth Schüssler Fiorenza concludes:

> The "house" of Israel is not guaranteed in and through patriarchal marriage structures, but through the promise and faithfulness of Israel's powerful, life-giving God. . . . In God's world women and men no longer relate to each other in terms of patriarchal dominance and dependence, but as persons who live in the presence of the living God. . . . The Sadducees have "erred much" in assuming that the structures of patriarchy are unquestionably a dimension of God's world as well. So, too, all subsequent Christians have erred in maintaining oppressive patriarchal structures.[29]

The Sadducees come to Jesus to make a mockery of his authority and his grasp of Scripture. In response, Jesus makes a mockery of their abuse of authority and challenges, not their knowledge but their understanding of Scripture.[30]

The clash between Jesus and the Sadducees ends with two Greek words—

---

26. On the Sadducees, see also Josephus (*Jewish Wars* 2.8.14; *Jewish Antiquities* 18.1.4).

27. Myers, *Binding the Strong Man*, 315.

28. Horsley presents a persuasive argument for reading Mark 12:18–27 as a polemic against gender and economic exploitation and privilege (Horsley, *Hearing the Whole Story*, 222–23).

29. Elizabeth Schüssler Fiorenza, *In Memory of Her: A Feminist Theological Reconstruction of Christian Origins*, 2d ed. (New York: Crossroad, 1994), 145.

30. Williamson notes the modern relevance of the distinction between knowledge and understanding: "Jesus speaks of something other than Bible content, of which the Sadducees had good mastery. . . . They were proud of their conservative doctrines of inspiration and interpretation. In what sense, then, did they not know the Scriptures? They seemed not to know the Scriptures as the powerful word of the living God, a word which accomplishes what it says and sustains all who hear it" (Williamson, *Mark*, 224).

polu planasthe ("You are being deceived," 12:27). By already acknowledging the force of the demonic in the Temple (12:8, 15), when Jesus speaks in the passive voice—"you (pl.) are being deceived"—Mark identifies the cause of the Sadducees' confusion. Who has deceived the Sadducees? Readers will recall the source of this deception in Jesus' interpretation of an earlier parable: "These are the ones on the path where the word is sown: when they hear, Satan immediately comes and takes away the word that is sown in them" (4:15). Jesus has entered the house of the "strong man" and has bound the Herodians, Pharisees, and Sadducees in a web of their own design.

When read out of context (as it often is), the next encounter, between Jesus and a scribe (12:28–34), appears to be a softening of the Markan resolve to expose the erosive underpinnings of the Temple. Interpreters often see the scribe as a well-meaning soul who treats Jesus with respect and, in return, is respected by Jesus. When Jesus tells the scribe, "You are not far from the reign of God" (12:34), these same interpreters go in one of two directions. Either this scribe is "so near, but so far," or he is portrayed as one of the many unnamed characters in Mark just on the cusp of discipleship.

Taken narratively, however, this story lines up well with those that precede it in the Jerusalem Temple and those that will follow. By chapter 12, readers are aware that Mark associates the worst of institutional resistance and theological obstructionism with the scribes (1:22; 2:6; 2:16; 3:22; 7:1; 7:5; 8:31; 9:14; 10:33; 11:18; 11:27; 12:35; 12:38). From start to finish (14:1; 14:43; 14:53; 15:1; 15:31), Mark is consistent in his portrayal of the scribes as defenders of a religious tradition that has lost its theological moorings. Along with the Herodians, Pharisees, and Sadducees, Mark depicts the scribes as those whose authority is eclipsed by the coming of Jesus.

Prior to this exchange between the scribe and Jesus, there is a series of despicable tests of Jesus by Temple authorities (12:13–27), and then following this exchange, Jesus will warn his disciples about the religious duplicity of scribes (12:38–40). The key, then, to interpreting Mark's intent in this detailed exchange is not to read this scene romantically, as some sort of hopeful interlude to ease the narrative pathos, but tragically, in continuity with all prior encounters in the Temple. In the story of Jesus and the scribe, readers will encounter some of the sharpest Markan irony in the entire Gospel.

Addressing Jesus without using any customary title of respect (i.e., teacher or rabbi), the scribe concedes that Jesus has confounded the Sadducees (12:28). He then puts his own test to Jesus by asking Jesus a fundamental question about the ultimate source of religious authority (12:28). Jesus quotes from the Shema (Deut. 6:4f) and appends a citation from Leviticus 19:18 about obligation to neighbor (12:29–31). The scribe asks for one commandment and gets two.

Readers who are unfamiliar with the Old Testament may be tempted to hear the response by Jesus in a privatized manner: love God and treat your neighbor nicely. However, in Leviticus, "love your neighbor" was judicial shorthand for Israel not exploiting the less powerful and the stranger in its midst (Lev. 19:9–18). It meant that Israelites were to leave crops in the field for the poor and the sojourner, were not to enact laws that afforded political sanction to steal from those powerless to resist, and were not to slander those whose property could be obtained by abusing positions of privilege. "But," as Richard Horsley notes, "these injustices in violation of the Mosaic covenantal commandments are precisely what Jesus accuses the Temple rulers and their representatives of practicing almost systematically."[31]

In 12:32–33, the scribe seems to align himself theologically with Jesus. The scribe does not dismiss the importance of the sacrificial system, but he does put it in theological perspective. As in his initial exchange with Jesus, the scribe commends Jesus for his keen theological reflection. Jesus notes that the scribe has answered "wisely, sensibly" (12:34). In Mark, the scribe, then, is a "wise" *spectator* who is "not far from the reign of God." He will not get closer to God's reign by intellectual sparring with Jesus. Though "wiser" than his colleagues, the scribe is not "wise" enough to recognize that he is standing in a building that is about to crumble upon him (13:1–2), for this building houses a system that does not liberate "neighbors" but oppresses them.[32]

An assault on the theology and practices of the Temple scribes continues as Jesus asks how the scribes can teach that the Messiah is the son of David (12:35–37). On his way into Jerusalem, followers of Jesus shouted, "Blessed is the one who comes in the name of the Lord! Blessed is the coming kingdom of our ancestor David!" (11:9, 10). Once inside the Temple, Jesus responds to this misguided cheer. Jesus quotes Psalm 110:1 to insist that messianic authority existed long before David and so the Messiah cannot be an ancestor of David.

Why does Mark include this theological riddle? He wants to clarify for his readers that to follow Jesus is to resist the temptation to accommodate to Roman policies (Sadducees), to reform and purify religious practices (Essenes and Pharisees), or to overthrow Roman rule (Zealots). Mark insists

---

31. Horsley, *Hearing the Whole Story*, 200.

32. So Myers: "'Not far' once again implies that orthodoxy is not enough; it must be accompanied by the practice of justice to one's neighbor. Mark *appears* to reject the possibility of scribal discipleship. Why? Because however aware of biblical imperatives they might be, they are by definition committed to a *system* that oppresses. To repudiate that system would be to stop being a scribe within it" (Myers, *Binding the Strong Man*, 318).

that Jesus has not come to restore the Temple state to its earlier "glory" under David. Myers puts it clearly and succinctly: "Jesus is not disputing genealogy but ideology: to be 'David's son' is to stand in solidarity with the restorationist vision—that is, the relegitimation of the Temple state. . . . He will not rehabilitate the old imperial vision; indeed, the Davidic tradition must submit to the authority of the Messiah."[33]

Having attacked the theology of the scribes, in the next two scenes Jesus warns his disciples not to be duped by their liturgical splendor and pompous piety (12:38–44). Unfortunately, the New Common Lectionary often misses Mark's point when it treats this passage as two separate pericopae; in reality, they are narratively inextricable. Some scholars see 12:38–44 as an "example paradigm" in Greco-Roman rhetoric in which the scribes prove the negative example and the nameless widow the good example,[34] while other scholars see these two stories as the final repudiation of scribal practices as the widow is "devoured" (12:40, 42) by the Temple practices of the scribes.[35]

The Septuagint's version of Ezekiel 22:25 levels this charge against the religious leaders in Jerusalem: "Its princes within it are like a roaring lion tearing the prey; they have devoured (*katesthiontes*) human lives; they have taken treasure and precious things; they have made many widows within it." In Mark, the scribes are charged with behavior reminiscent of their ancestors as they devour (*katesthiontes*) the houses of widows under the guise of holiness. Donald Juel contends, "Far from offering a good example, the story of the poor widow gives an indication of why the Temple will be destroyed."[36] Juel is correct to point out the abusive institutional practices by those entrusted with care for widows and orphans (Deut. 16:11, 19–22; Isa. 1:16–17, 23). While the scribes (the powerful) focus on what special privilege they can garner, the nameless widow (the least powerful person in the Temple—a *woman*, a *widow*, an *impoverished widow*) gives away all she has to sustain an institution whose practices leave her destitute.

Juel misses, though, an important aspect of Markan irony in this story. Jesus points to this woman, not simply to condemn despicable practices of an institution charged with protecting "widows and orphans," but to direct his disciples toward her faith that is far greater than the Jerusalem "keepers of the faith"—a faith large enough to throw mountains into the sea (11:23).[37] In this

33. Myers, *Binding the Strong Man*, 319.
34. For example, Tolbert, *Sowing the Gospel*, 256–67.
35. For example, Myers, *Binding the Strong Man*, 320–22.
36. Juel, *Gospel of Mark*, 132.
37. Dowd argues against a strictly negative reading of this pericope that sees in it only a condemnation of the practices of the scribes: "[A. G.] Wright claims that Jesus *laments*, rather than *praises* her extravagant

widow, Mark reminds his readers that "those who lose their life for my sake, and for the sake of the gospel, will save it " (8:35) and prepares them for the passion narrative ahead. As Markan irony would have it, the disciples are too awed by the dress of the Temple leaders and the stonework of the Temple itself (13:1–2) to see the one disciple of note in the Temple.[38]

In 13:1–2 the scene shifts to the outside of the Temple, as Mark concludes the narrative flow that began in 11:1. Despite the withering of the fig tree and a stream of attacks on Jesus by the Temple hierarchy, when the disciples walk outside the Temple they are like schoolchildren set loose in the big city for the first time. In Mark 13, Jesus moves beyond parable and allegory and tells the disciples straightaway and with an apocalyptic pronouncement that this "beautiful" piece of stonework will be destroyed and replaced with a new "cornerstone."[39] For Mark's readers, this pronouncement challenged them to resist the nationalistic rhetoric of those who were calling for a restored Temple-state. As in Mark 11, so again in 13:2, Mark raises the most basic existential crisis for those whose faith has been centered in Temple life. Disciples/readers are left to ask themselves: How does one worship and serve the Lord without this "house of God"? Williamson sounds an alarm for followers of Jesus in any age: "Mark 13 warns against confusing religious institutions with the Kingdom of God or thinking God's future is tied to their success or failure."[40]

How are disciples of Jesus to live faithfully outside the Temple? What will happen to the One who takes on the Temple authorities? Who in their right mind would speak so defiantly against such a longstanding institution and its leaders? Given the chance, Mark might well answer those questions by suggesting that we reread the parable of the Tenants (12:1–12).

---

contribution to the corrupt and doomed Temple (Wright 1982, 262). But from her own point of view, the widow is giving, not to the scribes, the priests, or the Temple, but to God. . . . The Markan Jesus . . . points out that the widow has given to God 'that which is God's,' that is, her whole life. Her outward piety is completely consistent with her inward surrender (c.f. 7:6b). This is the example the Markan Jesus praises in 12:44 and follows in chapters 14–15" (Dowd, *Reading Mark*, 134).

38. Williamson sees the Markan symbolism in the story of the widow in the Temple: "Her gift foreshadows the one Jesus is about to make: his very life. In Mark this poor widow becomes a type of him who, 'though he was rich, yet for (our) sake became poor, so that by his poverty (we) might become rich' (II Cor. 8:9)" (Williamson, *Mark*, 234).

39. Noting a familiar pattern in Mark's rhetoric, Tolbert observes, "In structuring the opening exchange of the Apocalyptic Discourse with a chiastic repetition of the key words 'stones' (λιθοι) and 'buildings' (οικοδομαι), the implied author signals the authorial audience that the discussion to follow will explain how the rejected stone becomes the 'head of the corner'" (Tolbert, *Sowing the Gospel*, 259).

40. Williamson, *Mark*, 241.

View Two: "Nothing Left Behind" (Mark 12:38–44)
Gary W. Charles

[Introduction: For most Protestant congregations, autumn leaves announce the arrival of the annual stewardship campaign. Preachers are called on to inspire people to reexamine the grace of God and the claim of Christ on their lives. Certain biblical texts rush to the preacher's cause. One such text is what tradition has named "The Widow's Mite" (Mark 12:41–44; Luke 21:1–4). Ironically, the radical witness of this text has been lost over time. It has been used in Christian pulpits to defend that about which the text actually warns. While obviously a story that demonstrates sacrificial giving, most sermons miss Mark's biting irony that accuses religious institutions of creating destitute situations, thereby victimizing those whom they are charged to defend. Whenever we use this text and the one that precedes it (Mark 12:38–40), we need to do so with fear and trembling, praying that God will deliver the church from sacrificing the needy as we search for sacrifices. The sermon that follows was my annual effort in 2000 to give a biblical and theological foundation to a life of Christian stewardship.]

This story from Mark's Gospel is commonly known as "The Widow's Mite." Most often, though, the real name of this story is "The Preacher's Ploy." Violins play softly in the background as the preacher paints a scene that competes with the best weekday soap opera. The music grows to a swell as the wealthy in the congregation come forward and write a large check, and hits a crescendo as a poor widow drops in the meager remains of her husband's trust fund. The preacher then swoops down for the kill. She says, "Yes, the wealthy give a lot, but they also have a lot left over. The widow gives it all." A pregnant pause is followed by violins again that sound a long plaintive chord as the preacher pleads: "Dare you give anything less?"

A few years back, I was worshiping at the Riverside Church in New York City to celebrate Nelson Mandela's release from prison. The atmosphere was electric, the music outstanding, and the preaching stirred the soul. The African Methodist-Episcopal bishop of New York stood to call for the offering. He began by asking, "To what denomination do you belong?" A quick survey of the room would have revealed a rainbow of traditions, from Catholic to Pentecostal to Presbyterian. But before anyone could respond to his question, he said, "My experience is that most people belong to the Washington denomination." He held up a dollar bill and said, "Tonight, my friends, it is time to change denominations." You should have seen the dollar bills being stuffed back into wallets, the fives exchanged for tens and the tens for twenties. I have often wondered how much money "The Preacher's Ploy" produced that night.

You often hear some version of "The Preacher's Ploy" whenever this story from Mark is read during the fall financial campaign. The widow becomes the cover girl for anxious pastors trying to squeeze out every last pledge dollar to meet the budget. Poor Mark must cringe each time we reduce this story to a religious twist of the arm to get a higher pledge or some biblical lever to garner more cash for the collection. Such preachers' ploys, while popular, simply turn this profound story into an absurd moral lesson. Who in their right mind would tell their son or daughter, "I cannot put food on the table tonight, because I gave away our last dime at church this morning"? You see, "The Preacher's Ploy"—asking people to be generous like the poor widow—never really expects what it asks of people. It is often just a gimmick used by the church to put a holy face on trying to empty people's purses and pockets.

So, if this beloved story is not a simple moral lesson about giving until the bank account is empty, then what is it? To answer that question we must look back a few verses in Mark's Gospel. Looking closely, you see that Mark's story has been sliced in half—at least that is what most biblical translations and church lectionaries have done. First, they tell about Jesus publicly chiding the scribes in the Temple (12:38–40). Then, they start a whole new paragraph, and seemingly new story, about public offerings from the wealthy and a widow (12:41–4). To be fair, Mark is partly to blame for why these can easily look like two separate stories. He has a habit of telling one story in two parts that look, at first, to be two different stories; but as you dig deeper, you learn that you cannot understand one story without the other.

So, before you and I can see what Mark has in mind, we need to see that this story has two scenes and the first begins before we meet a poor widow. The setting for the story is Jerusalem, and in Mark, it is Jesus' first visit there. The place is the Temple, swarming with religious pilgrims in town for the high holy days. The time is just hours before Jesus will be arrested. The antagonists are scribes who enjoy their religious credentials, often at the expense of the weak and vulnerable.

People who think of Jesus as "meek and lowly" must blink their way through his tirade in the Temple. Jesus, in effect, does something like walking into the halls of Congress and saying, "Beware of senators and congresspeople who love their stretch limos but who close their eyes to the homeless stretched out on Constitution Avenue." Jesus enters the home base of the scribes and accuses them of fraudulent piety (11:15–19). He faults them for feeding upon accumulated privileges of their position while charmingly extorting the very ones the Mosaic laws charge them to defend—poor widows (12:40).

Jesus condemns scribes for growing hoarse in the face of oppression and need, and even worse, for conspiring to create human need. What were the scribes thinking? How could good, religious leaders remain quiet while widows were robbed of what little they had? Where was the "not far from the reign of God" (12:34) scribe when the widow dropped in her last two coins to support an institution that cared more for her money than for her? At the headquarters for religious observance, when this woman made herself destitute, what happened to these otherwise vocal scribes? Mark ends the first scene of his story with Jesus telling the Temple crowd, "They devour widows' houses and for the sake of appearance say long prayers. They will receive a the greater condemnation (12:40 NRSV).

The second scene of Mark's story (12:41–4) shifts focus but remains in the Temple Court. In those days, no collection plate was passed during Temple services. People made their offering by announcing the amount to a priest and then depositing it in one of thirteen shofar chests. These chests were designed like a tuba with a wide mouth and narrow tube to discourage busy hands from taking out rather than putting in. In this second scene, Jesus comes down from the podium, takes a seat inconspicuously in the Court, and watches everyday exchanges as people bring their offerings to the priest to be dropped into the shofar chest.

As Jesus watches quietly, many wealthy Temple members give impressive amounts (12:41). Then, he notices a widow enter the Temple court, just moments after he chastised scribes for their neglect and abuse of widows. She was not the widow of a wealthy Jerusalem Jew. She was poor (12:42), but "poor" does not do her situation justice. When Mark tells us that she gives her last two lepta, he is saying that she was down to her last dime. Like the widow of Zarephath in the reading from 1 Kings, who uses the last jar in the cupboard to feed Elijah (1 Kgs. 17:8–16), this widow in the Temple gives away all she has (12:44). There is literally nothing left behind.

Where are the scribes when this poor woman makes such an extravagant gift? Mark does not say, but, based on the first scene of the story, you might guess that they are polishing the shoes of the big contributors in the congregation, or playing golf at the country club with the Temple president, or sitting in the box seats of the hockey match with a top benefactor. Why? Because the scribes know well that it takes money to keep a religious institution alive, lots of it, and that while the public offering of a widow's last dime may be a sweet gesture, it doesn't make much difference to the institution; it won't pay the bills. Where are the scribes? They are not seeing what Jesus sees, for they are too busy pandering to the privileged. And on that count, they are not so exceptional. How easy it is for scribes and preachers and elders and congregations to lose sight of whose institution it is and why it even exists.

No wonder Jesus next takes his disciples outside and tells them, "Do you see these great buildings? Not one stone will be left here upon another; all will be thrown down" (13:1–2 NRSV). You see, the scribes were not evil people with stones for a heart. They were people like you and me who love our church and want the best for it and will do anything to make it better. Sometimes, though, we lose sight of what the church is for; we see people as a means to an end and so notice only those people who will help us reach that end. The scribes did not notice poor widows whose generous gifts to the Temple sent them home destitute; they were in the collecting business, and they welcomed every nickel and dime. Unfortunately, the widow had taken their rhetoric to heart.

The widow in the Jerusalem Temple gives to an institution that has forgotten that it is to care for widows and orphans and children, for the mentally ill and socially estranged, for the imprisoned and the physically unfit and for all those broken in body or spirit. The widow gives to an institution that no longer notices those who are in the greatest need. How easy it is for those with means not to notice those in need. Did you know that our Associate for Community Ministries spends more than forty hours each week on the phone with citizens of our city who are working two or three jobs and yet need $75 to keep their family from being evicted or to send their child to the dentist or to buy a prescription—all things we do, oftentimes grousing about the cost of housing and health care, without giving them a second thought? Did you know that hundreds of children in Alexandria cannot attend preschool because there is no more room in the superb Head Start preschool and there is too little room and there are too few scholarships in private and religious preschools like our own? Did you know that more children will starve in Mozambique this week than will die in our city during the rest of this year?

The widow gives to an institution that no longer notices those who are in the greatest need and has forgotten why it exists. And, yet, about *her*, Jesus says, "Truly I tell you, this poor widow has put in more than all those who are contributing to the treasury. For all of them have contributed out of their abundance; but she out of her poverty has put in everything she had, all she had to live on" (12:43–4 NRSV). For Mark, the widow is not unlike Jesus, who will also soon give his last red cent not to inflate the corrupt Temple treasury but to redeem God's beloved world. He will give it somewhere near the trash dump on the outskirts of town, on a cross at Golgotha, leaving nothing behind.

No wonder we like to turn this story into a nice moral lesson. After all, most of us can *spare* more money and time and energy and love for God's work than we now do. Wouldn't it be great if the Christian life could be reduced to a formula for giving that would make prayerful soul searching unnecessary? Well, this is not a nice moral lesson, and the Christian life does not come in black and white. It requires prayer and discernment and risk.

In that spirit, I hope you will respond to God's grace and the ministry of the Meeting House generously today, but *I do not hope* that you will respond like the widow. Pay attention to the whole story. Jesus does not want to leave us destitute, impoverished, unable to care for ourselves, much less unable to care for those in need. Neither does Jesus want from us the little we can *spare*, as if discipleship is a cheap and inconsequential commitment. Jesus wants from us abundant and sacrificial and extravagant lives of faithful and courageous discipleship, forever thankful for the One whose love sacrificed all for us, with nothing left behind.

View Three: Dead Man Walking
Brian K. Blount

Mark 11:1–13:2 is one of the most difficult for me to read. The poignancy of the impending pathos is almost too vibrant here. Like bright sun glare on a morning drive, it hurts my eyes to look; yet if I am to reach my destination, I must keep going. I squint and ride through it. What I can't do is avert my gaze; that is when a wreck happens. I must look into it; I must press on. In the case of Mark 11–12, that means capturing the rotting glory of the Temple and the beautiful breakdown of Jesus' ministry in one, single, paradoxical glance. Gary's exegesis sets the scene well. High up on a hill is the magnificent Temple. On the valley coming toward it is lowly Son of God. Both are vibrantly alive in this pre-Passover narrative snapshot. But at the same time, like a playful, laughing child in the final phase of comfortable hospice care, both of them are pretty much already dead.

Some years ago, the actor Sean Penn played the lead role in a film about a man on a U.S. prison's death row. The movie highlighted the angst of someone condemned to die, waiting out his time incarcerated, losing more and more of his humanity as each day passed and the moment of his killing drew near. The last and perhaps the saddest ritual of his experience was that final walk from his prison cell to the death chamber that would host the forfeiture of his life. They had a name for a man on this short walk, another character in the movie confessed. Since his end was already foreordained, since it was only now a matter of timing, even though he walked and breathed, his life had, for all intents and purposes, come to an end. He was a dead man walking.

I think of that incongruous description whenever I read these stories about

Jesus entering the city of Jerusalem in the midst of that jubilant parade and walking up to that vibrant Temple alive with the majesty of Herod the Great's financial and architectural prowess. The Temple, because it is so grand and magnificent (as Jesus' disciples note, 13:1–2), captures my attention first. It is Passover and there are thousands of pilgrims celebrating the festivities of God's power to conjure freedom in the midst of the darkest enslavement and oppression. Anticipating a most ironic show of sacrificial piety, they are readying themselves to slaughter individual animal life as the way of commemorating God's gift of their national life as a people.

The Temple, though, is not just a grand architectural marvel. It is the seat of the people's religious and secular governance.[41] It is also the symbol of their existence as a people before God. Built by Herod on the same ground as Solomon's original "house of the Lord," the Temple fostered in the people's minds the same sense of tangible connection with God's Holy Presence. God was here, and when the people came here too, they were caught up in the glory and hope of God's promise for their present and future.

There was more. The Temple also represented God's care for humankind. It was to act as a center for the kind of teaching of God's will that demonstrated how God expected the people to live before God and live with each other. This literal ground of their being was also supposed to be the symbolic guide for their living, so that the people could know God's intent for the structure of their communal living as well as Herod's architects knew the infrastructure of this building.

Clearly, though, Mark believes something had gone wrong. When Jesus enters Jerusalem and walks up for a reconnoiter of the Temple, he apparently leaves with a sense of dismay rather than joy. Mark narrates that dismay by an appeal to the only tradition of Jesus cursing something anywhere in the Gospel record (11:12–14). The fig tree that he saw on the way to the Temple also conveyed by its grand, leafy appearance that it could fill the hunger of a person in need.[42] Just as a people hungry for direction from God were flocking now toward the Temple, so Jesus, seeing this tree at a distance, drew near to seek its

---

41. Palestine was, of course, under Roman rule. In the provinces, that rule had been delegated to regional overlords like the sons of Herod the Great. In Jerusalem, the Romans ruled directly through the presence of appointed governors like Pontius Pilate. The Romans did, however, allow a certain level of secular and religious self-determination among the people of its conquered regions. In the case of Palestine, this meant allowing a limited measure of governance to the Sanhedrin, the Jewish court located at the Temple.

42. Scholars, of course, point out incessantly that it was not the season for figs. Since no one has satisfactorily explained why it was the case that the tree had leaves but not figs in an infertile season, I won't try to close the case here. I point instead to what clearly was Mark's point in the narration: Because the tree had leaves it conjured the imagery of fruit; that is the parallel between the tree and the Temple (see View One above).

sustenance. Both Jesus and the people had been fooled by appearances. Neither the tree nor the Temple were able to make good on their ostentatious displays. As furious with the tree as God was no doubt furious with the leaders of the Temple, Jesus cursed it. From that moment on, though still leafy and inviting, it was already dead. So, too, was the Temple. Jesus wouldn't formally announce its demise until Mark 13:2, but his expulsion of the merchants and overturning of the tables (11:15–19) were a prophetic premonition of God's housecleaning to come. This place was supposed to have been a house of prayer for all the nations. With its grand court of the Gentiles, it appeared to make good on the bearing of this vital fruit. But the placards around the inner walls that threatened trespassing Gentiles with death belied the deception.[43] Occupied by pious leaders who wielded purity rules as a weapon of separatism and zealous forces dedicated to the expulsion of Gentiles from the land, the Temple had become a staging ground for division and rebellion instead. For that betrayal of God's vision, the fact of its destruction had already been set. Only the timing now was in play. The Temple was a demolished building, standing.

Jesus was a dead man riding. Like the Temple, he, too, seemed so powerfully alive on the surface of Mark's narration. The scene that surrounds his entrance into Jerusalem on the back of that colt is one of the most electrifying and affirming in the Gospel. Whether they were gathered by Jesus, whether they gathered spontaneously when they saw him coming, whether they were gathered for the Passover and Jesus just happened to wander fortuitously into their mix, the fact remains that in this moment he looks every bit the Messianic Son of God Peter had proclaimed him to be (8:29). Riding in on the prophetic nostalgia of Zechariah 9:9, he is, quite simply put, a prophetic vision. The crowd knows it. That's why they sing out with those acclamations of praise, "Hosanna." "Save Now, God." "Save, now that the one who comes in your name comes to reestablish the glory of our people as when David was our king." I have heard the adulation of crowds. I have seen them stand at sporting events to signal their joy. I have been a part of them at grand events of worship as they proclaim their awe. I have been once or twice the recipient of their admiration and praise. I know that at such a moment there is no greater feeling of being alive, of being an important part of some measure of human living. Odd, then, that at just such a moment, we see the foreboding narrative shadow. We know that Jesus is already dead.

---

43. Everett Ferguson, *Backgrounds of Early Christianity* (Grand Rapids: Eerdmans, 1987), 446: "A low balustrade separated the Court of the Gentiles from the temple proper. Placed in the wall were stones bearing the inscription, 'No man of another nation is to enter within the barrier and enclosure around the temple. Whoever is caught will have himself to blame for his death which follows.'"

There are two notable points about Jesus' death. First, whereas the Temple's death is sealed by its failure to bear fruit, Jesus is a dead man riding because his life produces too much fruit. He doesn't just feed the hunger of the people; he overwhelms it. This ostentatious display of God's miraculous, transformative power is symbolized by the outrageous feedings of five (6:30–44) and four thousand (8:1–10) people from meager scraps of food. Such efforts are too much for the limited, institutionalized faculties of the leaders of the time. It is not just the quantity of the abundance, of course; it is also its quality. In a world tethered to a Temple determined to protect its identity by shunning the impure and locking out the foreigners, Jesus' symbolic distribution of "the children's bread" to both Jew and Gentile alike was not very well received. Nor were the accompanying activities that challenged food laws, Sabbath laws, and holiness codes interpreted to limit rather than open community. Motivated by a rule of God that he believed would draw all people together before God, Jesus proclaims the demise of any institution—even the Temple—that would stand in the way of the inclusive vision this rule foresaw. Here is where Mark saw the paradox come. By proclaiming the Temple's death, Jesus signed his own death warrant. Nowhere is that clearer than in his trial before the Sanhedrin when, absent of any real evidence against him (14:55–59), the high priest is stymied in his prosecution of Jesus until Jesus himself provides him with all the proof he needs (15:60–65).

The second thing about Jesus' status as a dead man walking is that Mark doesn't end the irony with his recognition that Jesus' proclamation of the Temple's death signals his own. The greater and more hopeful irony is that this dead man's death is the only hope there is for the people's communal life before God. Through him, people walking through life separated from each other and God, and therefore by definition themselves dead people walking, have an opportunity to see the pathway back to God, and therefore back to life (15:38). Sean Penn's character was a dead man walking because he was on a final, short journey to the death chamber. Ironically enough, any character who chooses to follow Jesus on his way to the cross is, according to Mark, a dying person coming to life (8:34–38). Only the reader who knows Jesus' story already can know that, even as he hangs upon the cross, Jesus is on his way to life rather than death. This one-time dead man walking hangs on the cross as a man dying to life. How odd that this very odd story gets even odder at the end. Not just for Jesus, but according to 8:35, for Jesus' followers as well. Those who follow him in his challenge to institutions like the fruitless Temple, and who therefore risk losing their lives, will save them. That, apparently, is what it means to take up one's cross and follow. That is how one dies to life.

10

Watch Out!
Mark 13:3–14:72

View One: From Text to Sermon
Brian K. Blount

*T*here would be signs. I remember that. Now that I'm a teacher, I wonder sometimes whether my students examine my preclass calisthenics with the same care I once employed in inspecting my instructors. They were always carrying something: a briefcase, lecture notes, class rolls. First thing you'd check, then, was the load. Was she bearing more than she usually bore? More papers, perhaps? Or maybe just a sterner facial expression? A longer than normal huddle with the teaching assistant was especially intriguing. What were they talking about? Why was the teaching assistant sharing the professor's paper load now? Why was he subsequently breaking toward the class while the professor retreated to sanctuary behind the lectern? You had an inkling, but now that the teaching assistant had invaded desk territory at the front of the class, you knew. He was moving fast, bombing every desktop in reach with a single sheet of paper. The handout flaunted a few lines of challenging propaganda on the top and a wide clearing below upon which you could commandeer a pen and stage a response. An unannounced quiz was popping out. Your class standing was being fired upon. Your GPA was at stake.

There was no time to prepare. Now was too late. You remember her warning you about a moment like this at the beginning of the semester. You don't remember it sinking in. Not the way some of your associates felt sunk now. She'd told you to watch out for just this kind of moment. Then she'd explained the way to watch. Watching means you don't sit passively while the semester slides comfortably by. Watching means you always do your work. Watching means you're always prepared. Watching means no matter when a moment like this one comes, you're ready. For anything. Watching means that when the test comes you won't get caught sleeping. Were you?

Were you sleeping through the semester when your moment came? Or were you ready?

The disciples weren't. Not according to Mark. Time and time again, throughout the narrative course of Mark 13–14, at one crucial moment after another, the evangelist fears that they will be caught napping. So, in many of these two chapters' major subsections, a climactic introduction or conclusion is punctuated by the imperative "watch!" (*blepete*, 13:5, 9, 23, 33). Mark builds on each of those moments until the entire episode crests with Jesus' climactic and despondent query that offers an answer even as it poses its question: "Could you not watch one hour?" (14:37). No, they couldn't. When the moment came, they weren't ready. They weren't prepared.

As early as 13:1–2, Jesus tries to ready them. Focusing on their eyes and what they can (if they keep them open) see, he directs them to look back at the grand Temple buildings they've just been ogling. "Watch them," he says. "Go ahead and watch them. People will soon watch them fall." Even though his parabolic association of a cursed, unfruitful fig tree with the cleansed, equally unfruitful Temple (11:12–25) had pretty much prefigured the Temple's doom, now Jesus comes right out and, shockingly, says it. His words ultimately spread further than his circle of friends. At 14:58, those who bear witness against him at his trial before the Sanhedrin testify falsely that he said he would himself bring the edifice down. Understandably astonished at both Jesus' prediction and the boldness it took to declare it so openly, the disciples ask when the events culminating in this dire thing will take place. It is at this point that Jesus' "look, see," turns into "watch out!"

He knows what they are looking for. In fact, his own ministry has heightened the anticipation. Because the events surrounding the Temple's destruction will be cataclysmic, he is concerned that they will read more into the chaos than they should. He therefore warns them to watch out (*blepete*) for those who will come peddling it as the moment for which they have been waiting, the dawn of God's reign. His message from verses 5 to 23 revolves around this single theme; the false messiahs who, in verse 5, attempt to take advantage of the political and military disorder, resurface in verse 22. In between, Jesus unleashes an historical review that chronicles exactly the kind of upheaval that is under way when Mark writes decades (c. 68–70 C.E.) after Jesus' death; Israel is being consumed by a war with Rome. Mark uses Jesus' earlier prediction to speak to his people's current circumstance. The watching that Jesus had commended then Mark champions now. As Werner Kelber commented, "The primary function of the first part of the speech is to refute the prophets and to discount all kingdom expectations from the war years. The war will bring suffering and death, not the full time of the kingdom."[1] Watch out for (*blepete*) anyone saying otherwise; his or her prophecy will be false.

Like Jesus, Mark is concerned because he knows that belief orders action. Anyone persuaded that the war to humble Rome was the prelude to the reign of God would feel compelled to do battle. After all, at first at least, the warlords seemed to be right. By the outbreak of hostilities in 66 C.E. a sense of apocalyptic insurrection had already reached a fever pitch. Many Jews perceived the attempt of the Roman governor Florus to pilfer gold talents from the Temple treasury to have been more than they could peaceably bear. Rome greeted their rebellious response as a declaration of war. When the initial counterstrike of Roman loyalists was defeated and driven off, competing messianic claimants and provisional government authorities dared dream of a miraculous victory. Hunkered down, and squabbling viciously over space in their Temple command base, several competing factions of Jewish freedom fighters were intoxicated by what Jesus foresaw and Mark knew was a false hope. "God," they proclaimed, "is once again fighting on our side."

That declaration seemed somewhat premature when the Roman armies of Vespasian followed up by cutting down through Galilee in the North and laying siege to the capital. Then, more good news! Just as Vespasian's forces were making a push in 68, the Emperor Nero died in Rome, and Vespasian was called back to a capital city in civic and political turmoil. Once again the rebel leaders proclaimed God's involvement and issued the invitation that all loyal Jews should join the effort to reestablish the Davidic kingdom and thereby initiate God's reign.

This projected reign seemed all the more enticing since one of its primary objectives was Gentile eviction from the land. As Joel Marcus points out, because of their literal interpretation of Zechariah 14:21, the revolutionaries were certain of God's desire for the expulsion of Gentile influence and presence.[2] Mark, because he writes to and for a community already mixed with Jews and Gentiles—presenting the Jesus who founds this community as the narrative satisfaction of Gentile hunger—finds himself in a bit of a bind. Marcus writes:

> [He] is confronted with an Israel that has taken up the cudgels against the non-Jewish world in a desperate fight for survival. In the heat of the war, and fired by apocalyptic visions of victory by a purified Israel, some Jews

---

1. Werner H. Kelber, *Mark's Story of Jesus* (Philadelphia: Fortress Press, 1979), 69.

2. Joel Marcus, *The Way of the Lord: Christological Exegesis of the Old Testament in the Gospel of Mark* (Louisville, Ky.: Westminster/John Knox Press, 1992), 160.

are prepared to take drastic steps against Gentiles and against Jews who advocate coexistence with them—that is, the sorts of people who made up Mark's community.[3]

This is what, at 13:14, Mark wants readers to understand. The abominable desecration of the Temple is caused by the Jewish rebels who, in their zealotry, misread God's intent and turn what was supposed to be a house of prayer for *all* the nations (11:17) into a staging ground for a war whose goal was to kick all the nations out. Marcus continues:

> In response to the Zealot occupation of the Temple and similar acts of "purification" of the holy land from Gentile influence, Mark tells his community—which perhaps has experienced first hand the drastic effects of these acts—that the revolutionary purge is actually a defilement, that it will precipitate divine judgment, and that the inheritance of Israel will be taken away from the Jewish leaders and turned over to a new people that prominently includes Gentiles in its ranks (12:9).[4]

These *new* people, Mark suggests, are *us*! That is why we must watch out!

Reactionary Roman soldiers would be indiscriminate in their rage against the people, *all the people*, of Israel. Mark's people included. Zealot Jews would find Mark's community equally despicable for its unpatriotic, boundary-disturbing stance. Caught in the middle, they could therefore not afford to be caught off guard. And so in 13:9–13, the text framed by the watch commands (*blepete*) of 13:5 and 13:22, Jesus' "watch out, don't be misled" turns into "watch out, take care!" The imperative "see" (*blepete*) in 13:9 has switched from a concern about general historical travails that will beset all of Israel to troubles that will specifically afflict the readers in Mark's community.

At 13:10, the center point of this central text, Jesus clarifies for Mark's readers precisely why they will have become such pariahs. In this fragile world of Jew/Gentile disruption, they must preach a gospel of universal inclusion, precisely the kind of gospel no one on either the Zealot Jewish or the imperial Roman side wanted to hear. The command to preach *this* good news is the glue that ties this apocalyptic chapter together. As Timothy Geddert puts it, "We should pause before accepting the commonly held position that Mark 13:10 is an intrusive element weakly tied to a tightly knit literary pattern. Perhaps it is part of a pattern as well. The mission question, especially as it relates

3. Joel Marcus, "The Jewish War and the Sitz Im Leben of Mark," in *Journal of Biblical Literature* 111 (1992): 453.
4. Ibid., 455–56.

to the Gentiles, might prove to be more significant in Mark 13 than is usually noted."[5]

The eschatological significance of the verse is established by Mark's choice of wording; Mark's community *must* act, for as G. R. Beasley-Murray puts it, "The Gospel is to be preached at all costs."[6] This is no mere indicative statement of what their future *may* bring; it is a command that the listening/reading community participate in the universal preaching task at hand. *This* is *how* they watch! They must not be misled into fighting for the exclusion of Gentiles from the land. They must instead do all they can to preach the contrary news (gospel) that the invitation into God's coming reign is every bit as sure for Gentiles as it is for Jews.

That is why, in the second half of this sermon (13:24–37), Jesus unleashes the highest concentration of purely apocalyptic symbolism in the entire book. Particularly in verses 24–27, where the overtly mythical language describes the darkening of the three celestial lights (Isa. 13:10; 32:7; Amos 8:9; Joel 2:10) and the coming of the Son of Man (Dan. 7:13) on the clouds of heaven to gather the elect (Isa. 11:11, 16; 27:12; Zech. 2:6–11; 10:6–11; *1 En.* 57; *Pss. Sol.* 11:3), the focus shifts from historical review to apocalyptic vision. The command to watch (i.e., to preach this good news about God's coming reign to *all* the nations) obtains its urgency from that vision. Unlike the earlier cataclysms, this event *is* the end; it will be precipitated in verse 26 by Jesus' return as Son of Man. This is the same return to which he testifies in open and hostile court at 14:62. He will return to gather those who remain true to the course of resisting the impulse of segregationist rebellion (watch out, don't be misled!) and preach the good news of God's eschatological invitation to all people despite the cost (watch out, take care!). Therefore, despite your fear, despite the hostility, preach Jesus' inclusive word. When he returns as Son of Man, *this* is what you want him to find you doing! Watch out; don't get caught off guard!

Mark 13:28–31 appears to suggest that there will be time to prepare if one stays awake to the signs popping up all around. Jesus' mini-parable directs his followers and Mark's readers to pay attention to God's eschatological clues with the same vigor they pay to seasonal indicators in nature. It seems there just might be a way to anticipate the sudden coming of God's reign after all. This was certainly good news; the person who could anticipate could also prepare. But then, remarkably, verse 33 eliminates the very security Jesus'

---

5. Timothy J. Geddert, *Watchwords: Mark 13 in Markan Eschatology* (Sheffield: Sheffield Acadmic Press, 1989), 146.

6. G. R. Beasley-Murray, *A Commentary on Mark Thirteen* (London: Macmillan, 1957), 41.

preceding words had just offered. Now Jesus explains that no one except God will know the hour of his return as Son of Man. Not even him! The implication is certain; don't try to anticipate it.

Still, the resulting emphasis can't be "don't look for it," since Jesus clearly declares that signs of its coming will be evident. He must mean that there is instead no way to anticipate either it or the signs that will come immediately prior to it. By the time one sees the signs, the event itself will be so close behind that there won't be time to prepare. You will know it is coming, but if you haven't already been preparing, in that moment you will not have time to do so. The message, then, must be Get Ready Now! Be Ready All The Time! *That* Time Can Come, It Will Come At Any Moment!

A subtle but potent shift emphasizes the point: without warning, Jesus' vocabulary for "see!" changes. Up to this point he has depended on the Greek verb *blepō*. In fact, he will introduce this new section with it at 13:33: "Watch Out!" he will repeat. "You don't know when this reign of God moment will come." Apparently, though, Jesus now requires a word that can do heavier verbal lifting. Though he maintains the imperative emphasis, he switches now to a different verb *(grēgoreō)*. There is a distinction between the two words for watching as Mark's Jesus uses them. *Blepō* refers to the kind of correct spiritual discernment that protects a disciple from being misled by external appearances (4:14, 24; 8:15, 18; 12:38). *Grēgoreō* has a different function; it deals specifically with correct behavior (14:34, 37, 38). In the parable that follows, verses 33–37, Jesus leans upon this new "see" verb in order to make the case that his people must, in their anticipation of his return, watch, which is to say, *act* in a new way. What appears on the surface to be perhaps a counsel to wait in passivity is actually a call to move. According to Timothy Geddert, "The Markan parable seems to speak its message most clearly if the primary call is to be a faithful watchman [*sic*] *on the master's behalf* because he is away, rather than to be a faithful watchman [*sic*] *for his appearance* because he is returning."[7] The disciple must concentrate not on looking for the return but on his or her actions prior to it. "The point at issue is not whether or not a disciple will be found faithfully at his [*sic*] post at the single and precise instant of the master's return," argues Geddert. "The point at issue is whether or not he [*sic*] has been faithful *right through* the long night of waiting."[8]

Mark, then, by placing these terms in the same narrative context, has developed the understanding that accurate spiritual perception (*blepō*) must lead directly to faithful behavior (*grēgoreō*). The evangelist does not advocate

7. Geddert, *Watchwords*, 105.
8. Ibid.

spiritual perception for its own sake but directs it forcefully, through the plan of the entire chapter, toward active behavior. Knowing (discerning), that is to say, seeing the reality of the reign of God, the disciple is called to "watch," to act, to preach the universal reality of that reign.

At 13:9–13, Jesus had, of course, promised that faithful believers would pay a heavy price for the proclamation of this universal reign of God. Now, in the very next chapter, Mark reminds his readers just how much it will cost Jesus. Mark 14 opens with a narration about the efforts of the chief priests and scribes to arrest and destroy Jesus during the Passover (14:1–2). He follows up that narration with the bad news that Judas, one of Jesus' twelve confidants, will deliver his teacher into their hands (14:10–11). The narrative that once had Jesus telling his disciples to "watch out!" now seems to be playing the message back to Jesus himself. "Watch out, they're coming to get you!"

Mark doesn't dwell long here, though, because he knows Jesus needs neither warning nor instruction. He has seen his coming death all along and has tried to prepare his obtuse followers for it (8:31; 9:31; 10:33–34). Three times, though, following three clear predictions about his upcoming trial, death, and resurrection, his disciples miss the point and act in most unfortunate ways (8:31–9:2; 9:33–37; 10:35–45).[9] No one seems capable of doing what Jesus kept telling them to do in chapter 13; no one seems able to "watch/see" (*blepō*) sufficiently so that he or she will be able to "watch/act" (*grēgoreō*) appropriately. It is at just this despondent point that Mark wants us to "watch" the dubious dinner behavior of a rather unusual woman (14:2–9).

Her story starts with Jesus once again acting like a messianic maverick. Mark tells his readers that the Messiah, the one who will come on the clouds of heaven to initiate the holy and pure reign of God, is sitting at meal in a leper's house. The language of leprosy entered Mark's narrative story at 1:40–45 where, in equally outrageous fashion, Jesus demonstrated a complete disregard for the purity laws by touching a leper before cleansing him. Now, according to Mark, he's even taken to eating with such people. As Morna Hooker notes, "The words [Simon the leper] probably shocked Mark's original hearers, reminding them once more that Jesus deliberately associated with outsiders."[10]

Still reeling from this recognition, Mark's readers are now introduced to a character who is as much a troublemaker as the teacher himself. Out of nowhere, she intrudes on the meal of these men, who certainly would have had much more important matters at hand than dealing with anything *she* had

---

9. See chapter 8, View One.
10. Hooker, *Gospel according to Saint Mark*, 328.

to do or say. One can almost hear the disciples muttering in the narrative background, "Watch out! What's she up to?"

She is up to something obviously unreasonable. Without hesitation, she dumps what is apparently almost a year's worth of wages, money that could obviously have gone into mission, onto Jesus' head (14:3). She has wasted a precious resource. The attentive reader, the one who "sees," knows, however, that her unreasonable action fits right in here. After all, this isn't a reasonable text. First, the leaders of God's people are trying to kill the emissary God has sent to lead them (14:1–2). Second, the emissary God had sent to lead a holy and pure people is sitting in the impure, unholy abode of a man marked by impurity. And third, there's this unnamed, unannounced, unanticipated woman flitting about. Given all this, a reader shouldn't expect reason, at least human reason, to dictate Mark's plot. We get this point immediately, of course, when Jesus says, "Let her alone" (14:6). When he asks them, "Why do you trouble her?" he appears to miss their point about her waste. Jesus, it appears, is now the one who does not "see." He seems to be the one who does not understand. Haven't they already made it clear that her actions do not jibe with Jesus' own orientation of his ministry toward the poor?

That, though, may well be Mark's point; they are presently focused *too much* on the poor. Jesus' ministry was really about the reign of God and human preparation for it. This is the same point Jesus made at 2:18–20, when he taught that fasting, though a way to respond to the presence of God's reign, was not equal to that reign itself. Therefore, in the presence of the one who represented that reign, appropriate response to him was more appropriate even than this most vital ritual act.[11] Just so, one way to prepare for that reign was to help the poor. But that aid, as great an act as it was and is, was only a response to the nearness of the reign; it was never to be equated with the reign itself. This is a crucial point. Even such noteworthy activity as caring for the poor does not take first place; being ready for the reign takes first place!

One gets ready, of course, by "watching," by seeing what others miss. The female protagonist of 14:2–9 is an outsider; she's not one of Jesus' named Twelve, and she's a woman interacting with men in a public space.[12] Yet, she can see something that the insiders miss. She can see the moment, Jesus'

---

11. So Hooker: "The contrast in both Mark 2 and 14 is between those who rejoice in the presence of Jesus and those who are concerned—however sincerely—to do what the law requires [e.g., fasting and almsgiving]" (Hooker, *Mark*, 329).

12. As R. E. O. White explains, "The superiority of the male was assumed—in *religion*, as in the heart of the synagogue liturgy the Jew thanked God that he was not made a woman; in *law*, in the rules governing inheritance and divorce; and in *social custom*, as illustrated in aloofness towards women in public places—even relatives" (R. E. O. White, *Biblical Ethics* [Atlanta: John Knox Press, 1979], 59).

moment, coming. She is watching while, even now, they are sleeping (cf. 14:37, 40–41). It could be that she sees what is going to happen to Jesus, that she reads the signs, recognizes the predicament Jesus' behavior has put him in, and anoints his body for burial. Jesus implies this by the way he speaks at 14:8. She knows this story is not going to end well.

But the implication of Jesus' words could also be that she sees who he is and what his life means. Therefore, even if she doesn't have a direct sense that he is about to die, she knows that what and who he represents is more special than everything else there is in life, *even* raising money for the poor. Seeing properly, she therefore acts appropriately. Like the poor widow at 12:41–44, she gives everything she has; she not only pours out all her oil, she breaks the jar that held it. She responds completely to Jesus because she sees the reality of God's reign in him. This is where she knows she must place her best resources, knowing that God will respond to that gift in transformative ways. Perhaps this, in the end, is the meaning of Jesus' troubling statement at 14:7 (NSRV): "You always have the poor with you." You will not always have this moment. Respond, therefore, to this moment. This moment will transform you so that, empowered by it, you will do much more for the poor than 300 denarii ever could.

Such an interpretation fits the unreasonable logic of this passage. This outsider woman, who sees what the insider men miss, anoints the body that is soon to be broken in everyone's (the poor's particularly) service (10:45; 14:22). Mark uses the word body (*sōma*) only four times (5:29; 14:8, 22; 15:43). Only once does the term not refer to Jesus' body (5:29). In the other three it refers not only to Jesus' body but also to his death. Verse 14:22 makes Mark's point clear by connecting "body" with the adjective "broken" and the corresponding noun "bread." The bread terminology connects the body emphasis back to the feeding of broken bread to the multitudes in 6:30–44 and 8:1–10. There the bread satisfied the hunger of both Jews and Gentiles. The story in 7:24–30 emphasized that universal point through the Syrophoenician woman's inclusion at the Jewish table.

So does this story. Before Mark closes it, Jesus makes the point that the woman's ability to see and act will become an integral part of the very good news about God's reign that her behavior salutes. When Jesus explains that her act will be memorialized whenever believers gather to tell the story (14:9), he goes out of his way to say it in exactly the kind of provocative, boundary-breaking manner that fits the 13:10 theme. News of her watchful behavior will be preached universally, in all the world. The rupture of the boundary between Jew and Gentile before the presence of God's reign that was promised in 7:1–8:9 will happen as promised. The people who courageously "watch," who preach toward that unreasonable end will preach about the watchful courage of this unnamed, outsider, out-of-place woman. For she becomes a model of the very attentiveness to the moment that the disciples fail to show.

Jesus will appeal to this critical watch language one final time at 14:32–42, the tragedy at Gethsemane. The emphasis on action, on watchful behavior, picks up here where it left off at 13:33–37. Just as there Jesus pleaded with his disciples three times to watch (*grēgoreō*, 13:34, 35, 37), so here he pleads with his disciples in the garden three times to watch (*grēgoreō*, 14:32, 37, 38) with him for the moment of his arrest, trial, and death. The troubling triads continue when the disciples meet this watch hour three times not with alertness but with sleep.

Echoing the kind of grief the psalmist declares (Ps. 42; 43), Jesus slips off by himself to pray, under the supposed watchful eye of Peter, James, and John (14:32–35). Readers remember from 9:14–29 and 11:22–24 that the power of prayer is palpable. As then, so now Jesus shows that prayer is the energetic ingredient that sustains faith even against the most improbable of odds; he is certain at 14:35–36 that God can alter the trajectory of his life even at this late moment (cf. 14:8). Instead of seeking that out, though, he models another key characteristic of his ministry, his recognition that prayer is the antidote to sleeping during one's posting on God's watch. At his crucial moment of decision, Jesus prays for the power to endure the course God has set, and receives it (14:36). Like the unnamed woman of 14:2–9, he is ready when his moment comes. His disciples, unfortunately, are asleep. Three times (13:37, 40, 41) they are caught off guard because they have nodded off to the critical nature of the situation facing their Lord. This is all the more tragically ironic since these are the same three who at different points in the narrative boasted that they would be able to share Jesus' suffering (10:35–40; 14:29–31) with the appropriate resolve.[13]

Jesus symbolizes his rebuke of them all by reclaiming the new name, Peter, he had bestowed upon his lead disciple when he recast and renamed the Twelve (3:13–19) as a new, countercultural Israel.[14] When he finds them snoozing, it is the old Simon he sees, not the Peter he had once envisioned (14:37). Mark lays out the case of Peter's sleepiness in triplicate yet again when he chronicles the lead disciple's denials of Jesus at 14:66–72. While Jesus stands fast before the great movers who want to shake the life out of his ministry, Peter wilts before a rabble of maidservants and gardeners. Like his brothers, Peter heard the sermon in Mark 13, saw the object lesson of the

---

13. Hooker, *Mark*, 329.
14. See chapter 2, View One.

woman at 14:2–9, and was warned that this moment was coming (8:31; 9:31; 10:33–34). Still, they were all unable to muster the resolve to stay awake.

No doubt this narrative failure represents real and troubling historical lapses for Mark the evangelist. In this depiction of disciples who fail to watch are surely historical disciples who were unable to resist the call to battle by the false prophets and thus joined the Jewish war against Rome rather than the Jesus movement. No doubt there were others in the Jesus movement who were unable to shake the threat of persecution and death and failed to preach the good news of God's transformative reign that would include Jews and Gentiles as one people gathered before God. No doubt, there were, and are, many who don't see where God is present and how God is acting in their lives and who thus stick to the old ways of doing the rituals and attending the services of worship and following the laws of holiness and love, but who fail to respond radically to the wonderfully new thing that is God's reign in their midst. No doubt there are many contemporary Christians who cannot see what that unnamed woman saw, that perhaps the time for acting reasonably is at an end. That is why Jesus' message at the end of Mark 13 (13:32–37), apocalyptically driven as it is, remains historically viable. The moment of God's reign will come suddenly and unannounced. You don't want to be caught unprepared. You want to be ready. You become ready by preaching the reign of God in radically transformative ways, ways that transform you even as they transform your world. When that moment comes you want to be transfigured enough to become part of it. That is why what Jesus says he says to all (13:37), and he says over and over again: "Watch. Watch out!"

View Two: "Inside Out" (Mark 14:3–9)
Brian K. Blount

[Introduction: I preached this sermon at the Witherspoon Street Presbyterian Church in Princeton, New Jersey, where my family and I are members.]

I've only had one real fight in my life. I was eight. My opponent was also eight Incredibly, she was *also* a girl. We were in the third grade. At recess. On the playground. In the 1960s, in Smithfield, Virginia, on the playground, there was a wonderful kind of equality between boys and girls. We treated each other pretty much the same, even though our parents and teachers were desperately trying their best to socialize us, to make us realize the differences and how differently we ought to be treating one another. But on the playground we were all the same. And in the language of eight-year-old boys, that means "winner takes all." Girls were bigger at eight and that gave them a physical advantage. But boys couldn't be backing down in public, not to other bigger boys and certainly not to girls.

So, when Carolyn, one of my best friends growing up, wanted my swing seat before I was finished swinging in it, there was bound to be trouble. Wars, you know, are fought very often over territory. Some country wants more land than it has; that means it's got to take it away from some other country it thinks has more than it needs. That other country wants to keep what it has; that means it's got to stop that other country from taking it away. And that means there's going to be trouble. Countries call it war. Eight-year-olds on a school playground call it a fight. Carolyn and I were about to have a fight. I grew up in a house of three boys. Anyone who's grown up in a house of all boys knows that territory isn't surrendered. Territory isn't given away. Territory must be taken. I knew instantly that Carolyn wanted to take mine.

I don't remember a whole lot about the actual battle. I remember that Carolyn was a whole lot bigger than me, though. And that gave her a sizable advantage. She was also standing on solid ground while I was going up and down, up and down on a swing, which meant she had secure footing and I didn't. That gave her yet another advantage. But that didn't mean I was backing down. I hadn't ever been in a fight before that moment, but I was ready for whatever was coming. I'm not counting all the battles I'd had with my older brother. Those weren't fights; they were massacres. He was older, more experienced, and much, much bigger than me. And though my parents would never have admitted it, I also think that, back then, he was partially insane. So even if I hadn't ever been in a public fight before, I knew what fighting was like. I just wasn't used to any of my wild swings making contact. That's why I remember being awfully surprised when Carolyn pulled me off that swing and the first fist I launched landed squarely against her eye.

There was a bit more to it, I think, but that's all I remember. I guess I've repressed the rest. I just remember that single swing and the black eye she wore for about a week after that playground altercation. What I remember even more vividly is the brief period of time that followed. You've heard that saying, "win the battle but lose the war." Well, that was me, and I knew it. I'd won the battle with Carolyn, but there wasn't any way I was going to win the public relations war to come. I remember being scared and ashamed. Funny how I'd never felt ashamed when my older brother beat me up. Then, I just remember being mad. Now, having accomplished what might pass for a win for once in my life, I was feeling not pride but shame. So I didn't go back to the classroom after recess because I knew what was waiting. I wanted to put it off as long as I could. I went to the bathroom and just sat there, trying as best I could to buy some time. Ashamed. Because I knew I'd just been fighting not only Carolyn but everything my mother and father stood for. Ashamed, because I knew how disappointed they'd be in me. Scared, because I knew punishment was coming. There was in that world no excuse for what I'd done, and I knew it. Even in the third grade I knew it. I felt humiliated. I felt alone. I felt outside.

Maybe then it's not so funny that I thought about that playground fight with Carolyn as I meditated about this passage about the woman with the alabaster flask of pure nard. I kept trying to think what it would be like to be a woman like her. I kept trying to identify with her. I kept trying to feel what she must have been feeling as she walked in on holy Jesus and his holier-than-thou disciples. And I kept coming up empty. And then, all of a sudden, I came up eight years old and frightened and alone in a bathroom because I wasn't who and what people wanted me to be.

Look at her. Nothing about her is what folk in Simon the leper's house expected her to be. If there were any women around they ought to be shuffling around doing the kinds of things women were supposed to be doing. Working the kitchen, herding the servants, rounding up the chillun'. You know the kinds of things men expected of women then. Some men expect it still. At best, women were second class, not citizens, mind you, because that designation usually belonged to the men, so, just second class. In ancient Jewish circles it could even be worse. Some rabbis had a nice little prayer that went something like this: "I thank God who has not made me a sinner, a Gentile, or a woman." Sinners, Gentiles, and women, you see, were unholy. So, how do you guess this woman felt walking in on Jesus and his holy boys?

But Mark likes her. There's no doubt about that. She's kind of a heroine in his story. But you'll note she's an outsider even to him. He doesn't even use her name. Doesn't have it. Or won't use it. Either way, when somebody won't use your name, you know you don't rate very high. Don't think it matters? How would you like it if your pastor, your boss, your doctor, the people you wanted to be your friends, didn't know your name? Remember that old television show *Cheers*? Remember its opening song. It went like this: "Sometimes you want to go where everybody knows your name." That would be special, wouldn't it? To have such a place. How would you feel if the place you thought was most special, the place where your Lord sat eating at table, the place where you turn every day and night to read about that Lord, were all places where *nobody* knew your name. How would that make you feel? How about second class? How about inferior? How about outside? Even though I got into a fight with her, even after some thirty years, at least I remembered

Carolyn's name. After they verbally tried to beat this woman up, they still didn't have the decency to ask her for her name.

Maybe it was because of the kind of woman they thought she was. Legend has it she was the wrong kind of woman. In Luke's very different version of the story, he says she's a sinner (Luke 7:37). We all know what kind of sinner he means. Though none of the Scriptures do, some later church fathers believed she was Mary Magdalene.[15] We know what line of work some of those church fathers thought Mary was in. What's clear is that she's not one of Jesus' inner circle, and she's carrying around some very expensive ointment, and the disciples want to know where it came from and how she could afford it. There are a whole lot of folk who think she was something other than a PG-13 kind of girl. Working with the Lukan version of the story, Joel Green is more direct: "She is a sinner in the city—that is, a woman known in the city as a sinner. Undoubtedly, this characterization marks her as a prostitute by vocation, a whore by social status, contagious in her impurity, and probably one who fraternizes with Gentiles for economic purposes."[16] Now, in a world where even mothers and daughters, where so-called *good* women were bad, how would it have felt to be a woman like her? No wonder they don't even remember her name. They don't want to. They want to forget her. Forget she was there. Especially there hanging around their Lord.

When Ched Myers writes in his commentary about this passage, he says that even here Jesus is being the radical teacher. He's trying to teach his unreceptive disciples about receptivity. All along he's been hanging out with lepers, sinners, tax collectors, children, and women as if they, too, belong unconditionally to God's reign. Now he's hanging out with her. Trying, evidently, one more time, to get them to see life, to live life from her perspective. From the perspective of an outsider.[17]

No doubt Mark wants from us what Jesus wanted from those disciples. He wants us to identify with folk like this woman who are so far outside the *acceptable* circles that people don't even take the time to ask them their names. She is exactly the kind of ostracized, misunderstood, *poor* person about whom the disciples *profess* to be so concerned. She represents those impoverished by economics, anonymity, gender, and reputation to whom they allegedly want to target their gracious fund-raising efforts. While they mouth off about helping the poor, this woman, impoverished by her station in life,

---

15. See Joseph A. Fitzmyer, *The Gospel according to Luke, I–IX* (Doubleday: New York, 1979), 688–89. Joel Green refers to her as an "intruder" (Joel B. Green, *The Gospel of Luke* [Grand Rapids: Eerdmans, 1997], 309).

16. Green, *Gospel of Luke*, 309.

17. Myers, *Binding the Strong Man,* 440.

stands before them apparently invisible. They can't help her because they can't see her. To help her, to help those whom she represents, they must identify with her. *Be* with her. Identify and be with them. That takes time, though. And effort. At this point in Mark's story, with this woman, they apparently have neither.

Do we? Do we take the time, exert the effort to identify with the unnamed people suffering all around us? Does it matter to us? Or are we so busy trying to help them, trying to strategize for them, trying to build programs around them, trying to raise money for their cause, that we don't get to know them? That would be tantamount, I think, to being so busy working for God that you have no time to pray with God. I've seen many a Christian go nova, just burn out like that, like a bright star whose fury had turned in on itself. And as they do, God's people, the nameless ones, the unnamed women, and the countless poor still cry out for light and warmth.

We know them; at least we see them. Struggling on the street begging for money. Standing on the side of the road beside a broken-down car. Living down to the lowest expectations in overcrowded, improperly cared-for public housing. Shivering from fear, bleeding ignorance in schools where violent students are more plentiful than honor students. There are others. The ones on welfare who live right around the corner, or the ones who've gotten off welfare and yet struggle in working poverty while the government celebrates the lowering of the welfare rolls. What about the children who are shot in the belly going to day care? Do we know them? Do we take the time to ask them their names? Just a few summers ago there was a six-year-old boy with two bullets in him struggling for his life because some madman who hates Jewish people went gunning indiscriminately in his daycare center. When you said a prayer for that little boy that night, did you know his name? There's that black man who was dragged down a road chained to a pickup truck in Jasper, Texas, until his body broke apart and shattered on the roadside. When you said a prayer for him, I wonder, did you use his name? Who are we like? Are we like Jesus, who wanted to know about such people, know their names, and know *them* in their struggles and gave his life trying to change theirs, or the disciples, who wished such people would stop cluttering up their Master's itinerary with their unholy existences. It's hard to keep focused on God's agenda when all the problems of the world are nipping at your heels. We know how the disciples dealt with that situation. They tried to ignore the problems, tried to forget their names.

In seminary we give tests, you know. And many students treat us professors after the tests the way people treated me after my fight with Carolyn. We don't win popularity contests that way. Sometimes, you know, they get downright angry with us. If we ask them questions that they think are too petty. If we ask them questions that they think aren't worth learning. If we ask them questions they don't think have anything to do with ministry. There's one question that's legendary. It was on the midterm for the "Introduction to the New Testament" class. I won't tell you why we put it on there, but I'll tell you what it was. It was about Alexander the Great. Everybody knows who Alexander the Great was. Everybody knows that in his twenties he captured the entire world. Legend has it he was so powerful that at one point he stooped beside the bank of a river and cried because he had run out of countries to conquer. Well, we asked them, what were the names of Alexander the Great's parents? By the time the uproar had died down, I felt like I was back in that bathroom after that playground brawl with Carolyn.

Of course, Philip and Olympia, Alexander's mom and dad, were a king and a queen and they ruled over a mighty province in their own right. A province that had a great impact on Jesus' Palestine. They were not insignificant people. But still, the legitimate question was raised: What does knowing the name of Alexander's mother and father have to do with ministry? Who cares who his mother and father were, what their names were? We really don't even care all that much about Alexander himself. We want to save souls; we don't want to know about two dead people a long time ago. We don't want to know their names.

Half of me thinks they're right, you know. The other half grieves. I wonder about their inattentiveness, our inattentiveness. If you're studying history but don't want to learn the names of two very important people then, when you're doing history, when you're living it will you care about learning the names of unimportant people now? When the big, big mission of the cross is in front of us, little things like learning somebody's name, identifying with their problems and fears, seem like grunt work.

I'll tell you one thing: I would bet that the people who start pushing for better controls on assault weapons now will be people who know the name of that little Jewish boy who was shot in the belly. The rest of us will forget him and the circumstances that helped allow his shooting. I'll bet that the people who fight for just welfare reform are people who know the names of the unimportant, insignificant people living in poverty. I'll bet that the people who make the big changes in our lives tomorrow are the people who are learning the names of little people being hurt today. Those are the people who know that the details matter. Those are the people who'd understand why Jesus didn't start his ministry in the big-city lights of Jerusalem but in the dim and dark corridors that housed Galilee's unnamed lepers, sinners, tax collectors, and women.

In fact, in this respect, we can follow Jesus' lead. Before he heals for them, before he exorcises for them, before he calms wind and wave for them, before he dies for them, before he rises from the dead for them, before all of that, he takes the time just to be with them. I think we take the Christian thing too seriously, and in the wrong way sometimes. We start to think we're Jesus. Our first order of business seems to be to change somebody, to rehabilitate somebody. And if we can't rehabilitate them, we exile them, push them to the outside. We can't be with them, unless we can find the power to transform them and make them become like us. That's the disciples. They talk about how they're mad with her because she's there wasting all that ointment and stuff. They're mad because she's there, period. Not Jesus, though. He lets her come near. Just as she is. We sing that song, "Just As I Am," all the time. The truth is, we don't want nobody just as they are. We want them just like we want them to be. Which is usually just like us.

Jesus, really, truly, called people just like they were. Look at him. Isn't there something about this story that bothers you? It bothers me. If you take the time to get to know the details of the thing, it's going to bother you too. When the story opens Mark tells us that it's two days before the Passover and the Feast of Unleavened Bread. This is a high holy period in Israel, one of the holiest in fact, when the people celebrate the exodus from Egypt. It's like Christmas and Easter for us Christians. We preacher types get our robes pressed and cleaned. All the children want to be on their best behavior. You know the song, "Better watch out, better not cry, better not pout, I'm telling you why, Santa Claus is coming to town." We all want to be our best. Our purest. Our holiest. Even the most fighting of families try to put on their best family face for such special occasions. Such holy occasions.

Given all of that, the *last* place you'd want to find your priest type during such a period would be in a leper's house, at a party, with a woman of questionable reputation pouring expensive ointment all over his head. And just two days before the highest holy day of the year. What's Jesus thinking? In Leviticus it says a leper is unclean for as long as he is a leper (Lev. 13–14). So why is Jesus staying at a place Mark calls the house of Simon the leper? Okay, let's try to rehabilitate this story before it scandalizes us all. Maybe he *used* to be a leper. Maybe that's it.

So why doesn't Mark make everybody feel better and say the home of Simon the *ex*-leper? No, he says home of Simon the leper. Mark not only remembers his name, he remembers the name of his disease. He's a leper. And Jesus is in his house, sitting at his germ-filled, flesh-falling-off, got-to-be-unkempt, unclean, and unholy table eating his food. And with just two days before the holy feast. How's Jesus going to participate in the *holy* feast with the remains of such an *unholy* person still clinging to him?

Well, maybe he can wash up. He's got two days, after all. If he doesn't get out of the tub for two days, maybe that'll do it.

But in Leviticus it says you need a whole week to clean up from being around a leper. A whole seven days (Lev. 14:38). And on the eighth day there's *still* stuff you've got to be doing. What's Jesus going to do in *two* days? He's going to be unclean; that's all there is to it. He's going to be unholy on the holiest day of the year because he spent the night at an unholy man's house and his unholiness is now Jesus' unholiness.

But wait! There's even more. There's a party going on! There's a dinner party at the home of a leper, and presumably Jesus is sitting at table with him. We're talking about a world where you weren't even supposed to eat at table with a man who hadn't washed his hands![18] Jesus is sitting there eating with a man whose hands are being mauled by a flesh-eating disease. And then, that woman walks in! Let's see if we can count up all the transgressions: In the house of a leper. Having a dinner party. Being stroked by an anonymous woman. Maybe even, if the rumors are true, an anonymous woman of the night. How's he ever going to get cleaned up behind this? Ain't no shower in the world going to cleanse him from all the dirt he's touching right now.

Jesus must have something different on his mind than the rest of the holy people have on theirs right now, though. I tell you what he's got. He's got God's commission that the first thing you do after seeing someone in trouble is to learn their name—who they are and what they feel—and the only way you can do that is by being with them. That's why all through Mark's story Jesus is intentionally with the wrong kinds of people, the kind of people the good people in Israel thought were unclean and unworthy of a place before God, not to mention a place setting next to God's son.

And so the good people, represented in this story by Jesus' good disciples, want to get the questionable people out of the picture. That's why they're really angry with this woman. The disciples want to do with the woman the same thing they earlier wanted to do with the children who'd been brought to Jesus—get them, and her, out of the way (10:13–16). They belong outside because they are outsiders.

But Mark's story wants us to be different. To be unlike the disciples. It's asking you to identify with those who are struggling, those who are different, to learn their names, to be with them, and, I think, to realize that we're one of them. Realize that to God, we're just like them. We're like a leper. We're like that woman. That's when we really begin to work for people, without looking

18. Cf. Mark 7:1–5.

down at them, without patronizing them, without humiliating them. When we realize that we're all eight-year-old boys and girls hiding out in the bathroom because we know we haven't lived up to what God has expected from us. We've all fallen short.

So, what do we do with this realization? We do what this outsider woman did. We don't sit somewhere pouting because we aren't as good as we thought we were. We give what we have. We give like she gave. We do the very best we can with what we have in us to make a difference. Whether or not people know our name.

That's what that woman's ointment symbolizes for me. It's symbolic of somebody poor living like they were rich. We all feel like outsiders sometimes. You've got your midlife crisis, your bad day, your bad week, your bad month, your bad year . . . sometimes, even your bad life. How do you deal with it? You deal out of it. Like she did. When you realize nobody knows your name, when you feel like an outsider looking in, you take whatever you have and . . . you give it away. That must have been what she was thinking. That's how she found her redemption.

I think of this because of all the folk I know who ask when reading a biblical story, or after hearing a sermon, or a Bible study, "Where's the grace? What's in this story for me? Where is the point in this text that makes *me* feel good, *me* feel better, *me* feel closer to God and Christ? Where is it?" Maybe, I want to say, it just isn't there. Maybe this whole Christianity thing wasn't first thought up just so you and people like you could feel good. Could that be possible? Maybe the God who sent God's son to die on a cross didn't have feeling good as the first thought in mind. Maybe what's more important is giving of one's self even in those moments when you don't feel good. Maybe that's where redemption lies. Like this woman. At her worst moment, she gives what she has to Jesus in a way that seems wasteful to everyone else. But Jesus notices it as something special. He notices that she has noticed his impending agony and his present need and has addressed them both with what she has, the most precious thing that she has. As Lamar Williamson writes:

> Christian stewardship as a regular pattern of life is a good and challenging ideal, but this anonymous woman's response to Jesus moves on different grounds. Her deed springs from a personal love for Jesus which, on occasion, breaks all patterns, defies common sense, and simply gives. Spontaneous, uncalculating, selfless, and timely, her gift calls us to love Jesus in this way too and not to judge the way others express their love for him.[19]

19. Williamson, *Mark,* 249.

Unlike Jesus' own followers and disciples, she has seen in his circumstance something that reaches out for consolation and warmth. She can't name it, she can't heal it, but she can identify with it. Like his, her life is a struggle. On that basic level of anonymous hurt, she reaches out to him. She identifies with him. She touches him. She consoles him. She readies him with her love for the moment coming before him. This woman who needs so much herself sees Jesus' need and puts that first. So she gives him the only material resource she has. And she gives it all. Not to make him richer. But to make him feel loved. And soothed. And so, prepared.

Perhaps that's the lesson for us. When we're down and out, instead of coming to God to look for a pick-me-up, as though God were a spiritual drugstore and we'd written out ourselves a prayer prescription, perhaps we ought to come looking for ways to identify with someone in trouble, and give of ourselves, even when we feel given out. Perhaps it's in the giving to others that we get the peace we seek. Perhaps that's the mystery even Jesus' disciples didn't understand. Here was a woman "talked bad about sure enough," and yet despite that, she moves into a place where they were bound to talk about her even more. And she doesn't come asking Jesus to give her peace; instead, she gives Jesus everything she has. And in that giving, Jesus says, she will receive something special. From now on when people talk about him and his God, they will also mention her. You talk about things turning topsy-turvy and inside out. Jesus doesn't say the disciples will be remembered wherever the gospel is preached. He says we'll remember her. Because she represents God's grace. She *became*, she *is* the very grace she went looking for. There's a lesson there, if we have ears to hear it.

View Three: You Better Watch Out!
Gary W. Charles

Mark 13 arrives at the same time every three years in the New Common Lectionary. The turkey's barely off the table, and Mark 13 shows up like that crazy uncle who embarrasses everyone at the table. It ushers in Advent—a crazy enough season itself! Have you ever noticed that malls don't even bother with Advent? The season just won't sell. How do you market quiet faithfulness? You can't, so you don't. Society simply skips Advent, blithely oblivious to the bizarre warnings in Mark 13.

Christians often skip Advent as well. Churches may light four candles and pass out devotions to read each day, but they're swimming upstream. People want to sing carols and hear about a decree that went out from Emperor

Augustus; they don't want to hear warnings about the sky falling and the world turned inside out. So, even Christians skip Advent. No sooner do they stack the Thanksgiving dishes than they set the table for Christmas.

Who needs Advent, anyway? In John Updike's remarkable novel *In the Beauty of the Lilies*, Essie, the young protagonist, is finally old enough for her parents to allow her to walk to the Saturday matinee alone. She emerges from the dark confines of the Roxie Theater, and Updike writes, "Outside the Roxie, the day had gone on being Saturday. Days were so long she couldn't see how people could ever get old, the future was so far away."[20] As a child, all I remember about Advent are those torturous days leading up to Christmas when, as it was for Essie, time was stuck in a jar of molasses. As Christmas approached, each day seemed to last a month.

Whatever attention my church gave to Advent—and it was not much—Advent was the time-to-get-through-as-fast-as-possible season. It was like those old double exposures, when one image would be imposed on top of another. As a child, Christmas was always spread all over Advent. I do not appreciate Christmas any less as an adult, but now I wish Advent would last longer. It's not that I like waiting any more at this age than at a younger one. I don't. I want a longer Advent, because I am convinced there is something crucial about Advent that gets buried when the season is lived only in anticipation of Christmas.

That brings me back to Mark 13. It's a strange chapter filled with eerie images of coming attractions—persecution, families torn apart, betrayal, nature unleashed, armies on the march, and life ripped open at the seams. It's a Markan remake of the Egyptian plagues—without the frogs. Another reason why Advent won't sell! *This* is the church's "welcome mat" to the season of Advent? No wonder we skip it.

The editors who compile the readings for the New Common Lectionary give us a break when we land on Mark 13. They begin the Sunday reading for First Advent near the end of this chapter—on a much calmer note. Gone are the images of cataclysm and terror we see when the tornado hits Kansas in *The Wizard of Oz* and Dorothy sees her house spinning in a funnel cloud, her neighbor riding a broom, and all those she loves tossed to and fro in a fierce whirlwind. By Mark 13:32–37 the wild, apocalyptic images are gone—at least until they are fulfilled in the horror of Mark's coming passion narrative.

Shifting out of doom-time gear, in Mark 13:32–37 Jesus tells another, seemingly simple, parable. A lord leaves his house and entrusts his estate to

20. John Updike, *The Beauty of the Lilies* (New York: Fawcett, 1997), 243.

his servants, telling the doorkeeper to "stay awake." The servants must "stay awake" through the four Roman watches of the night; evening, midnight, "cock crow," and dawn.[21] They must "stay awake" because it is unknown when the lord of the house will return and *no one dare be found sleeping*.

Mark switches verbs in this little parable. As Brian noted earlier, "Up until this point he has depended on the Greek verb *blepō* ... apparently, though, Jesus now requires a word that can do heavier verbal lifting. Though he maintains the imperative emphasis, he switches now to a different verb (*grēgoreō*)." *Blepō* means to "pay attention, beware of, keep alert to," while *grēgoreō* means to "keep watch, be vigilant." Vigilant disciples do not waste time speculating when the lord will walk through the door; they keep doing the lord's business—preaching, praying, worshiping, healing—no matter the month, no matter the time of day—evening, midnight, cock crow, or dawn.

Unfortunately, this "verbal heavy lifting" is obscured in most English versions of the Bible, as translators use a variety of English synonyms to translate *blepō* and *grēgoreō*. *Grēgoreō* is a verb used rarely in classical Greek texts, and even less in Scripture. Yet Mark uses it *three* times in this parable (13:34, 35, 37) and *three* times again in Mark 14 as Jesus addresses the familiar trio of disciples in the Garden of Gethsemane (14:34, 37, 38). Mark is using red ink here! He wants readers to notice. He wants readers to *grēgoreite!*—stay awake![22] Three times the servants are called to *grēgoreite* and three times Jesus tells his servants—Peter, James, and John—to *grēgoreite* as he himself goes off to pray—the last time in Gethsemane. In 13:32–37 Jesus calls for vigilance in discipleship, but in 14:33–37 he gets only sleeping disciples.

This subtle shift of language calls readers to pay attention to verbs in Mark, especially the verb *grēgoreite*. *Grēgoreite* is a call from Jesus to lead a life of faithful vigilance, to avoid looking beyond today for Christmas to come and the Lord to return. We are to live confidently in the provisions of God *every day*, even when the lord is away. For, in the parable, the lord gives the servants "authority" (*exousia*) to do what is necessary while the lord is not with them, just as Jesus gave his disciples such *exousia* in 6:7–13. Tragically, though, those best prepared to heed the command *grēgoreite* fall

21. Myers notes how Mark parallels the four "watches" in this parable with the four "watches" of the passion narrative: "It was Lightfoot who first recognized that these watches correspond to moments in the passion: 1. evening (*opse*): the time of the Last Supper (14:17), and the time after the crucifixion (15:42); 2. midnight (*mesonuktion*): night (*nux*) is the general time of Peter's denial (14:30); 3. the 'cock crow' (*alektorophonias*): specific time (*alektor*) of Peter's denial (14:30,72); 4. dawn (*proi*): when Jesus was handed over to the Romans (15:1). No proleptic reference to the passion story is stronger, however, than the parable's warning not to be found 'asleep'" (Myers, *Binding the Strong Man*, 347).

22. Four of Mark's six uses take this more forceful, imperative form of the verb (13:35, 37; 14:34, 38).

asleep on the "watch," leaving Mark's readers to heed the command *grēgo-reite* themselves.[23]

That brings me back to Advent. Mark 13:32–37 was a call for Christians to switch out of the passive mode. *Grēgoreite* is Mark's trumpet blast to introduce Advent. Advent, then, isn't a pensive season to get our spiritual affairs in order before Christmas returns. Advent is a time of movement, a time to "stay awake" *now* for a God-on-the-move. Advent is a season that kicks us off our couches, turns off our TV screens, and pushes us outside our gates to pray for and preach for and live for a God who has given us more than enough authority to do so.

When my children were very young and I was fed up with their impatience during Advent, I would pointedly sing to them, "You better watch out, you better not cry, you better not pout, I'm telling you why." Maybe God and my children will forgive me in time for such exploitative parenting. Hopefully, in time, they and God will forgive me for advancing such woeful theology, reducing Advent to nothing more than a prelude for the *real* religious season to come.

The next time Mark 13 heralds in Advent—as well as *every day* in between—consider the call from Jesus to *grēgoreite! Watch out!*

"You Better Watch Out!"

You better watch out
Not for stodgy Santas
And rugged reindeer

You better watch out
Lest awe dull over time
And passion smolder in ashes

You better watch out
For courage to act
And faith to trust

You better watch out
Not for pale riders
Or skies that turn black

23. Myers draws a critical parallel between the parable calling disciples to watch and the disciples in Gethsemane, who do not: "In Mark's story line, the tragedy is that the disciples in that episode will not 'stay awake' with Jesus in Gethsemane; they will sleep. They will betray and finally abandon him at each 'watch' of his final night because they do not understand his call to the cross" (Myers, *Binding the Strong Man*, 347).

You better watch out
For a sentry call
To a life of prayer and love

You better watch out
With children's eyes
For Advent.
       (Gary W. Charles)

11

Hand-ed Over
Mark 15:1–47

View One: From Text to Sermon
Gary W. Charles

I begin each Holy Week with a visit to the church garage. After moving aside a year's worth of "treasures," a group of us makes our way to an eight-by-four-foot wooden cross. We then debate the best way to carry the cross from the garage to the sanctuary a half block away. Having decided on our strategy, we carry the cross to its appointed destination. Once inside the sanctuary, we debate how best to secure the cross and where best to shine the spotlight on it. Within an hour of the final "Amen" to the Good Friday service, the cross scene is repeated in reverse, as the cross is removed from the sanctuary and safely stored for the coming year.

While it makes perfect theological sense for Christians annually to focus on the cross during Holy Week, to revisit the pain and suffering of the cross and crucifixion, Mark is not the church's most helpful ally among the four evangelists in this effort. For in his Gospel, Mark does not focus so much on the cross and crucifixion as on the people and events leading up to and following that dark hour. Not unlike the majority of Rembrandt's depictions of the death of Jesus, in his passion narrative Mark positions his readers to look less at the crucified Jesus and more at those along the way to and stationed by the cross.

In a series of handoffs, Mark's crucifixion narrative begins long before any account of the cross. At the opening of Mark 15, Jesus is *handed over* to Pilate by the duplicitous chief priests, elders, and scribes (15:1) who earlier had found Jesus guilty of blasphemy (14:63–65). Later in this chapter, the crowd asks Pilate to *hand over* the prisoner Barabbas (15:11), a long-standing tradition of political appeasement (15:6). Pilate asks the crowd if they want him to *hand over* Barabbas, a convicted murderer, or this Jesus.

The crowd tells Pilate to *hand over* Barabbas for freedom and to *hand over* Jesus for execution. So, Pilate *hands over* Jesus to be ridiculed and tortured. Then the soldiers *hand over* Jesus to be crucified (15:12–15). Meanwhile, the soldiers *hand over* the crossbar for Jesus' execution to Simon of Cyrene (15:21). While hanging from the cross, the crowd *hands over* drugged wine for Jesus to drink (15:36). After Jesus has breathed his last, Pilate *hands over* the body of Jesus to Joseph of Arimathea for burial (15:42–47).

Though it does not occur in every instance cited above, Mark frequently (on ten occasions in his passion narrative)[1] uses the same verb for "hand over" (*paradidōmi*). This verb, often expressed in the passive voice,[2] gives Mark's passion narrative a sense of dual movement—both presenting the inexplicable and unconscionable actions of comrades, crowd, and chief priests, as well as suggesting the inexorable and mysterious movement of the divine.[3] Ched Myers notes, "Bracketed by the term 'handed over' (15:1, 15), this second hearing [in the Praetorium] is patterned after the first."[4] Surprisingly, though, Myers drops this cogent line of thought and fails to explore further this important Markan literary and theological marker.

Unlike the pre-Jerusalem narrative, Mark 15 is carefully framed by chronological signals: early morning (15:1), nine o'clock in the morning (15:25), noon (15:33), and evening (15:42). Though written in a series of episodes, the chapter is a neatly woven narrative in which Mark is less concerned with conveying information[5] than with fueling the readers' indignation and buoying their faith. Mary Ann Tolbert provides a critical insight into understanding Mark when she contrasts the modern way of reading a literary text with the ancient way: "Our contemporary obsession is with the *meaning* of a text, whether we choose to locate that meaning in the text itself or in the reader or somewhere in between."[6] She then proceeds to quote from the literary critic, Jane Tompkins: "From an ancient perspective, 'The text as an object of study or contemplation has no importance, . . . for literature is thought of as existing primarily in order to produce results and not as an end in itself. A literary work is not so much an object, therefore, as a unit of force whose power is

---

1. Mark 14:10, 11, 18, 21, 41, 42, 44; 15:1, 10, 15.

2. Mark 1:14; 9:31; 14:21, 41.

3. Vincent Taylor remarks that *paradidōmi* "may represent the point of view of one who sees behind the actions of men [and women] the fulfilment of the fate of the Suffering Servant" (Taylor, *Gospel according to St. Mark*, 578).

4. Myers, *Binding the Strong Man*, 378.

5. Notice how Mark covers certain details of the crucifixion with the three-word sentence *kai staurousin auton* ("and they crucified him," 15:24).

6. Tolbert, *Sowing the Gospel*, 289.

exerted upon the world in a particular direction.'"[7] Mark, then, wants us to *respond* to this crucifixion narrative—and to respond differently than the majority of characters in the story.

The character of Mark 15 is that of high tragedy. As the curtain rises on the day the sky went dark, Mark presents us with a familiar cast of antagonists. As did the Pharisees and Herodians in 3:6, so here the chief priests, elders, scribes, and whole Sanhedrin hold a *sumboulion* (council/consultation/meeting),[8] not to better understand Jesus but to devise ways to be rid of him (6:6; 9:14; 9:24). These Jerusalem religious leaders gladly *hand over* their "problem" to Pilate. Without a narrative pause, the scene shifts from the religious leaders to the political leader. Mark tells his readers nothing about the initial exchange between Pilate and the leaders from the Sanhedrin. The scene begins with the implied charge against Jesus stated as Pilate asks the defendant, "Are you the King of the Jews?" (15:2).[9] Jesus, who is simply one more Jew in Palestine with his own religious philosophy, is hardly a threat to Rome. Pilate's concern is with Jews who are prepared to incite religious and civil unrest.[10] In Mark, unlike in John 18:33–38, Jesus does not enter into a complex theological debate with Pilate. On the contrary, Jesus gives Pilate a non-answer (15:2) and then no answer at all (15:5). Remarkably, as the religious and political leadership in Jerusalem confront Jesus, he has nothing to say. Beyond any historical referents, this exchange in Pilate's praetorium reminds

---

7. Ibid. The quote is from Jane P. Tompkins, "The Reader in History: The Changing Shape of Literary Response," in *Reader-Response Criticism: From Formalism to Post-Structuralism* (ed. Jane P. Tompkins; Baltimore: Johns Hopkins University, 1980), 204.

8. Raymond Brown discusses the possible meanings of *sumboulion* and how each reading affects the reading of this Markan text (Raymond Brown, *The Death of the Messiah: From Gethsemane to the Grave: A Commentary on the Passion Narratives in the Four Gospels* [New York: Doubleday, 1991], 629–32). Assuming a consultation of the Sanhedrin, Ched Myers comments on *sumboulion* to make an important literary and theological connection: "The Sanhedrin's 'consultation' (*sumboulion*) brings to a close the subplot of the conspiracy, which opened with a similar 'consultation' (3:6)" (Myers, *Binding the Strong Man*, 302–5; Horsley, *Hearing the Whole Story*, 387).

9. Richard Horsley makes an extended argument for distinguishing what Mark means by *hoi ioudaioi*: "The Greek term *hoi ioudaioi* cannot be translated simply as 'the Jews'. . . . Ancient Judean writers such as Josephus . . . fairly consistently distinguish between Judeans and other peoples who had lived at points under Jerusalem rule, such as 'the Idumeans' to the south and 'the Galileans' in the north. . . . Significantly, in the narrative of the crucifixion of Jesus, it is the Roman governor and soldiers who name and mock Jesus as 'the king of the Judeans' (15:2, 9, 18, 25), while the Judean chief priests and scribes mock him as 'the king of Israel' (15:32). . . . Thus the conflict here is not between Jesus and his movement and 'all the Jews' or 'Judaism' generally, but only between the Jesus movement and the Pharisees and other Judeans" (Horsley, *Hearing the Whole Story*, 167).

10. Donald Juel discusses the significance of Mark's use of "King of the Jews": "Romans are interested only in political implications [while] to the religious authorities, the claim to be 'the Christ, the Son of the Blessed' (RSV), enthroned at God's right hand, is pretentious to the point of blasphemy. To the Romans the claim is seditious (there can be only one king in Caesar's realm) and absurd [while] for readers who know that Jesus is 'Christ, the Son of God': it provides testimony to the truth" (Juel, *Gospel of Mark*, 146).

readers of the roots of the "King" on trial, as Lamar Williamson notes: "[I]n the silence of Jesus two Old Testament themes converge: the righteous sufferer of the Psalms (cf. Ps. 38:13–14) and the suffering servant of Second Isaiah (cf. Isa. 53:7)."[11] Pilate is "amazed" (*thaumazō*) at the silence of Jesus, thus adding to the list of characters in Mark for whom Jesus prompts "amazement" more than faith (see 1:27; 2:20; 5:20; 5:42; 10:32; 12:17; 15:4; 16:8).

The second scene echoes an earlier scene in Mark 6. With no attempt to soften Pilate's complicity in Jesus' death, Mark's account of Pilate's decision recalls for readers an earlier decision made by Herod. Like Herod in 6:14–29, so now Pilate in 15:6–15 rules on the basis of political expediency, for he both realizes that the charges against Jesus are fraudulent (15:10, 14) and wishes to satisfy the crowds (15:15). Just as John the Baptist was *handed over* for execution in 6:17, and just as Jesus was *handed over* to religious expediency in the Sanhedrin trial (14:42, 53), so now in the praetorium Jesus is *handed over* to political expediency (15:15).

While biblical scholars and Hollywood directors sometimes focus on the role of Barabbas, Mark does not. Barabbas (meaning "son of the father") is chiefly a Markan foil to advance the story by emphasizing the dramatic injustice being done to Jesus. The tragic irony is advanced when the same crowd that had shouted "Hosanna" at the entrance to Jerusalem (11:9) is now manipulated by the chief priests to shout "Crucify him!"(15:14). Ironically, Jesus, the one who *can* save lives (*Hosanna* means "Save now" in Hebrew) is rejected in favor of one who has taken life and, according to Myers, "was in prison with the rebels who had committed murder during the insurrection" (11:17).[12]

The second scene ends with words that leave readers with the same disdain for Pilate as earlier they had had for Herod: "So Pilate, wishing to satisfy the crowd, released Barabbas for them; and after flogging Jesus, he handed him over to be crucified" (15:15).[13] This verse is a tragic fulfillment of the seed sown in rocky soil in 4:19: "The cares of the world . . . come in and choke the

---

11. Williamson, *Mark*, 270.

12. Myers posits that Barabbas was likely a member of a terrorist group known as the Sicarii. By naming Barabbas, Mark forces his readers to make a choice between violence and nonviolence: "What Mark calls 'murder' (cf. *phonos*, 7:22) would have been characteristic of the modus operandi of the Sicarii or 'dagger men,' who were infamous for their stealth in political assassination. Thus Mark's narrative concern here is to dramatize the choice. Jesus and Barabbas each represent fundamentally different kinds of revolutionary practice, violent and nonviolent, both of which have led to a common fate: prison and impending execution" (Myers, *Binding the Strong Man*, 380).

13. Williamson notes an important Markan referent in 15:15: "'Scourged' and 'delivered' both recall Jesus' third passion prediction (10:33–34) which, along with Old Testament scripture, will be further fulfilled in the following paragraph" (Williamson, *Mark*, 272).

word." The cumulative narrative effect is devastating. The Twelve are nowhere to be seen. The religious leaders are well on their way to achieving their stated objective since 3:6. The crowd, which had played a neutral to positive role in Mark until now, has proven itself sorry soil (4:1–9, 14–20). A known insurrectionist and murderer is now free while a guileless defendant is given the death sentence. Once again, the political establishment in Rome ignores justice in the interest of keeping the peace. In just fifteen verses of Mark's crucifixion narrative, readers are left with the realization that Jesus has been abandoned by friends, family, religious community, and society.

The third scene (15:16–20) quells any desire for readers tempted to sympathize with soldiers "just doing their job." It is a brutal scene of unabashed torture and ignominy, flavored with Old Testament allusions and Markan irony. As Jesus is draped in a purple cloth and his head pierced with a crown of thorns, soldiers salute him as "King," spit upon him, and beat him. The scene brings to mind Isaiah 50:6 and the promise of a coming Suffering Servant: "I gave my back to those who struck me, and my cheeks to those who pulled out the beard; I did not hide my face from insult and spitting."[14] Readers are struck again by Markan irony in this scene as the soldiers are ultimately mocked, because, in fact, they *are* paying homage to the King. Having shown the suffering of Jesus at the hands of Pilate and now his soldiers, Mark is ready to shift scenes.

As the fourth scene (15:21–4) opens, the soldiers compel Simon of Cyrene, the father of Alexander and Rufus, to carry the cross (crossbeam) of Jesus.[15] This is the only mention of Simon, Alexander, and Rufus in Mark's Gospel, and it is the first mention of the cross in Mark 15. Scholars have a field day speculating about Simon,[16] but in keeping with the limited information Mark provides readers about this drafted disciple, Brian Blount best captures the tragic irony of this scene: "In a world where discipleship is defined by the act of taking up Jesus' cross and following, the scattered disciples all fall short. The burden falls upon a previously unknown interloper who just happens upon the scene and this critical discipleship role at 15:21."[17]

Ched Myers sees Mark's irony less in a "previously unknown interloper" than in a specifically named interloper. The first disciple called by Jesus was "Simon," who later confessed Jesus as "the Christ" and who was among the

---

14. Williamson suggests that this scene had a powerful resonance for the religiopolitical situation of Mark's readers: "A . . . probable reason for the prominence of mockings in Mark is that this Gospel was written for Christians who were themselves undergoing ridicule and abuse for their faith. They could identity with Jesus, because Jesus had identified with them" (Williamson, *Mark*, 272).

15. Taylor writes, "It was customary for the condemned man to carry his cross beam (*patibulum*)" (Taylor, *Gospel according to St. Mark*, 587).

16. Brown offers detailed speculation about Simon of Cyrene (Brown, *Death of the Messiah*, 913–16).

17. Blount, *Go Preach!* 97.

inner circle included in Jairus's house (5:37) and atop the Mount of Transfiguration (9:2–8). Prior to his three denials of Jesus, readers would logically expect him to take up this cross. Tragically, though, it is a stranger called Simon who is forced to bear the cross of Jesus. "Yet," as Myers notes, "again it is an outsider (Simon was father to Alexander and Rufus, names from which we must infer that he was a gentile) who, however unwittingly, answers the call to discipleship, while the twelve are nowhere to be seen."[18]

It is within this fourth scene that the readers are taken outside the city to Golgotha.[19] There, details of the crucifixion are announced in a terse three-Greek-word statement: *kai staurousin auton* ("and they crucified him," 15:24). The crucifixion has long captivated the religious imagination of biblical scholars, painters, and musicians. Mark, though, is not especially fascinated by the crucifixion itself. He offers no details about nails being driven into the hands of Jesus or blood gushing from his side. Instead, Mark's focus is elsewhere as he again stresses the Old Testament roots for what is happening. The offer of drugged wine and then the casting of lots for Jesus' garments remind readers, respectively, of the words of Proverbs 31:6 and Psalm 22:18. Through scriptural allusion Mark states what Matthew will make explicit— that even in the death of Jesus, the Word of God is being fulfilled.

The fifth scene (15:25–32) is largely a change of camera angle. In this scene, Mark reminds his readers of the time of the crucifixion. He states that it was nine o'clock in the morning when Jesus was crucified (15:25). By this time notation and the use of the historic present tense, Mark pulls readers closer to the action.[20] Again in this scene, Mark tells his readers that the charge against Jesus is sedition as the sign above the cross reads "The King of the Jews" (15:26). And again, readers experience Markan irony as they know that what is written as mockery is, in fact, the truth: Jesus *is* the King of the Jews. This scene does not focus on the physical misery of the crucified Jesus but on the unrelenting taunts and verbal assaults of Jesus by known and anonymous opponents.[21]

Scriptural allusions and Markan irony also dominate this scene. Having

18. Myers, *Binding the Strong Man*, 385.

19. Pheme Perkins writes, "*Golgotha* is the Aramaic term for 'skull.' The more popular name, 'Calvary,' comes from the Latin term *calvaria* (skull)" (Perkins, "Gospel of Mark," 722).

20. Taylor explains: "The use of the historic present is a striking feature of the Markan account of the crucifixion. In 21–7 there are five examples. There are also three imperfects in 23–32. . . . This use of tenses gives great vividness to the scene; we see it before our eyes" (Taylor, *Gospel according to St. Mark*, 588).

21. Brown traces origins in Mark for this "blaspheming" of Jesus: "At the beginning (Mk. 2:6–7) Jesus was accused of blaspheming because he forgave sins, a power appropriate to God alone. At the end in his trial by the Sanhedrin (Mk. 14:61–64) Jesus was convicted of blasphemy because he said he was the Messiah. . . . Now at the end as Jesus hangs on the cross, passersby blaspheme against Jesus, challenging his power to destroy the sanctuary and build it in three days. Thus the picture of hostile misunderstanding is consistent in Mark from beginning to end" (Brown, *Death of the Messiah*, 986–87).

rejected the cause of Jewish insurrectionists, Jesus is hung indistinguishably between two of them (15:27). In 10:37, James and John ask Jesus if they may sit at his right and left in his glory. They assure Jesus of their ability to remain always faithful to him (10:39). Five chapters later, these self-assured disciples are conspicuous by their absence, having been replaced with anonymous insurrectionists. The insurrectionists join the chief priests and crowd in mocking Jesus, especially in relation to the Jerusalem Temple (15:29–30). But what those who mock Jesus do not yet realize is that, upon his death, Jesus' prediction of the demise of the Temple (13:1–2) was not an idle threat. For in the next scene the Temple's curtain will be split apart (15:38) and with it all former sanctioned religious segregation.

The common chorus throughout this mocking scene is "save yourself" (15:30–1) even though it was Jesus who had taught the crowds, "For those who want to save their life will lose it" (8:35). The chief priests are unrelenting in their opposition to Jesus as they mock his "Kingship" while insisting that if he saves himself, they will "see and believe" (15:32). "But the Marcan readers have already heard Jesus speaking of such outsiders in Isaian language (4:12 = Isa. 6:9): 'they may indeed see but not perceive.' "[22] Mark's readers also know that the religious leaders have seen multiple wonders at the hands of Jesus, and yet this has not led to faith but to a hardening of their opposition.[23] As Myers notes, "Jesus' opponents have once again exegeted the central messianic truth. Jesus was indeed committed to 'saving' life (3:4), and he did indeed warn his disciples against trying to save their own life (8:36). The tragedy of the story is that no one has understood this paradox; his enemies ridicule it, his disciples have abandoned it."[24] There is no penitent thief in Mark as in Luke's crucifixion narrative (Luke 23:39–43), no one who stands faithfully by the cross as does John's beloved disciple (John 19:25–27). Mark ends this scene of the death of Jesus with even the guilty joining the chorus of mockers. Thus, with echoes of Lamentations 2:15 and Psalm 22:8, Mark's crucifixion narrative makes a masterful use of irony to make foolishness the wisdom of the world (1 Cor. 1:18–25).

Apocalyptic signals introduce the fifth scene (15:33–39) as the sky dark-

---

22. Ibid., 995.

23. Tolbert uses the irony of the mocking of Jesus on the cross to discuss Mark's understanding of faith and salvation: "They [Jesus' opponents at the cross] demand a miracle, a sign, upon which to found their faith, but faith is not something an action of Jesus can give to them; faith is something within them that responds to Jesus. Indeed, when Jesus interacts with those of faith, they are saved, not by Jesus, but by their faith. . . . Miracles will not come to those who seek them *in order to believe*; for the Gospel of Mark, *miracles occur as the fruit, not the cause, of faith*" (Tolbert, *Sowing the Gospel*, 276).

24. Myers, *Binding the Strong Man*, 388.

ens from noon until three in the afternoon. Lamar Williamson explains, "A recurring theme in apocalyptic literature, the darkening of the sun, suggests the eschatological import of the crucifixion of Jesus. The reference is not only to tribulation and judgment, but to the time when, after the great tribulation, the sun will be darkened (13:24) and the Son of Man will come with power and glory."[25] Pheme Perkins suggests that Mark's readers were accustomed to cosmological signs accompanying the death of great persons: "Mark's readers probably knew the story that the sun had grown dark when Julius Caesar died as well."[26] Surely, Mark's readers also remembered the Exodus story and how God blotted out the sun in Egypt for three days (Exod. 10:21–29), as well as comparable apocalyptic texts in Joel 3:4 and Amos 8:9–10.

In consummate Markan irony, Jesus' cry of dereliction (15:34) quotes directly from Psalm 22:1.[27] However, those standing by the cross mistake "*Eloi*" (my God) for "*Elias*" (Elijah, 15:35–36). Mark's readers know that Elijah has already come in this Gospel, first at the baptism of Jesus (1:3–8) and then at his transfiguration (9:2–8). Elijah, then, will not return to rescue Jesus from the cross (6:29; 9:13). No one in heaven or on earth will stop this miscarriage of justice as Jesus is now finally *handed over* to death. In Mark, Jesus dies completely abandoned by the voices of heaven and earth while surrounded by those who had every opportunity to understand him but did not. As in many Greek dramas, the tragic hero dies abandoned and misunderstood.

Unlike most Greek tragedy, though, Mark does not close this scene with the death of Jesus, even as he does not end the crucifixion narrative with a focus on the last breath of Jesus. Instead, Mark next introduces his readers to events and reactions in response to the death of Jesus (15:38–39). How one understands what happens in this crucial scene in Mark 15 directly impacts how one understands the dramatic and homiletic intent of Mark's Gospel.

The first event following the death of Jesus is both apocalyptic and a prophetic fulfillment. Mark writes that upon the death of Jesus, "the curtain of the temple was torn (*eschisthē*) in two, from top to bottom" (15:38; cf. 1:10).

---

25. Williamson, *Mark*, 276.

26. Perkins, "Gospel of Mark," 723.

27. Tolbert provides an important argument against those who assume that when Jesus utters Psalm 22:1, it is simply Markan shorthand for the entire psalm, thus absolving Jesus of any genuine cry of dereliction from the cross: "That Jesus should suggest that God has forsaken him on the cross has disturbed many Markan commentators. Since the words Jesus uses, 'My God, my God, why hast thou forsaken me?' are a close rendition of the opening verse of Psalm 22, which begins in sadness but ends in assurance, some have argued that the whole psalm is being called to mind, and consequently the cry should be interpreted as triumph over desolation. Such a view, however, does little justice to the words as they stand. Had Mark wanted Jesus to express triumph or confidence from the cross, his final words could have been shaped quite differently, as in fact they are in the Gospels of Luke and John" (Tolbert, *Sowing the Gospel*, 282–83).

The passive voice of the verb *schizō* indicates that this rending is the divine response to the death of Jesus; the tense and meaning of this verb suggest a violent, completed, and decisive action. As God rends the veil (*katapetasma*)[28] of the sanctuary (*naos*),[29] that which divided the holy from the profane is removed. The Temple can no longer serve as "a den of bandits," as a house for zealous, nationalistic movements, or a house for accommodation to the dominant political forces, or a house for a malignant tradition of ethnic and ritual exclusion. Myers observes:

> Mark's narrative of subversion regarding the efficacy and authority of the temple cult now is given closure. Jesus' death has unmasked the fact that the "tear" (*schisman*) in the "old garment" is irreparable (2:21); the symbolic order as it is centrally embedded in the sanctuary has been overthrown. . . . The strong man has *not* prevailed, his "house" *has* been ransacked.[30]

As at Jesus' baptism (1:10), the rending (*schizō*) of the sanctuary curtain is a Markan aside intended for his readers. Again in Mark's narrative, readers know something that other characters in the story do not. Readers know that upon the death of Jesus, as in Jeremiah 7 and Ezekiel 10, the Temple is no longer the repository for the holy, for even though the Temple is temporarily standing (either at the time of Jesus or the writing of Mark), it is already effectively dead to the roots (11:20). The divine rending of the *katapetasma* signals, not a renovation of the Temple and its cult, but a rebirth as envisioned in Isaiah 56 in which God's house will be "a house of prayer for all nations" (11:17).[31] The grace of God is accessible now to all people.[32]

After the death of Jesus, Mark first tells of the rending of the Temple curtain and then shifts back to the cross and a "confession" by a nameless cen-

---

28. Brown writes, "The general function of such a veil [*katapestama*] would be to shut the holy place off from the profane, and rending the veil would mean destroying the special character or holiness that made the place a sanctuary" (Brown, *Death of the Messiah*, 1101).

29. Brown provides a detailed exposition of the function of the *naos* in *Death of the Messiah*, 1099–1102.

30. Myers, *Binding the Strong Man*, 390.

31. Juel (*Gospel of Mark*, 147–50) for a helpful discussion of the cursing and then later rending of the Temple veil.

32. Sharyn Dowd suggests an additional function for Mark's account of the tearing of the "temple tapestry." She writes, "It signifies the royal stature of Jesus; a Greco-Roman audience would expect the death of a ruler to be accompanied not only by astrological portents, but also by supernatural events associated with cultic places or images. . . . The statue of Jupiter at Olympia laughed aloud before the death of Caligula (*Caligula*, 57.1), and a statue of Jupiter was struck by lightning before the death of Domitian (*Domitian*, 15.2). . . . The tearing of the temple veil at Jesus' death would have meant to Markan audiences that this was indeed the death of a king" (Dowd, *Reading Mark*, 162).

turion (15:39). It is at this point that many scholars neglect Mark's consistent and clear literary intent.[33] As I have already argued, in Mark 15 the religious authorities, the political authority, the soldiers in charge, the crowds present at the cross, and even convicts contribute to a collective denial of what readers have known to be true about Jesus since 1:1 and know to be true even upon the humiliation and death of Jesus on the cross. While readers grasp the identity of Jesus, they are the only ones at the foot of the cross who do. The centurion makes his "confession" only for Mark's readers, as Dowd notes: "On the level of the story it is a sarcastic comment on the lips of a jaded professional executioner who has just watched one more Jewish peasant die calling on his God."[34] Here, as throughout chapter 15, Mark's irony and bitter sarcasm makes the abandonment of Jesus complete and the death of Jesus tragic.

Some scholars argue, however, that the "confession" of the centurion is the breaking of the messianic secret. They too understand Mark's use of irony and suggest that the intended irony at this point is that the first "real" confession of Jesus comes not from one of the Twelve, but an anonymous soldier—not from a Jew but a Gentile. Tolbert represents this view when she writes:

> The centurion, standing opposite the cross and observing the sudden death after the loud petition to God, speaks for the authorial audience as well as for the author of Mark when he declares: Truly this man was Son of God (15:39). God's Son is reunited with the divine Parent; God does indeed save those who endure to the end (13:13), regardless of the rejection, betrayal, and failure provided by most of humanity in this corrupt and hard-hearted world.[35]

While such a reading of the centurion's "confession" has a definite interpretative appeal, it is finally unconvincing because it neglects too much of Mark's consistent style and theology and fails to provide adequate narrative logic for such an epochal confession. As Tolbert herself notes, miracles in Mark, such as the rending of the Temple curtain, do not produce faith; they are the fruit, not the cause, of faith.[36] And, even if such an apocalyptic and prophetic sign were capable of producing faith, in Mark's Gospel the centurion does not see the sign; instead, he's facing the cross.

Raymond Brown argues differently. He suggests that the rending of the

---

33. Matthew 27:50–54 resolves the ambiguity of Mark 15:38–39 by placing the centurion's "confession" after a series of apocalyptic and eschatological signs.

34. Dowd, *Reading Mark*, 162.

35. Tolbert, *Sowing the Gospel*, 287.

36. Ibid., 182.

katapetasma tou naou ("the Temple veil") is concurrently an apocalyptic sign and a transforming and redemptive sign for the centurion. Brown argues, "There is no reason to think that the ancient Marcan audience (any more than most people today) would have had a problem with the centurion's seeing the rending of the veil."[37] While that statement may or may not be true, it is certainly true that Mark himself would have had a problem with such an assumption on at least two counts. First, to reiterate what has already been said, Mark makes a literary point to his readers to portray the centurion as facing the cross, not the Temple. The centurion's "attitude is the same as that of the others at the foot of the cross," argues Dowd. "If Jesus had really been anyone special, he would have been translated to heaven before dying such a shameful death (Origen, *Ccel* 2.68)."[38] Second, Brown's argument ignores the idea that the rending of the *katapetasma* in Mark functions more as a literary aside intended for his readers than as motivation for the centurion to confess his faith. Mark then gives his readers no narrative logic to lead them from Jesus' death on the cross to the rending of the *katapetasma tou naou* to an unambiguous confession of faith in Jesus as the Son of God by the Roman centurion.

Looking again at Mark's crucifixion narrative, readers are introduced to the centurion not in relationship to the rent curtain but in apposition to the crucified Jesus. Readers alone, certainly not a member of the cohort that had tortured and crucified this religious fraud, are the only ones who know that the crucifixion was not the tragic end to Jesus and his challenge to the religious and political authorities in Jerusalem. Before and during his crucifixion, those facing Jesus taunted him as "the King" (15:26, 32). The centurion simply continues this sequence of taunts. Facing the tortured and limp body of Jesus hanging from the cross, the centurion adds an exceptionally bitter taunt: "Truly this man was God's Son." In continuity with the preponderance of irony in Mark's crucifixion narrative, what the centurion "confesses" as farce readers know to be as true now as it was when they first learned the identity of Jesus in 1:1.[39]

---

37. Brown, *Death of the Messiah*, 1145.
38. Dowd, *Reading Mark*, 162.
39. Juel offers a similar reading of the centurion's "confession" and a convincing rationale: "Like the chief priest, the guards who taunt Jesus to prophesy, the mockers at the foot of the cross, Pilate, and the rest of the Roman soldiers, the centurion may say more than he knows. If the confession is sarcastic, it would fit the general tone of irony. Nothing in Jesus' ignominious death would convince anyone that he was the King. In fact, it would seem to be a final disqualification. . . . And there is equally good reason for understanding how the last comment functions ironically as confirmation for readers who watch the story from another place, appreciating what players in the drama cannot. The confession of the centurion is true, whether or not he understands what he says. And in fact it is even more 'true'—even more realistic—if he does not understand what he is saying" (Juel, *Gospel of Mark*, 146–67).

Some scholars argue that having the women "looking on from afar" (15:40) is Mark's way to contrast the faithfulness of women in Mark[40] with Mark's male disciples, who disappear altogether in Mark 15. It is true that women play a significant role in Mark's narrative, and it is therefore tempting to see these women as the good soil upon which the church will be built (4:20). Unlike James and John who looked for glory (10:37), Mark tells us that since Galilee these women have done what true disciples do—they have "followed" Jesus and "served" him. Myers speaks for any number of contemporary scholars when he argues, "The women now become the 'lifeline' of the discipleship narrative."[41] Unfortunately, Myers woefully understates how tenuous is both this "lifeline" and this line of interpretation.

What does Mark tell us about these women? While we hear discipleship qualities about them—that they followed and served—we hear no confession from their mouths. Ominously, Mark tells us that these women observed the crucifixion "from a distance" (*makrothen*). In Mark's Gospel, Peter, in the midst of a triple denial, was the last observer of Jesus "who followed him from a distance" (14:54, 66–72). This Markan parallel of failed discipleship provides a difficult interpretative problem for those who contend that the women are the faithful remnant of Jesus' followers. More likely, though, as happens throughout the crucifixion narrative, Mark here echoes a psalm, in this instance the Septuagint's translation of Psalm 37:12 (Ps. 38:11 NRSV): "Those who were close to me stood *from a distance* (*makrothen*)."

Another ominous narrative sign appears as Mark gives us specific names for some of the women. Characters in Mark who are given names typically do not fare well as disciples. Often, they are portrayed as seeking position, glory, status, or authority. What about these women? It is impossible to discern Mark's final assessment of the faithfulness of these women on the basis of chapter 15 alone. For in Mark 15 these women do not interact with Joseph; they simply mark the site of Jesus' burial (15:47). It is not until chapter 16 that any argument for the women as the faithful remnant of Jesus' disciples crumbles. First, they come not to celebrate a risen Messiah but to anoint a dead Jew for burial (16:1), in itself a redundant act since proleptically an anonymous faithful woman has already done so (14:9). More important, the divine messenger at the empty tomb confirms that the three predictions of Jesus are true. He has suffered and died and now is risen and will meet them in Galilee (16:6–7).

---

40. For example, Peter's mother-in-law (1:29–31), the hemorrhaging woman (5:25–34), the Syrophoenician woman (7:24–30), the widow in the Temple (12:41–44), and the anonymous woman who anointed Jesus for burial (14:3–9).

41. Myers, *Binding the Strong Man*, 398.

How do these women respond to this astounding news? Tolbert ends any romantic interpretation of the enduring faithfulness of these women in Mark when she writes, "Here in the final irony of the Gospel, with all need for secrecy gone, those who are directed to go and tell run away in fear, saying nothing to anyone."[42] While Mark commends these women who have *followed* and *served* Jesus since Galilee more than the male disciples who do not even merit mention in the crucifixion narrative, these women also finally fail in the discipleship to which they are called. So, as the Gospel ends, male and female followers, despite their initial enthusiasm, each fall on rocky ground (4:16–17).

What about the last hope for transformation at the foot of the cross in Mark's crucifixion narrative? What about Joseph of Arimathea (15:40–47)? In Matthew 27:57 and John 19:38, Joseph is described as a disciple of Jesus, while in Luke 23:50–51 Joseph is seen as a Sanhedrin insider who objected to their treatment of Jesus. Yet, in Mark, *all* members of the Sanhedrin, especially during the passion narrative, are opposed to Jesus (14:64). It is the members of the Sanhedrin who begin the fateful string of events in which Jesus is *handed over* to be executed.

Like the women who viewed the crucifixion "from a distance" and, more to the point, like the scribe who was judged by Jesus to be "not far" from God's kingdom (12:34), Joseph engenders initial sympathy from readers. After all, he is willing to get involved with a person whom he and the Sanhedrin have deemed blasphemous. In addition, he endangers his ritual purity by dealing with a corpse on the eve of the Sabbath.

If we look more carefully at Mark's narrative, however, our sympathy for Joseph soon wanes. As a faithful member of the Sanhedrin, Joseph is surely not alone in waiting for the coming reign of God. Readers know that the reign of God has been at hand since Jesus began his public ministry in 1:15. As Dowd concludes, "The fact that Joseph is still 'looking for the kingdom of God' shows that he, like so many in this story, has missed the whole point."[43] Unwilling to view Joseph unsympathetically, some point to Joseph's burial of Jesus. Look again. What does Joseph do? He asks Pilate if he may bury a fellow Jew immediately (and without the traditional Jewish rites of anointing for burial) lest the Sabbath be profaned (Deut. 21:22–23)—not because he has found the coming reign of God revealed in Jesus. "Joseph, in other words, is simply attending to a matter of ritual purity," argues Myers. "In the end, the Sanhedrin has successfully repelled

---

42. Tolbert, *Sowing the Gospel*, 295.
43. Dowd, *Reading Mark*, 164.

Jesus' challenge to the symbolic order; the one who claimed to be 'Lord of the Sabbath' (2:28) is subjected to the ultimate insult—improper entomb-ment—for the sake of the Sabbath order."[44] Like the young man who fled from the scene when Jesus was arrested, leaving his linen cloth (*sindōn*) behind, so now Joseph wraps the crucified Jesus in a linen cloth (*sindōn*)— a haunting allusion to the desertion of nearly *all* in Mark's cast who have *handed over* Jesus to death. Quite simply, then, there is no convincing lit-erary or theological logic to view the centurion or Joseph of Arimathea as repentant military and religious figures.

So, as the curtain falls on chapter 15, Mark's readers are left in a quandary. They know Jesus to be the Son of God and they have heard repeatedly that on the third day Jesus would rise to new life, and yet no one in the story seems to grasp this "Gospel." No one by the cross has shown through word or deed that they are prepared to "take up their cross and follow" Jesus. What are read-ers to do?

View Two: "Is That Your *Final* Answer?" (Mark 14:32–15:47)
Gary W. Charles

[Introduction: What sense is a preacher to make of Mark's passion narrative when the New Common Lectionary divides it into separate, seemingly unre-lated, scenes? The sermon below is an attempt to address the literary and theological challenges to readers/listeners in considering all of Mark's pas-sion narrative. The sermon tries to enter into a conversation with Mark's passion drama and so ends much at the same point that Mark 15 ends—with far more questions than answers. I hope however, that the sermon triggers a desire to enter more fully into Holy Week and to venture into the miracle of Easter.]

They sit eyeball to eyeball on a small, circular pedestal. Regis asks, "Is the capital city of Italy (a) Buffalo, (b) Madrid, (c) Tokyo, (d) Rome?" If Marva answers correctly, she wins it all. She has used all three of her lifelines in prior rounds and now must answer this question on her own. The audience can hardly hold itself back from shouting out the answer; the music stops and the silence is deafening. Marva whispers her response. Regis waits a dramatic minute and then asks, "Is that your final answer?"

Oddly enough, this spoof on the popular game show *Who Wants to Be a*

---

44. Myers, *Binding the Strong Man*, 395.

Millionaire? corresponds in an important way with the passion story from Mark. For in the course of two chapters, one hundred and eleven verses, Mark puts us in the contestant's seat, has us listen to a series of questions, and at the end, will ask us for our final answer. He starts with this question from Jesus to the disciples in the garden called Gethsemane: "Could you not keep awake one hour?" At the end of Mark 13, just a few verses earlier, Jesus tells his disciples a parable that ends with this one-liner: "What I say to you I say to all: Keep awake" (13:37 NRSV).

Soon after this parable, Jesus ruins a perfectly good Passover meal when he tells the disciples that not only will one of them betray him but they all will desert him. Peter protests and Jesus says, "You will not only desert me, Peter, but you will openly deny me three times in one night." Yet, despite his harsh assessment of the reliability of his colleagues, Jesus takes Peter, James, and John with him to the garden, just as he had earlier taken these three with him into Jairus's house and up the Mount of Transfiguration. In the garden, Jesus asks that they stand watch while he prays. He returns to find them sleeping and asks the rhetorical question, "Could you not keep awake one hour?"

In Matthew's Gospel, Jesus renames Simon *petras*, which in Greek means *rock*. He even goes on to say about Peter: "Upon this rock, I will build my church." Mark shows us how porous is the rock upon which the church is built, as any of us who love the church know only too well. But before we can get too disgusted with three sleeping disciples, another one arrives in the garden. Judas has the nerve to kiss the man he has come to betray. Porous rock, indeed, upon which the church is built. And, as Mark tells the story, it only gets worse.

The second question from Mark's passion story comes when Jesus addresses the armed crowd accompanying Judas: "Have you come out with weapons to arrest me?" In the garden, Judas is joined by an armed crowd and after his infamous kiss, a nameless disciple of Jesus, no doubt thinking he was doing the noble thing, attacks one of the armed guards. He cuts off someone's ear for the sake of Christ.

Motives today are not nearly so noble, but violence is just as near the surface. We curse the driver tailing our rear bumper or toss an insult at a waiter who does not serve us fast enough or smack a child who refuses to do just as we wish or point a gun to scare some sense into someone. Before long, we do not even see the violence outside and within us, or worse, we defend our violence as a necessary, if regrettable, way of the world.

In my childhood and youth, my generation watched so many hours of bombs and raids and fires in Vietnam that we no longer saw the human being in the helmet or the child of God running for shelter through the rice fields.

We no longer saw violence. As an adult, the dulling effect continues. After a while, every movie and commercial, every front-page lead and video game, begins to look and sound so normal, so real, that when a teacher is shot in her classroom or a car bomb explodes in a residential neighborhood or a mother is knifed in broad daylight for drug money our eyes glaze over and our hearts grow one more layer of callus. Common sense rules out any other kind of good sense or God's sense claiming that sometimes violence simply must be met with more violence.

It strikes me as more than strange that the Lord of our church was a victim of senseless, sadistic, ruthless violence and capital punishment and yet on these subjects the church often acts as if it had nothing to say. Many well-meaning Christians argue, "Leave legal and judicial matters to police and attorneys and legislators and judges and juries who know better." But as soon as that is said, you can hear the irony dripping from Mark's pen as he writes a story in which the legal process was fixed, the attorneys corrupt, and the jury tampered with. If the passion of Jesus teaches the church nothing else, it must teach us that good people sometimes do the wrong thing and that bad people almost always do bad things but make them sound good. At this time of year, I often hear religious nonsense that turns the death of Jesus into some sort of positive, innocuous event. To that line of thought, I can only ask that God forgive us when we make the excruciating crucifixion of Jesus sound as if it were really a good thing.

G. K. Chesterton was never wiser than when he suggested that the most important question you could ask a seaside landlady when looking for holiday accommodations was not "How often do you change the sheets?" or "Do you turn eggs when frying them?" but "What is your view of the universe?" Andrew McLellan writes, "The idea was that if she got her theology right she would be likely to get the clean sheets and the bacon and egg right."[45]

There are lots of theories today about the decline of the church in America. I've got a couple of my own. One is: bad theology. We have somehow convinced ourselves that we can speak *about* God without speaking *for* God's people in need. We can have our own "sweet hour of prayer" without living a life of prayer for those whose lives are anything but sweet. As many of you know, a favorite spot of mine is the small isle on the west of Scotland called Iona. Thousands of people come there from across the world each year on a spiritual quest. Norman Shanks, the leader of the Iona Community, responds

---

45. Andrew R. C. McLellan, "Garden Theology," in *Preaching for These People* (London: Mowbray, 1997), 71.

to Iona's seeming success with this thought: "People come to us seeking peace and quiet and we try to send them away seeking peace and justice."[46]

The third question from Mark is uttered by Pilate about Jesus to the complaining crowd: "What evil has he done?" Unlike John's Gospel in particular, Mark spends little time describing Jesus before Pilate. Pilate knows Jesus is innocent, but he also knows that he has a crowd to please and you don't keep people happy by ignoring their wishes. Justice is fine, but for most people, justice means seeing that things go the way they want them to. So, Pilate does not delve deeply into his question to the crowd or ask it of them a second time. He is far more concerned with expediency and calm than with justice or truth. So, he gives the maddening crowd the one for whom they clamor and then moves on to the next case.

Another of my theories about the decline of the church in America is that like Pilate, churches have come to worship expediency and calm. As churches struggle to keep members, the last thing they want to do is to upset the apple cart, to make someone mad and have them storm out and take their friends—and their money—with them. So, inside our churches, we talk about safe subjects and we engage in comfortable mission projects and we bend over backwards not to search for truth or to insist on justice but to make sure everyone is happy. Mark will not let us forget that Pilate sacrificed an innocent human life to make an unreasonable crowd happy. And, far too often, ever since the church has done the same.

The last question of the passion story from Mark is spoken by Jesus on the cross: "My God, my God, why have you forsaken me?" By this point, Peter has already denied Jesus three times. Judas has sold Jesus out for a bag of gold. Loyal followers have fled so far from Golgotha that a total stranger has to help Jesus haul his cross. Pilate has cowered at the notion of doing justice. Scribes and Pharisees have played their religious trump card. Soldiers have tortured an innocent victim and the crowds have called for the release of a known murderer. Jesus hangs like a limp dishrag and cries, "My God, my God, why have you forsaken me?" Mark asks us: Is this the way the world ends, as Tennyson writes, "not with a bang but a whimper"? Is a disconsolate, abandoned, betrayed, beaten, broken Jesus and a world seething with violence, immune to injustice, glad at the misfortune of another, the final answer to the question "What's life all about?"

If you think it is, then stay home on Maundy Thursday. Do not walk into this sanctuary at Friday noon and, certainly, walk anywhere but into this

---

46. Norman Shanks, *Iona: God's Energy: The Vision and Spirituality of the Iona Community* (London: Hodder & Stoughton, 1999), 83.

Christian sanctuary next Sunday. If you think the first fifteen chapters of Mark's Gospel give final answers to the questions, "What's life all about?" and "Which disciple should I emulate?" then you have wasted your time listening to Mark and to me. If instead you would follow and serve this Jesus and his beloved even to the grave, then the story is not yet over. It will be over soon, at least Mark's part of it. And at the end, then, and only then, will you and I be asked to make our final answer.

View Three: Will the Real Son of the Father Please Stand Up?
Brian K. Blount

Maybe you're old enough to remember a television show called *What's My Line?* Off to one side stood the obligatory host who moderated the session. More centrally located was a bank of three semicelebrity figures whose analytical and guessing powers were to be put to the test. In the focus of attention stood three or more "regular people," contestants whose job it was to fool the celebrity panel into thinking each one of them was the only one who represented a particular occupation. Which one of them was the real writer, or truck driver, or airline pilot? Each of the contestants was coached by handlers in the background with the kind of information people in his or her particular profession would naturally possess. The real airline pilot, of course, knew all there was to know about altimeters, rudders, yaw, and pitch. The others would have to fake it. The better they faked it, the more money and status they won. At the end of the interrogation, after the celebrities had made their choices as to which person actually represented the highlighted profession, the host, amid a calculated air of tension and drama, would ask, "Would the real . . . please stand up!"

Gary's excellent exegesis gives us a similar kind of unscripted, frighteningly real, and incredibly tense scenario. Clearly, in this first-century time, Pilate is the host. The background handlers are the chief priests, elders, and scribes who have bound Jesus before the Roman governor. The crowd, stirred to hostile intent by the handlers, play the role of the semicelebrities who must make the critical decision about the identity of the contestants. The contestants themselves are played by a man whom Mark has identified as the Son of (God) the Father (1:11; 9:7) and a man whose name, *Barabbas*—from the Hebrew *Bar* ("son") *Abba* ("father," cf. 14:36)—means Son of the Father. The decision will be crucial; there will be no consolation prize for the loser this time. The winner will live; the loser will die. The crowd must choose.

As I sit and write this final of my responsive reflections to what Gary has done in his exegesis and sermon, our post–September 11 world is in a state of political anxiety and military dis-ease. Although our U.S. military has effectively annihilated the regime that harbored the sponsors of terrorism that befell New York and Washington, D.C., pilots and soldiers remain still in harm's way. On the ground, days of inactivity are punctuated by intense moments of fearsome fighting, whose sights and sounds are brought back live via satellites hovering miles above the fray. In Israel, tanks sweep through occupied Palestinian lands and fixed-wing aircraft and helicopter gun-ships lock in on a regime allegedly harboring the sponsors of a terrorism whose suicide bombings have shell-shocked an entire planet.

The great Western powers are the hosts. The background handlers are the political spin masters who tell us that violence is wrong when someone else perpetrates it against us but right when we must counter them by whatever means we deem necessary. On both sides the situation is spinning out of control. Even as it does, we are brought before our television sets, we semi-celebrity, innocently bystanding, can't-change-the-channel onlookers of carnage as the decision makers who must choose. By our inaction we sanction what we see. Only by our protest and movement do we actively prosecute a contrary vote. Finally, there before us are the options. The violence of terrorism to find justice. The violence of war to destroy the terrorism that has taken justice away. Or the peace of violent protest that stands defiant before empires; the peace of resistant citizens who demand that their powerful governments find a political and diplomatic solution to the warfare their armies and their surrogates impose. The decision will be crucial; there will be no consolation prizes for the loser this time. The winners will conquer; the losers will die. You must choose.

That's how Tom Skinner, an African American preacher of a generation ago, interpreted the tragic scene that surrounded Jesus' final trial. I have found his work both provocative and useful as an example of how a person's context can influence the meaning he draws from the biblical material he reads. Though his issues were particular to his time, his counsel lives in a way that can be effective for ours. He, too, writes for a world that must come to a decision about what kind of power it will choose to back, what kind of Son of God it will choose to follow. He, too, is waiting to see what the people will do. He wants them to know, though, that their choice isn't the end of things. God's action is. Their choice will say something about them; it will not say anything about God. God will speak for God's self, at that moment when the real Son of God stands up. His identification of himself will enthrall many. It will certainly convict some.

Here's how Tom Skinner saw it: "I've been there," he writes. "I was born in Harlem and have lived out my life where exploitation, oppression and violence are a way of life."[47] This early life situation, conditioned by circumstances of inequity, produced a worldview that looked favorably upon revolutionary attitudes and tendencies. "Yes, I am a radical; I am committed to revolution. I am committed to doing something about the suffering, shame, and misery in America."[48] He therefore reads the Bible with a program of sociopolitical change in mind. "Everywhere I go people say, 'The system's got to go, man,' and 'we gotta do away with the system.' People are fed up. Blacks and whites are sick of the hypocrisy and corruption. Young people are fed up with the world their parents are handing them. Poor and middle-class citizens are reacting to the inequities they see in society."[49]

The critical question is, what is the proper mode of revolution? What is the appropriate way to respond to the injustices a person or an entire people must endure? It is this question that connects Skinner's twentieth-century observations with our twenty-first-century cyclical crisis of violence and counterviolence. Skinner believed that a proper understanding of the biblical text could guide readers toward the proper kind of future conduct for inaugurating productive social transformation. Because of his own encounter with the biblical story, this onetime youth gang leader dedicated to violence embraced an adult life committed to nonviolent engagement and change. Called upon to make a choice, with the means of violence and nonviolent protest before him, he chose the direct action of peace. It is the choice championed by Jesus. Make no mistake, the real Son of the Father stood up to the injustice and the violence in his own world; that was why he became a threat that had to be stamped out.

> Now any time a man starts talking that strong, there are going to be problems. When a man starts shaking up the religious, political, and social system, the people *in* the system feel they have to stop him. . . . Jesus came along and began to threaten both their systems [Pharisees and Sadducees— the Jewish leadership] and denounce them both. Strangely the Pharisees and the Sadducees suddenly got together. Now they had a common enemy. They conspired to have Jesus locked up because He was "dangerous."[50]

---

47. Tom Skinner, *Words of Revolution: A Call to Involvement in the Real Revolution* (Grand Rapids: Zondervan Publishing, 1970), 7.

48. Ibid., 9.

49. Ibid., 7.

50. Ibid., 73.

He was dangerous, but he was not violent. To be sure, there were alternative ways of responding to the injustices in Jesus' world. To the particular injustice of Roman occupation, many of Jesus' contemporaries resorted to a kind of guerrilla warfare that the Romans termed banditry. Today, we might call it terrorism. Barabbas represented this option, this choice for many first-century Jews who sought justice and freedom.

"And Barabbas began to rap to his people, 'There is only one way to get that Roman honkie off your back—burn him out!' So Barabbas and his band of guerrillas burned Roman homes, jumped Roman solders on the streets, and killed Roman soldiers whenever they could do it without great risk."[51]

Jesus and Barabbas agreed that there were significant oppressions of God's people. In fact, as far as Skinner was concerned, Jesus would have agreed with present-day revolutionaries. *I'm not so sure that Jesus Christ is interested in preserving a corrupt [American] heritage.*[52] It was and is at the point of choosing a response that Jesus and Barabbas came to a radical parting of the ways and thus provided a clear choice for the crowd called upon by Pilate to vote. Jesus recognized that the victims of societal oppression could be as evil as the perpetrators of that oppression. It was therefore necessary to change more than systems alone; people themselves had to change.

It is at this point that we must make our choice, that we must decide which way—Jesus' or Barabbas's—is truly the way of the Son of the Father. There will be revolutions. The conditions in our world demand it. The question is, what kind of revolution will it be? Who is going to lead it? *We do have an option.* We can decide between Barabbas and Jesus. Either one of them will change the system. One will do it the wrong way and one will do it the right way. Either way the system will be changed. It's up to you to decide who will do it."[53] The choice belongs as much to us as it did to the crowd gathered that Passover season in Jerusalem.

Pilate knows there is a choice to be made, and he knows the crowd must be allowed to make it. So he allows them a prime opportunity. Even so, the governor is not a sympathetic figure in Skinner's interpretation. Recognizing the parody and irony in the text, Skinner interprets at this point with a literary, ideational skill worthy of the best academicians. Mark, he argues, is not trying to make the Roman look good at Jewish expense. His offerings of amnesty are, in reality, calculated taunts.

---

51. Ibid., 69–70.
52. Ibid., 71.
53. Ibid., 72.

[Pilate] gets up in front of the Jews and says, "Look, I've got two revolutionaries in jail. And you know how much I love you dear Jewish people. I've always loved the dear Jewish people. In fact, some of my best friends," says Pilate, "are Jews. And not only that, the guy who ran my bath last night was a Jew. I even had lunch with one last week. So I have nothing against you dear Jewish people."[54]

Pilate's taunting betrays a scheme. The choice he offers is really no choice at all. He wants the crowd to opt for Barabbas, the more visibly active revolutionary. This is because Barabbas, for all his terrorizing, is a part of the status quo. The Romans know they will always have a Barabbas. They are prepared to deal with a Barabbas. They are confident that their armies will always be able to defeat a Barabbas. So freeing Barabbas will appease the large festival crowd, it will make them feel as if they have made a difference, and in the end that liberating act will have maintained the very oppressive system against which the crowd thought they were mounting a challenge. "You can always stop Barabbas," Skinner writes. "But the question is: *how do you stop Jesus?* How do you stop a Man who has no guns, no tanks, no ammunition, but still is shaking the whole Roman empire? How do you stop a Man, who—without firing a shot—is getting revolutionary results?"[55]

The question is as pertinent for Skinner's readers and our readers as it was for the Roman governor. In fact, Skinner's interpretation of this ancient text, as we can see from the references to tanks and ammunition, is designed to shed light on the contemporary world. He switches from the ancient to the contemporary context without really seeing any change in meaning. The choices presented to the Jerusalem crowd are presented anew in his twentieth and our twenty-first century. Which way, which Son of the Father, will we choose?

We know, of course, how the story ends. The Jerusalem crowd selects Barabbas. His affectations of angst to the contrary, Pilate can't help but be pleased. He has maintained the peace and assured the continuity of the status quo precisely because he got the oppressed liberation fighters to choose the violence they thought was their only way out. Pilate knows it is his method of keeping them hemmed in. In the end, every terrorist action terrorizes its own cause and people with much more oppressive brutality than it ever could impact its oppressive Rome. The Jewish leadership is pleased as well; this Jesus who had threatened their institutional control was now under the control of a death sentence.

---

54. Ibid., 73.
55. Ibid., 74.

On the surface, it appears that the effort was lost. And yet, Jesus' eschatological claims, voiced at 14:62, were initiated with his resurrection that, for Skinner, became a political event: "Three days later Jesus Christ pulled off one of the greatest political coups of all time. He rose from the grave, saying, 'All power is given unto Me in heaven and in earth. And with this power, I'm prepared to radicalize men [*sic*] for God. I'm prepared to make revolutionaries and radicals for the kingdom of God.' "[56]

This is Mark's promise. In the eschatological moment after we make our choice God will make God's judgment; then, the real Son of the Father will stand up. At that moment, depending on our prior vote, we will find ourselves standing with or against God. Even before that moment we will find ourselves either embroiled in violence from which we can see no escape, or, like Gandhi's Indians or Martin Luther King Jr.'s African Americans, standing side by side with revolutionary-minded people who would see oppression end and productive, transformative change come. But who will choose the way of peace to do it? It is our time now. Will the followers of the real Son of the Father please stand up?

---

56. Ibid., 75.

12

Happily Ever After
Mark 16:1–8

View One: From Text to Sermon
Brian K. Blount

Go ahead,
Drive the nails in my hand,
Laugh at me where you stand.
Go ahead,
Try to hide the sun,
One day you'll see that I'm the One.
'Cause I'll Rise Again
Ain't no power on Earth can tie me down.
'Cause I'll Rise Again
Death can't keep me in the ground.[1]

It is one of my favorite musical selections. The church I pastored had a gifted organist; he wrote a special arrangement that our choir and a talented lead baritone sang with tremendous feeling and power. If you closed your eyes you almost felt like you were there watching them taunt Jesus. You could sense the pathos that cloaked the tragic end of what had become a desperate life. And yet, there was that defiant glimmer of hope flashing in his eyes. There would be, despite the horrific goings-on, a triumphant, happy ending. The song buoyed my faith. If Jesus rose again, certainly I who believe in him, could—would—rise from the big and little horrors that plagued my life and the life of my church and community. His happy ending helped assure me of my own.

---

1. Dallas Holm, "Rise Again," © 1977 Going Holm MUSIC/SESAC (administered by ICG). All rights reserved. Used by permission.

I call it the "Walt Disney effect." Over the past several years I have paid big money to go to the movies to see cartoons. My children love them, so my wife and I love them. We cheered for Ariel in *The Little Mermaid,* Belle in *Beauty and the Beast,* Aladdin in, well, *Aladdin*, and Simba in *The Lion King*. One thing that makes these movies special is their happy ending. Walt Disney Studios has for several generations now been in the business of making children and their parents believe, if just for a moment, that there is such a thing as "happily ever after." Part of our faith in the whole Walt Disney ethos is its ability to make us believe in happy endings, and then, especially for children, to somehow transfer that belief to our own fragile, often very tragic lives.

And so it is with the life of Jesus. Because our faith in the outcome of our own lives is so often tied up in the outcome of his, we need to believe in a happy ending. Well, if not happy, at least victorious. What if the happiness ever after, the victory after the defeat, isn't so clear-cut? We would be like little children caught up in successive fairy-tale nightmares. Ursula the sea witch conquers Ariel and Eric her prince. Gaston, the self-absorbed, egomaniacal lunatic kills the heroic beast and forces Belle to marry him. The evil vizier, Jazar, destroys Aladdin and takes over Agrabar and establishes a rule of pure evil. The manipulative, slithery Scar rules forever triumphant in the Pride Lands while Simba lives out the rest of his days in defeated, despondent exile. We would feel lost.

That is precisely why Mark's original ending at 16:8 is so hard. As Ched Myers aptly puts it, "It is not a 'happy ending' in which all is resolved. . . ."[2] The early Christians were like latter-day Walt Disney; they couldn't abide such a curt, stark, open ending. They needed happiness. They needed victory. They needed triumph. *They needed a few more verses.* So they supplied them. They supplied the kind of ending they figured Mark would have supplied had he understood the kind of consternation *his* kind of ending ultimately caused.

Returning to the example of modern Hollywood, I offer another case in point: the movie *Fatal Attraction.* Glenn Close and Michael Douglas played the principal characters. Douglas's character, who is married, has an affair with Close's character. When he tries to end it, the Close character irrationally and destructively maneuvers to save it. In an effort to gauge audience feedback, the film's first incarnation was planned, shot, and then field-tested at a few movie houses. The procedure is called a prescreening. The originally scripted ending did not fare well; it finished on a despondent, somewhat open-ended note. In order to punish the Douglas character for jilting her, the Close character committed suicide. She left behind evidence that implicated her

---

2. Myers, *Binding the Strong Man;* 397.

lover as her murderer. Apparently, the test audiences didn't like that ending; they thought it was anticlimactic. So Hollywood went back to the cinematic drawing board. The cast was recalled, the movie was returned to production, and the ending that eventually electrified movie audiences was put in place. They fiddled around until they got the ending just right.

So did the early church—fiddle around—that is, until they got the ending of Mark just right. Christianity, too, has a fatal attraction to happy endings. Faith, too, it seems, depends on Jesus' ending being a clear cut-victory, not the kind of mystery Mark leaves for us at 16:8. So, how to clean Mark up? The early church fathers could not go back and rewrite the Gospel. So they did the next best thing. They added some *good* to Mark's rather *ambiguous* news.

D. E. Nineham therefore starts his discussion of Mark 16:1–20 with a definitive statement:

> The undisputed facts are that everything which follows 16:8 in any surviving MS. can confidently be declared non-Markan on grounds of attestation, style, and content; thus the Gospel in the earliest form in which we can trace it ended at 16:8.[3]

The evidence is overwhelming. Neither Matthew nor Luke shows any signs of having met the material in 16:9–20.[4] Additionally, Eusebius and Jerome in the fourth century agree that 16:9–20 were omitted in the best manuscripts known to them. Most decisive is the fact that the style and vocabulary smack of the second century, well after Mark had composed his work. All of this leads Nineham to conclude:

> The emphasis and point of view reflects the conditions and needs of the post-apostolic Church, especially the need for unhesitating faith in the gospel of the risen Christ on the basis of the reports of the original witnesses.[5]

In other words, they needed a happier ending.

Why the need to question the ending Mark originally gave us? Nineham notes a host of objections. First, the ending does not fit the rest of the Gospel. The rest of the Gospel promised us a happy ending by claiming to be the *good* news of what God accomplished in Jesus Christ. But the ending at verse 8 leaves us to believe that not much was accomplished after Jesus' death. We

---

3. Nineham, *Gospel of St. Mark,* 439.
4. Hooker, *Gospel according to Saint Mark,* 382.
5. Nineham, *Mark,* 450.

are left on a low note without any impression of victory. The disastrous ending on the cross appears to have the last word and, therefore, the last laugh. Second, there are too many loose ends left at verse 8. Mark 14:28 and 16:7 suggest postresurrection appearances in Galilee. How can that occur given the tragic ending in verse 8 where the women are too afraid to let the disciples know the fact and the location of those appearances?[6] "Surely," the early church must have thought, "Mark must have intended to give us more. Since we don't have it, we must manufacture it ourselves." Thus we have verses 9–20; Myers calls them "imperial rewrites."[7]

Whether they are imperial or not, these rewrites do, as Myers suggests, betray the intent of Mark's original ending. He points out that this is exactly how many of the Greek tragedies ended in the ancient world. Perhaps Mark was influenced by that style of writing and attempted to use such an expressive ending to present his own unique take on the Jesus story. The rewrites move us away from *that* message to the "happy ending" message of the early church.

> The "dilemma" of the ending is precisely what Mark refuses to resolve for us; he *means* to leave us to wrestle with whether or not the women at the tomb (that is to say, we ourselves) overcame their fear in order to proclaim the new beginning in Galilee (16:8). To provide a "neat closure" to the narrative would allow the reader to finally remain passive; the story would be self-contained, in no need of a readerly response.[8]

In other words, missing Mark's intent in the ending, that of an invitation to respond, the early church treated the ending as a scandal that had to be resolved. The church's ending therefore reported Peter's restitution as the head of the community. Jesus successfully met the community and sent it on an apostolic mission. Everything happened "happily ever after."

In creating this happy ending, Myers notes that Mark's original ending is betrayed in three ways. First, the happy ending "suppresses the central contradiction of Mark's story; the genuine struggle of the disciples to 'believe.'"[9] Now unbelief, which Mark used only three times in the Gospel,[10] becomes the villain. While in the Gospel proper belief was always a dialectical endeavor, interacting with unbelief and overcoming it (cf. 9:24, "I believe; help my

---

6. Ibid., 439–42.
7. Myers, *Binding the Strong Man*, 401.
8. Ibid., 401–02.
9. Ibid., 402.
10. Mark 6:6; 9:14; 9:24.

unbelief") in the rewritten, happy ending, unbelief becomes a primary sin. Faith becomes a static reality. Only the one who believes will be saved; Jesus will upbraid the unbeliever. According to Myers, this new take on faith was the early church's way of building a boundary between Christians and pagans. That is exactly the kind of goal Mark spent his gospel effort writing against.[11]

Myers sees the second betrayal as the restoration of *thaumaturgy*, or miracle working, as a guarantee of belief. In saying "These signs will accompany those who believe," in 16:17, the ending suggests that to be a Christian "means to demonstrate visible power."[12]

As the third betrayal, Myers points to the transition from earth to heaven in 16:19; Jesus is moved "upstairs." This exchange allows readers to make a similar transition; concentrating all their efforts on a spiritual Jesus in a distant heaven, they can tone down the call to follow Jesus in active, boundary-breaking discipleship on earth. Certainly Myers is correct at this point when he writes, "The power of Mark's Gospel ultimately lies not in what it tells the disciples/readers, but what it asks of them."[13]

It asks them, to use yet one final Hollywood term, to *fade to black*. Television programming uses this technique in quality drama when, at the point of a powerful dramatic interlude, the screen dissolves into darkness, giving viewers a moment to ponder the resolution of the crisis. Then, instead of coming back with the resolution, the programming breaks to a commercial, attempting to leave viewers on the edge of their seats, hungry for more and asking, what is going to happen next? The difference between Mark's Gospel and the quality television programming is that Mark, after fading out, never fades back in. The screen goes permanently dark. Readers are left hovering on the precipice of an expectation that will not be fulfilled, at least not through his narrative. What will readers do?

Evidently, if you are an early church leader, you change the ending. That, we've already discussed. Modern biblical scholars have another option. They can ask a critical question: "Did it really happen the way Mark says it happened?" Nineham, like many earlier form critics, suggests that Mark borrowed this material from tradition and placed it here without much literary skill, the implication being that the evangelist didn't really know what kind of ending he was getting himself into. He argues that the kind of intentional sophistication someone like Myers applies to the ending would have been beyond any writer of the period.

---

11. Cf. 9:40, "whoever is not against us is for us." Also, chapters 6 and 10, View One.
12. Myers, *Binding the Strong Man*, 403.
13. Ibid.

If St. Mark did intentionally end his Gospel with this paragraph, he was certainly behaving with considerable literary sophistication and making great demands on the understanding of his readers, whom he expected to find the whole of the resurrection gospel in his eight allusive and enigmatic verses. In that case he would have in fact hit on a way of ending his book which just happens to "suit the technique of a highly sophisticated type of modern literature."[14]

One might counter that Mark has, throughout his work, presented us with thematic literary innovations; they indicate the capability for such a unique literary twist. He has treated women, Gentiles, lepers, the law, and outcasts in novel ways for this patriarchal, often legalistic culture. There are also contemporary, first-century parallels to the ending. The Greek tragedy, as I have noted, often employed just this kind of ending.

There are, however, other narrative infelicities that bolster the form critical cause. At 16:1, the women are reintroduced when they had already been introduced previously at 15:40, 47.[15] This redundancy suggests that Mark is adding a traditional account to the end of chapter 15 without comprehending the consequences.

The women's visit to the grave is also unusual. Crucified criminals were usually buried in mass graves. Had Jesus been buried in a mass grave it would have been difficult for them to find his body. The Joseph of Arimathea story may well, then, have been crafted to overcome this crippling narrative obstacle. The counterargument is that Joseph of Arimathea, who is mentioned in all four Gospels, may well have acted historically exactly as Mark portrays.

Still, other difficulties with the text remain. It is possible that the women wanted to find Jesus' burial site; it was customary to visit a grave for three days after burial. Is it logical, though, that they'd want to anoint a body already decaying two days? And what about that angel? "Young man" is used as a designation for angel in other biblical literature,[16] and the wearing of white robes is symbolic of the clothing for heavenly beings. All of these details suggest the possibility that Mark may have taken a traditional legend about Jesus' burial and placed it here at the end of his Gospel, perhaps without understanding the consequences such an ending would have for later readers.

Ultimately, of course, we cannot determine whether Mark's presentation is

---

14. Nineham, *Mark*, 442.
15. It should also be noted that the names of the women vary in the different accounts. This, too, suggests a Markan uncritical joining together of different traditional sources.
16. Second Maccabees 3:26, 33.

rative, the end provides a kind of closure that makes perfect sense.[24] Everything turns on the theme of discipleship. Mark wants his readers to stop gazing up to heaven looking for apparitions and get down to the business of following the way of Jesus in boundary-breaking discipleship. The only way he can force this is to focus on an empty tomb that leaves questions rather than resurrection appearances that provide happy endings.

Petersen therefore tells us how Mark achieves closure with this discipleship motif in mind. He notes that the women's failure to follow through in 16:8 would not be remarkable if their failure was followed by something else. But Mark has ended here with creative intent.

However, the narrator's unexpected withdrawal from communication with the reader is such that the reader is compelled by the narrator to respond. The juxtaposition of the expectation introduced in 16:7 with the terminal frustration of it in 16:8 requires the reader to review what he has read in order to comprehend this apparent incongruity and its meaning for the narrator's message.[25]

The end of the text, then, is not the end of Mark's work. The narrator has left the story with unfinished business because he intends that his readers will complete that business. The shocking ending is shocking precisely because it intends to propel readers into the responsive role of filling the void created by the fear of the women and the disciples.

Mark achieves this effect skillfully. Petersen notes that in 16:7 we do have closure of a sort; there is the expectation of a meeting in Galilee between Jesus and the disciples. Like the one shoe dropped on the floor, he says, we are left with an open-ended expectation until the second shoe drops. Yet in 16:8 we are dumbfounded. Mark not only tells us that the second shoe fails to drop; he counsels us to forget about it. But the frustration is too great. We can't forget. We must do something. We must *not*, however, write another ending.

Mark has, in fact, set up his work exactly so that we would expect the drop of the second shoe. One of his principal plot devices is prediction and fulfillment. "Through predictions he generates expectation and through fulfillment he satisfies them."[26] Verses 14:28 and 16:7 predict a meeting in Galilee. Why, then, does 16:8 guarantee nonfulfillment?

Petersen tells us that if Mark is to be consistent there must be fulfillment

24. Norman R. Petersen, "When Is the End Not the End? Literary Reflections on the Ending of Mark's Narrative," *Interpretation* 34 (1980): 151–66.

25. Ibid., 153.

26. Ibid., 155.

somewhere. That means that on some level 16:8 can't be the real ending; there must be an ending consistent with the text thus far. It does not come in the literal reading of the text but in an ironic understanding of it. Petersen notes that for Mark the will of God and his son always overrides the will of human beings. Jesus makes the prediction in 14:28 about Galilee knowing that the disciples will fail him, and so, in 16:7, despite their failure, he is still on his way to Galilee.

> Consequently, it would appear from our narrator's representation of his characters' actions that the behavior of neither the establishment nor the disciples, that is, of men [*sic*], has any finality about it. It is Jesus who has the final word and the final act. Thus our narrator leads us readers to expect something other than what we find in 16:8 and finding 16:8 to disbelieve that he means it. The end is truly not yet.[27]

It is "not yet" in an ironic sense precisely because the reader is expected to provide the ending in his or her own life of discipleship. In fact, Myers calls it the "Third Call to Discipleship" in Mark's Gospel. He argues that the narrative in this way functions not to close the discipleship story but to reopen it by turning the reader's attention back to Galilee and the opening of Jesus' ministry and the call to discipleship.

> This "future" point of reference is the same as the "past" one: Galilee. And where is that? It is where "the disciples and Peter" were first called, named, sent on missions, and taught by Jesus. In other words, the disciple/reader is being told that the narrative, which appeared to have ended, is beginning again. The story is circular![28]

But circular to what end? To provoking in the reader an active response. That's why Myers notes that "the openness/ambiguity of 16:8 cannot be resolved 'aesthetically,' but only by practice."[29] This is why the women are afraid. The young man's invitation *should* cause fear, just as this ending should cause fear in readers. The narrative concern also reaches out to us. The question, what will the women do? must necessarily become, what will *we* do?"[30] Will *we* follow, or will *we* flee? Will *we* spread the word, or will *we*, who can talk all we want when we want, keep our traps shut at precisely the time the demands of discipleship need us to open them? Myers is correct when

27. Ibid., 156.
28. Myers, *Binding the Strong Man*, 398–99.
29. Ibid., 400–1.
30. Cf. Tolbert, *Sowing the Gospel,* 299.

he says, "This cannot be resolved in the narrative moment, only in the historical moment of the reader."[31]

This is ultimately why attempts to provide a happier ending with resurrection appearances is a betrayal of Mark's Gospel. In attempting to demonstrate that Jesus was victorious, such endings dilute the point that the victory resides not only in the resurrection but more concretely in the discipleship which that faith in, but not necessarily witness of, the resurrection compels. No wonder Myers concludes,

> [N]o one can convince "nonbelievers" of the resurrection as an abstract proposition. Mark, at least, offers no "proof"; did Jesus in fact appear to the disciples? We are not told. For Mark, the resurrection is not an answer, but the final question. There is only one genuine "witness" to the risen Jesus: to follow in discipleship. Only in this way will the truth of the resurrection be preserved.[32]

Petersen says Mark's ending can be described in this way: "The song is over but the melody lingers on."[33] It's like the music that keeps playing over and over again obsessively in your head. No matter what you do you can't stop it. It breaks in, breaks your concentration, infuriates you, overwhelms you. This ending was intended by Mark to be exactly like that. A song that won't stop until we get up and change our own tunes of living. Until we stop looking for happy endings and, living a life of discipleship, start creating them. Perhaps this is why Mark doesn't have Jesus—who has appeared throughout this narrative—appear again. Maybe he wants the reality of discipleship in his followers—which has been invisible up to this point—finally to appear instead. Maybe that's the appearance he's really looking for. He is looking for it from us, the readers. He wants *us* to finish *his* Jesus story.

View Two: "Finish the Story: A Charge for Ministers Being Ordained" Brian K. Blount

[Introduction: The name of the ordinand used in this sermon is fictitious, but the text refers to an actual ordination service. Students often ask if their teachers

---

31. Myers, *Binding the Strong Man*, 401. See also Tolbert, *Sowing the Gospel*, 297: "If the women frustrate the hopes of the authorial audience for individuals to prove faithful to the courageous example of Jesus and follow his way by going out and sowing the word abroad [preaching], is there anyone else available to fulfill that task? Of course there is: the audience itself."

32. Myers, *Binding the Strong Man*, 404.

33. Petersen, "When Is the End Not the End?" 163.

could participate in the worship service wherein they are ordained to the ministry of the Word and Sacrament. I was happy to offer this word as a charge to the new minister on one such occasion.]

For the past three years, David, you have labored through the rigors, tumults, trials, tribulations, triumphs, and joys of a theological education. No doubt your time studying the Gospels has acquainted you with the dispute over where the Gospel of Mark originally ended. As you know, most of the earliest manuscripts of the Gospel ended with chapter 16, verses 1–8. The early church fathers Eusebius and Jerome wrote that as far as they could tell the Gospel originally ended at 16:8. Indeed, it appears when you study Matthew and Luke, even they apparently thought Mark chose to end his work at 16:8.

So, why is there a problem?

Well, you know from your studies, David, that there's a problem with saying Mark ended at 16:8, because in all our Bibles there are an additional twelve verses, verses 9–20. If Mark didn't write them, where did they come from? And even more important, why did they come? It's almost certain we'll never be able to answer the first question, but we know the answer to the second. Those last twelve verses are there because the earliest readers of Mark's Gospel couldn't believe he ended it at verse 8. I call it the "Walt Disney" effect. Over the past several years I have been paying big money to go to the movies to see cartoons. And Disney's cartoons have one major thing in common; no matter how dark things get in the middle of the movie, by the end of the movie there comes a happy ending. Ariel, Belle, Aladdin, Simba, Tarzan all eventually win. Everything eventually becomes all right. And we and our children can sigh with relief and go out of the theater comfortable, happy, and satisfied that everything worked out in the end.

Mark wouldn't have been able to work for Walt Disney Studios. Mark didn't know how to create the proper kind of happy ending. Look at how he ended the story at 16:8. Jesus has been crucified. The women come to visit his tomb, but his body is gone. Sure, a young man tells them that he has risen, that he goes before them to Galilee, that they should go and tell the disciples to go meet him, but the women are more afraid than they are believing. When the story ends they have fled with fear and trembling; they say nothing to anyone. No one sees the risen Jesus; no one even knows to look for him, because the women are too afraid to pass the message along. That's it. That's where Mark stopped. As one commentator puts it, this is not a happy ending in which all is resolved. The earliest Christians couldn't take this kind of curt, stark, open ending. They needed happiness. They needed victory. They needed triumph. *They needed a few more verses!* So they supplied them. They supplied the kind of ending they figured Mark would have supplied had he understood the kind of consternation his ending ultimately caused.

I suggest to you, though, David, that this is exactly the way Mark wanted to end his Gospel. No mistake here. He knew exactly what he was doing. As one theologian writes, "The 'dilemma' of the ending is precisely what Mark refuses to resolve for us; he *means* to leave us to wrestle whether or not the women at the tomb (that is to say, we ourselves) overcame their fear in order to proclaim the new beginning."[34]

In other words, Mark wants us to finish the story in our words and deeds of discipleship. He has left the ending open, so that we, so that you, David, can write it in the way you live out your ministry, even though you know that in your living out that ministry you may, like Jesus, be subjected to the pain of following One whose truth was nailed to a cross. That's why it's right that he leaves us with a tone of fear as he closes his Gospel. This fear is appropriate not only to this ending but to the entire Gospel. It is the natural reaction to a discipleship whose content is the way of the cross. Anybody who truly understands what it means to be a disciple of Jesus is afraid. *If you're not afraid, you don't understand.* That's why Mark doesn't want to wipe out the fear with happy-ending assurances. He stresses the call and the challenge which that call represents. He's about calling disciples, about calling you, David, to walk through the darkness in order to pull God's people into the light. He is calling on you, David, to help finish the story. The question, what will the women do? has necessarily, today, become, what will *you* do? In this dangerous world where those who speak up for truth are often tortured by lies, where those who try to expand the light are often shoved into the darkness, where those who are dedicated to life are often hounded by the powers of death, where fear and pain are as palpable as the needs of God's people, Mark is asking you to put yourself in the place of the women and he is asking you, as we who read the Gospel are asking them, what are you going to do? Will you finish the story? How will you finish the story? At this moment you are saying that, even knowing the costs, you are dedicating yourself to do just that. So, finish the story!

Finish the story by not being afraid to take on the big challenges. I'm reminded of this book titled *Makes Me Wanna Holler,* by a young black man named Nathan McCall, who describes his horrible life growing up in inner-city America. At one point he is describing a conversation he has in jail with

---

34. Myers, *Binding the Strong Man*, 401–2.

another prisoner who, for a moment, becomes his mentor. The mentor, named Mo Battle, is teaching him to play chess. He writes, "One day, I made a move to capture a pawn of his and gave Mo Battle an opening to take a valuable piece. He smiled and said, 'You can tell a lot about a person by the way he plays chess. People who think small in life tend to devote a lot of energy to capturing pawns, the least valuable pieces on the board. They think they're playing to win, but they're not. But people who think big tend to go straight for the king or queen, which wins you the game.' I never forgot that. Most guys I knew, myself included, spent their entire lives chasing pawns. The problem was, we thought we were going after kings."[35]

Lots of Christians, ministers and laypeople, devote their time, David, to going after pawns. You can't finish the story that way. You finish the story by reaching far, by digging deep, by dreaming visions of God's coming reign, and then stepping out into reality, even amid the fear, to bring a piece of that reign to the people who so desperately in our day seek it.

Don't be afraid to believe in the visions God gives you and don't be afraid to pursue them on behalf of God and God's people. Go after the kings, David. When God's people holler out in need around you, don't be afraid to holler out with your life and ministry an answer to their prayers, no matter how much those prayers require. And especially, don't be afraid to holler God's message, even when even the Christians around you plug up their ears because the message is too hard for them to bear, requires too much for them to give. Let your life become a sermon that in its living finishes the story Mark left open for you.

I remember when I was growing up and the minister was speaking, especially at one of those hot, humid, summer-night revivals, people would talk back all during the sermon. And I thought I noticed a pattern. Whenever the minister was speaking against something that wasn't something our church was involved in, when he was speaking about people who didn't appear to be our church's people, when he was speaking against the abuses and neglect of the governments which certainly did not involve people in my church, then I'd hear these loud affirmations. "Preach! Preach! Preach!" They'd shout it out from the pews. They'd stand up and shout it from the aisles. But when the preacher turned, when his focus shifted to what he knew about our church, when he started stepping on rather tender, present toes, then the loud cries to the pulpit turned as well. Then people were saying things like "Watch out, now" or "Help him, Lord," and no doubt probably a few were thinking, "Shut him up, Lord."

Now, it seems to me, in the light of passages like the one we're talking

---

35. Nathan McCall, *Makes Me Wanna Holler: A Young Black Man in America* (New York: Random House, 1994), 148.

about from Mark, that there are voices out beyond the walls of this church and every church in every community of our country and, for you, our world, shouting today, perhaps not in good English or good Italian, but in striking, powerful cadences nonetheless. They aren't crying out in affirmation, though. Often, they're crying out in their anguish, begging in their need, soliciting from their pain, "Preach! Preach! Won't somebody talking in there come out here and PREACH!" The preacher's job inside is to step on so many complacent toes in such a fiery, sincere, and enacted way that even those tempted to say, "Shut him up, Lord" will rise up, chastened, encouraged, challenged, and inspired, to get up and help him to help them, Lord. To go with him to the people crying in the streets and homes, tenements, and alleys for preachers to come with the words and actions, and thus the power of the reign of God.

God needs people to fight with cutting and living words. God needs people to live out sermons of life and hope for people who have none. Sometimes churches and Christians want their word, not God's Word, spoken from pulpits, or lived in Christian lives. Your job, David, if Jesus is to be any guide, is to give and live God's Word, anyway.

It won't be easy, though. I know that. You know that. Finishing Mark's story, God's story, is no simple thing. If it were, those closest to Jesus surely would have managed a way to conclude it. Fear overwhelmed them; fear will stalk you. But you mustn't ever believe that a faithful person is a fearless person. Faith for Mark is not being without fear; it is refusing to let fear silence you and the gospel message you've been commissioned to carry. Faith is what God makes possible in you so that you can see your way through God to the goals God has set for your life and the lives of God's people even in the midst of darkness.

So, with God's help . . .

Finish the story, David. Finish it strong. In your strength the weak will find comfort and the strong will find God's challenge.

View Three: Galilee
Gary W. Charles

In Mark 16:1–8, the women come to the tomb looking for death. They had watched death from a distance. They had seen Joseph of Arimathea take the corpse of Jesus from the cross and wrap it in linen cloth. Now, at dawn, they leave their homes to do what loved ones do when death comes.

We do the same whenever death comes. We call the undertaker and then visit a funeral "home" and its unmistakable odor of death. We pick out a handsome coffin or a lovely urn. Check out a vault. Decide on the limo. Get the bill. Write the check. The whole affair is beyond bizarre, but we do what's necessary whenever death comes.

In 16:1–8, the women worry most about how they will move the stone blocking the tomb. It's that way when death arrives. We worry about the details and walk around stunned, immune to advice or comfort. Writing about such times, Ann Weems, poet and mother of a murdered son, writes:

> O God, what am I going to do?
> He's gone—and I'm left
> with an empty pit in my life.
> I can't think.
> I can't work.
> I can't eat.
> I can't talk.
> I can't see anyone.
> I can't leave my house.
> Nothing makes any sense.
> Nothing seems worth doing.[36]

What Weems is describing is the "death walk." Though numb inside, we tend to the details and do what's necessary to complete that walk.

So it was with three women at dawn outside Jerusalem. Mark does not praise or criticize them here. He simply states that they come to the tomb on a "death walk." They come prepared to anoint his body for burial. No men come along to help. It is three loving women who arrive at the tomb—looking for death. Anyone who has read the rest of Mark's Gospel knows that this presents a problem. Jesus told his followers on three separate occasions that he would die but on the third day would rise to new life. And, just before entering Jerusalem, a nameless woman in Simon's house had already done what these three women have come to the tomb to do.

Inside the abode of death, a young messenger tells the women: "Go tell his [Jesus'] disciples and Peter that he is going ahead of you to Galilee, there you will see him, just as he told you" (16:7 NRSV). On a "death walk" all our senses are dulled, including our hearing. People say things, sincere things, words intended to help; we nod politely, but we don't really hear them. At the tomb, the women hear the messenger's words, but they don't *really* hear. Easter has come too soon for them. They are on a death walk and they can't yet hear anything new, no matter how good the news. So, told to go and shout, they run in fear and hold their tongues.

---

36. Ann Weems, *Psalms of Lament* (Louisville, Ky.: Westminster John Knox Press, 1995), 20–21.

That's it. That's how Mark ends his Gospel. The risen Jesus does not whisper Mary's name or appear through locked doors to some disciples and then later to Thomas. He doesn't build a fire and fix breakfast for the disciples on the beach. What we know of the risen Jesus in Mark is no more than what the women hear in the empty tomb. Just when Mark shines the spotlight on three women—a rare enough occurrence in any literature of its day—the women duck into the shadows and flee from the tomb, just as earlier three men had "fled" in the garden.

The women, we are told, run away in *fear*—the most intractable opponent of faith in Mark's Gospel. Grief has no closer ally than fear. Fear constricts our thinking to the most fundamental level. Grief does the same. It leaves us haunted by the specter of "How will I get through the next hour?" "What will become of me?" "How will I pay the bills?" On their death walk, these women are far more open to fear than the glad tidings of faith toward which they are called. Mark's Gospel closes, then, on the all-too-human chord of grief and fear.

No wonder the early church did some editing. "This ending just won't do!" As Brian says so well in his exegesis, "The early Christians were like latter-day Walt Disney; they couldn't abide such a curt, stark, open ending. They needed happiness. They needed victory. They needed triumph. *They needed a few more verses*. So they supplied them. They supplied the kind of ending they figured Mark would have supplied had he understood the kind of consternation *his* kind of ending ultimately caused."

Mark doesn't need copy editors; he needs careful readers ready to "stay awake" and "pay attention." Mark 16:1–8 is not a *literal* ending; it is a *literary* one. Mark is not making an historical point—three women came looking for death, heard about resurrected life, and were too scared to tell anyone. He is making a *literary* point. "Here in the final irony of the Gospel, with all need for secrecy gone, those who are directed to go and tell run away in fear, saying nothing to anyone."[37]

If the three women had had their wits about them, I bet one of them would have asked, "Why Galilee?" Again, Mark's interest is not principally geographic or historic. *Galilee* is a regular, though silent, character in this Gospel:

"In those days Jesus came from Nazareth of *Galilee* and was baptized in the Jordan" (Mark 1:9).

"Now after John was arrested, Jesus came to *Galilee*, proclaiming the good news of God, and saying, 'The time is fulfilled, and the kingdom of God has come near; repent, and believe in the gospel'" (Mark 1:14–15).

---

37. Tolbert, *Sowing the* Gospel, 295.

"As Jesus passed along the Sea of *Galilee*, he saw Simon and his brother Andrew casting a net into the sea" (Mark 1:16).

"And he (Jesus) went throughout *Galilee*, proclaiming the message in their synagogues and casting out demons" (Mark 1:39).

"They went on from there and passed through *Galilee*. He (Jesus) did not want anyone to know it; for he was teaching his disciples, saying to them, 'The Son of Man is to be betrayed into human hands, and they will kill him, and three days after being killed, he will rise again'" (Mark 9:30–31).

The young man instructs the women at the empty tomb to "Go, tell his disciples and Peter that he is going ahead of you to *Galilee*; there you will see him, just as he told you" (Mark 16:7).

Mark's Gospel begins and ends in *Galilee*. In Mark, *Galilee* awaits us. The risen Jesus goes before us. Our death walk is over. That is the glorious news of Easter. In Galilee, Jesus awaits the Judas in us, that part of us willing to betray a close friend for the noblest of reasons. Jesus awaits the James and John in us, that part of us consumed with achievements and recognition. In Galilee, Jesus awaits Peter, who confessed Jesus as Christ in Caesarea and who denied knowing him in Jerusalem.

At the turn of this century, Albert Schweitzer closed the chapter on the first "Jesus Seminar" with his pivotal book *The Quest of the Historical Jesus*. Schweitzer wrote:

> He (Jesus) comes to us as One unknown, without a name as of old, by the lakeside, He came to those who knew Him not. He speaks to us the same word: "Follow thou me!" and sets us to the tasks which He has to fulfil for our time. He commands. And to those who obey Him, whether they be wise or simple, He will reveal Himself in the toils, the conflicts, the sufferings which they shall pass through in His fellowship, and, as an ineffable mystery, they shall learn in their own experience Who he is.[38]

Schweitzer then asks: "Where is *Galilee*?" He answers this question saying that *Galilee* is "in the toils, the conflicts, the sufferings" of this life. That is the Easter destination to which the messenger calls the disciples in 16:1–8. *Galilee* awaits all who are open to God's future. *Galilee* awaits people who have lost their bearings, whose faith flickers at best, who compromise their integrity for a buck, who sit in the pews most Sundays yet still are mostly confused about who Jesus is or how to follow him.

The good news that Mark promises us is that the risen Lord awaits us not

---

38. Albert Schweitzer, *The Quest of the Historical Jesus: A Critical Study of Its Progress from Reimarus to Wrede* (New York: Macmillan, 1968), 403.

in an empty tomb or in some distant future or remote place; the risen Lord awaits us in *Galilee*—on our city streets, in the halls of our schools, in the wards of our hospitals, and behind the bars of our prisons. The Lord awaits us in the market and the gym, when we sit down to dinner and when we lie down to sleep. Want to find the risen Lord? Want to serve the risen Christ? Mark says, "Then go to *Galilee*."

However, the women don't head to *Galilee* in Mark's story. For them, as dawn breaks, Easter comes too soon. After hearing glad tidings, they cannot run and shout loud "Alleluias" or shout at all for that matter. I know these women as kin. When I stood beside the grave of my father and later spoke words in an unfamiliar chapel in remembrance of my brother and most recently, planned the funeral for my mother, bearers of the Easter faith surrounded me. People from current and former churches, college and the old neighborhood, distant places and nearby all witnessed to God's transforming love in this world and hope in the life to come. They shared with me the same good news as the young man sitting at the entrance to the empty tomb shared with the women. How did I respond? I accepted each gesture and expression like one more casserole for which I had no taste. Why? Not because I have no faith, but because I'm far better acquainted with Golgotha than *Galilee*.

For Mark, Easter comes not at an empty tomb with a mysterious messenger announcing resurrection news, nor with women on a "death walk" exiting the tomb in mute fear. Easter comes not in sterile funeral parlors, nor when standing beside freshly dug graves. For Mark, Easter comes when we set our face toward *Galilee* to sow hope where despair rules, to speak consolation where desperation dwells, and to break wide open all tombs that the righteous have built to keep God only for themselves. Easter comes not in discounting 16:1–8 by thinking it a fragment and desperately hunting for Mark's *real* ending. Easter comes when 16:1–8 does not leave us confused, afraid, and silent but prepared to end our "death walk" as we walk toward the risen life that awaits us in *Galilee*.